FLOWER OF SCOTLAND?

A SCOTTISH FOOTBALL ODYSSEY

ARCHIE MACPHERSON

highdown

FOR JESS

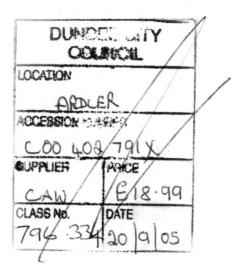

Published in 2005 by Highdown,
an imprint of Raceform Ltd
Compton, Newbury, Berkshire, RG20 6NL
Raceform Ltd is a wholly-owned subsidiary of Trinity Mirror plc

A CIP catalogue record for this book is available from the British Library.

ISBN 1-905156-11-1

Cover designed by Tracey Scarlett

Interiors designed by Fiona Pike

Printed and bound in Great Britain by William Clowes Ltd, Beccles, Suffolk

CONTENTS

ACKNOWLEDGEMENTS

I am deeply grateful to the many people who talked to me about Scottish football. Once again I relied heavily on former librarian Pat Woods's research and advice, without which I would have been lost in the labyrinth of memory. Walter Smith, Scotland's team manager, was of great assistance and spoke candidly about some of the problems facing the development of the game in Scotland. The following former players and managers all gave of their time to recall the events the narrative covers: John Greig, Billy McNeill, Jim McLean (former manager of Dundee United), Sandy Jardine, Davie Provan, Frank McGarvey, Allan Rough, Alex MacDonald, Joe Jordan, Hamish McAlpine, Eamonn Bannon, Bobby Shearer, Gordon Smith, Willie Miller, Peter Weir, Maurice Malpas, Terry Butcher, 'Dixie' Deans, Lou Macari, Murdo MacLeod, Roy Aitken, John Robertson, Paul Sturrock, John Hewitt, Tommy Craig (former physiotherapist at Rangers) and two players from the now defunct Third Lanark, Mike Jackson and Tony Connell.

Former SFA secretary Ernie Walker and ex-Scotland team manager Craig Brown were extremely helpful, allowing me to dig into their recollections about many of the events surrounding the World Cups – the good, the bad and the ugly. Hamish MacBean, former inspector with Strathclyde Police and match commander at Hampden Park in his time, and Joe Black, formerly of the Scottish Police Federation, were immensely helpful too, providing background information to an infamous match. My thanks also go to Third Lanark historian Bob Laird, for setting me right on one of the biggest iniquities in the history of the Scottish game, and Robert McElroy, the Rangers historian, who also clarified important elements for me. John Cole of The Celtic Internet site was of great assistance also.

The Souness revolution at Ibrox could not have been adequately covered without the full co-operation of the former chief executive of Rangers, David Holmes. Similarly, to have attempted to explain the complexities of the transformation of Celtic under Fergus McCann would not have been possible without the advice of former directors of the club Willie Haughey and Brian Dempsey, financial consultant David Low and lawyer Brian Jackson.

Friends and colleagues from journalism and broadcasting also offered me both advice and invaluable information, and I thank Allan Herron and Dixon Blackstock (formerly of the *Scottish Sunday Mail*), Iain Scott (sports news editor of the *Daily Record*), Alex Montgomery (author of *Martin O'Neill – the Biography*), Ray Hepburn (*Scottish Sunday Mirror*) and football historians Peter Rundo of Dundee United and Kevin Stirling of Aberdeen FC. From broadcasting I have to record my gratitude for information provided by Hazel Irvine of the BBC, Colin Davidson of Setanta, Craig Millar of Grampian Television and the inimitable comedian Andy Cameron.

Michael O'Neill, Director of Education for Lanarkshire, and former schoolteachers John Gold, Bob Doherty and John Watson reintroduced me to the tender shoots of Scottish football. Dennis Canavan MSP kindly lent me some political insight into the problems facing the national sport. And from the SFA, David Little, National Secretary of the Scottish Youth Football Association, and Sandy Bryson provided information that greatly aided the conclusion of the book. I must also thank the staffs of the Mitchell Library in Glasgow, the British Newspaper Library in Colindale, London, and the photographic desk at the *Daily Record*.

Finally, my long-suffering wife chose the right wine to keep me going, and it is to her that this book is dedicated.

INTRODUCTION

One November night in 1993 there was a riot around the fountain in Porte de St Cloud in the 16th arrondissement in Paris. The French police, grotesquely fattened by their padded riot-prevention gear and huge boots which made them look like computer-generated creatures in a blockbuster film, were taking on Marseille supporters with all the finesse of a seal-cull. It was brutal to watch, and for the innocent onlooker, who comes to Paris expecting to sample the sophistications of life, it would have been wholly shocking and surprising. But I had watched it before. The City of Light was no stranger to mob violence after football matches. During preparations for a normal Paris St Germain league match, the area around the Parc des Princes could look at times as if the French were preparing for a Panzer strike down the Marne valley from the north. Riot squads and their equivalent of Black Marias were always stationed around this plush area, certainly when bitter rivals Marseille came to town. It was especially rough that night: they were dragging men to the vans as if they were vermin. My French colleague sitting in the café beside me certainly thought they were. 'These folk from Marseille,' he said, 'they come up here thinking not about football but about how to cause a riot. They have no respect for a beautiful city. Just think of that miserable place they come from with all their drugs and blacks. Hooligans, you know, like you have with Celtic and Rangers.'

Ah, so! You could probably imagine what was going through his head, as images stuck out like obelisks. Glasgow. Scottish football. Celtic and Rangers. Bigotry. Riots. That was the thought process. I had heard it all before. Not just here, but in Argentina, Peru, Brazil, Mexico, USA, Hong Kong, Australia, Italy, Spain and Israel; in stadiums, bars, restaurants, streets and homes. I thought I had become inured to the totality of this universal response whenever Scottish football was mentioned, and at first the implied slur on my native city had little effect on me. The first priority, after all, was to duck as another bistro chair left its moorings and sailed through the night. But as time went by and order was restored, his words lingered.

It is not easy to admit even now, but what my French colleague said about the Old Firm had a corrosive effect on me. I began to recall all the times I had defended Scottish football, tried to explain it, developed arguments with foreigners in an attempt to rationalise the 'guid conceit' we had of ourselves as a small nation, which once upon a time seriously thought it could win a World Cup. But all they wanted to hear about was the Old Firm. That night I tried to explain to my friend that he needed to know more about us than the wildly exaggerated notion they had of Old Firm hostilities, although they most certainly existed in different forms. I pointed out to him that I had never seen football violence on such a scale in all the years of covering those occasions when Celtic played Rangers as I had in this fashionable arrondissement. Yes, there had been one infamous riot in 1980 at Hampden. And yes, in various localities there could be venomous hostilities between the opposing Old Firm legions. But still I found it difficult to explain to my Scottish friends back home the deep-rooted hatreds (mostly racial) and brutalities I had observed at football matches in the Parc des Princes.

As far as football was concerned, Scotland inhabited a tiny niche in the foreign mind as a nation that exported only notoriety. We certainly had our share of it, as I will recount, and I wouldn't have boasted about some of the Old Firm traditions. You may as well try to justify child molestation. But my colleague's glib dismissal of Scottish footballing culture bothered me, even though I knew that our status in Europe had declined to such an extent that you might have thought we had been airbrushed out of existence. And it's a fact that the French public were not educated by their media. Apart from the occasional brief mention of an Old Firm game, so seldom was Scottish football reflected in the famous sports newspaper *L'Equipe* that to come across any reference was as surprising as finding an advert for a malt whisky in the Salvation Army's *War Cry*.

There and then that evening my indignation mixed with a doleful nostalgia for the 'dear, green place'. In the early days of exile in Paris I honestly felt relieved to have put the unquenchable bigotries of the Old Firm behind me. But after that night I felt I needed a whiff of that very acrid atmosphere they generate, as a relief from watching a form of football that was often brilliant but remote and almost academic. It was like feeling the lust again for an old flame to whom you had previously shown the door. I suppose it was an admission to being an addict of my native game. Coming back from the continent one Saturday after having commentated for Eurosport on a technically sound but goalless and bloodless UEFA cup semi-final between a German and Russian side, to watch Clydebank against Falkirk as the Bairns attempted to get into the Premier Division, was like coming upon a delightful country store, with its pleasant aroma of the good earth and sweet fruits of honest toil – such a contrast to the glossy supermarket of European football I had been trundling about in. It was a tonic.

People to whom I tried to explain this at the time, and probably those reading this now, registered puzzlement. But however comprehensive a coverage of some of the best teams on the planet, no matter how skilful the football product, I felt little affinity with it. It was a job. There was no passion in it. A Scottish football junkie on his own, even in a glorious city such as Paris, is in dire danger of making a pathetic spectacle of himself in trying to explain the symptoms to people whose *politesse* could simply be a preface to open ridicule. Sometimes it was fun; other times it hurt. But it was simply an epitome of all that I had experienced through the years. Home thoughts from abroad were the most aggravating of all. Being on the touchline of Scottish football for four highly significant decades, I experienced, and witnessed in others, elation, depression, excitement, fear, joy, sadness, sleepless nights, boozy nights, confrontations, blazing rows, solid friendships, backstabbing, deceit, courage, success and failure. We ran the gamut of emotions from A to Z.

Indeed, there is a mantra used by colleagues of my generation, repeated frequently when we stumble across one another and survey what we now see as a game in crisis, having watched with dismay the importation of mediocre foreign players and suffered as our national team came through the nightmarish Vogts years, as if the man had come from Hamelin, not Mönchengladbach. We mutter amongst ourselves something like, 'Thank God we were around to see the best of times.' We were the fortunate ones – or so we now think. In the presence of a younger generation it might sound like, 'We had caviar, you have mince.' There was much disappointment, certainly, but there was also greatness. We saw Stein majestic, Waddell triumphant, McLean tactically superb, Fergie omnipotent, England whipped at Wembley – just to mention a few treasures. To be sure we were intoxicated by our self-belief at times, well beyond the means of a rational assessment of our standing in the world. But the tantalising ingredients were there, so often, to encourage us to a presumption of greatness. It also induced the natural corollary – remorse. Listen to novelist Gordon Williams's drunk man – fictional, but real – upstairs on a Glasgow bus returning from seeing Scotland play the Auld Enemy at Hampden:

> I mean, just as the teams are coming out I could die for Scotland. Honest. Tears, the lot. What else is there? See if we get an assembly or a Parliament? Want a bet it'll be the same bigmouths and windbags and chisellers? You think they'll do as good a job for the country as they did for football? The big sell-out – we're so familiar with it you could almost call it genetical. Greatest talkers of rubbish in the world. Scots? Wee boys looking for fairy tales. (From the mid-1970s short story *See Scotland?*)

Are we wee boys looking for fairy tales? Hopefully this odyssey will go some way to helping the reader come to terms with the distinctive Scottish football mentality. There is the paradox to start with. Most of us are certainly enjoying greater personal wealth than we were 40 years ago, yet football is generally impoverished. Why have we not marched onwards in tandem? Towards the end of my trail through the decades, in the spring of 2005, I sat with the Scotland team manager Walter Smith in his office at Hampden Park mulling over the state of Scottish football. He explained his problems in social terms: 'If you look at one generation, my kids can play tennis better than me, they can swim better than me and play golf much better. Great! But they only ever played a tenth of the spontaneous football I played when I was growing up like them, if they were lucky. A tenth! Are they better off? Sure. Society is better. But in football we also have a big, big problem, because we've stopped playing the game in the streets.'

We will come to that problem eventually, after we have dropped anchor at places such as Lisbon, Barcelona, Gothenburg, Seville and the World Cup countries, and looked as closely as we can at some of the events and personalities that made us what we are now as a football nation. This work might also be seen as an epistle to my French friend who admitted to loving the sound of the 'Flower of Scotland' being sung by the Scots at sporting events. I have to explain to him that the flowers I have in mind are those blossoming and largely unexpected moments when Scottish football transported you to your own personal nirvana. Hopefully you will be able to pluck out those flowers from amongst the weeds as the journey unfolds.

CHAPTER ONE

SETTING SAIL

It is late afternoon on Friday, 28 April 1967. A packed minibus of professional footballers sets out from the south side of the city of Glasgow on a journey that will take the occupants down the River Clyde to the town of Dumbarton. After crossing the river in the city they make their way through Clydebank, and looking to their left they see, amid the towering derricks of the shipyards, that the ugly duckling of steel-sheets and rivets has been transformed into the swan which will be christened five months later as the QE2. This is providing a sheen of prosperity to an area heading for darker days inside an economy that will see the devaluation of the pound in only a few short months' time. The travellers certainly do not feel as if the re-election of Harold Wilson a year earlier, with his promise to modernise Britain, has done anything significant for them. In fact, they feel they are subject to conditions in their present employment that would not have been out of place in the feudal system of medieval Scotland. But right now, shoehorned inside the vehicle, they are not in a reflective, philosophical mood. Part of their chat during the bumpy, claustrophobic journey centres on a week in which history has been made.

Three days earlier, on 25 April, Celtic became the first British club to reach the European Cup final. The week before, Rangers, playing the first leg of a semi-final in the European Cup Winners' Cup, beat Slavia Sofia 1–0 away from home; they now look certain to reach another European final. Kilmarnock are to contest the Fair Cities Cup semi-final against Leeds. Having three semi-finalists in European competitions in the same season is something that has never been equalled by the more powerful base of English football. So, in contrast to the clouds gathering gloomily around the economy, Scottish football seems to be in for a period of self-sustaining growth, and in general terms looks so buoyant that on 19 June the Berlin newspaper *Neues Deutschland* will carry the headline 'Das Schottische Jahr' (The Scottish Year). The game is being noted in parts other Scottish news never previously reached. Harold

Macmillan's electoral boast 'You've never had it so good' might easily be applied to our national game at that period.

Not for the men in the minibus it can't. For as much as they may be fully aware of the growing respect for Scottish football, there is one thing of which they are entirely ignorant as the large volcanic hump of Dumbarton Rock hoves into view. They are not to know that this will be the last time they will ever travel together. Indeed, most of these men will never see one another again. And throughout later decades they will curse the fact that they did not realise the implications of that evening. For as they descend from the minibus, make their way to the dressing-rooms, don their gear and run out in blazing scarlet jerseys, they are not to know that Third Lanark, the football club they represent, a founder member of both the Scottish Football Association and the Scottish League and one of the oldest professional clubs in Scotland – having been formed in 1872, a few years after the oldest club of all, the amateur Queen's Park – is about to play its last ever game.

They lost 5–1. A man called Drew Busby became the only player in British football to put his name to the final historic goal of a club whose name would completely disappear from existence; other clubs that failed in senior football in the UK managed to retain their names at different levels of the game. Third Lanark's former players are still revered as faded photos in albums, or on the walls in the homes of a dwindling band of romantic enthusiasts, who keep the club alive in their minds, just like those who feel Elvis did not expire but is still out there somewhere, strumming away immortally. Hardly anybody cared in 1967. Many people, however, cared in the early 1990s when a club only a few miles from Cathkin looked into the abyss that had faced Third Lanark in the 1960s. Indeed, they cared so much about the future of Celtic that they massed their battalions and fought a financial, intellectual and guerrilla war against l'ancien régime of the Kellys and Whites, which I will examine later. By comparison, Thirds went with barely a whimper, owing £60,000 to debtors. For me, time, events and the extreme passions which reveal the love of football link these two clubs indelibly to that period of the 1960s when I first stepped into the media.

Understandably, those of us who were at the beginning of our careers then were caught up in the euphoria surrounding the success of the Scottish clubs. So what did I care about this footballing vagabond passing away, to be buried in the pauper's grave? Shamefully, a tiny passing thought of regret was all I could muster at the time; not until many years later did deeper thoughts surface. The Third Lanark–Hibernian match in November 1962 was the first of my television broadcasts, so I owed them something, if only an occasional pang of nostalgia. Moreover, I had had more than a sneaking affection for Thirds long before television. In my boyhood I would travel all the way across the city with my grandfather to watch the Hi Hi's, as they were called, and became infatuated with one player in particular, whose memory I still revere – Jimmy Mason. Fragile-looking, nimble, astute, and with an accuracy of passing that an astrophysicist might have admired, he contained all the elements with which the traditional Scottish inside-forward stamped his unique imprimatur on world football. Mason and his like identified the Scottish game with craftsmen who sprang from the purity of natural, uncoached, God-given talent that could emerge miraculously from, say, single-end tenement living – 'wee headies up the close', dustbins for goals, gravel-rash from an ash-pitch, cramp in the back row of the cinema on a Saturday night, a high tolerance level with the 'bevvy', and a 24-hour obsession with the game. Being able to play like Mason seemed to be nature's way of conferring a blessing on the virtues of working-class life. But, as I said, few cared about Thirds' death. The feeling, in a way, was that they had it coming. That attitude helped bring about the most scandalous death in British football.

Five years after my Cathkin debut, and long before I should have been promoted, I had graduated from rookie commentator to a vantage point alongside Kenneth Wolstenholme at a European final. As these finals do not happen all that often to Scottish sides, it was like jumping a long queue of tired hopefuls for a passport to the Promised Land. That event and others might convey to a contemporary generation the glow of a golden age, considering the achievements I have already referred to. But, of course, it depends what you are looking for. Delve deeper and wider and you might see portents that are inconsistent with such a romantic reverie about those days. These two clubs in particular, Third Lanark and Celtic, represented the strengths and faults of the era, neither of which can afford to be ignored. In the first four years of my professional life their respective fates contained elements that have affected the Scottish game ever since. Both the unprecedented triumph and the miserable expiry of a venerable club are not unrelated, for the respective fates reflect the stewardship of Scottish football. Who in their right senses, that May day in 1967 in Lisbon, could have imagined that nearly 30 years on Celtic would be struggling for its very existence?

I am reminded of the night in the early 1990s when I drove their manager at the time, Liam Brady, home to the village where he lived from the television show *Sport in Question*, which actually thrived on the Celtic crisis of the time. Just before he left the car he turned and asked me solemnly, 'Do you really think Celtic will go under?' He was genuinely scared. Lisbon, at that moment, seemed like a figment of the imagination. I told him about Third Lanark. He did not know who they were. You could not blame him. Many Scots in 1967 did not worry about Thirds' fate. You felt then, as crowds rolled up in relatively abundant numbers, that time would stand still. Football seemed as firmly anchored to its base as a redwood forest. But the men who ran the game then couldn't see the wood for the trees, and we were all, through time, to suffer.

Only boffins in back rooms had colour television in 1962, when I entered the fray. It was the lull before the storm. As I watched Third Lanark play Hibs on my television debut, Jock Stein was still at Dunfermline. He had not yet burst on to the scene with Celtic to rip into the norms of Scottish football. We knew he was good. We had watched his side take the Scottish Cup from his old club Celtic in 1961. There were rumours flying around that he would leave Dunfermline, and the club he was linked with was the Edinburgh side I was watching that day. Scot Symon, almost inevitably neatly suited and wearing his trilby in public to denote his rank, commanded Rangers with the same aloof self-assurance his players showed for the whole of Scottish football. Celtic were then no competition for them. Indeed, as the Celtic community became increasingly alarmed at the club seemingly sinking well below the Plimsoll line as the burden of recurring failure, particularly against Rangers, began to weigh even more heavily, certain prominent supporters were shortly to mount a rebellion against the dynastic control of the Kelly family. It was led by a councillor, Bailie James F. Reilly, Labour member for the Townhead district of the city of Glasgow. This seedy lawyer, playing heavily on the Catholic vote in his political life, was later to become a director of Third Lanark. As we will later show, it is just as well for Celtic that the revolution petered out as ridiculously as the one in the Bay of Pigs.

In season 1960/61 Third Lanark had glowed with the promise of more to come. They had scored six in their last league game against, curiously enough, Hibernian to achieve their 100th goal of the season and to finish third in the table. That was 12 more goals than Rangers, who won the title that season, and a staggering 36 more than Celtic. What these bald statistics reveal, in light of the fate which was to befall Third Lanark, is that footballing success bears no automatic correlation to the handling of the finances of a club. The names indelibly associated with that particular year were Hilley, Harley and Gray, a trio abundant in goalscoring certainly but in a free-flowing, swashbuckling manner which elevated the club to a status that showed no inferiority when they played against the Old Firm. They had beaten Celtic twice that season after all, 2–0 at Cathkin and 3–2 at Celtic Park. These results, indicative of Celtic's slump, would have been noted in the managerial office at Dunfermline where an ambition was being quietly nursed by the man who had been advised to move on from Celtic Park because he would never become Celtic manager.

It is one of the curious aspects of Stein's views that when, as Celtic captain, he was asked to nominate his favourite Scottish player, the name he gave was George Young, the former Rangers and Scotland captain. It was as if he wished to retain evidence of the sympathy he had held for Ibrox as a young man in Burnbank, Lanarkshire. On 12 December 1962, Stein was in Valencia with Dunfermline. They were to face the holders of the Fairs Cities Cup. On that same evening, George Young was seated on the platform at a Third Lanark AGM on the south side of Glasgow in the Dixon Halls, Cathcart. The night went badly for both men. In Valencia, Stein's side lost 4–0; in Glasgow, Young dramatically put on his coat, handed in a letter of resignation as manager of Third Lanark, and in front of snapping photographers walked away from the club and out of football for ever. Stein made a comeback; Young never did. Dunfermline then staged one of the great European recoveries in the replay, overcoming the Spaniards 6–2 on a night when a new ice age seemed imminent and the pitch, hard enough to resist a comet strike, was unplayable – until Mr Stein told the referee that it was. The former Celtic player's reputation was now beginning to soar. Young, a magnificent defender and principal exponent of route-one football with the famous Iron Curtain defence at Ibrox in the immediate post-war years, was simply making his way out of the game into a successful business career and a complicated love life which saw his wife throw his girlfriend's goods and chattels out of a hotel window one night after deciding on a showdown over who owned whom. But his experience, and above all his geniality and kindness, made Young immensely popular in the trade, and particularly with supporters of Thirds, who were shocked when he walked out so dramatically. He did so for one reason: his deep mistrust of a man about to return to the board as a director – William Hiddleston.

To those deeply, incurably hurt by the extinction of Thirds, Hiddleston's name causes the sort of revulsion you would find in south-east Asia at the mention of the name Pol Pot. He was one of the seminal figures of that era – unfortunately in the most negative way. In 1955 during one of the continually recurring financial crises the club faced, when they had to sack their manager and his assistant, Hiddleston was appointed to the remarkable role of director/manager. After he uttered the usual platitudes about ensuring a glorious future for the club, the press were not only kindly disposed to him, they enthused over a man who seemed to have different ideas. After all, Thirds were in a fix. The fact that they continued to be hammered by opponents after the appointment did not seem to matter. It was the long term they were thinking about. That is why another couple of statements he made at the time passed without too much attention. When asked if he could make his club a success in 1956/57, he replied, 'Of course, although football is no longer a game. It is all about finance now.' Not a year has passed, up and into the new century, without my hearing a statement like that being uttered by somebody involved in having to pay bills to keep the game alive. You might therefore have conferred on this accountant, who owned pubs and clothing companies as well, the quality of prescience, were it not for another of his utterances which revealed a more acquisitive than philanthropic slant to his role. Pointing to another part of the spacious Cathkin ground at the time, he said, to an acquaintance, 'A well-known builder wants to erect houses there, and maybe we'll let him, because we own the ground.' Bland or even astute, whichever way it might have been received at the time it now sounds like one of the most sinister remarks ever made about a football club.

The passing of events made it even more so. Two years after becoming the 'saviour' of the club, and not without support from many Thirds people, Hiddleston resigned, as adverse fortune continued to dog them. When he acquired the majority of shares and returned on that fateful night of 1962 to take overall control and force Young's resignation, there began the period, to which I was close witness, during which a long-running tragi-comedy was virtually airbrushed out of existence by the coming of one man from the east to initiate the most historic renaissance in Scottish football.

Hiddleston and co. were peripheral to the agony being suffered by Celtic in the early 1960s, which was as painful to their supporters – if not more so – as the tortures being endured by those following Thirds. From the very low enclosure commentary position just in front of the Celtic directors' box you could hear, from time to time, the abuse being directed at chairman Bob Kelly, who under his trilby hat sat there courageously, like a man honoured to be so beset by the 'slings and arrows of outrageous fortune' but determined to cheat the gallows. Faces would turn in the enclosure to look over our camera position and scream upwards at the board of directors, helplessly complicit in Kelly's ways, utterly devoted to the club but too often obdurate and sometimes eccentric. On one occasion in the early 1960s, while travelling on the team bus to a game at Airdrie, he spotted the reserve goalkeeper Willie Goldie standing at a bus-stop wearing a Celtic supporter's scarf and heading off on his own to back the team. Kelly ordered the bus to be stopped, invited Goldie on board, and impressed by the man's loyalty to the club decided to play him in the team that day, to the astonishment of Pat Crerand. 'I could not believe it. It showed you how that club was run in those days. The best you could say about it was that it was a shambles. But you just accepted it. It just happened to be Celtic's way, and because you were dyed-in-the-wool Celtic, you just went along with it. But, honestly, I got pissed off with all of that eventually.' 'Pissed off' might have been the motto of their supporters' association at the time.

Then, on 31 January 1965, Celtic announced that Jock Stein was to join the club as soon as the vacancy created by his current club, Hibernian, could be filled. He returned in March. But that announcement hid the protracted talks that went on with Stein, as they offered him first the assistant managership, then joint managership with Sean Fallon, and eventually the full job, thus revealing the historically reflected initial reluctance to appoint the club's first ever Protestant manager. The first interview I ever did with him was terse. To compare it to the genial approach of his predecessor Jimmy McGrory, it was like approaching a shark instead of feeding your pet goldfish. The sharpness he demonstrated in those early skirmishes clearly indicated that this man would add a whole new dimension to the game. Celtic and Scottish football were about to be transformed.

Third Lanark would lend impetus to that change because by then they had become a cause célèbre, filling the front as well as the back pages of newspapers. On 10 January 1965, just a few weeks before the Celtic announcement about Stein, the *Scottish Daily Express* reported that 'Mr Hiddleston, principal shareholder in the club, covered his face as he went into the hotel'. Well he might have, as he headed into another crisis meeting of shareholders, for by this stage the media were reporting on this club as if a stench was being emitted from Cathkin Park throughout the land. The finances and the mystery surrounding the way the balance sheets were presented meant that the directors, including the chairman Bailie Reilly, were constantly being pursued to provide answers about the future. They seemingly had the knack of survival, with slippery explanations and last-minute infusions of money to alleviate overall debt, which astonished the players who from time to time simply did not receive wages.

One of them, Mike Jackson, had left Celtic in April 1963 to go to St Johnstone; ten months later he joined Thirds, the club he had supported as a boy having been brought up in nearby Allison Street. He did not know what he had let himself in for. Although he was fielded 78 times for Celtic and played alongside (now Sir) Alex Ferguson at St Johnstone (and thus would have been prepared for anything), he and his colleagues were to go through experiences as bizarre as any encountered anywhere else in football. 'I signed for £27 a week,' he said, 'and I did get the money, for at that time everything seemed to be running smoothly. But after just avoiding relegation that season I got the sense, at the beginning of the next one, that things were going wrong. We had a good, experienced side and Ally MacLeod was still playing then, but we were struggling to win games. Then I realised that things were going down the Swanee. At training they would only produce one decent ball; they would paint some of them just to make them a bit more reasonable-looking. Bobby Evans, the ex-Celtic player, was manager and trainer all in one, but they couldn't afford medical stuff. I remember we went to Dundee to play one day and Bobby asked me if I knew the trainer there, Sammy Kean, which I did. He then asked me if I would go to him and tell him we had forgotten our medical bag and ask if he could give us some bandages and bits and pieces. We went begging around the country. It was depressing. Well, when we got relegated that season and went part-time, that's when things started to go disastrous.'

The means of travel shrank. The team bus became a minibus. Wherever they went they were packed uncomfortably into this vehicle, alongside the hamper. In the lower division they had to endure treks to places like Arbroath and Montrose, stopping at convenient fish and chip shops for sustenance, while in addition asking some players to travel by car. The only playable ball they had for matches at Cathkin Park was painted white, but because of the nature of the Scottish climate it rapidly lost its camouflage on a wet day, to the surprise of opponents who were beginning to believe Thirds had just invented the chameleon ball. Sometimes they acquired a ball at a cheap discount rate with a defect known only to the retailer, which would pass muster even with some of the more fussy referees before the match, as their painted monsters sometimes might not have. They knew it would only last a couple of minutes in its pristine condition. So when it strangely deflated at the first decent kick, or landed like a squashed pancake on somebody's head just after kick-off, on would come the painted orb which the referee would have to accept just to keep the game going. Third Lanark's players were becoming skilled in the arts of deception which had nothing to do with the tactics board, and their technique was to reach heights of great creativity.

One Friday the players were asked to assemble to be told that for various reasons they might not be able to put out a full-strength team. In order to avoid any embarrassment about the fixture, the players were provided with pails and asked to cover the pitch with water. Somebody with foresight on the board had seen the weather forecast for a heavy frost that night. The following morning the referee, Tom Wharton, found a pitch fit only for the Toronto Maple Leafs ice hockey team. Game postponed; pressure eased. But with the con-tricks came indignities. Tiles began to fall off in the bathrooms. There was no hot water anywhere in the pavilion, to the disgust of away sides. Players would start fires on the stone dressing-room floor with any appropriate material, just to get some heat. At training, Hiddleston economised by refusing to put the floodlights on, so players were running around in the dark, Inspector Clouseau-like, looking for clues as to where the ball might be. The absurdity of his almost manic attempt to cut costs was exposed, in all its insensitivity, during a friendly against Clydebank on a bitterly cold, foggy day in January 1966. A young player called Kinnaird was being fielded as a trialist. He sustained a shocking break to his arm on the hard surface.

People watching said it was dangling, sickeningly, in several places, and he must have been suffering intense pain. Mike Jackson was on the touchline. 'I was told to get an ambulance and accompany the young lad to the Western Infirmary. Now when you saw the arm you were frightened even to touch him for fear of hurting him. Yet I can recall Hiddleston's very words to me: "When you get to the hospital make sure to tell the doctors to lift the effing jersey over his head and not to cut the sleeves, for we'll need it for next week."'

When ex-Ranger Bobby Shearer became manager in 1967 he had to pay the players by going to the gatemen, collecting the turnstile admission money of threepennies, sixpennies and half-crowns and dispensing these in the dressing-room to men whose tolerance of this and a £6-a-week wage now seems incredible. But there was a breaking point. They knew that all clubs presented Third Lanark with a cheque after playing an away game, but they were not receiving any wages for playing outside their own stadium, laughable though these payments were. The news was spreading about this and they realised their professional reputations were at stake, quite apart from their own desperate need for money. They rebelled. Tony Connell, who would play in that last match at Dumbarton, recalled the Good Samaritan who surprisingly came to their aid. 'It was an away game against Morton, and just before the match we refused to go out unless we were guaranteed a wage for the game. We told Hiddleston that in the dressing-room. He just turned on his heel. But shortly after that, as we were sitting there, in came Hal Stewart, the owner of Morton. Now you know what Hal was like. You could say he was the same kind of animal as Hiddleston. So anything he would say about our man would be like the pot calling the kettle black. But he held up a cheque and said that is what he was paying Thirds, and he would guarantee we would get money. We did go out, and we did get paid the following week.'

By contrast, the relative wealth of Celtic at the time did not mean that the coming of Stein would suddenly turn the dressing-room there into a cornucopia of earnings. Desmond White, the club secretary at the time, was an astute accountant in his own right, and with Stein slavishly devoted throughout his career to keeping a tight purse, the players at Celtic Park were being exploited just as shamelessly as they were at Cathkin. They certainly had a different status in life with the more famous club, but like the Thirds players they just took what life offered. It was the age of innocence, after all. They simply wanted to play football. A player like Billy McNeill, who had become frustrated at the lack of success at the club and was looking to earn more money elsewhere, changed his outlook when Stein arrived. Just one taste of the Big Man on his return to Parkhead, and like the others he was hooked. So Celtic and Thirds players were essentially serfs, albeit in different circumstances, operating within a system they felt was unchallengeable. Both sets of players were young, naïve and simply in a swoony romance with football. That played well with supporters and accountants. And in Celtic's case, the aspiration that emerged from it created Lisbon.

When we first saw them emerging from the dressing-room area in the Estadio Nacional in Portugal on 25 May 1967, Celtic's green and white jerseys, set against the more sombre tone of Inter Milan's outfit, looked refreshingly more in keeping with the incandescent nature of the day. Television, I knew, would never be able to capture that essence of blossoming colour and the infectious mood of anticipated celebration, for it was the age of the black and white camera. Yet within six weeks of that date in Lisbon a television development occurred that was to influence all our lives, and particularly the transmission of sport, when five continents were hooked up by satellite in a one-off, two-hour Sunday evening programme entitled *Our World* of which the *Radio Times* proudly proclaimed 'Live TV circles the globe for the first time'. Six days after that innovation, the BBC took its first step into colour with Centre Court pictures from Wimbledon. So although we were not aware of it at the time, we were also on the cusp of a new television age. But on the spot, in that stadium, the added disadvantage for Wolstenholme and me was that the sun was shining into our large television monitor, making viewing of the pictures on it quite impossible. To add to our discomfort they had put a roof above the bench in front of us, which together with the bulk of the television set meant that we both watched this European final through a space which was the equivalent of a large letter-box.

The confession, which I make now but did not before the game to colleagues, is that I would not have been sent into misery if the game had been drawn. Astonishingly, Wolstenholme had been assigned to cover the Austria v. England friendly in Vienna, leaving the replay in the hands of yours truly who had to enlist the aid of the late Labour MP Jimmy

Hamilton to persuade the Lanarkshire Education Authority for special release from teaching to travel to Lisbon. I quaked inwardly at the prospect, but equally it's something I coveted. Going solo nationwide seemed like a fine career move. Television puts the fine edge on ego.

That thought had gone well out of my mind by the time Celtic were leading 2–1 and were edging towards their unique triumph. Each time a goal was scored the Celtic official party would jump up in front of us, blanking out the pitch entirely; and since they would not sit down again for at least a couple of minutes we had to screw up our eyes and try to determine what was happening on the field using the quite inadequate monitor. At the end, amid the throng on the park and minus a piece of my white shirt, ripped off my back in the maul that surrounded Stein on the pitch as I tried to get him for an interview, the extremes of euphoria reminded me of being in George Square on VE night as a kid, buffeted in a delirium that left you breathless and pleasantly marked for life. The deed was done. No replay. That potential career leap would have to wait.

As Celtic had been building up their resources under Stein in the two years leading up to Lisbon, Thirds were surviving like tramps feeding off handouts. That naïvety of players I spoke about was something Hiddleston in particular was ruthlessly exploiting. I only bumped into him once, and that was in the toilet just outside the boardroom at Greenock Morton's Cappielow. He came in with Bailie Reilly, his henchman. He always wore a soft hat, indoors as well. He moved towards the loo muttering to his companion a couple of sentences that stuck with me because of the reputation he had amassed: 'They're effing mean in here. You cannae even get a half of whisky out of them.' That would have amused his players, who had had several showdowns with the board over non-payments and who from time to time had had to bring in the Scottish Players' Union man Johnny Hughes to intercede on their behalf.

Hughes was simply a stepping-stone to the next crisis though. It was the sheer audacity of Hiddleston that aided his survival. Sometimes the players were complicit in this, for they were forced into being masters of deception. This reached its apotheosis one morning in 1965 when Mike Jackson turned up with the rest for training, which took a highly original form. 'They had just built the new stand,' he recalled. 'Of course the boardroom looked magnificent, but the dressing-rooms still hadn't been touched. Around 14 full-time players turned up to train under Bobby

Evans that day. But before we started Hiddleston came in to talk to us. "I'll tell you what I want you to do this morning," he said. "The Customs and Excise men are coming in today to examine us. Now there are some things they don't need to see. I want you lads to help me shift the fruit machines out of the lounge." He was referring to about half a dozen one-armed bandits in this big lounge in the boardroom which somebody had obviously told the Inland Revenue about. So all fourteen of us gathered in the lounge and proceeded to lift them all, carry them right across the pitch, up the terracing to the enclosure on the other side of the pavilion, dump them and hide them. It took us all morning, manager and players. I felt as if I had a double hernia. We were covering up for him. God knows what the Inland Revenue would have thought.' In truth they would hardly have credited a training session with felonious acts.

Stein also used a native cunning, but to much more productive effect on the field. During those first four years of commentating I witnessed the demise of the old-style manager, as personified by Scot Symon of Rangers, who was sacked by the club in late 1967. He was certainly not an unsuccessful manager, as his track record revealed; Stein had simply made him seem inappropriate. The new Celtic manager was establishing a sometimes tyrannical regime with players and press which was on a different scale and dimension from those which an odious figure such as Hiddleston was attempting at the lower end of the market. Players Stein had a great fondness for, like his captain Billy McNeill, were shown no mercy when it came to negotiating terms. John Hughes, then a prolific striker for the club, once approached him with the idea of asking for 15 per cent more in the pay-packet. Whether or not he had already whispered that around the dressing-room, when he saw the manager he was told to sit down and his play that season was praised. But then Stein added, 'Sometimes in life you've got to be shown how to keep your feet on the ground and not get carried away with things. So I am going to suggest you take a 15 per cent cut for this season.' Hughes, flabbergasted by the audacity of this, was then left having to argue not for an increase but for what he was already earning. Stein's masterly deflation of players might have seemed cruel at times, but it reinforced his command of all that he surveyed, for the benefit of the club.

Compare that to the scene when Mike Jackson decided to have a showdown and proposed to Hiddleston that he buy out his own contract, which was the method by which the director extorted money from the unenlightened. Jackson, though, was dealing with a different animal. 'I told him I wanted a transfer and I was prepared to buy myself out. He just looked at me and said, "Who would want to buy you? You're effing useless!" I reacted, stood up and bent towards him in anger. He shouted at me, "You touch me and I'll have you sorted out. You'll be done in. You'll regret it!" So there was this man in the soft hat in front of me trying to threaten me with violence. You know, I just burst out laughing!'

So pseudo-gangsterism was alive and well in that little corner of the south side of Glasgow at a time when we were all being dazzled by achievements elsewhere. Jackson did have to buy himself out, as others did, but as in so many cases it was never recorded in the accounts. The missing money from those sources, the negligent handling of the books, the mysterious transactions over shareholdings and the suspicion that Hiddleston and his directors wanted to sell out Cathkin and move the club to the new town of East Kilbride because the valuation of the ground had risen from £6,000 an acre in 1962 to £25,000 an acre in 1966 – all of this pushed the club further towards public opprobrium and eventual financial collapse. All the occupants of that minibus heading for that game in Dumbarton on 28 April 1967 learnt two days later that Third Lanark would never play again. They were shocked and bewildered, and felt quite powerless. They had all believed that this was what Hiddleston had been after all along – to run the club into the ground, then sell and move on to make himself a handsome profit.

Nature, though, was not going to let him get away with it. In November 1967, while on holiday in Blackpool, Hiddleston died of a heart attack. As Tony Connell afterwards commented, 'We were surprised by that, because we didn't think he had a heart.' It was the most drastic way to avoid the consequences of his actions, but the law would have got him in the end anyway. On 1 July 1968, four former directors, including Bailie Reilly, were found guilty of contravening the existing Companies Acts and fined £100 each. Later that year, an investigation by the Board of Trade of the affairs of Third Lanark Athletic Club Limited castigated the directors but particularly William Hiddleston for blatant corruption, confirming that he ran Thirds 'as an inefficient and unscrupulous one-man business without regard to the provisions of the Companies Act, the articles of association of the company, or the interest of shareholders'. Then they concluded that in relation to certain transactions 'the circumstances merit police inquiry'.

How could this sordid phase in Scottish football have been allowed? There was no such thing as the process of administration in those days, the life-raft for so many clubs today. More importantly, there simply was no willingness on the part of other Scottish clubs to come to the rescue, because it was the age of relative plenty and Third Lanark's fate did not seem to contain the seeds of a financial contamination about to spread through the rest of the sport. Another factor was the old Scottish cultural distaste for debt, which prudes might have considered the by-product of dissolute living. After all, before 1918 in Scotland you could have been put in jail for personal debt, such was our puritanical scorn for it. So Thirds became a pariah, and the only former British senior club whose name has entirely disappeared from current football activity. There is barely any consolation to be rescued from their passing, other than that it reminds us that fighting for a community's love of a club is eminently worthwhile. Celtic and Rangers left that era behind, seriously clueless about what would lie ahead in a rapidly changing world, but with a continuing belief in their own abilities to reach the heights. This they did in the new decade, on a single night, when together they created a new European record.

CHAPTER TWO
A CITY OF TWO TALES

'I felt fine at first. But I'll tell you what killed me. The walk. We had never done this before. It was that 50-yard walk that got to me. It seemed all right at first. I remember walking the first ten yards or so, then I started to jog, then I slowed down a bit as I got nearer. You could hear a pin drop. It was unbelievable, scary. There had never been anything like this before. We just didn't know what it would be like. It was the first time, of course, that this had happened. It was raining that night.'

The inner musings of a troubled man, looking back on a night he will never forget. Raymond Chandler might have written that script for him. Except this was no gumshoe but a man much less shifty, and one who could find no hiding place. It suggests torment. It was. For a while, anyway – he is made of stern stuff, as we shall discover. His contribution on that evening of 19 April 1972 was historic, whichever way you look at it. But I will return to him, and name him, later.

Glasgow was a city of two tales that night. One story tragic, the other euphoric. By midnight, the footballing city faced in two directions. One face looked to a final in a Mediterranean city about which there was only cursory knowledge. We knew only that there was a statue there to Columbus and an odd-looking church which someone said resembled 'faither's' attempt at a sandcastle 'doon the waater'. The other face of the city became numbed in the knowledge that the night would end up in the history book as a crushingly painful statistic. Some 155,000 watched all this unfold, on the same evening, within a matter of a couple of hours that rent Glasgow in two, and afterwards triumphalism at one end of the city bounced off mass incredulity at the other. The city, though, conveyed to the rest of Europe the entirely neutral but unambiguous message that even as a western outpost of the game the sport enjoyed public support few if any cities on the continent could equal. The sheer magnitude of that aggregate attendance – 80,000 at Ibrox for the Rangers–Bayern Munich second-leg Cup Winners' Cup semi-final, 75,000 at Celtic Park for the equivalent stage of the European Cup against Inter Milan – suggested that if you had to seek a centre of gravity of the European game it would be in George Square, Glasgow, roughly a few feet away from that statue of Sir Walter Scott. No other European city has ever again assembled such a throng on one single night. Nothing in the city commemorates that public achievement – partly because not even Epstein could have come up with a work of art that adequately conveyed the defeat and triumph experienced that night.

At the time, our media were not slow to drum out the message. Malcolm Munro of the *Evening Times*, learning of the tickets being snapped up for both venues within hours of their opening sale, commented in his paper, 'No city anywhere else could pull out 155,000 fans on the same night. Glasgow is the most football-crazy city in Europe. No, make that the world.' Alex Cameron of the *Daily Record*, on the eve of the matches, noted that UEFA officials in Berne described it as 'the number one crowd-pulling city in Europe, at least for matches in their competitions'.

Not domestically, though, for the story of that night was the contrasting appeal of Scottish and European competition. The public were deserting the old First Division in droves. People would look at the European matches, note the crowds they could attract, particularly on that evening, and use that point in the prolonged discussions on league reconstruction as an argument for radical change to the domestic game. After that night they would come to a conclusion that in hindsight can be seen as momentously short-sighted, by opting for a tight league system that would effectively encourage defensive not attacking football, and which would contribute in the long run to the dearth of talent in this country.

This, though, was the age when such a correlation between the huge crowds for European games and the advance of Celtic and Rangers to finals was taken for granted. Were not these clubs conceived to do exactly that, and had they not done it all before? In 1967 they'd fought for these same two trophies in Lisbon and Nuremburg. Now, this was both attempting to reach their third European final. Lisbon still transfused Celtic, and bugged Rangers. It was never going to be allowed to go away, especially as Stein had been able to record his seventh league title in a row by beating East Fife 3–0 the weekend before the Inter Milan semi-final. Alex Cameron had taken up a campaigning posture for the club in the *Daily Record* when he wrote, 'Celtic should be allowed to keep the handsome Scottish League Championship trophy to mark their seven astonishing years at the top.' This was as unlikely to happen as the League asking Rangers to play in green and white. But, although he did not mind the praise for the seven-in-a row achievement, Stein himself wanted to divert attention to the Inter Milan match by responding to Celtic's seventh title with this dismissive remark, one made to sound rather odd in hindsight: 'It'll never happen again in my lifetime. But there is no time to look back.' It was as if he was resigned to the fact that he could sense the creaking of a juggernaut, about to suffer mechanical failure. In fact it was another three years before the club looked as if it had only three wheels on the wagon.

Lisbon had fortified Celtic. It was as if they had rewritten a constitution that gave them the right to refer back to that famous May afternoon as a clause of indemnity against failure in Scotland. Celtic's air of superiority stemmed from that. It had given them unprecedented stature, and the belief that they were simply better had clearly been passed on, through those five years, like some apostolic succession to a new generation of players. You felt that success, necessarily breeding more success, was a prototype first tested by Celtic. Rangers, having dispensed with two managers as casualties of Stein's throttling grip on them, could still do nothing to usurp him. This was more than a hex on Ibrox, it was a condition of mind. Alex MacDonald, a key player for them who had lived part of his boyhood on the terracings at Ibrox, coming as he did from nearby Scotland Street, felt the full brunt of Rangers' flagging fortunes domestically. 'When you are not doing well as a Rangers player, the postman tells you, the grocer tells you, the street-sweeper tells you, your granny tells you. Half of Glasgow is angry with you, the other half is laughing at you. It can be painful, and we were coming near the end of our tether. It was only in Europe we seemed to find that extra-special lift. Thank God for that. For life was becoming intolerable.' Indeed, in that season of 1971/72, Europe had looked like an escape hatch for them through which they could elude the clutches of the man demonised around Govan.

It was Stein himself, no less, who used to say to me, with that suggestive, knowing smile, when referring to the long-drawn-out talks about league reconstruction occurring around that period, 'They're trying to devise something that'll make it difficult for us to win.' But even Celtic must have been worried themselves about the decline in interest in the First Division, as it existed. Their sixth consecutive league title achievement had been watched by 47,000 fewer than had watched their fifth. Season 1970/71 saw a total decline in the top division's attendances of 143,000; and on Saturday, 24 April 1971 only 39,000 watched the sixteen teams play (the Celtic match was postponed that day). Part of the problem was the continuing domination of Celtic, who were making the league seem a mere preamble to their coronation every season. The corollary was that the Rangers support was less inclined to show up around the country. It was the uncompetitive league producing Celtic supporters' apathy and Rangers supporters' disgust that distorted the overall figures. Of course there were other strong social factors influencing footballing attendance. Nevertheless, had Rangers during that period mounted a much more robust challenge to Celtic, the attendances around the country would not have dwindled as much, leading to the false conclusion that the public as a whole was losing its taste for the game.

It is no wonder, then, that after he became general manager of Rangers in June 1972, Willie Waddell would take the initiative in discussions with representatives of other clubs in order to find a formula that would bring people back to the domestic game. But in their panic they were eventually to go down a route that would effectively stifle much creative football through the emergence of a more defensive mentality in a smaller, tighter, elitist league where demotion could spell financial disaster and the avoidance of defeat became the prime motivator in the game. Now, in the new millennium, we scratch our heads and wonder where the classy Scottish ball players have gone. And all clubs shared a common belief that a monster was stalking the land, one that would devour the sport completely in an age of apparently waning interest. Its evil eye was the cathode-ray tube. Television was to be treated as the ultimate menace.

In fact, 19 April 1972 was the evening when football completely surrendered to the blandishments of television, and its relationship with the Scottish game was never to be the same again, whatever public display of hostility was mounted from any source. The two companies, the BBC and Scottish Television, were at first flummoxed as to how to cope with two major games dropped in their laps. Obviously the major tournament would have been given precedence under ordinary circumstances, but they were far from ordinary on this occasion. Italian

Television, weighing in heavily with their battalions of lira, demanded an eight p.m. kick-off at Celtic Park. Celtic chairman Desmond White, whose favourite melody was that played on a cash-register, responded swiftly.

Celtic succumbing to any television demand of any sort at that time was like hearing of a man of the cloth being caught in a brothel. It seemed completely out of character for a club whose hardline attitude was that John Logie Baird was basically responsible for letting loose a deadly virus that would leave the terracings devoid of life. This trenchant attitude stemmed from previous chairman Bob Kelly, later Sir Robert, who despised television's presence in a football stadium. He had travelled to the States in the 1950s and returned absolutely convinced that he had seen the death throes of baseball, which had, in his terms, sold its soul to network television and allowed attendances to plummet. Whenever we talked about television coverage of his games in the 1960s, I felt like I was a first lieutenant to the Grim Reaper. And the power of his personality, allied to the influence he had wielded through his presidency of the SFA, made him a resolute foe of the medium. Desmond White, picking up the baton from his now departed leader, relayed the same fundamental message at a meeting of the SFA on 19 March 1973, albeit a year after selling out to Italian Television: 'Live spectators come first, and while we regret that the elderly and the sick should be deprived, we must not pander to the lazy and indifferent and encourage an armchair audience.'

The rest of Scottish football was also heavily influenced by that tone and attitude. During the period from the mid-1960s until that evening in April 1972, it was quite easy for anybody from television to enter a football ground and realise how it felt to be the fox being pursued by the Beaufort Hunt on Boxing Day. We did gain entry most of the time, and dealing directly with players and managers caused little difficulty. But if you met anybody at boardroom level you encountered barely disguised contempt from time to time. One man continued to exercise his right simply to bar television, which individual clubs could do in those days. He was the chairman of Hibernian, Tom Hart. This self-made builder detested the medium, and when you faced his crude belligerence, as I was forced to do on occasion, you felt there was as much chance of Arthur's Seat moving to Easter Road as cameras being allowed entry to his fiefdom. Indeed, when Celtic clinched their 30th League

Championship in April 1977, it was not covered by television because the game was played at Easter Road. The loquacious and amiable Jack Steedman, chairman of Clydebank and an executive member of the Scottish League during that period, once told me with almost admirable candour as we stood on the pitch at the old Broomfield Park, Airdrie, before a game involving his club, that if he could have his way he would expel me from the ground, there and then, and send the cameras packing. 'What good are you doing football?' I recall him asking rhetorically of me, before sweeping aside what he must have considered my attempt to justify something akin to housebreaking.

The press followed meekly in the wake of such views. At any excuse they would heap scorn on television. And admittedly during the first primitive attempts at putting on sports programmes, in the late 1960s in particular, much scope was given for derision. Some of our efforts looked as though we were filming the Keystone Cops chasing a piece of tumbleweed rather than a Scottish football match, and there were edits on film that looked as if they had been made by the knife of Sweeney Todd. On one occasion, to cover a technical hitch in a recording, football noises from the sound library had to be dubbed on over a shot of Celtic supporters expressing jubilation after a goal had been scored. Unfortunately the tape was from a Rangers archive. The clearly distinguishable sound of the Orange anthem 'The Sash My Father Wore' coming from the mouths of those in green and white elevated ecumenism to a dizzy height. Such blunders were not infrequent. Indeed, you might have thought that the opponents of television would have taken some comfort out of seeing the awful lapses that did occur to conclude that this medium was as innocuous a threat to the Scottish game as the alternative sport of haggis-throwing. But they worried about its potential, and were right to do so.

Scotland's growing appetite for televised football reflected what was happening south of the border. When *Match of the Day* was first screened in August 1964 on the new BBC2 channel, which was very much a minority viewing platform, it was screened only in the London area and watched by a mere 20,000. This was half the attendance at the game itself, Liverpool v. Arsenal at Anfield. When the programme switched to BBC1 in August 1966 in the wake of the World Cup held in England that year, six million tuned in. Kenneth Wolstenholme announced on that first programme after England's World Cup triumph, 'Welcome to those who have followed us from BBC2 to BBC1. But a special welcome to those new viewers who have been won over by the World Cup. We hope you will go along to watch your local team as well as watch *Match of the Day.'* And then he added a few words which to succeeding football commentators must sound endearingly quaint: 'And in response to many requests, I will explain some of the more technical points of the game as we go along.'

The stances of the football authorities in Scotland had been extreme, though. Television was perceived to be a potential bully which, if given its way, would ride roughshod over all the essential trappings of the traditional game. We were pariahs, we of the cathode-ray tube. I had made enemies of some of the written press for no other reason than that I represented television. But I detected a thawing in the five years or so leading up to that night in 1972. It was coming about because only the most myopic could fail to detect the growing public interest in watching football on the box. So, this was to be the night when, depending on your point of view in the debate about television, either the medium came of age or the evil genie was let out of the bottle.

The complications in terms of providing fair and adequate coverage to both games were immense. The eight o'clock kick-off at Celtic Park made it awkward for both the BBC and Scottish Television, but did not prevent complaints from Celtic Park that they, being in the premier competition, ought to have had precedence of coverage. It was easy to dismiss that on the basis of first come, first served. And there was one major obstacle for BBC Scotland – the *Nine O'Clock News*. Within the corporation this news slot was regarded as sacrosanct; nothing short of a direct hit from an ICBM could have taken it off the air. To have covered the whole Celtic game live would have meant knocking that news bulletin wholly from its slot. We pleaded for an exemption, but the insularity of BBC London has always been a major aggravation for provincial broadcasting and they bluntly rejected our requests. Scottish Television took full advantage of this scheduling nightmare and covered the whole Ibrox game live, leaving the BBC to transmit highlights later. We could, of course, cover live anything from Celtic Park – but only once Robert Dougall had said goodnight from his London news studio, by which time the Rangers game was over.

7.30 p.m. The Rangers match at Ibrox kicks off. At Celtic Park, at exactly that time, I am sitting above the 'Jungle' with song after song wafting up towards our platform, hitting us the way a warm air vent from the Glasgow subway sweeps through you. The multitude below is impatient for their game to start in half an hour, and they are in full throttle. Then something happens. There is a hiatus of sorts. The song suddenly becomes a strangulated buzz, like a grasping for something other than song. It is a mere momentary blip, and when the voices let rip again it is with an almost defiant tone. Through the miracle of the 'trannies' they have heard that Rangers have scored after exactly 60 seconds; the hiccup was caused by their seeking quick confirmation of the dreaded news. They have been hoping for Bayern to triumph.

In a sense I felt cheated by that opening goal because my colleague George Davidson, the commentator at that Ibrox match for the highlights to be transmitted later that evening – one of the most colourful men in broadcasting, and a retired merchant sea-captain who had been the first man to land with a relief boat at Yokohama after the great earthquake there of 1923 when 142,000 people perished – was getting in on the dramatic action even before we had started. Was I sitting on top of a major anti-climax by comparison? I sat there, itchily envious. I could barely believe that Rangers would score at all, let alone beat a side comprising a group of players who would go on after that season to dominate European football. I had been in Munich to cover their semi-final, which had ended in a 1–1 draw. I had seen a Rangers side defending so desperately at times that you had to think they were simply no match for the aristocratic bearing of so many of the Bayern players. But they had not buckled. It was the last ever European game Bayern played in their old stadium before moving to the splendour of their new home within the complex built for the 1972 Olympics. 'Splendour' is not the word they would have attached to their visit to Ibrox that night; that other German word 'Blitzkreig' might have passed through their minds when Rangers struck so early in the game.

Sandy Jardine, the goalscorer, had no inhibitions about taking a little of the shine off the manner in which he executed his strike, because actually puncturing the Germans with hardly a drop of sweat having been spent was what drove a wedge between Bayern and the final they had assumed they would reach. 'I've got to be honest,' he said. 'I would love to say I drove a superb shot all of 25 yards into the roof of the net. But, in fact, I hit this looping ball towards goal and I didn't really expect anything out of it.

Remember, they had the famous Sepp Maier in goal. To my astonishment he let the ball swing over his head. He really should have saved it. I could scarcely believe it. But it went in, and we were on our way.'

But with Beckenbauer as the elegant leader, and players like Breitner, Roth, Schwarzenbeck and Müller around him, such a start elicited fears of a backlash rather than hope of a Rangers romp. However, there was another factor which to this day Alex MacDonald feels degraded the play of the Germans. 'The pitch. At that time the pitch at Ibrox was in a terrible condition. It had taken a battering over the season and it was all uneven and bumpy. Compared to what the Germans would have been used to, it was awful. They just weren't passing the ball the way I knew they could. Take Beckenbauer. You know the player he was. He hardly ever placed a wrong pass. That night he was all over the place. It was him who misplaced a pass that went to Sandy for his opening goal. Beckenbauer would try one of those little chips of his towards the wings and you would see the ball running out of play. Time after time. His first touch was terrible that night. Beckenbauer, of all people. Sandy's goal had certainly rocked them and we were all inspired by that, but the Germans did not settle down on that pitch at all.'

Twenty-two minutes later, 18-year-old Derek Parlane swept in a shot off the underside of the bar, after Stein had head-flicked on a Johnston corner. Parlane had come into the side for injured club captain John Greig, who had begun to look like an ally of Pancho Villa with his long hair and unshaven face, which he had determined not to reunite with a razor until Rangers brought the cup to Ibrox. (Some, less sympathetic to Rangers, suggested that if that were the case Greig would end up looking more like Methuselah.) If anybody personified the tenacity of the Waddell–Wallace years it was the boy from Edinburgh who diverted his childhood affection for Hearts into a missionary zeal on behalf of the Ibrox club. Such conviction brought him the honour of being selected as The Greatest Ever Ranger by the worldwide support in later years. Rangers had been prepared to gamble on his fitness, but his ankle let him down. Still, his replacement Parlane's goal meant that the festival at Ibrox was now well underway before anything had stirred in the east end of Glasgow.

8 p.m. Celtic kick off. At last. Half an hour's wait for us while another struggle is taking place and a Scottish team is in a strong lead against the famed Bayern side on the other side of the city feels like you are being held in a detention centre. But once it starts the acoustics of Celtic Park suck you into the middle of the play and you begin to sweat as the massed body heat of the packed Jungle and the adrenalin pumping put you on a state of alert, waiting for one of those erupting moments for which Parkhead under Stein have become renowned.

The first 20 minutes saw a flood of expected Celtic attacks. But a nagging worry was the memory of how they had been sucker-punched in a game in 1969 by the other Milan side, AC, as Jim Craig explained: 'I thought we had a great chance to win the European Cup in 1969 when we went to the San Siro and drew 0–0 in the snow. It was a great performance. But back we came to Celtic Park and it took just one bad throw-in by me and a misjudgement by Billy McNeill for Prati to come in and kill us. I shied the ball to Billy and called on him to boot it. He tried to kill it but lost control, and Prati stepped in to score.' I recall that night – the Italians simply acting like a landslide in the Brenner Pass, blocking everything that was thrown at them, and then the figure of Prati getting that break, streaking towards goal like a tarantula, followed by the inevitable sting. A solitary incident knocking Celtic out of the cup. And if I could remember it distinctly, you can understand how the classic Italian counter-attack must have preyed on the Celtic mind that night, three years later, even though they had returned from the first leg with another no-score draw, against Inter. They were meeting Italian defending at its best. The Jungle was a mix of exasperation and anxiety.

9.20 p.m. With the conclusion of the Ibrox game and the triumph of Rangers confirmed, the BBC makes its switch to the Celtic match. Little do they realise that they have just struck gold. For, leaving aside the implications of the eventual result, a drama falls into our laps which despite many other evenings of gut-wrenching intensity in that stadium turns out to have a quite unique assault on the nervous system.

One name kept popping up in commentary. Facchetti. The man who had been stared at almost in awe by Bertie Auld as he stood beside him in the tunnel before the game in Lisbon in 1967 was still at the helm for Inter. He strode through the game like a Greek god assuring those around him that Fate was on their side. His superb marshalling of the Inter defence meant there were few clear chances for Celtic to score. One glaring miss by Tommy Callaghan probably signified for him a rejection by the terracings ever after.

Time wore on. The pace slowed. The Italians obdurately refused to entertain and we went into extra-time thinking it inconceivable that these two teams could play two entire games plus an extra half-hour without finding the net. But the night had a character all of its own. Jim Craig recalled Celtic's preparations for this eventuality. 'We were down at Seamill [Hydro Hotel] as usual, and the day before the game Jock had us take part in a penalty shoot-out competition. Dixie Deans won it out of the park. So we picked our five: Dixie to go first, then Pat McCluskey, Jimmy Johnstone, Bobby Murdoch, then me. Actually, as things turned out I was promoted up the order just after Facchetti had scored with his penalty. Why, I'll never know, and as I walked up to take it I could hear a kind of mutter of disbelief in the crowd that I was taking it – which does your confidence a world of good, doesn't it? But anyway, I scored. But what was going through my mind, as a defender, was that we had held them at bay for 210 minutes and had been let down by our forwards.'

This was the first penalty shoot-out ever seen in Glasgow. The scene spread before us was of initiates being introduced to a new ritual; we knew where the altar was, but didn't know how to approach it. It was this perhaps more than anything else that placed such great stress on the player who was to make the historic first move. Dixie Deans, a prolific goalscorer signed from Motherwell earlier that season, a chunky, mobile, aggressive leader, had always conveyed the impression of being a nerveless scorer of goals. Even decades later his testimony to me, which I recount at the start of this chapter, sounded almost like that of a penitent still keen to unburden himself of a sense of lingering guilt. 'At the end of extra-time big Jock talked to us at the halfway line and he said to me, "How are you feeling?" I said, "Nae problems, boss, nae problems. Brand new, boss, brand new." If it had been an ordinary game, you are all around the box when a penalty is awarded and you just step up and take it. But we were all congregated on the halfway line and I had never anticipated what the procedure was. The referee blew his whistle and it was me for the first penalty.' Then came that walk. 'I put the ball on the spot. I lifted it again and wiped it on my jersey, and to be honest I think I froze a bit, and a bit of panic set in. I remember thinking to myself, "Oh, for God's sake!" I decided where I was going to put it, and to this day, watching the videos, I believe I was right in thinking the keeper moved just before I hit the ball, and I tried to loft it over him. But over the bar it went. I never heard anything after that as I walked back to the halfway line. There seemed to be that deathly silence again. I remember saying to Jimmy Johnstone, "Say a prayer for me, wee man." He just looked at me, smiled and said, "It's mair than a prayer you'll need noo!"' All the other penalties were scored, so Celtic were eliminated 4–5 on the shoot-out.

At Ibrox, the Rangers players gathered round their dressing-room television to watch the demise of their great rivals. Some of them, according to Sandy Jardine, felt sorry for Celtic. They were in the minority. Most, as Jardine honestly admits, felt it added to their feeling of euphoria, and they cheered every Inter penalty.

At Celtic Park, the first thing Jock Stein did was to commiserate with Deans and point out that the losing of the game was not down to the missing of a penalty but much else in the match. It wasn't until a couple of days later that Stein became angry. For on match night, photographers had pursued Deans and tried to trail him to a pub where he was having a drink after the game. He'd become aware of this and had tried for the rest of the night to duck and weave away from them. He'd phoned his wife and told her he wouldn't be returning home, for the press had parked outside his house. He'd stayed overnight with a friend, but they'd caught up with him the following day, unknown to him, as he recalled. 'I went to get a bus home in the morning, having stayed out all night, and I just stood for a while waiting for it. I didn't want to stand beside anybody. I just wasn't feeling like talking to people. But the next day I opened the papers and there was this picture of me standing at a bus stop and it looked as if the queue was looking the other way, shunning me, and that is the way it was written up. I couldn't believe it. When I went back to the park, Jock went ballistic. He tore into me and just didn't accept that I hadn't posed for this. But I hadn't. He never really believed me.'

To a generation of people – those who were inside Celtic Park and the vast audience watching on television – that miss would be positioned in the gallery of cruel anti-climaxes alongside Doug Sanders' missed putt on the 18th at St Andrews in 1970, Don Fox's front-of-posts, last-gasp, missed conversion in the 1968 Rugby League Cup final, and Devon Loch failing at the final hurdle at Aintree in 1956. But, as I pointed out, Deans was made of stern stuff: nearly three weeks later he scored a hat-trick as Celtic beat Hibernian 6–1 in the Scottish Cup final.

Midnight. It is all over. It has been no ordinary evening. Though nobody in Scotland realises it, television has effectively set the agenda for the future and taken over effective control of the major games. The public has warmed to it regardless of the contrasting results of the ties. Their reserve about television's influence on the game, stoked by the press, has been blown away. Their appetite for more will never be sated. Sponsors have woken up to the mighty potential within their grasp. Why, only days later we hear the preposterous suggestion that players might actually wear advertising on their shirts one day. How arcane! Scottish football's legislators are now even keener for reconstruction, as they puzzle over how to tap the huge crowd potential that European football demonstrates does exist. But at the time we put the night behind us, little thinking of the consequences to follow.

By the morning of 20 April the Rangers legions were already bombarding travel agents for the mass exodus to Barcelona, avidly intent on outdoing the Lisbon festival of their great rivals. The rest of us firmly believed that such evenings would be a regular occurrence, so confident were we of the robustness of Scottish football. In fact Celtic would have to wait 31 years before reaching another European final, and Rangers have not managed one since that night in the Camp Nou. Crowds would never reach that peak again. Twenty-two full-blooded Scots played for the Glasgow clubs that night, whereas now that birthright has been sold out. We were unaware we were looking down the other side of the watershed.

There is a postscript to the evening that points again to a future of great significance to the Scottish game. Thousand of miles away in Toronto an expatriate Scot and Celtic fan wishing to take advantage of the new technology of satellite transmission hired Toronto's famous Maple Leaf Gardens to allow 12,000 Scots and Italians to watch the Celtic–Inter game live. Unfortunately, whether through optimism or not, he only booked the satellite for a 90-minute transmission and had to pay out more to cover the dramatic conclusion. It is also said he lost money on the venture. Embarrassment was obviously no impediment to his progress in life. Two decades later, when he surfaced again to take over a moribund Celtic, he would suffer little embarrassment, and he certainly would not be out of pocket. His name was Fergus McCann.

CHAPTER THREE
OLÉ OR NOT OLÉ

On 20 May 1972 the American Navy invaded Barcelona. A task force just off the coast had decanted the upholders of democracy into a city still under the totalitarian heel of Franco, on a mission of relaxation and debauchery. Barcelona was festooned with the evidence that shore-leave could bring a city to its knees just as effectively as a barrage of two-inch shells. In the Ramblas, droves of plain-clothed sailors jostled passers-by as they wove drunkenly up and down the broad thoroughfare, which they seemed to be claiming as their own through *force majeure*. In the narrow lane leading to the famous restaurant Los Caracoles, Americans were only ceasing their gyrations when nature forced them to crouch and vomit. Their style of negotiation with the prostitutes in the doorways lining the lane was simply to reach out and try to drag them by the hand. They were meeting unexpected resistance, as Catalan prostitution seemed to be proving that it did have certain standards: a public blitzkrieg of this sort and the potential of a gang-bang was not to their taste. At least not with sailors who were the werewolf versions of Kelly and Sinatra in *On the Town*. Screaming echoed along the lane occasionally and the stench of vomit and urine competed with the aromas of resplendent cooking from the open doors of the various cafés and restaurants.

Walking beside me, Gerry Pullen, a senior cameraman for the BBC, was in a state of professional agitation. Not that he was squeamish by nature. Cameramen rarely are. Snappers love a maul. It was simply because he had no camera with him. It was his night off and we were going out to eat. His statement there and then, as we were about to make our escape into the restaurant, resonates through the years. 'Bloody hell,' he said. 'You don't often have it laid on for you like this. I've missed the real action.'

He was, of course, spectacularly wrong. For four nights later, on 24 May, Glasgow Rangers played Moscow Dynamo in the Camp Nou in the European Cup Winners' Cup final, the aftermath of which made the onshore activities of the American Navy seem like peaceful fraternisation. A force was unleashed that night which stunned, mortified, puzzled and ultimately saddened anybody concerned about the image of football. And in a strange way, the riot that ensued might be traced back both to the conditions the Catalans had had imposed on them since the Spanish Civil War of the late 1930s and the nature of Glaswegians' unwillingness to lie down meekly in the face of outright intimidation. I base this observation on the comments made to me by Reuter's correspondent at the time, as we overlooked the mayhem that turned the Camp Nou from a sporting into a gladiatorial arena.

When we'd arrived several days before the Rangers official party and their supporters to make a documentary film as a preview for this final, we'd fallen in love with a city that held the Mediterranean at bay with resplendent self-confidence. This was, of course, before the major clean-up and renovation of the seaboard side for the Olympics of 1992, which dramatically altered the character of the port and harbour. Columbus, though, was still up there on his pedestal, still waiting to head out for the horizon, and looking down on a harbour too bustling and busy to be concerned about the past. And the broad sweep of elegant avenues from the harbour to the centre of the city added to the impression of sophistication and urban restlessness. Naturally, we assumed a busy, thriving city like this would barely notice a European final comprising a side from way up there in the north-west of Europe and one from behind the Iron Curtain. Indeed, the locals did turn their backs on the game, as if a source of plague had been identified at the Camp Nou. But there would be supporters arriving from abroad looking for more than a game of football. Not many from downtown Moscow, though. The only ones we were to encounter, apart from the players, were po-faced team-minders who fitted the caricature of KGB thugs. We were barred, for example, from filming the Dynamo training sessions in Espanyol's stadium prior to the match, when large men stood in our way wagging menacing fingers at us. No language, plenty of clear intent. But after a discreet withdrawal Pullen, a Londoner, returned with a camera hidden under his raincoat and marched through the ranks of the ungodly like one of those mad-dogs-and-Englishmen we have heard about, to shoot them secretly, as if he were an innocent bystander. The video revealed plenty of shots of the lining of his coat, as well as a team revealing absolutely nothing that would be of interest to anybody.

Glaswegians not only take kindly to the pleasures of the flesh, they can winkle them out even if dropped into the middle of the Gobi Desert, and since 26,000 of them were heading our way it seemed likely that the leisure business would thrive in a city geared up to varied entertainment. It would certainly be a dramatic change for those discovering for the first time the delights of the combination of constant sun and cheap booze. But the area off the Ramblas with its narrow, twisting lanes did convey a constant air of menace and impropriety, of which we certainly had plenty of warning as we watched the Americans at play. But this was the age of innocence. This was a time when spectator violence was not the preoccupation of anybody in Europe as a potential epidemic. My television producer John Coleman made the passing comment to me on that first night, 'The Rangers supporters will have a ball here.' That must now go down as one of the finest examples of dramatic irony since the about-to-be-assassinated King Duncan in *Macbeth* uttered, 'This castle hath a pleasant seat.'

The pleasantest seat of all was where Rangers decided to settle for the three days before the game. It was the Don Jaime Hotel, half an hour's drive from the stadium, on a hilltop in Casteldefels on the coast, with views over the Mediterranean you would die for. One of the preliminary boasts of this establishment, uttered almost proudly to me by the receptionist, was that the famous Hollywood actor George Sanders had committed suicide in one of their rooms. There was no rush to draw lots for that room, and after a couple of days experiencing the slowness of room service we had to assume that Sanders had in fact died of malnutrition. We were also living cheek by jowl with the players. This is a practice that went out of fashion in the next decade as managers strove to separate their players from the consequences of a more demanding press, in the wake of tabloid competition. Trust between media and clubs began to evaporate from about that time. But we were in it together then, and the mix of media, officials and players seemed natural, pleasant and productive. Interviews were granted at will, and the manager, Willie Waddell, would hold court with many of the journalists he had worked alongside as a football writer himself, with the *Scottish Daily Express*. He loved that because he had crossed the threshold, which gave him the upper hand in any argument with them. Previously they could treat him as one of 'them'; now they had to hold their tongues when he spoke. And the press were deeply conscious of the fact that he had both influence in

European football and the thrust of personality to exploit that.

I had witnessed a happening in Munich after the first leg of the semi-final of the tournament against Bayern on 5 April which included a corollary of note to those who avidly pursue conspiracy theories. At the end of the game I suddenly became aware of a bustling figure coming up the stairs from the direction of the pitch. It was Waddell, in a state of great agitation. He rushed past our commentary position, his usually immaculately-Brylcreemed hair flapping in rhythm to his mood. I had no idea what was perturbing him, but eventually that cameo was to fall into place. Colin Stein had been officially cautioned by the referee in the game, which meant he would miss the return leg in Glasgow. Now Stein was an important element in the Rangers side of that time. The eleven goals he was to score that season does not seem a huge total by modern standards, but it was his presence and grafting, and his ability to score at vital times, that made him important. It was his drive and aggression that night that had caused Zobel to head past his own keeper for the Rangers equaliser. To lose him for the return leg was unthinkable.

So Waddell was making tracks to find the UEFA delegate at the game, one Sandor Barcs. This Hungarian not only knew Waddell from past meetings, but had such an affection for the Ibrox club that it was said he wore a Rangers scarf and tie from time to time. Journalists knew that something was brewing, for after what seemed like an eternity we heard rumours to the effect that the referee might have got his booking wrong. Journalist Allan Herron of the *Sunday Mail* tracked down Barcs, after midnight, at his hotel. After some questioning, UEFA's delegate informed Herron that the referee had made a mistake and had booked the wrong player. It was a case of mistaken identity. Stein was in the clear to play in Glasgow. A Waddell coup? We never really got to the bottom of that, although it did leave you with an uneasy feeling that a power game had been in play off the pitch.

Now, in Barcelona, Waddell was within 90 minutes of a triumph that would consolidate his football reputation, which had shrunk to a great extent in the shadow of Jock Stein. They might not have articulated it openly, but there is no doubt that everyone associated with the club in Barcelona, from Waddell right down to the legions in red, white and blue, wanted to outdo Lisbon in celebration. They were having their problems though. The first one centred on their captain John Greig, who still wasn't fit. 'I thought I would be able to rest well enough in the days between [the semi-final] and Barcelona and get it right,' he said. 'But a couple of days before the final we trained on a local pitch which was bone hard. The following morning I woke up and the pain in the sole of my foot was unbearable. Nobody at that time had got to the root of the problem. I just didn't know what was causing it, but I knew I was in trouble. I told Deedle [Waddell] I wouldn't be fit to play. He just said, "You're playing." I knew what he meant. I had to be there just for the rest of the lads. They all expected me to be there, and I knew I would just have to deal with the pain and get on with it.'

To add to that, Colin Jackson, who had been indispensable in central defence, had problems with his ankle. Derek Johnstone, still only 18 at the time, recalled the decision which affected him more than any other. 'Bomber Jackson was so important to us that Deedle left it to the very morning of the game to decide. But I'll always remember when Bomber had to admit to himself he couldn't make it. He was in tears. It was to be the greatest game of his career, and here he was missing it. It was then they told me I was to play at the back. I had been up front as a striker against Bayern, but the change didn't bother me all that much. Remember, I was young and up for anything, although just before the game I felt very nervous. But that was nothing new. I had that feeling before every game, even when I got much older.'

I watched Jackson sitting by the side of the pitch as the others trained on that last day, distraught and inconsolable. He looked almost like a symbol of Rangers' season, which had been fraught with difficulties. They had won nothing. This was their last chance. But now they were seriously under-strength and likely to play with a captain with only one good foot. Still, this cup competition had seen them rise above domestic angst. They'd had so many bizarre moments you might have concluded their name was on the trophy from round one.

Sandy Jardine, who had opened the gates for them in the semi-final that April night in Glasgow, recalled vividly what happened in Lisbon in the game with Sporting in the second round which inspired their belief that they would go far in the competition, and which astonished UEFA because of its bizarre outcome. 'We had beaten Sporting 3–2 at Ibrox and we thought we had a right good chance. But after 90 minutes [in Lisbon] it went to extra-time and we ended up being beaten 4–3, which made it 6–6 on aggregate. The referee automatically ordered the penalty shoot-out, which we naturally went along with. The Portuguese won that, and you should have seen the celebrations as their crowd went mad and their players danced about. We just trudged off thinking that was that. It was only when we got into the dressing-room, all of us just sitting around in the gloom, when in came John Fairgrieve, who was, as you know, a very respected journalist and had been up in the press-box doing his reports. Something had occurred to him as we went to take the penalties and he checked up the new UEFA rules. And there it was in black and white. The new rule had just come in. The [extra] away goal we had scored counted double. We had won the game legitimately on the new away-goals rule. Willie Waddell went straight for the referee, showed him the book, pointed out to him the error of his decision, and he had to accept it. We were through, not them. So you had the unique situation of us going mad with joy in the dressing-room while outside the Portuguese players and their supporters were doing exactly the same, thinking they were through. I doubt if that has ever happened again in European football.' Rangers left the stadium in safety that night with the locals none the wiser, for UEFA did not officially announce the outcome until the following day.

So when they took the bus to the Camp Nou in the late afternoon of 24 May, they could claim to be battle-scarred veterans. But they were still in for surprises. For when we all arrived at the complex and made for the pitch, we discovered that hundreds of Rangers supporters had beaten us to it. One of the greatest stadiums in the world barely had a security system. Fans were strolling about on the pitch as if it was a Glasgow Corporation public park. The police were standing around watching this with complete unconcern, and striking a pose of false geniality which I think, there and then, was breeding the notion amongst the fans that the men in uniform were a soft touch. This again encouraged the anarchy that ensued. Although they were armed for action with bulging gun-holsters, these little men, who looked like a flock of Spanish welterweights, seemed to me menacingly innocent.

From a commentary position only a few feet above the touchline, even though the Camp Nou towers up to the stars, I was a close witness to this extraordinary evening. What took the edge off the broadcast was that because of the international match between Scotland and Wales at Hampden Park that night, at about the same time, no permission had been granted by the SFA to transmit this European final live. Astonishingly we had to content ourselves with a deferred relay: the whole game was shown to viewers back home only after the final whistle had sounded. It added another unsettling factor to the night as you realised that by the time they listened to what we were saying they would know every kick of the ball through the universal radio transmissions. It was, for us, the second-hand final.

Not for the Rangers players, though, who summoned up extraordinary bursts of early power to surge ahead of the Russians, who looked quite taken aback by the pace of the game. Derek Johnstone lost his early nerves thanks to the man who played beside him, Dave Smith. 'Dave told me just to go for every ball first time and not to worry about what might happen because he would be right behind me. And he was. But he did more than that. He had the ability and the nerve to get forward.' The Russians, robotic and initially lacking in pace, could not master Smith as he pressed forward, whenever he could, and his immaculate passing brought Rangers their first two goals. He sent Colin Stein clear in the 24th minute to drive strongly past Pilgui in the Dynamo goal for the first, and from an even more advanced position he chipped across for Willie Johnston to head the second, five minutes before half-time. Nine minutes after the interval the same player ran on to a long ball from goalkeeper Peter McCloy and, quite unchallenged, scored a third against a defence that looked as if it had lost all hope of retrieving the situation.

That would be a bare reading of the events up to then. But that would not be enough to illustrate the spill-over of emotion. For after each of Rangers' three goals there was a crowd invasion as hundreds ran on to the field in frenzied celebration. The police did nothing to stop it. At that juncture it was simply a takeover by robustly happy people who ought not to have been on the field but who took flagrant advantage of the total lack of marshalling. The game was held up while they were gently shepherded off each time. However, a certain constraint on celebrations suddenly developed as Dynamo, as if to prove they were not the quitters they had seemed earlier in the match, scored twice: Eschtrekov netted with half an hour to go, and then three minutes from time Makovikov brought it back to 3–2. John Greig had an almost terminal attack of nerves in those dying minutes as he watched, as we all did, tired limbs succumb to renewed Dynamo strength. '"Good God," I thought to myself. "We're not going to blow it again, are we?" That passed through my mind maybe more than some of the others, for I had been with the side that lost the last final in 1967 in Nuremburg, against Bayern, to an extra-time goal.

I knew we were near the final whistle but I also felt that if it was anything like ten minutes left then we were going to go under.'

At the commentary position several Rangers supporters, getting ready for take-off into celebration, sat near us, and one kept reaching across and shoving a bottle of the Spanish brandy Fundador under my nose and asking me to take a slug, even as I tried to convey the mood of those last convulsive moments. The Rangers players were suffering, not just from the sapping of their energy, but from an all-enveloping heat – a situation not helped by the jerseys they were wearing. They had ordered special light aertex jerseys, but when they arrived from the manufacturer Waddell had rejected them. 'They're the wrong colour of blue,' he'd bluntly told his players, dredging up some traditionalist value. So they wore their normal polo-neck jerseys, which were more suited to insulating players from a north-east wind sweeping in from the North Sea during a Scottish cup-tie at Arbroath. For them it was like playing in chainmail. They were not only tiring, they were melting.

Then the referee blew his whistle for an infringement. The crowd assumed the final whistle had blown and invaded for the fourth time that evening. For a moment it looked as if the referee would simply abandon the game, construing the interruption as a deliberate attempt to influence the outcome, as Rangers were hanging on desperately. But after a delay they restarted. Another agonising couple of minutes later the final whistle did eventually sound. The invasion, real and authentic this time, then began. As did Rangers' nightmare.

Within seconds the Rangers players were engulfed in a tidal wave of fanaticism. This was a support determined to have their celebration to equal that of Lisbon. They went at it with gusto, just as anybody might have expected, on the back of a hard-won triumph. The players were waiting for the cup to be presented. This was obviously being held back because of the congestion around the touchline, just in front of us. The players were then ushered back down the stairs, from which they never reappeared, as John Greig bitterly recalled. 'We had no idea what was happening up on the pitch and just went back to the dressing-room where we were in great spirits. But as time wore on we wondered about the cup presentation. Then a Spaniard came to the door and asked me to go with him and told the others to stay where they were. The Camp Nou is a big place, and I just followed him along corridors, went through different doors, and at last we came to this room where there were some

UEFA officials. This man had the cup in his hands. He just said to me, "This is the European Cup Winners' Cup. Take it." That's all. That was the cup presentation. I walked back to the dressing-room where we certainly were elated to get it. But I felt angry about the way this had been done, and that my team hadn't seen the presentation. And I wondered what the hell was going on.'

What was going on was to hit newspapers around Europe. The police in their folly had decided to clear the pitch using tactics we had never witnessed before. The supporters, desperate to see the cup being presented after spending so much money to witness exactly that, would not budge. By this time I had climbed to a higher vantage point beside several journalists scribbling furiously in their notebooks, and I surveyed the bizarre scene from there. We had noticed that just to our right there was a commander-in-chief of the police who seemed to be directing operations. I remember him distinctly raising his arm and then bringing it down like someone starting a Formula One race, and in unison the charge came, the batons were raised, and they started to strike out wildly. The crowd retreated. But not for long. Back they came. Forward again went the police line, driving them away, this time even more harshly. Next, we saw supporters arming themselves on the far side of the pitch with wood they had broken from stadium seats, and back they came in a mass charge. The police turned and ran, got to the touchline, reassembled and mounted a counter-charge. The wave and counter-wave of attacks were, I have to admit, a bewildering but fascinating spectacle in their own right.

At its peak, as we saw the police laying about the fans, one of the journalists expressing his disgust at this identified himself as the Reuter's correspondent in Barcelona. It was clear whose side he was on. 'What you're seeing down there is the fascist police in action,' he told me. 'That is the only way they can handle any disturbance. They are the experts in ruthless suppression. They are not even local police. They are not Catalans. That is why they are so hated in this city. They are Franco's men. They are recruited from Castile or Murcia. Anywhere but Catalonia. They are in this area to maintain a dictatorship. They have regarded these supporters from their very first invasion like an assault on the Caudillo, Franco himself. That is how they are conditioned to act. Respond to command, don't think. These supporters simply do not understand their lives could now be at risk.'

It might be lending new meaning to the phrase 'extenuating circumstances' to suggest that the rise of Spanish fascism through the Civil War, and the instruments of the police state that emerged, lay at the root of a particular episode of football hooliganism. But it is worth bearing in mind that the immediate reaction of the media was to lump this episode along with the kinds of violence which seemed to be on the rise in England, principally through the conduct of Manchester United supporters, who during that period were a continual source of hooliganism. Alex Cameron in the *Daily Record* of 26 May wrote, 'The sight of hordes of them racing out to attack a baton-charging line of police struck a new note in outright hooliganism.' Jim Parkinson in the *Glasgow Herald* on the same day recorded how he had been asked by young Rangers supporters to help them get out of the main gate to get away from the baton strikes of the police. He added that 'the cancerous evil of hooligans' was damaging the image of Scottish football, and went on to say, 'As our prestige soars at club and international level, our stock is plunging crazily by this disease on the terracing.'

But this episode palpably was not a symptom of a spreading disease. The malevolent spirit that existed amongst English hooligans drove them on to perform acts of violence that were largely premeditated. It was becoming systemic. The scenes in Barcelona were of an entirely different nature. They were utterly avoidable and, of course, in terms of the fans' extreme behaviour, inexcusable, but there was a rush to judgement that virtually ignored the specific parameters. To be fair, what considered analysis could be applied when stories were being spread instantly around the world that supporters were wielding improvised weapons against authority? It is something you can hardly defend. We also noted that whenever the police charged, the television producer directed his cameras away from the scenes, to a side-street outside the stadium. This was probably an automatic response from the politically correct state television company.

Back at the hotel afterwards, as the players let their hair down and enjoyed the fruits of success, the party was split into two. There were the players, who still had no idea what had transpired, and then there was Waddell and the media, who knew full well that big trouble lay ahead for the club. It was not until we boarded the plane to go home with the cup and the Scottish newspapers were handed around that it all hit home to the players, especially when they read the banner headline on the front page of the *Daily Record*: 'The Shame in Spain'. Later, on the aircraft taking us back to Scotland, one player, Alex Miller, who later became a manager in Scotland and a coach in England, looked at me ashen-faced as I passed up the aisle. 'Are they going to take the cup off us?' he asked.

That possibility preyed on Rangers' minds in subsequent weeks as Waddell took on the unenviable task of seeking clemency of sorts from UEFA, for a ban of two years from European competition had been imposed on the club in the immediate wake of the final. He attended a meeting of their Appeals Court in Zurich on 6 July. According to Jim Blair in the *Evening Times* a day later, 'The word is that Mr Waddell's factual appeal and general concern for the well-being of his players and the thousands of honest, decent Rangers fans was the basis of the ban being cut in half.' He had clearly impressed the court. No other figure on the Ibrox board could have achieved that, so not only did they have much to thank him for, it also placed him in a unique position of authority within the club from which he was to exercise power ruthlessly.

But there was another factor that intruded on the court's deliberations on the riot. They were fully aware that since the final in Barcelona, and before their meeting, they had clear visual evidence of West German fans 'boxing in' the players during the final minutes of the European Nations Cup final on 18 June and invading the pitch at the end of the game in full view of the UEFA top brass (including the trophy presenter Hans Bangerter, who had condemned Rangers after the Barcelona match) and, of course, a massive TV audience. It is clear that they had before them a phenomenon of crowd disorder which was not purely intrinsic to Ibrox; it had a European dimension, and it had to be addressed in as equitable a way as possible. No sanctions had been imposed on the German FA for their crowd's rowdiness. This very probably influenced UEFA's thinking and produced what they thought might be considered an act of clemency in the Rangers situation.

Barcelona is not a template from which we can study the growth of football hooliganism. It had its own unique characteristics; indeed, as we will touch on later when we consider the Hampden riot of 1980, each example of crowd disorder has its own particular configuration. That there were undisciplined drunken elements within the Ibrox support that day is unquestionable, and their over-reaction to the police was inexcusable. The moronic element played a huge part. But so did Franco's stooges. Too many people jumped too quickly on to the high-morals bandwagon of outright condemnation, without studying the profile of the evening in more detail. If they had they would have concluded that the riot was eminently avoidable. The fact that it occurred, though, besmirched the name of Scottish football.

We thought then that the route to the 1974 World Cup finals in Germany would lend us an opportunity to refurbish Scotland's footballing image. It was at a time when club football had not yet eclipsed the widespread interest in the national side, as eventually it would. Optimism come 1974 was not in short supply therefore. Sadly, common sense was, to such an extent that the pre-World Cup trip to Europe compelled one of Scotland's leading journalists, Hugh Taylor of the *Daily Record*, to coin an appropriate phrase to reflect its eccentricities: The Tour de Farce.

CHAPTER FOUR

TAKING ON THE WORLD

When the official Scottish party for the 1974 World Cup arrived in West Germany on Friday, 7 June, they were supervised with the vigilance you might associate with the transporting of bullion to the Frankfurt Central Bank. In fact they could easily have been offered greasepaint and a local theatre to put on one of the farces they had clearly been rehearsing on the long, circuitous road to these finals. At various stages in this traumatic journey, we experienced that age-old Scottish dilemma of not knowing whether to laugh or cry as we watched a process of disintegration that left us wondering if we should surrender to events and go back home, before we suffered more. West Germany increasingly seemed as exhilarating a prospect as taking up residence in a gulag in Siberia. But here we were in Frankfurt, suddenly aware of helicopters offering a shield above our heads, men with rifles circling the airport, armoured cars at the airport surrounding our buses, and mechanical German officials trying not to think of terrorist threats by offering the sort of forced smiles you find on men wishing to make light of their irritable bowel syndrome. Underneath all the civilities it was deadly serious. We had made it, though at several stages we had thought we never would.

It had all started off well on Saturday, 18 May, had it not? What sweeter way to have a World Cup benediction than to trounce the Auld Enemy at Hampden Park before you set off for the unknown? To say 'trounce' might be a slight exaggeration, although when a 2–0 space between ourselves and the great foe is achieved – something that has occurred too infrequently in the past – a slight hyperbole is permissible. To the 94,487 watching that day, there was a canyon's width of difference between the two sides. That Scotland were the better team was beyond dispute. England were non-qualifiers for the World Cup finals after all, and exhibited no sense of urgency, no pride. They were the underclass you had to deal with in those days. But there was another game at play. The players had fallen out with the media. Diplomatic relations had been broken off as we were likened to a bunch of quislings ready to undermine morale. The principal cause of this was that lovely wee man Jimmy Johnstone.

Our unstinted admiration for one of the most exciting players ever to don a jersey did not extend to his seafaring skills. When he embarked one evening on a small boat without oars, heading westwards, when the Scottish team were shoehorned into a tiny family hotel, the Queen's at Largs, preparing for the England game, it seemed harmless enough. Players have got up to much worse. Gazza would have thought it a jape unworthy of the girls of St Trinians. Except that 'Jinky' was breaking curfew and his seamanship – he hailed from landlocked Tannochside in North Lanarkshire – was nil. Losing his oars did not help. So when the currents took over, there was the possibility of his being swept out of the Firth in the dark and, after the Gulf Stream Drift had taken over, making landfall in the Faroes. That, in any case, is the generalised overview the press took. Denis Law was there at the time and pled not guilty to being an accomplice. 'I couldn't believe it, but there he was drifting away from shore. I can't swim a stroke so there was nothing much I could do. It was left to me to call out the coastguard.' They came in strength, and the newspapers had their story. They wallowed in it, not quite knowing whether to take it seriously or not.

Jinky and his colleagues thought it all a gross exaggeration. The 23-year-old Joe Jordan woke up that day to find the hotel swarming with police and air and sea rescue people. 'I knew something had gone wrong. With all those rescuers about, I knew it couldn't be all that light-hearted. Of course it all became clear what had happened, and it is true we did think the press had made a meal of it. We didn't like the way they put the emphasis on that, instead of how we were preparing for the game. I knew that Jimmy was a lovely man and wouldn't hurt a hair on your head, but we were being ridiculed and didn't like it. It's not that they could have ignored it. It was just the tone. It seemed well over the top.' When Johnstone appeared at breakfast the following morning his mates greeted him with a chorus of 'What Shall We Do With the Drunken Sailor?'

But if a player makes himself fair game, the gloves come off. This too was an age when the press in particular had yet to acquire the tabloid *modus operandi* of vultures. The Scottish players were incensed because it seemed to indicate that not enough serious attention was being paid to

World Cup preparation. So we waited for an explanation that this piece of rowing was in fact part of a cardiovascular programme that would stand Jinky in good stead when he played in Germany against the great blond Brazilian defender Marinho, who had a kick like a mule and the pace of an antelope. None came. But they showed their indignation to the press by moving en masse towards the centre circle at Hampden at the conclusion of the England match and, in unison, offering an unambiguous two fingers to the press box. Jinky tried to join them but found it difficult to do so, for at the end of the game he had swapped jerseys with Martin Peters, the bigger-framed English forward. The Celtic player's hands failed to emerge from the shirt; all we could see were two flapping sleeves being semaphored at us. The result even had a political consequence, as one figure conscious of the rise of nationalism latched cutely on to the match. At the Scottish Conservative Party conference, Edward Heath took the trouble to start his speech by announcing the half-time score from Hampden (Scotland were leading 2–0) to great cheers of enthusiasm from the audience, then added, 'This is when I cease being an Englishman and become a representative of the UK!'

The Scottish manager, Willie Ormond, did not seem at that stage like a man in charge, more a helpless figure caught in the middle of a needless feud. Now, if the meek really were to inherit the earth, Ormond could have laid claim to most of the northern hemisphere. He was, as you say of men who give the impression they would go through a personal hell before showing malice to you, a gent. Small, rotund, neat in dress and immaculately groomed, you felt he deliberated over the degree of hanky he should show in his top pocket, even when preparing for a press conference. There was nothing of the bombastic manager about him: he spoke about the game intelligently and cogently at times, coming as he did from the great generation of Hibernian players of the 1950s (he was one of their Famous Five forward line). He had made a success of management with the provincial club St Johnstone, taking them to the 1969/70 League Cup final, where they were beaten 1–0 by Celtic, and ousting Hamburg from the 1971/72 UEFA Cup. His credibility was stretched to the limit, however, when he made his debut as Scotland manager, on a cold and frosty evening at Hampden Park on 14 February 1973. England breathtakingly ran over his side, and won the SFA Centenary match 5–0. In my commentary I studiously avoided using the word 'humiliation' because I allowed my liking for Ormond as a person, and the fact that this was his first national game, to sway my judgement. I was also thinking this was freakish. Just ponder some of the names wearing Scotland's colours that night: Dalglish, Macari, Morgan, Bremner, Lorimer, Graham – enough already! In the post-match press conference his almost jolly, things-can-only-get-better line was swallowed a great deal more readily than the first homily on defeat doled out by Berti Vogts a few decades later. It was simply because we wanted it to be true, whereas with Berti we knew inwardly it could not possibly be.

Ormond had been bequeathed a strong foundation by Tommy Docherty, who had given up his Scotland job to move to Old Trafford after managing two World Cup group qualifying victories against Denmark. So Scotland had been well placed to qualify for West Germany before Ormond took over. When they did, on that eventful night at Hampden on 26 September 1973 by beating Czechoslovakia 2–1, the 5–0 drubbing by England was forgotten. The euphoria was preceded by intense support from the 100,000 crowd, which inspired Jim Holton and Joe Jordan to score the two goals and prompted my good friend and commentating counterpart on Scottish Television Arthur Montford to emit a *cri de coeur* which in broadcasting terms must be the equivalent of Jenny Geddes' famous interruption of the service with 'Whaur's your Wullie Shakespeare noo?' As a Czech player advanced on Bremner at one stage, Arthur found himself bellowing to his live countrywide television audience, 'Watch your legs, Billy!'

That in itself would have demonstrated to Ormond the enormous fund of goodwill that existed, which could even transcend broadcasting objectivity. There was a spiritual communing that night around the whole of Hampden, which might have furnished justification for journalist Brian Glanville's famous remark of us, the Scottish media, that we were simply punters with typewriters, although experience tells me that the English media kick every ball for their team too, until they start kicking their managers. Perhaps all this backing made it tougher for Ormond. For the level of expectation after that was not one whit less feverish than that which was to follow for Ally MacLeod and Argentina, although for a variety of reasons that South American venture seemed uniquely overwhelmed by hysteria.

But the wee man from Musselburgh seemed a vulnerable personality. The first long conversation I had with him was in a hotel in Perth, when he was going strong as a club manager, had taken St Johnstone into Europe and was being touted for various other more illustrious posts. As he opened up to me I wondered if he would have the steel to take on anything at a greater level. He told me of the time he thought his number was up. St Johnstone had gone to Yugoslavia to play a tie in the winter of 1971. On take-off for the return trip, the aircraft struggled. 'I could see we weren't going to make it,' he said. 'The branches of the trees were brushing against the wings and the whole plane was shuddering. I thought this was going to be it. I don't think I even prayed. I was too terrified to think of anything. Then, somehow or other, the pilot swung the plane round and I kept my eyes shut. But we landed. We got off the plane and I remember they told us they were going to have another go at taking off in about another hour. "Not on your bloody life," I thought. But I knew I had to get back somehow so I went into the lounge bar and drank it dry. I was paralytic when I boarded again and I remember bugger all about anything else until we landed back in Edinburgh.'

It was beginning to be said of him, after that, that his remedy for a fear of flying – a hearty drink or two – was becoming too much of a habit. You need only take a drink or two, in this business, to be made a habitual drunkard by word of mouth, and he had to withstand constant talk about that. You had to wonder, then, when the time eventually came, if this homely little man could stand up to the likes of Rinus Michels of Holland, Miljan Miljanic of Yugoslavia, Helmut Schoen of West Germany and Mario Zagalo of Brazil, all of whom were giants preparing for battle. I certainly felt that he was playing no part in either encouraging his players to rebel against the Scottish media or in trying to play peacemaker. At first he gave the impression he could not care less, although as we shall see he eventually broke cover and took on the media. But because of the travel arrangements for the trip to West Germany, nothing could be done about the fact that the squad and the media would be sharing an aircraft on the journey firstly to Belgium, then onwards to Norway (both staging posts for friendly preparatory matches), and thereafter to Frankfurt.

As modes of travel go, this British Airways aircraft was at the opposite end of the spectrum from the *Love Boat*. We were, of course, separated; the players at the front, the enemy at the back. BA's idea of making us feel comfortable was to offer hospitality on a scale equivalent to a bacchanalian orgy of Ancient Rome. Even before we had reached the first layer of cloud, champagne had been downed by everyone, and a constant supply followed. In our non-athletes area this was lapped up eagerly as we wondered what kinds of thirsts were being slaked at the front of the plane. As subsequent events were to prove, many of them up there had not asked for mineral water as a substitute. As I tramped down the gangway at Brussels Airport I held two bottles of champagne in either hand, and my bag was full of assorted miniatures. The players were no different. We were all aglow. As we travelled by bus towards Bruges, flat and dull Belgium was now appearing to us the way Judy suddenly saw technicolour Oz after the monochrome of Kansas. The entire Scottish party was, in fact, heading for the World Cup like bus-trippers bound for Blackpool and the September weekend break.

It was not clear how much alcohol had been imbibed by the players, although we knew some of them were teetotal and never touched a drop. But not many. Most of them came from the thriving footballer's booze culture to which managers, and indeed British society as a whole, largely turned a blind eye. Drinking after a game was assumed to be macho and desirable, a therapeutic exercise that did little harm to the system. That belief endures to this day. But harm was being done, if not to their physiology then to the rapidly fraying relationship with the media. We knew that some of the players were indulging heavily, and in a way that tainted the rest of the World Cup experience because it was felt, rightly or wrongly, that it was another indication of the carefree, undisciplined approach to the most important event of their lives. Things could only get better, you felt. But that thought came only through alcohol-induced euphoria. For they suddenly got worse, on hangover day.

Scotland had to play Belgium, as part of their World Cup preparations, in the Klokke Stadion in Bruges on 1 June. I watched on my television monitor from the platform of the little ground a close-up of the face of Billy Bremner coming to the centre circle for the toss-up with the Belgian captain. He looked as if he hadn't slept for a week. There was a tired, weary air about him. Now, it is possible that that is how the Leeds player looked prior to any game. But the point is, we were now so influenced by the skirmishes that had gone on since before the England match, and by observing what seemed like a wholesome 'happy hour' on the aircraft, that we were assuming the worst of this squad. It would have helped had they played well. The performance of the players that day, though, never rose above the level of sleepwalking.

It was cumbersome, they lacked any sense of unity, and they went down 2–1 to a very mundane Belgium side. When Jimmy Johnstone scored the consolation goal, there was again a clenched fist directed towards the press box. That charming gesture convinced us that only a bridge-builder like Thomas Telford could span the chasm between us.

He certainly did not show up at our next port of call, Oslo in Norway. It is to the credit of the squad that they did not rebel outright when they saw their accommodation – a students' hostel attached to the University of Oslo. None of the players had even been to prep school, let alone lived on a campus, so spartan accommodation did not conform to their idea of what the World Cup was all about. They started to grumble. Not about everything. There were consolations. The campus seemed to be alive with tall, willowy blondes who looked as if they were studying Dior rather than Descartes. And there was a typical students' howf that served huge beer tankards, designed along the lines of the Old Man of Hoy. Trappist monks might have remained impervious to such an environment; randy footballers stood less of a chance.

At first, though, all seemed to have settled down. Players and media did have some conversations and met in a kind of no-man's land, much like the Allied and German troops in the trenches during the First World War when they held a Christmas truce and all they threw at each other were snowballs. So there was a kind of hiatus during which, thankfully, as far as we broadcasters were concerned, nothing much was happening. It was too good to be true. One evening John Motson, another BBC commentator and a friend and colleague for years who, like me, was at his first major tournament, accompanied me to one of the student taverns to sip a beer or two and to enjoy the less studious side of the campus. We were there for about half an hour when we heard raucous singing. It was coming from the mouths of Jimmy Johnstone and Billy Bremner.

The Scottish captain and the most brilliant winger of his generation had their arms round each other's shoulders, probably to aid their equilibrium, for they were both in the final stages of a mammoth binge. I remember Mottie muttering to me as they headed straight towards us, 'What are we going to do? Shall we leave?' He was nervous. He had probably led a sheltered English middle-class life up till then; two Scottish drunks must have seemed like an uprising of the Visigoths to him. But I knew that exiting there and then might be construed as an insult to the two men whom we were going to have to deal with, professionally, in the coming weeks.

They sat beside us, ordered beers, and sang a ballad lustily while the tavern came to a hush, probably perplexed even more than we were at the sight of two men, a couple of days away from another international match, letting it all hang out. Those students reading anthropology could have read something into it. The unease I felt was for the two players. We were the only two media men in the place, but news of this would get back. These things always do. Worse, I knew they were certainly breaking their curfew and that somebody would be out looking for them.

About 20 minutes into their increasingly discombobulated evening with us, a figure appeared at the top of the stairs leading to the tavern. It was Willie Ormond. He looked across at the raucous but, to be fair, not unpleasant scene, even though two of his stars could not have walked a straight line any longer even had they been rewarded by their next game bonus. He then turned on his heel and left, which I felt was odd. About five minutes later the SFA and Celtic doctor, Dr Fitzsimmons, made his entry, walked across to the two players and put his avuncular arms around them. After some gentle words in their ears they stopped singing and left with him.

I was haunted by that episode throughout the World Cup. It seemed to be key to understanding what influences were shaping the players' destiny. Had a Stein or a Waddell been in charge these players would have been hauled out of there manually. Ormond had side-stepped that responsibility, which left me with the feeling that if you were going into a World Cup you must have a leader who at least can show he can dirty his hands, without leaving it to others. Managers have to induce fear from time to time, if not on a permanent basis. That did not obtain here. It is one thing to set out a tactical stall and pick a team; it is quite another to galvanise it into positive action. It was difficult not to perceive Ormond as a weak figure who left you pondering who really was in charge.

These were the days before press officers, so everything was controlled by the secretary of the SFA, Willie Allan, whose ideas about public relations seemed to come from readings of the Victorian penal system. He hovered around the scene like a warrant-sale officer, waiting to pounce with the letter of the law. He would dispense his decisions with a soft politeness which belied their severity at times, and was about to show that side of him to great effect. For the press, alerted to the scenes in the bar, as I knew would happen, plundered the news. After all, things had become a little too uneventful and boring of late, despite the animosity openly expressed by the players. Having this story fall in their laps was like finding caviar in a bacon sandwich. It made the expected splash.

We awaited the decision of the SFA on the two players, and we knew that within their ranks a view was held that both Bremner and Johnstone should be sent home. Some of the press were so fed up with the lack of co-operation that they would not have minded seeing the backs of both players either. Others felt they were indispensable to the cause, regardless of how they felt about them personally. Bitter arguments ensued as the press, previously united against the shambles of the SFA, became split. Those for and against awaited the decision. It came the day after the incident: Bremner and Johnstone would continue onwards to West Germany and would be available for selection for the friendly against Norway. Ormond had declared that sending them home would be counter-productive and would engender the wrong sort of publicity. Something told us that there was still volatility in the air.

While standing in the foyer of the hostel one morning we saw John Mackenzie of the *Scottish Daily Express* being pulled to one side by Willie Allan. There was a brief, whispered and apparently casual conversation between the two before Mackenzie wandered over to tell us, 'I've been banned. I won't be allowed on the official flight to West Germany and I won't be able to talk to the players again.' The reason given by Allan was that Mackenzie was 'muck-raking' and 'causing distress to the players and their families back home' with 'misleading reporting of the Oslo bar incident'. It is true that the journalist was not in the bar at the time, but there were enough reports of what happened to ensure that exaggeration was virtually impossible. Banning a prominent journalist was, anyway, like handing an Armalite to a sniper. His newspaper lapped it up, and duly made him out to be a hero of campaigning journalism, while his competitors looked on, wishing they had suffered a similar fate. The newspaper led on 7 June with the banner headline 'The Man They Can't Gag!' The SFA were simply selling papers for them.

The players, meanwhile, were hardly selling themselves well to the commercial world. A large man who smoked large cigars called Bob Bain, who was reputed to have graduated into PR work through trying to promote the Bunny Club in London (which obviously qualified him for this assignment), had been appointed to look after their interests. He was a large-scale flop whose participation merely added to the feeling of incompetence about the way the SFA had approached these finals. So the players stumbled unguided into trying to deal with matters themselves. Jim Terris, the pleasant sales chief of Umbro, arrived to ensure that his boots were going to be worn prominently by the players. But I recall watching him, as he sat with me eating a thick steak on a sizzling platter, with a doleful expression on his face. 'I wish I didn't have to deal with these bastards,' he told me. For, because of a dispute about money over an official World Cup photograph that was to be sponsored by a brewery, the players had taken knives from the breakfast table and ripped out the identifying trademarks on their boots just before appearing in front of camera, much to Terris's disgust.

My personal problem was what the press were thinking about me. For Ormond, who openly described journalists – some of whom were my personal friends – collectively as 'vermin', was easily accessible to me in front of a camera virtually at any time of asking. It is not that he had a personal liking for me. He had been bribed. A couple of weeks before we had set out on this trip, Jonathan Martin, the editor of the BBC's World Cup presentation, asked me to arrange a lunch with Ormond. Before we sat down to the meal he talked to me, privately in the toilet, and warned me that he had an envelope to give to the Scottish manager which he was going to pass under the table, for me to pass it on to Ormond during the lunch. My first thought was that he had been reading too much John le Carré. But no. Halfway through the tournedos Rossini I felt this pressure on my thigh. I slipped my hand under the table and felt a bulky envelope being pressed into my palm. Trying to look as nonchalant as one can when chewing a mouthful of meat, I slipped the envelope towards Ormond, who having clearly been warned about what was coming, slipped his hand down, missed first time and caressed my thigh, as if searching indiscreetly for a lady's garter, then grabbed the envelope and whipped it into a side pocket away from us. To this day I don't know how much was in it. But he had been bought. He was now at our beck and call, regardless of what he thought of the rest of the media.

This was to produce another embarrassment on the eve of the game with Norway. For when we turned up dutifully for a boring training session we were met by a large Norwegian security man at the stadium who announced that nobody was to gain entry. I couldn't explain to this massive rock of a man that we, the BBC, had special dispensation or else I would have been mauled by my press colleagues. So we waited for them to come out. Except they played games with us. They sent the team bus to a gate and we followed, hoping to catch them as they came out. Suddenly it reversed and made for another gate with all of us in pursuit, like a scene from the Keystone Cops. Then it went back to the other gate. Tempers rose amongst those with notebooks. How Ormond thought that such actions might endear him to the press corps is beyond understanding. For when he eventually emerged, leading his players, he was savaged during a battery of questions such as you might direct to a murder suspect, and he barked back, his face becoming redder and more defiant. At that moment I believed we were as mentally prepared for the finals as a maiden would be tied to rail-lines, waiting for an oncoming express.

That Scotland beat Norway 2–1 would ordinarily have been a matter of no significance, because in the 1970s the Norwegians had not yet matured as a footballing country. But given all that had gone on prior to the game, the victory induced a sense of relief that carried us all the way on an escort-laden journey into the Taunus mountains to the ski-lodge in Erbismuhle which was to be the Scotland squad's base. It was also a stronghold of the West German security police who were everywhere in the area, carrying their guns openly and mixing pleasantly enough with the players, but employing the trick of looking beyond you when they spoke to you. After all, two years earlier the Munich Olympics had suffered the Black September terrorist attack, and they were going to extremes to prevent a repetition. And there had been, so we were told, an added and specific threat to the Scottish party from the IRA. Nobody took that seriously. Coming, as most of us did, from the West of Scotland we knew that if that organisation were to inflict any hurt on a party including both Protestant and Catholic players it would set back their cause for ever. We let the Germans think it was for real.

David Coleman and a vast entourage of BBC personnel invaded the country, even though no English side was in attendance. While on the one hand you could tell some of them did not like having to pay such attention to Scotland, people like Coleman were far too professional to allow such feelings to interfere with their work, and he built up a good relationship with Jock Stein, employed by the corporation for the occasion, and the rest of us. Others, behind the scenes, gave a clear indication of being patronising. Even Coleman baulked at that, on one occasion bawling out Jonathan Martin, effectively his boss as editor of the whole shooting match, when the latter burst rudely into a conversation the commentator was having with Stein and me. He called his editor the 'biggest little wanker in the business' in front of everybody in a crowded restaurant. I was impressed by the naked show of commentating stature. Coleman, in fact, was such a major figure at that time within the corporation that he gave the impression he answered to no one.

We were all together for that opening game in Dortmund on 14 June against Zaire, or the 'wee darkies' as Ormond referred, somewhat affectionately, to them. We simply did not know what to expect. Defeat was unthinkable, but by the same token, given the recent fiascos, perfectly thinkable. Ormond sent out David Harvey (Leeds), Sandy Jardine (Rangers), Danny McGrain (Celtic), John Blackley (Hibernian), Jim Holton (Manchester United), Peter Lorimer (Leeds), Billy Bremner (Leeds), Davie Hay (Celtic), Kenny Dalglish (Celtic), Joe Jordan (Leeds) and Denis Law (Manchester City). There was no Johnstone. He was not to play in West Germany. In my view, despite all the censure placed on him, he should have been tried. Two goals by Lorimer and Jordan in the first half put the outcome beyond doubt, but it left them open to a new criticism: they hadn't scored enough. It was a sultry evening in Dortmund and in the confines of this new, compact stadium, which was to become the model for the new Ibrox being developed by Willie Waddell, the heat was intense and legs began to weaken. Some of the press did not see it that way, though, and felt that a modest scoreline might come to haunt us eventually. Frankly, any win satisfied most of us at that stage, for Brazil was the next game, four days later.

One outstanding image burned into my mind from that game. It had many moments, of course, that linger in the memory: a Rivelino free-kick from 30 yards that flew and bent like a heat-seeking missile and tipped the Scottish bar; a thundering Davie Hay shot that brought out the best of a sometimes lazy-looking goalkeeper, Leão; the power of the blond defender Marinho, the flashy style, quick turn and menacing run identifying him as the prototype for the emerging wing-back style. There was sheer hard grafting by Scotland against a side that had set aside its samba heritage for a more European, more physical approach to the game, to everybody's regret. And the Scottish hard work paid off. Despite all the fears about their class, Brazil were neutralised. But what I sometimes mull over is the image of the Bremner miss. To call it a miss is perhaps to do less than justice to it. It was more an admission of our lack of self-belief at crucial times. A ball played into the box finds Bremner without cover, a couple of yards from the line, near the Brazilian left-hand post. You feel as you watch it that it is within the human capabilities of even a pub player to reach out and prod it home. The word 'Goal!' is deep in the lungs waiting to surface for the huge audience back home. But then you watch, as if in a dream, as Bremner's legs fail to function. There is a pause. The ball moves. His legs don't. You have to retain a certain calm as you watch this, although a note of hysteria creeps into the voice as you see the sudden anguish Bremner suffers.

The game ended goalless. Despite the Bremner incident, we cheered ourselves up by realising that something approaching a miracle had prevented us from the sound beating we had all anticipated. I interviewed Ormond on the lawn of the hotel the day after, and he admitted he had had a few drinks after the game, which probably meant he had just stopped short of a huge bender. He beamed and smiled, and everybody seemed to be his friend. But it didn't last. During the interview he could not avoid another swipe at the press. He was still bitter. He had not rung many changes in the side from the first match against Zaire. In the view of many he had persevered with Kenny Dalglish far too long, although he was to substitute him twice. At that stage, his huge club reputation was acting as a shield against the obvious realisation that he was having a poor World Cup by his own standards. Denis Law had been dropped after the first game to be replaced effectively by Willie Morgan of Manchester United, and John Blackley was deposed by Martin Buchan of United. So going into the last match, again in Frankfurt, there were only two changes from the opening game.

A win on 22 June would have put Scotland through. It was 1–0 to Yugoslavia until one minute from time, when Joe Jordan equalised. Here was the birth of another special agony. You knew at the time that it was too late. There wasn't even a hint of one, brief shining moment about it. Seconds later, Scotland were out. The best World Cup Scottish squad ever, in my estimation, had blown it. There might have been kinder things to say, and were, because they had recovered from the shambles that had preceded the event to achieve tolerable results. But that was the only reason. They had failed, and failed badly if you take into account preparation, attitude, self-interest and lack of self-discipline. Stein, too, thought they were the best of all the squads to have been sent to the World Cup finals, and if anybody doubted him – and few did – then you need only consider the words of Joe Jordan. 'I was a youngster and was in awe of players like Denis Law, Danny McGrain, Sandy Jardine and Billy Bremner when I came into the squad. But it was the best, now that I think back. And one of the ways of judging that was that Jimmy Johnstone never played a single game in the finals. If you could leave out that ability . . . perhaps there were other factors involved, but if you could leave him out, for whatever reason, then it gives you an indication of the strength that was there.'

We all flew back together, enmities for life established between the media and certain individuals in the SFA party, including the manager. And when we looked out of the window and saw the thousands at Glasgow Airport waiting to greet a team that had failed, it was difficult to comprehend. At that moment, truthfully, it was bizarre but not wholly shocking to see the conquered greeted, not with compassion but apparently as heroes, upholders of a great footballing tradition. It was only afterwards, once it had sunk in, that you felt an unhealthy passion had been let loose. Tom McGrath, author and writer of the play *The Cheviot, the Stag and the Black, Black Oil*, had already placed the German adventure into a political context when he said in an interview on 6 June with James Cox in the *Daily Record*, on the subject of nationalism and 'Scotland's oil', 'There is this feeling in Scotland that we don't need England so much. Oil has helped encourage our self-awareness. So has Scotland's success in the World Cup. Football is the working man's culture and success in that really helps us to believe that we can be successful in other fields too.' On the other hand, Andrew Marr reported in his 1992 book *The Battle for Scotland* that 'on the day Scotland played Yugoslavia, in Frankfurt, eighteen of the twenty-nine members of Labour's Scottish executive proved themselves patriotic enough to fail to turn up to its meeting that day – which happened to be when it was discussing devolution. But of the eleven who did arrive at the meeting, six were anti-devolutionists and voted against all the Home Rule schemes put before them.'

There was obviously no limit to where the effect of supporting Scotland's national team would take you – in the latter instance, upsetting a government's plans for a new constitution for the United Kingdom in order to counter the threat of the SNP. Football was clearly a potent force that could be hooked up to, to catch the conscience of a nation. It was ripe for exploitation. And a man was to turn up in the following four years to do exactly that, as he turned football management into a new form of fanatical evangelism.

CHAPTER FIVE
BROKEN CROSSBARS

Within three weeks of Ally MacLeod being appointed manager of the national team, the Scots pillaged Wembley. We knew things would be done differently under him, but we had not realised how quickly and dramatically his reign would become associated with mass hysteria. The smashing of crossbar and posts, the ripping up of turf in a stadium to which even Scots had become endeared over the years, marked the beginning of an era for Scottish international football characterised mainly by fanaticism and, ultimately, self-destruction. By the end of his reign you had to wonder if Ally bore stigmata, such was the crushing manner of his demise. Failure seemed to visit itself upon him and upon all of us caught up in his jet-stream in a way that might have lent special credence to the saying 'Those whom the gods wish to destroy, they first make mad.'

In his first press conference as manager, MacLeod adopted the tone of a redcoat at Butlin's, shattering the dawn with a wake-up call. In a self-deprecating touch, which despite his supreme confidence he was fond of lapsing into, he touched his large and prominent nose and declared in his first statement to the press, 'Concorde has landed.' It is not as if we did not know what his general approach to life was. In his days as a player on both sides of the border, and in his demeanour as a manager at Ayr United and Aberdeen, his self-belief was as pronounced as his proboscis. He did not use the English language sparingly, but in amazing flows, sounding at times like an old-fashioned evangelist at Hyde Park Corner, duelling with heckling atheists. It is not surprising, given what you heard at press conferences, that he was a marvellous raconteur. His style fell somewhere between that of Uncle Remus and Blind Harry. He used to recount one story frequently to people when I toured the country with him, handing it out like a verbal business card. It was about an incident that occurred when he was playing with Blackburn. One night before an important game, as the unique non-drinker in that notably hedonistic group, he had acted as minibus driver for Derek Dougan and his carousing team-mates. They picked up a group of nurses at a pub and brought them back to their hotel. One of the nurses then broke her leg while trying to climb down a ladder in an attempt to sneak out of the establishment, and an ambulance had to be called. This fracas ended without the soundly-asleep manager Dally Duncan ever finding out about it. The players managed no sleep, but went on the following day to trounce the opposition and score five goals.

He seemed to me to be indicating that while he was very much an experienced professional who could mix in the dressing room with anybody, he was also a slight cut above all of that. He was a semi-participant, a pragmatist, worldly without being dissolute. I do not know whether he over-emphasised the sobriety role he played in the Blackburn squad, who certainly would become renowned for their night-clubbing, but he was making it clear he was not an absolute ingénu. After all, he was coming into an arena where, at least amongst the media, there was full awareness that pulling a Scottish jersey over your head did not mean at the same time that you had signed the pledge. The drink culture still abounded. No fool he, then, he seemed to be stating. Perhaps he was also hoping that nature would deny him the same kind of profundity of sleep Dally Duncan had enjoyed.

That sense of urgency which he himself exuded to start with, was enhanced by the timing of his appointment. The newly structured Home Championship was looming for him. On 28 May 1977 Ally MacLeod entered international football for the first time at the Racecourse Ground, Wrexham. It is not the most attractive of venues, and only 14,469 turned up to watch the game that day. It might have been more, but for the innovation. Television had taken over. The championship format, in which all games would be played over one week, was designed primarily for television. All games were to be live. This day was notable, not for the utterly negative banality of the match itself, but for the sheer arrogance of television's intrusion. For when I arrived at the commentary position at the back of the grandstand, I was astonished to see the intricate scaffolding the BBC and ITV had jointly constructed to house, atop it, David Coleman and Brian Moore respectively. It ran the whole length of the perimeter of the stand. My position, behind the fretwork of the temporary rostrum, was exactly similar to spectators paying handsome money to see this game. Unlike my colleagues above me, I had to unravel the game from amid this frontal intrusion, much as I used to do when I was a kid, unable to climb over the fence to see a junior football match. Yet, as I can recollect, although there were some obvious initial mutters of astonishment and grumbles, there was no real sense of outrage, as I thought there might have been. I can only put it down to the acquiescence of the public, to the fact that people were still a bit in awe of television and the personalities involved. If Coleman and Moore wanted this, then that's what they should get. They had arrived imperiously on the pitch, after all, by helicopter, thus stamping television's imprimatur on the entire proceedings.

I met Ron Greenwood, later to be the England manager, after the game as we both waited for taxis, and quite unsolicitedly he offered his views on the new format. 'I can't see this lasting,' he said. 'Three games in a week at the tail-end of a long season? It'll take its toll. You'll see injuries mount, and the most important thing is you won't see the best football. Players will be too tired.' All he needed to offer, as evidence, was the game that afternoon, which was a case of a new and proud manager who had long been associated with attacking football, but minus two main strikers in Joe Jordan and Andy Gray, manfully geared up to avoid defeat. As Ally himself admitted of the goalless draw with Wales, 'It wasn't attractive, and I wasn't particularly proud of our tactics. But they were proved right for the occasion, and that no-scoring draw served the purpose of getting me off the mark. I would have hated to be labelled a failure after the first match.' That was his ego talking, and it was a nonsense. A honeymoon period would have seen him through a baptismal defeat, even though he had prefaced his first remarks to the players by saying, with due modesty, 'I am a born winner!' A defeat in Wales would not have meant umbilical strangulation at birth. That fund of goodwill which is naturally preserved for all new managers was enhanced by the nature of the man himself, who had always been seen as a genial enthusiast. Some, though, even from the outset, thought he was nothing but a buffoon. Jock Stein never would bring himself to criticise Ally in public, but privately I recall him saying to me, quite brutally, 'That appointment is a joke.'

Ally did survive that first game, but he needed a win to fortify him for Wembley, which he got on 1 June against Northern Ireland at Hampden, when a couple of goals by Kenny Dalglish and one by Gordon McQueen secured a 3–0 victory. After the final whistle, as he admitted to me, his stomach began to churn. Wembley was only three days away. And in the background to that was the additional worrying thought that in recent years the greatly treasured tradition of that special weekend in London had been corrupted.

I remember, as a boy in the late 1940s, watching the menfolk assembling just off Shettleston Road in the east end of Glasgow before boarding the bus that would take them to Wembley. Relatives and friends would surround them, wishing them well, as if they were about to board a troop-train for the front. By and large, though, we knew they would come back safely to their loved ones, having suffered damage only to their pockets and their livers. It was the same in hamlets and towns throughout the land. Men saved up for two years for this in the Wembley clubs that they ran. 'Have you been to Wembley yet?' was a notable question in many a discussion about football; if answered in the negative it could be seen as an admission of immaturity, or of uncertain sexuality. Scots saw this as a rite of passage you had to undergo if you had any desire to unravel the complexities of nationhood and our relationship with the English, who needed a reminder in those alternate years as to how we could puncture their sense of superiority. That being a tall order, it was not just the game that mattered, it was the whole adventure. It was about being able to live for a couple of nights in a doss-house of a London hotel, trying to sleep on a floor while the other six of you shared the single bed; never sleeping a wink, in fact, for three days; being able to give yourself a full-scale bath in a wash-hand basin; living on a diet of fish and chips or bacon rolls; sluicing out your insides with the tepid mouthwash they called English beer; singing until the throat was like emery paper; and coming out the other end as an ordinary bloke who certainly wanted to drub, destroy, eliminate and annihilate the English, but without in those days being capable of turning into a raving racialist lunatic. In 1955, for instance, there was, in one London court, a solitary recorded offence by a Scot, who was considered to be drunk and incapable. In that more civilised era the magistrate bound him over for one night only and emphasised to the police that he must be given back the two pennies they had found on him and his return ticket to Glasgow, adding, 'But take care that he's out in time to see the match.' A Daniel come to judgement? More likely a reflection of a more decent age. Our behaviour then had more to do with the constant hope of surmounting the odds stacked against us and the pride in our forbearance when things did not work out well. All that went to hell in the 1970s.

In 1973 a railway guard called Joseph Wireko was seriously injured when he was thrown against a moving underground train as he tried to clear rowdy fans from a train leaving Wembley Park after Scotland had lost 1–0 through a goal by Martin Peters ten minutes into the second half, a defeat aggravated by the fact that Peter Shilton had brought off the save of the season from a Dalglish volley five minutes from time. Two years later, in 1975, Sid Weighell, the general secretary of the National Union of Railwaymen, wanted the match called off altogether after a whole series of train incidents in the previous fixture. Since this was not possible, the drivers and guards did indeed withdraw their services. Everybody unable to gain any form of transport had to walk the eight miles from central London out to the stadium. For the first time, some people were beginning to realise that we were not considering high jinks but serious misconduct. The Tory MP for Brent North (which constituency covers Wembley) declared on the front page of the *Evening Standard*, 'Lock up your doors, and batten down your windows, for the Wembley-bound Scots are dangerous.' At any time in the period leading up to the 1977 fixture, had I been called as a witness to any inquiry into Scottish fans' behaviour in London I would have sinned my soul had I not recounted the rampages I used to see: attempts to overturn cars in Soho, throwing anything they could get their hands on at shop windows, abusing passers-by, arrogantly blocking pavements to anybody who didn't wear tartan, and chanting their hatreds of the English. There is no doubt that some Scots felt annoyed by the attitude of certain English people. One fan from Glasgow, Kenny Forbes, gave an interview to the *Evening Standard* for its 23 May issue and was reported as saying, 'The people here are all stuck up. You can walk into a pub with a good jacket and your best trousers on and they still look at you as if you were scum.' No doubt that existed. There were people within top BBC management in sport in London, as we shall see, whose best shot at trying a relationship with Scots was to patronise them, rather like handing out food parcels to the needy. It infuriated me, but nothing could excuse what had been going on.

Can you imagine, then, in this inflammatory environment shortly before the 1977 Wembley game, how well Ally's statement about our Anglo-Saxon cousins at a press conference went down? I was present south of the border to hear him declare with that characteristic self-amused snortle, 'I don't dislike the English. I hate their guts.' It bombed, even then and there in the press room. Yes, there was a ripple of laughter from the Scottish press, who knew Ally was a bit of a card who only meant it as a joke, and anyway he could get away with statements like that. But after only a few minutes you began to realise how this might play in other parts, and how it might look in print. He even repeated it to me for a television camera, after he had dealt with the press, and tried to invest it with the same so-called spontaneity of his first airing. Some of us felt then that perhaps the SFA should hire Red Adair as a consultant, because out there in the nooks and crannies of our land there were some fine specimens of patriots who would regard that kind of talk as the verbal equivalent of the fiery torch encouraging those to regard a London pub as a symbol of English oppression, and thus fair game. Ally was pandering to a discernible change taking place in the Scottish political mood. As I have previously noted, nationalism was on the rise at that time. It had been shaped into a legitimate potent force by the SNP. I was beginning to experience anti-English sentiment in my travels around the country, even outside a footballing environment, of a degree of bitterness that transcended any decent political ambition. Nationalism was lending it booster rockets, whether the believers in that cause liked that accusation or not. Football was a perfect conduit for it all.

The couple of days leading up to this particular game, when the mass debauchery around Piccadilly and Soho in particular – windows were broken, cars overturned, pilfering was rampant and passers-by terrified – would have required a regiment of soldiers to regain control, showed that our fears were well grounded. Taxi drivers went home early, pubs remained shuttered, and the *London Evening News* reported that on the morning of the match 59 supporters were charged at Bow Street magistrates court with a whole range of offences. The *Daily Mirror* reported that on the eve of the match a 24-year-old fan had climbed to the top of the fountain in Trafalgar Square 'to the cheers of a jubilant crowd. But the cheers turned to gasps of horror as he suddenly plunged head-first into 18 inches of water, fracturing his skull on the marble base.' As you witnessed much of this, and read of such things, you became convinced that this could not be allowed to continue. Our image as a nation was being dragged into the gutter. Beating England seemed less of a priority.

On a beautifully sunny day on 4 June, Ally took his team to Wembley. Inside the stadium there were approximately 75,000 Scots. I joked with my English cameramen high on the gantry, just underneath the roof of the stand opposite the royal box, that rather than play a game of 'Spot the Ball' we could legitimately play 'Spot the Englishman'. If any were there, just before kick-off, then they were hiding amid a choppy sea of Scottish flags and banners. The faith in Scotland on display, despite the nauseating scenes we had witnessed prior to the match, was actually quite moving. You did feel again like a boy on his first Wembley trip. But nervous too, as you always were on first seeing the pitch. For Scotland had not won at Wembley for ten years.

And it showed in the early stages, as England, needing only to draw this match to win the Championship, looked like favourites. But towards the interval the momentum swung the other way, and to a tumultuous response Scotland went ahead when Gordon McQueen headed in an Asa Hartford free-kick two minutes before half-time. The celebration of that goal engulfed the rest of the game. From then on it was a seemingly endless cacophony of Scottish sound – a fact not lost on the players, particularly goalkeeper Allan Rough, who before the game had been almost lampooned by the English media. 'I had a good save early on in the game from Greenhoff,' he recalled, 'and that settled me. But when we scored and the crowd went wild, I knew we couldn't be beaten. It was astonishing to look around and see these sights. It did affect you. You felt you couldn't let such a mass of people down. I had never experienced anything like it, and I believe the English players were astounded. They had no support here in their own pad. Then, of course, when we scored again it was seventh heaven.'

That second goal, 16 minutes into the second half, came from the tip of the boot of Kenny Dalglish, who threw himself in front of Mick Mills to prod a Willie Johnston cross past Peter Shilton. To a Scot, even one charged with objectivity behind a broadcasting microphone, a scrappy goal like that against the English can look like a work of art. There was nothing coded about the implication of it though: Scotland under Ally were on their way. Mick Channon did score from the penalty spot with three minutes to go, but it only served to remind the crowd that England had actually been present that afternoon. MacLeod's name was being chanted in loud hosannas at the final whistle. All that was lacking now were palm leaves to be strewn across his path as he danced his way towards the tunnel.

It was only a few minutes, though, before we realised that the first trickle of a pitch invasion by the crowd had turned into a flood. From on high we saw them streaming down from all angles until it was virtually impossible to see a blade of grass on the pitch. It was then that we noticed the first climbers on the crossbar away to our right. As they bounced on it, it sagged. My honest reaction at first was that it all seemed like good, innocent fun, but as the competition went on between the climbers and the Wembley crossbar I realised that another interpretation was developing behind me. I heard Jonathan Martin, the BBC's Head of Sport, bawling instructions to 'get the focus on the mob on the crossbar'. When I saw it sag for the last time and snap, the instructions to the cameramen became fiercer and with a sense of indignation I knew that this was doing our image no favours. This was all going to be transmitted around the world – Scottish fans are a riotous mob. I was caught between conflicting emotions. On the one hand I desperately wanted the Scots to enjoy themselves out there. Indeed, I was euphoric myself. However, while I was annoyed at the almost gleeful way in which BBC London was intent on exposing this, I knew that they were professionally right to do so, even though they would edit it in a way that would show every shred of damage as an end to civilisation as we knew it. They were relishing it. They had not enjoyed the sight of England being eclipsed and for the rest of that night they were queuing up to shower me with indignation about the invasion of the barbarian hordes.

When the field was eventually cleared, Wembley looked as if it had been hit by a tornado. The goalposts were like used matchsticks, and the impeccable pitch, which had always held Scots in awe, had developed blotches as if hit by a plague, ripped and torn up in patches. It was ruined, as was the Scottish reputation. To this day some of the Scottish players, who had struggled to get to the dressing room, believe it was all good-natured and harmless. Indeed, Ally himself found it difficult to get back to join his players after doing press interviews because the police barred him from re-entry into that area. When eventually he returned to the dressing-room, he discovered to his astonishment that a fully clothed Scots fan was splashing about in the team bath with the players. Anarchy reigned.

If anybody was in any doubt about how we should all have reacted to that day, they ought to have read the statistics in the cold light of dawn, as revealed in the *Daily Mirror*. In the words of the Wembley groundsman Don Gallacher, 'a hundred pieces of turf gouged out, cans and beer bottles and glasses smashed all over the pitch, razor-sharp ring caps from beer cans pushed into the turf, goalposts smashed beyond repair, nets shredded and corner flags stolen'. Ernie Walker, when he eventually became secretary of the SFA, never forgot that day in his assessment of future relationships with the English. He enjoyed beating the English, but not at the cost of losing our dignity and making fools of ourselves. He would tell me in later years that the fixture was in mortal danger and that he would in fact be glad to see the back of it, rather than have our name dragged through the mud again. The contrast with others who felt it was all over-hyped by the English media could not have been greater. From that conversation with Walker I knew that this oldest of all international meetings was doomed as a regular occurrence. It would be another twelve years before the last of such meetings took place, and by that time the English had developed a greater interest in their international side, and in an attempt to outdo us as a volatile force were supporting their lads with techniques derived, it seemed, from the Vietcong.

The immediate concern for Ally was to translate all that massive backing for him into something really tangible. After beating Czechoslavakia 3–1 in a World Cup qualifier at Hampden on 21 September in which yet again Joe Jordan scored (as he had in September 1973), in addition to other goals by Hartford and Dalglish, the crowd roared for the Scots to come back on to the field. Rather uncharacteristically, Ally eschewed such appeals for he knew that the Welsh still represented an obstacle to their progress to Argentina. The Welsh, however, surrendered their right to play on their own soil, which is like forsaking your birthright, and chose for commercial reasons to play a 'decider' in Liverpool. Scots, by devious means, managed to get their hands on the majority of tickets, and by the evening of 12 October the area around Anfield resembled a medieval fair, with pickpockets plundering the great and the mighty just outside the ground, people shouting and bartering for tickets, and others making arrangements for the journey to Argentina – most of that latter category with Scottish rather than Welsh or Liverpudlian accents. They were particularly boisterous, but there was a blatant, aggressive and intimidatory edge to the Scottish supporters that sounded quite sinister. Perhaps it was because we had witnessed what so many of them had done in London. Perhaps it was just a naked display of brute nationalism. Any crowd that can drown out the Welsh Guards Band in the warm-up does require respect. But my co-commentator Jock Stein and I shared an anxiety. Stein summed it up succinctly. 'I hope to God we win,' he said. 'If we don't, I think they'll take Liverpool apart.' He gave interviews to others before that game, talking about its importance in a footballing sense, but underlying it all was his concern for Scotland's image. Ally, on the other hand, was on fire. He knew the support did not want a diet of realism. They wanted to be spoon-fed by the super-optimist, and he accepted that role as if he could feed the multitude with five loaves. The possibility of defeat was unthinkable.

For Joe Jordan, the game survives as the moment he entered a witness stand from which he has never really re-emerged. For they still ask, 'Did you handle the ball, or didn't you?' I have met Jordan hundreds of times since then, but only once or twice has the subject arisen. He remains adamant that when a hand rose to the ball in the penalty area in the 79th minute it was not his. The referee immediately accepted that it had been the hand of Welshman David Jones, and our television replay was not conclusive, although after watching the incident Stein gave me a long, knowing look, smiled in a curious sort of way, and said nothing other than he thought it was a penalty. We all wanted it to be a penalty, of course. Consequently, although I was talking to the largest television audience for a football match in the history of BBC Scotland broadcasting to that date – almost 95 per cent of the available public – I admit I am still an unreliable witness to the event. I do not know who handled, although the case against Joe, it has been said by others, has been proved.

It mattered significantly. In a nervous game, which saw one of the best saves of his career by Allan Rough when he tipped a magnificent dipping shot by John Toshack over the bar, it needed something special like a simple throw-in from Willie Johnston on the left into a cluster of players to turn the match and begin one of football's longest controversies. The second Scottish goal three minutes from time, a header by Kenny Dalglish, playing on his own patch, from a cross by Martin Buchan on the right sent me into a paroxysm of commentating delight for which I deserved the Pavarotti award for hitting one of the highest notes in broadcasting history. So, I had been infected like everybody else. I had dropped all reserve and insisted it was a penalty, even though I was being dragged to a monitor to be shown the handling could not have been by Jones, and I'd adamantly refused to believe that Dalglish had been offside for his header. If I was being struck by the Ally virus, then what chance could there be for a sense of realism amongst the multitudes about to be officially dubbed 'Ally's Army'?

There was little chance of that. Something had been let loose in the atmosphere that seemed to spread wildly in the ensuing months. When I looked back to the day when Celtic supporters had invaded the pitch in 1967 in Lisbon it was like summoning up an age of innocence. The crowd on the pitch there had acted with a simple air of exuberance, not wanton destruction, even though swards of the Lisbon pitch had disappeared as horticultural memorabilia. But, paradoxically, it had turned out to be an invitation for everyone else to attempt the same in the following years – the good, the bad and the ugly. The unrestrained manner of the support for Ally and his team was from the wrong end of the spectrum. It was negative. It was anti-English. It was potentially dangerous. It was so, most significantly, for Ally himself, although he didn't recognise it at the time. The danger signals were recognised by Jock Stein, who gave an interview to Patrick Collins of the *London Evening Standard* just before the tartan armada set sail for its Eldorado. 'We've qualified for the World Cup finals,' he said, 'England haven't, and people are turning handstands. That's madness. There's a big world out there and the English aren't the only people who live in it.'

We were about to find that out the hard way.

CHAPTER SIX

BEATING THE DRUM

Months before setting out for South America, in a hotel in Stirling, I watched Ally MacLeod jump on to a table in response to the adulation his presence had provoked at an 'Evening with Ally' – part of a series being sponsored by a brewery firm which I had been asked to chair. The searing smile on his face, the hand punching the air, the face ruddy, the tie askew, the hair ruffled – the mirror image of a man drugged to the eyeballs with self-belief. That night, in the question-and-answer session, I brought up a subject that was being given a tentative airing in the press, that some of his players, like Bruce Rioch and Don Masson, were no spring chickens and that they in particular might be past their best by the time of the finals. He turned on me as if I had accused him of personally harbouring geriatrics. I had built up an amicable relationship with Ally, so it was quite startling to observe the dismissive manner in which he responded to my question. And the reason was simple: the crowd. He was theirs and they were his. Bonded by hysteria, you might have said. He turned them against me for the rest of the night, and any mild criticism – and it certainly was mild, because I wanted to get home safely that night – of how things had developed since qualifying for Argentina brought hoots of derision, much to Ally's delight. One phrase I remember him using after one of my interjections was, 'Listen, hear that? That's what I have to put up with.' They would hiss or catcall. It was chilling. After the event, outside in the car, Ally turned to me, in front of the brewery sponsor, and said, slapping me on the knee like a parent trying to make up after too heavy a scolding, 'I've got to do that. I've got to keep them going. I've got to keep it up. They lap it up.' Oh yes, they did. I felt hubris coming on, that if Ally were to fail in Argentina he would fall with a monumental clatter.

In another sense he could always answer any criticisms, quietly rising to the surface, by pointing to the fact that he had taken his squad on a tour of South America. This, of course, is something that had been prepared well before he had taken over the post. Most of us had assumed that Scotland would qualify, and it was right and proper to take the preparatory step of sampling the special conditions out there. And on the back of the Wembley triumph in his first attempt against the Auld Enemy it was certainly a euphoric group that set off for Chile in the second week of June 1977 with the intention of making sure that if Scotland qualified for Argentina they would at least have experience of South American footballing values, which produced skills that could fill you with awe and attitudes that could terrify you. It seemed like a simple and straightforward idea.

But there was a problem. The SFA had included a game against Chile in their itinerary, as well as another two against Argentina and Brazil. Outside the CIA and the Pentagon, most of the world had fallen out with Chile. In 1973 the democratically elected Marxist president Salvador Allende had reportedly been gunned down during a military coup organised by a general called Pinochet. Years later I had my attention drawn by someone to this same man in London in Park Lane, where he was strolling with an entourage towards Hyde Park. He looked like a well-heeled, moustachioed pensioner, capable of no greater an outrage than dropping litter when nobody was looking. Yet he had been something of a monster. The Labour government of the time made it clear there would be no formal connections with that country and made manifest their opposition to any football match being played against them. What intensified the passions and raised the level of protest by the trade unions against the tour was that the first game was scheduled to be played in Santiago's National Stadium (now renamed the Victor Jara Stadium in honour of the folk-singer who had his hands broken by Pinochet's police so that he could never play the guitar again, before they shot him dead). That same place had been used as a temporary concentration camp for Allende supporters. The part this unfortunate arena had played in the history of the Pinochet revolution was dramatised in Costa-Gavras's 1982 film *Missing*, starring Jack Lemmon. The Soviet Union had refused to play in this stadium in a World Cup qualifying match in 1973, and had sent this message to FIFA: 'Soviet sportsmen cannot at present play at a stadium stained with the blood of Chilean patriots.' (Never mind the blood of Czech or Hungarian patriots *they* helped spill, you might say.) The stains might have been wiped clean four years on, but the images of oppression remained in the very bricks and mortar of the place. And these Soviet words were regurgitated at every opportunity by opponents of the tour, to appeal to the emotions of the SFA, and particularly to the media, to snub this particular fixture.

Frankly, although fine words were spoken about principles and the need to show solidarity against fascism, few of us were going to ditch the opportunity to witness what Chile and its people were going through. We were the better informed for having gone there. As for Ally and the players, they were sniffing the possibility of World Cup success and at first seemed insulated from the political dramas being played out between the SFA, Downing Street and the British Embassy in Santiago, which was advising that if we did travel we would be treated as if we were not there at all. We were to be considered 'non-people'.

However, if anybody was under any illusion that the Scottish players were utterly devoid of knowledge of the political situation in Chile, or insensitive to the plight of the downtrodden, then one tiny cameo demolished that. As we rested on our first day at the poolside after an arduous flight in a standard British Caledonian aircraft (these were still the days before wide-bodied jets), nobody wanted to indulge in any political cross-talk. Then we were visited by an elderly, silver-haired gent who in perfect English began to regale the reclining company with talk of how beneficial Pinochet was to the people, and that we had to pay no attention to the horrible propaganda that was being churned out by communists around the world about the country. Unfortunately for him he was principally addressing the nearest player in front of him, who happened to be Kenny Dalglish. He had not graduated *summa cum laude* in political science, but he could tell a phoney when he saw one. Dalglish just growled at him, 'Bugger off – we'll make up our own minds,' and then lay back again, to see if the sun would eventually penetrate the Santiago smog. The gent, who had probably had little experience of sophisticated Glaswegian repartee, headed slowly for the horizon, probably to tell his mentors that the Scottish party contained a strange-sounding Marxist rabble-rouser who had to be kept under surveillance.

Ally, meanwhile, was ebullient. In the saucer-shaped, smog-ridden valley that is Santiago, he held court with a panache that truly was enjoyable to behold. It was not as if we were learning all that much about how he was setting up his stall at that time, because he was simply feeling his way with the players, all of whom had joined him on the trip from his Home International squad with the exception of the injured Joe

Jordan and Gordon McQueen. In truth, he was so obviously enjoying his new role as national team manager that he sounded like a young kid playing with his new Christmas present. The fact that he had just beaten England and that we were abroad, not quite knowing how to assess the worth of this venture, meant that he was under no great pressure from the media. This holiday atmosphere continued virtually up to the moment we stepped inside the notorious stadium on 15 June.

It was a night that brought to me an instant recollection of the Ibrox disaster in January 1971, when 66 people died on stairway 13 at that stadium. There was a chilly, damp mist hanging around the ground, just as it had that afternoon in Govan, which seemed to thin the blood, or perhaps, in another sense, intensify the feeling of guilt about watching a game of football in a place where people had been tortured. The ghostliness was intensified by the meagre size of the crowd. In the official record for that game, it will state there were 60,000 present in the large oval bowl. One tenth of that number would be an exaggeration. As in other matters in that country, the Chilean FA was clearly complicit with the regime in attempting to use a football attendance to falsify reality. Allan Rough recognised that reality in the tunnel leading to the pitch. 'We could see the bullet-holes all over the walls where we were told they had had firing-squads. It made you feel a bit squeamish. But to be honest we had a football game to play. At that stage you just have to get on and play. I know there were a lot of protests about us going there, and now we could see why. But to be honest the players didn't want to get mixed up in the politics, they just wanted to play football.' The candour of that remark has to be respected, for footballers live mainly by the herd instinct, and the banding together, having been asked to play a particular match, even under some naked political pressure, was not surprising. The SFA wanted the game played, and that was that as far as Rough and his mates were concerned.

The game proved that Scotland's recent success was no passing phase. They won 4–2 with a couple of goals by Lou Macari and one each by Kenny Dalglish and Asa Hartford. The two Chilean goals, by Crisosto, were greeted with a ripple of sound more like gas quickly escaping from a balloon than anything else. Patriotism was obviously shrouded in more than the mist. The thick atmosphere made the game, in television, terms difficult to view and comment on. For example, Scotland switched their goalkeepers from Allan Rough to Jim Stewart at the interval, but did not tell us. In the murk we were still describing good work by Rough for about 20 minutes before we realised our error. In another sense, it was certainly shadow-boxing for a bigger challenge to come in Buenos Aires. But the mist of that night was for me a metaphor for the entire South American continent. Poverty and extreme wealth lived cheek by jowl in a tense, troubled stand-off. Everywhere.

We thought that getting out of that sadly depressed country – on one of our tours we were shown the bullet-holes where Pinochet's secret police had tried to kill the missionary Dr Sheila Cassidy, and we also heard about the insidious malnutrition affecting the poorer people in the slum areas – and into the cosmopolitanism of BA, as Buenos Aires is known colloquially throughout the continent, would come as a relief. Of course it did to a great extent, but we were still beset by beggars and by the appalling sight of bundles heaped on pavements near the fashionable Florida shopping district, which on closer examination would turn out inevitably to be women and children sleeping in a pitiful huddle. All this, and the armed escorts that accompanied the team and press buses to and from the airport and training sessions, lent the impression of a country desperately ill at ease with itself. The normal protocol of the team bus being first in the procession was reversed so that the press always preceded the squad. This was explained away drolly by the SFA's Ernie Walker, who had been informed in advance about the threat of the terrorist organisation the Montoneros. 'Well, you see,' he said, 'if the Montoneros were to attack, they would perhaps bomb the first bus in the convoy, thinking it was the team and officials. That is why they are putting the press up front.'

However, as in all cases of terrorist threats, nobody really took them seriously, even though we were rushed at breathtaking rates through the streets of Buenos Aires, escorted in fast cars by men with guns. That in itself was more scary, including the instance of a gun being raised out of a window to pistol-whip an elderly gentleman who had dared to attempt to cross the street and halt the procession. As we sped on he was left lying on the ground, helpless. It was not until we arrived at Boca Juniors' ground, where the game against Argentina was to be played on 18 June, that the light-hearted approach to all these threats suddenly evaporated. A brown parcel was found lying on a staircase at the back of the main stand leading to the main media area. Brown parcels left on their own, in that environment, do not for happy minds make. There was a panic, whistle-blowing, an emptying of the area. Men suitably garbed for the job delved into it and found a selection of meat sandwiches, dropped there by an attendant. For all the turbulence we had experienced at Wembley, it was never like this.

The game was a triumph of concentration for the Scottish team. This steeply sided, cavernous stadium, filled with 57,000 ranting Argentines, provided by far the biggest test of nerve and organisation any potential candidate for the World Cup would have to face. Kenny Dalglish was superb, although he was not to score. Rangers' Tom Forsyth, with a reputation lent to him by his opponents, one of whom said it would be more appropriate if he wore a butcher's apron (and that was largely the view of the Scottish media too), was impervious to an attack featuring names that would become famous as the year progressed – Luque, Ardiles, Houseman, Gonzalez. At the back the Argentines had that supreme technician Daniel Passarella, and in their famous broad vertical stripes they looked mightily impressive. Which is why Scotland came out of it creditably with a 1–1 draw. Both goals were penalties, the first scored by Don Masson 13 minutes from the end and the equaliser by Passarella four minutes later. There was no way Scotland were going to be allowed to leave that stadium with a victory.

We could barely suppress Ally after that. Ask him one question on camera about that performance against the host nation for the finals and what might spring from it, and he could turn it into an epic of boundless confidence that seemed as if you were listening to Cecil B. de Mille telling us how he made *The Ten Commandments*. It would be quite untrue to say we were unaffected by this. We were now beginning to be suckers for his preachings. We lapped him up. Back home, the roots of mass subordination to his every word were shooting up. Now we could face Brazil and a visit to the Maracana with impunity. What previously had seemed merely like a thrilling visit to one of the great cathedrals of football, with the expectation of simply enjoying the privilege of being there and even of being ritually slaughtered by the yellow jerseys, was now suddenly looking like an engaging match of football in which Scotland realistically stood a chance. We did, in all solemn truth, begin to believe that. A stroll along Copacabana beach watching a display of flesh that put a strain on your belief that man and woman were simply descended from the apes did not disabuse us of the steadily growing feeling that this Scottish team would be cowed by no one, certainly not by the Brazilians in their own famous home. It now feels ridiculous to have thought so, but the virtues of that hedonistic paradise 'with the cancerous centre', as Ernie Walker once put it to me, lulled us further into the delusion.

It made Ally feel quite invulnerable. One afternoon, a couple of days before the game, tempted by the crashing waves in front of our hotel on Le Blanc beach, Ally took to the water. It mattered not that he couldn't swim further than his own body length. When the first wave hit him about 20 yards from shore and he went into a tailspin, we, the spectators, fell about as if at a pantomime. I don't know how many seconds elapsed before we realised he had not come back up for air. Then we moved. As we entered the water to effect some kind of rescue, we thought we saw something approaching a bedraggled head reaching the surface and then going under again. Eventually a stunned Ally was hauled back to the beach, with us wondering who would draw the short straw to give him mouth-to-mouth. In fact he was not as bad as that, but he did claim he had hit his head on the bottom and had been stunned. It gave the press a marvellous pre-match story, for Ally, after recovering, did not hesitate to make it clear that at one stage he thought he was for a watery grave. It was the first time we had seen Ally speechless and fragile. He was something like that again when the Brazilians got their hands on his team.

On 23 June we were so prejudiced in our belief in the Maracana being arguably the epicentre of world football that we started off intending to overlook the ramshackle perimeter, the broken seats, the paint hanging off the walls, the dinginess of the areas under the stands, and the general impression of dowdiness and dereliction. But by the end of the evening, having watched Scotland being given the run-around by a superlative Brazilian side, we concluded that the stadium's fading glory was not reflected in the prime quality of football it could still house. Some 70 minutes of play had elapsed before Zico scored the opener, followed up by Toninho Cerezo five minutes later, but they had largely toyed with Scotland, who looked tired and inept. Spirits were not helped by a goalkeeping error, which happened before the match. Allan Rough, who had been outstanding throughout the tour and to this day proudly displays the trophy he won from the journalists for Player of the Tour, normally took a sleeping pill the night before a match. He did not on that occasion. The following day he had a headache and asked for paracetamol. However, around about lunchtime he took the wrong pill – the sleeping pill. It knocked him out. Just three hours before kick-off efforts were still being made to rouse him. He did make it and performed reasonably well under the circumstances, but the taking of pills by players was something that would come to haunt Ally for the rest of his life.

The failure against Brazil was cushioned by the veneration all of us show to their football, and that defeat by only two goals was deemed within the SFA to be almost a triumph. It did not sound a warning note to us, although it should have. After that came the year of stockpiling – of fantasies more than anything else. Just after qualification at Anfield in October, Andy Cameron, the Scottish comedian, wrote 'on the hoof', as he put it to me, the song 'Ally's Tartan Army'. They printed 2,000 copies of it, but within weeks requests for it to be played inundated radio stations, and more were rushed out. They thought of printing another 10,000, but that proved to be a modest estimate. Andy is no Michael Jackson, but he made two appearances on BBC's *Top of the Pops* dressed up like the caricature Scot beloved by those people who know nothing about us, belting out a tune which he said was derived from the one he sang about his favourite football team, Rangers. Between October 1977 and the end of March 1978, he sold 230,000 copies. The propulsion of a little-known club-comedian to stardom was a bizarre by-product of the Ally phenomenon. And he bred more.

In April 1978, BBC *Grandstand* asked me to pursue the story of an attempt to hire a U-boat to take fans to Argentina. It had not only been given prominence in the local press, but had been mentioned in dispatches in the south. The story had risen from the fertile mind of a man I knew very well, Jim Tait, an independent bookmaker from Hamilton whose sense of humour was of the deadpan kind, liable to take in the unsuspecting. He had spun this tale to one or two people and had made sure it was passed on to the newspapers. I knew it was absolute hokum, so when the request came to cover this as a story of some significance I was tempted to knock it back. But I also knew that the BBC in the south would not have liked that. They did not care whether the story was true or not; all that mattered was to show the eccentric lengths to which these Scottish hordes would go to follow their team. Given the distaste they had expressed after Wembley about the Scottish supporters, I knew there might be an element of ridicule in this, so if I covered it at least I would have some control over the final edit.

The trail led us to a well-known football redoubt, the Ballochmyle Bar in the east end of Glasgow, where a boisterous throng had assembled, organised by Glasgow businessman James Mortimer, friend of many managers and intimate of Sir Alex Ferguson. He was to hold a raffle whose winners would proudly board this U-boat and off they would go, unpursued by the British fleet, onwards to Buenos Aires. It was all done po-faced for the sake of the cameras, though I knew the whole thing was a joke. It was not a scam, I hasten to add, just a jape that had grown gigantic legs and was now running out of control. There was, of course, no U-boat, despite Tait's brilliantly lucid explanation of how he would scour the remnants of the German fleet in Hamburg and offer big money to somebody who used to torpedo our merchantmen to come out of hiding and steer the thing to Argentina's shores. He was almost poetic about it. Tait and Mortimer had simply and marvellously spoofed the whole Ally enterprise. As far as I know, the men who won the raffle that night, specially devised for BBC London, watched the World Cup finals drinking pints in the Ballochmyle Bar. The charade was shown throughout the land, most of the population wishing to believe it was true.

What certainly was true was that the hysteria was making it difficult to focus on the football preparation. Ally himself was now a face that could launch a thousand adverts. He was never off our screens, or billboards, as he milked, quite properly, the commercial potential of his elevation to sainthood. His wife Faye was even better at it than he was. She punted various products, using Ally's name as if they were in vaudeville together. But tremors there were in the background, some of a physical nature, because when he went to Argentina with Ernie Walker, secretary of the SFA, for the draw for the group sections, they suffered the consequences of tremors in all the cities they visited – Rosario, Cordoba, and particularly in Mendoza where, Ally claimed, his bed was thrown across the room, so violent was the quake. As portents go, that was one that might have registered in more sensitive minds. But, shaken as he was, he was reassured by the local authorities that it was the first such phenomenon in 50 years.

If that did not lodge in his mind as some kind of divine warning, a more earthly warning was delivered by a man whom he was to discover was no patsy. Amid all the daft nonsense surrounding the forthcoming finals, Ernie Walker remained a steady, sober voice in Ally's ear. It increased in volume one evening in Buenos Aires just before the actual draw was made. For a man who whipped up nationalist sentiment, it does seem odd now that when Ally was asked which flag should represent Scotland in the line-up for the ceremony he chose the Union Jack. His reasoning, after the event, was that it would be a gesture to the Anglos in the side as, after all, they played their football in England, and it would be an appreciation of how everybody in the British Isles would be supporting the Scots. An incensed Walker failed to see the sophisticated nuances of such an argument and, if I am to believe what Ally told me on one of our trips, told him where to stick the Union Jack. He ordered it to be taken down to be replaced by the Saltire. Then, at the draw, the journalist Ian Archer, broadcasting it live for Scottish Television, uttered words that would be cast up to him in later months. To be fair to him, he said exactly what we were thinking as the names came out of the bowls: 'The best draw in the world for Scotland, and surely a passport into the last eight. Iran and Peru, the two minnows. It could be that when we get to play Holland, we'll both have qualified already.'

The piece of trivia about the flags, as it may now seem, was at least an indication that in the background some disquiet about Ally's solo rousing of the nation was beginning to be whispered around the SFA. Another loud whisper was about Peru, our first opponents. We had learnt that Peru had arranged to play a friendly against the host nation Argentina in Lima, their capital. It seemed like the perfect excuse to get out there and cover both nations, for the price of one as it were, for television's maw becomes insatiable as a World Cup approaches and it wants as much video or film footage as it can get for previews. We offered Ally a free trip to Peru, during which we would make a short documentary on his spying mission and at the same time record as much of the play as we could. Initially he said he would make a late decision about it, and we found ourselves flying off to Peru in March 1978 knowing that the local media were waiting for Ally and were alerted to our coming. There was disappointment when he did not step off the plane with us. Once we'd settled in, our first duty was to make sure that we had information on any aircraft from the UK that might be carrying a Mr A. MacLeod. We did not hang around waiting for him, but.with a locally hired crew and with equipment that might have been used by the early silent-cinema pioneers of Hollywood, we strung together some pictures of a country that could barely feed itself – meat was rationed to one day a week – and I suppose making it seem highly unlikely to viewers that such a Third World nation could make any impact on this Scottish side. The local media continued to pester us for information about when Ally would arrive. It got so intense that I took it upon myself to tell one journalist that we were doing the 'spying' for Ally, and a photograph of me ended up on the front page of a prominent Lima sports paper with the caption, explaining my identity, 'El Espión'.

The day before the game, we gave up. Ally had not arrived. The local press could scarcely believe it, as other World Cup coaches had turned up for this one, as well as having watched previous fixtures. On 23 March we filmed Luque, Passarella and Houseman scoring in a 3–1 victory over a Peruvian side that looked swift and tricky but with little substance, apart from one man who certainly had ineffable touches of class, Teofilo Cubillas – a name that continues to haunt goalkeeper Allan Rough to this day. Ally had not travelled allegedly because he was simply making far too much money staying where he was. Peru, despite being watched on video, were not properly scouted. Not that anyone cared at that stage, particularly elements of the press who were too loudly fêting Ally to care about details, like finding out about the true quality of the opposition. A sobering-up process was to come, though regretfully it was too brief.

It began in the Home Championship on 13 May in Glasgow when Martin O'Neill, later to become the darling of half of the city, scored for Northern Ireland in the 26th minute to deliver a sharp uppercut to what looked like a complacent chin. It was a home game for the Irish because of Scotland's refusal to travel to the province as a result of the Troubles; they benefited hugely with a gate of 64,433, many more than could have been squeezed into Windsor Park. That Derek Johnstone equalised with a glorious diving header ten minutes later for a final score of 1–1 did not diminish the feeling that too many Scottish players looked as if they hardly cared. That flatness showed through again in the next game against Wales, even though another superb header by Johnstone put Scotland into the lead early in the game. If you were wanting to count up the ill omens for Argentina, being wise after the event as it were, you would surely include the Welsh equalising goal one minute from time when Willie Donachie, for reasons only players in these situations can explain, passed back to his goalkeeper, Jim Blyth of Coventry City, but with such force that the dismayed keeper could not prevent the ball from crossing the line. Much more significant was an incident that considerably affected MacLeod's plans: Gordon McQueen, the only recognised centre-half in the squad, collided with a goalpost and damaged his knee. He would go to South America, but only as a non-playing guest of a dismayed manager. When you add to that the unavailability through injury of Danny McGrain of Celtic, you can see the beginnings of a defensive problem.

However, Ally could only remain upbeat in public. After two 1–1 draws, he began his build-up to the final game of the series, and the last before Argentina, by stating, 'If we can beat England three times in a row we get to keep them.' The English players, I am sure, were not howling with laughter. The non-qualifiers for the World Cup went about their business professionally and briskly on 20 May. Backed by a crowd of 88,319, Scotland were enthusiastic but largely clueless and could not break the English house down. Steve Coppell, seven minutes from time, scored the only goal of the game. After the final whistle, Ally insisted that his players return to the field to respond to the crowd, which was refusing to leave the ground. The sight of a defeated team being fêted by a passionate crowd didn't seem to unnerve us, for, after all, wasn't this a show of fidelity, of not turning against the ones you loved?

And that was only a preface to the day for which, despite all logical explanations as to its arrangement, you still need to hide your head under a blanket when you recall it. On 25 May the Scotland squad, with all the SFA blazerati mustered dutifully as well, appeared at Hampden to be given an official send-off by a rapturous crowd of about 30,000. Both squad and players had turned up to do nothing other than wave at one another. For some people it was probably as emotional a farewell as that of Flora MacDonald bidding Bonnie Prince Charlie a fond adieu at Portree, as he continued his escape after Culloden. If that wasn't enough, a man, naked as the day he was born, rushed out of his house, soap suds spraying around him, to get to the roadside when he heard the Scottish team bus was about to pass on its way to the airport, just to give them a final wave. Not a magistrate in the land would have dared lay a charge of indecency against him for this almost terminal display of devotion.

So, as Ally came out to face the media for the first time in that Argentine hill-town of Alta Gracia in May 1978, the world seemed to be his oyster.

CHAPTER SEVEN

ARGENTINA

A dead dog lay at the side of the country road that ran from Cordoba to the little town of Alta Gracia in the foothills of the Andes. We passed it every day as we drove from our own base to where the Scottish squad had been housed. We got to calling it Pedro, even though we normally passed it in something of a blur, driven by a maniacal Argentine who believed that 100mph was dawdling. We got so used to the sight of it that we would have a bet on whether or not it would be there next time. It always was. Nobody came to clear it up.

For those of us on the front line who had to try to make sense of it all, Pedro sticks in the mind as a symbol for what the Argentina experience became. Decomposition hung in the air, not just around the corpse of the dog but around a deceased fantasy. A vivid memory is of the day towards the end of our stay when my cameraman said to me as we fast approached Pedro (yes, he was still there on his side, stiff as a frozen chicken), 'Maybe we should stop and interview the dog. We'd probably get more sense out of it than we would out of Ally.' That is how low we felt. We should have been feeling no more than the professional responsibility of reflecting dispassionately what was occurring in Argentina. But after a couple of weeks that was impossible. We had been rendered vulnerable to an assault on our personal feelings by having bypassed rational thinking en route to South America. Hysteria had cloaked reality. We were all guilty to some degree for that, and suffered accordingly. But it was only one man who was being hung out to dry. He was up there, every day, sitting principally on a basket chair as I recall, on a hill that afforded views which reminded me of the undulations of Perthshire. But Ally was far from appreciating the pleasant contours of Argentina. On our last visit up that hill, the tiny stream you could see in the distance must have resembled the River Styx to him. And the more he talked, the more it sounded as if he had booked a one-way ticket with the ferryman.

The players around him spoke about their residence, the Sierras Hotel, as if the only thing it didn't have in common with Barlinnie Prison was that they didn't have to swill out. Someone within the SFA had, apparently described it as the 'Gleneagles of Argentina'. That was like comparing the Taj Mahal to the public latrine at Bridgeton Cross. The players called it 'Château Despair'. It was a faded and rather decrepit-looking Spanish colonial-style building vaguely reminding you of a much sprucer and elegant era. But these complaints fell on the deaf ears of the media who wanted to hear from men dedicated to the cause, not from contributors to a *Michelin Guide*. Their saddest story of Dickensian austerity came from the dining-room. The players had to eat the same soup every day, they told us. It never varied. As the Scottish players supped at this concoction with increasing disgust, they cast their eyes balefully over an Olympic-sized swimming pool which might have provided them with useful recreational hours. There was a problem, though: it did not contain a single drop of water, and throughout their stay not so much as a trickle appeared. One of Lou Macari's suggestions at a team-talk was considered seriously: 'Why don't we fill up the pool with that bloody soup?'

If you combined the lack of basic amenities with the long periods during which players were doing nothing but lazing around after training sessions, surrounded by a fence guarded by security police still wary of the threats of the Montoneros, then you had a recipe for growing frustration and a fertile ground for the malcontents. In that last regard Ally had used some savvy in trying to pre-empt a potential powder-keg in his relationships with two key players, Archie Gemmill and Bruce Rioch. He had removed the captaincy from Gemmill and handed it to Rioch a year earlier, making him the first English-born captain of Scotland and the ninth overall in a two-year period. He decided to room them together for the trip, so that if the Nottingham Forest player had taken his downgrading badly he was with the man who was now captain, which might cap the gusher Gemmill could be, instead of his becoming a conspirator against him. Coming from the Clough stable at Nottingham, Gemmill needed no encouragement to speak his mind. For example, after the final game in Mendoza, when he came over to our cameras for interview, he put me considerably at ease by snapping at me in his high-pitched voice, 'I hope you aren't going to ask me any stupid effing questions!' One wonders how he might have fared against Paxman.

Hundreds of journalists would crowd into the press conferences, which at first were good-natured and utterly innocuous. There was not so much bombast from Ally. He was more a man still pleased with himself, whatever he was anticipating in the immediate future. There were two strands of journalists present: those who were there purely to snoop around for anything that might make a headline or two, and who had little interest in football; and those, of course, who were the 'specialists'. It would be wrong, though, to assume that the division between the two was strictly demarcated, for any self-respecting football writer presented with a story that would make the front rather than the back page would grab it with both hands, as some eventually did. So the idea that the 'specialists' were a supine bunch, only there to quiz Ally on team selection or the incidence of injuries, is to misinterpret the balance between the two. Everybody was after a story. The shenanigans of Scottish players in the past, particularly in the previous World Cup, was part of the baggage they had to carry with them to Argentina.

Even the BBC got caught up in the general tension surrounding the camp. For in their wisdom, or lack of it, they decided to house me in a small chalet just a couple of hundred yards away from the gates of the hotel grounds, with a brief to look out for any nocturnal activities. I was completely on my own in a village where not a single person spoke English, as far as I could determine, and my Spanish was limited to differentiating between two types of mineral waters, 'sin gaz' or 'con gaz'. That is not a linguistic credential that will open doors in a foreign land. Our Man in Alta Gracia, as they began to refer to me, drew an absolute blank. In the days I was there I did see one or two Scottish supporters, dressed like the squad and even with the names of particular players on their jerseys. Little did I realise at the time that this was a practice which would inflict heavy damage on the overall image of the tour.

The reason for the scarcity of players was simple: the Sierras Hotel had become virtually an armed camp, all because of one incident. One evening before hostilities really started, Allan Rough, Sandy Jardine and Willie Johnston went for a stroll. They exited properly by the front door, entered a nearby casino (only as onlookers), couldn't drink there because it was a 'dry' institution, and on returning tried to climb over a fence as a short-cut, and alerted the local militia in doing so. They could not prove their identities to the man, who was armed to the teeth. Now, perceiving

Allan Rough to be a Montoneros freedom-fighter demands a powerful stretch of the imagination. Still, a brief situation developed before identities were eventually established. It seemed innocuous enough, but back at their desks in Scotland news editors saw the first chink in the Scottish footballing mentality and jumped on the copy sent to them with professional glee.

After that the shutters came down, and the players became imprisoned in their steading. Boredom ate into their bones. Although the climbing-the-fence incident had been blown out of all proportion, it did unsettle those of us who had witnessed embarrassments before and did not want to go through it all again. We became nervous after that. 'We're on Red Alert from now on,' is how my editor, Alan Hart, put it. Hart, a delightful and powerful man who was to rise to the post of controller of BBC1, was one of the few Englishmen on site with us who did not give the impression that the Jocks' reputation had to be plundered and exposed for the riotous mob some broadcasters thought they were. However, our first thoughts were more about the stupidity of the players rather than the avidity of news reporters and the vulture culture of news desks. Even then, before a ball was kicked in earnest, we were beginning to lose trust, and we began to think the worst, especially after the first sortie of the entire squad to the press centre in Cordoba where accreditation was gained for everybody. I recall the milling, shoving pack, trying to get something from the players, a snatched word or two. Autographs were sought and gained, indeed in some cases forged, for some of the Scots supporters would admit they had scribbled down the manager's and players' signatures as they milked the mistaken-identity naïvety of the local population.

It was the photographs that caused the first real alarm. The players were assigned a pretty hostess each (and they are particularly pretty in Argentina) so that as a welcome to Cordoba they would be seen being kissed gently on the cheek by each señorita. It seemed a harmless gesture. In later decades, knowing how situations can be distorted, players would rather be snapped kissing a snake than pose with seductive-looking women. Innocently, each stepped up and had bestowed on them this secular blessing. One man suffered more than most, though. Joe Jordan, in his early twenties then, was a tall, handsome man who was about as photogenic as anybody in the squad. His photograph ended up on the front page of a tabloid attached to a story suggesting there was more to this than met the eye. The implication was clear – that Jordan had 'scored'. As a result, Jordan's wife, seven months pregnant at the time, had to endure a period of utterly groundless gossip about an affair that didn't exist. After that any lady wishing to consort with any player would have to have been parachuted in by the Argentine air force – in the hope that she did not land in that damned swimming pool.

What none of us realised on that day of accreditation was that Scottish supporters, enjoying the delights of an inexpensive city such as Cordoba, and dressed like the players, were being snapped by the paparazzi from around the globe, who started to pass around images that led to conclusions that the Scottish squad was flagrantly disregarding proper preparation for the tournament of their lives. The character assassination had started, and it soon got out of control. This was not a happy background in the lead-up to the first match against Peru on 3 June. Nor were our feelings of gathering tension eased when on our visit to the stadium to see a training session the first notable sight was that of a line of about 20 men, facing a wall, their hands above their heads, with three soldiers pointing guns directly at them. They were still there two hours later when we left the stadium, without us ever discovering who those poor wretches were, although it was a reminder that for all the airs and graces put on by the authorities and the transparent good nature of the ordinary people, this was, politically, a very unpleasant country indeed. It was about to become even less appealing.

Like any other manager, Ally had tried to pour the gallon into the proverbial pint-pot. It would not have mattered who had charge of the side at that time, for the same problems of who to select and who to leave behind at home would always have caused a dilemma. Ally's selection for the game against Peru produced misgivings. Joe Jordan, for instance, who had scored only two goals for his country in four years, was preferred to Derek Johnstone, who had netted 41 goals the previous season for Rangers and both of Scotland's goals in the Home Championship. Indeed, Ally was sticking simply to the side that had lost to England. Such loyalty can be breached, especially by men who, as I had dared to mention back in Scotland, were looking as if they might be past their sell-by date and palpably were out of form – players such as Bruce Rioch and Don Masson, both of whom had little respect for Ally. These two had been described by their manager at Derby at the time, Tommy Docherty, as 'bad buys', and he had put them on the transfer list.

Yet here they were, forming the nucleus of the Scottish side in midfield. Peru, of course, were ageing too, especially Hector Chumpitaz, Hugo Sotil and, above all, Teofilo Cubillas, all of whom had played in the side of 1970 that reached the quarter-finals. But they were ageing in a rather different way, as wine does, not to dull the taste but to invigorate it. The wine-tasting was to turn sour for Scotland.

In all honesty I saw this game through a red mist. When I put the microphone to my lips well before kick-off for some trial sounds, I could tell it was 'dead'. It was never to be resuscitated. I have never yet been given a proper explanation of how the circuit never made contact with BBC Scotland. I was told that somebody back in our office in Queen Margaret Drive, Glasgow, had not made the proper booking. Six months' preparation for this and now suddenly this opportunity being snatched from me in a rather mysterious fashion was like being debarred from a banquet. It is certainly true, though, that it was a vast and complex exercise to provide European viewers with live pictures from a country whose television service was nowhere near the standard of those on our own continent. So it was David Coleman's commentary viewers in Scotland heard. I watched the drama unfold as a wounded spectator.

Scotland's team that day was Allan Rough (Partick Thistle), Stuart Kennedy (Aberdeen), Martin Buchan (Manchester United), Tom Forsyth (Rangers), Kenny Burns (Nottingham Forest), Don Masson (Derby County), Bruce Rioch (Derby County, captain), Asa Hartford (Manchester City), Willie Johnston (West Bromwich Albion), Kenny Dalglish (Liverpool) and Joe Jordan (Manchester United). At first, it seemed as if everything was fitting into an acceptable pattern. Scotland were neat and confident, but they had to thank one special character for the breakthrough. Quiroga, the Peruvian goalkeeper, was so eccentric he would have made Fabien Barthez seem like a bore; I once saw him sprint into his opponents' half and take a shot at goal from just inside the centre circle, in a Copa America match. It was his failure to hold a powerful Rioch shot and letting it rebound to the feet of Jordan, who scored after only 15 minutes, that made the optimism soar. Here was a man about whose ability there were many doubts, scoring the first goal for Scotland in the 1978 World Cup, after having scored our last goal in the finals in West Germany four years earlier. The expected euphoria was not to last. Rather than lie down, the Peruvians unleashed their response in a mix of pace and breathtaking one-touch football that made the ageing Scottish midfield appear to be lacking in oxygen. Two minutes before the interval they equalised: some bewildering inter-passing between Cubillas and Velasquez provided Cueto with the opportunity to score.

Now, before this match I had heard Ally talk about tactics. He was giving an interview to Tony Gubba of the BBC about the blistering pace of the two Peruvian wingers, Munante and especially Oblitas. During that chat he had described how Martin Buchan would have a special role to play in subduing Oblitas. He said that several times during the interview, and at one stage I thought of interrupting and asking him if that is what he really meant. For the problem was that Buchan was at left-back and Oblitas played on the other wing, on the left side, and was therefore due to torment Stuart Kennedy, not the Manchester United man. Either Ally was confused about names or, as became clearer as he expanded on the subject, he had not a clue where Oblitas actually played. The point has to be reinforced that he had not seen Peru in the flesh before this actual game. Their pace became Scotland's downfall, even though 15 minutes into the second half the Scots were awarded a penalty when Cubillas, of all people, brought down Rioch. Masson's spot-kick was the kind that enrages – soppy, unconvincing, lacking in belief and eminently saveable. Quiroga hugged the ball with body language that suggested the phrase, 'Now you're for it.'

Indeed Scotland were. Cubillas, throwing off the shackles of age, played like a gazelle with boots. In the space of six minutes he scored two goals. The first came after he was given a glimpse of goal by passes from Munante and Cueto; he had the ball behind Rough before he knew it. Peru were now ahead and rising. Cubillas's second was a classic, and it is firmly implanted in the mind's eye, never to be erased no matter which remedy is attempted, for it sank Scotland and all of us gathered round that ground with one fell swoop. A free-kick was awarded to Peru, just outside the penalty area. Cubillas, we knew, would take this. What we didn't anticipate was the technique he employed. As he took his short run-up, his pacing to the ball involved a sudden quirky movement. He did not swing at the ball, he stabbed at it with his front foot, and it bulleted over the wall and beyond Rough. I had to admire the audacity of it, but I was devastated, and I prepared for a long night's sulk.

It did not work because we all had to face up to the world again the following day, as did the traumatised Ally, who had heard the Peruvian manager's after-match message to him: 'I would like to congratulate Scotland and Mr MacLeod for the team they presented to us.' Brutal in its simplicity and intent, it had made for a deeply ruffled Ally. 'A disaster, a disaster,' he said several times in the first moments of aftermath, and in his suddenly truculent mood there seemed to be the coded message 'There'll be no Mr Nice Guy next time.' For there is little doubt he felt that he had been undermined by journalism since he'd arrived in the country.

In another way he had good cause to present a flintier face to the public, not just in terms of the result but also because of the increasing volume of rumour based on remarks made by the Tunisian manager Majid Chetali, whose team for some time had shared the Scottish squad's hotel, and who was quoted in the press as saying, 'The Scots do no work. They lie on the veranda and drink and eat, drink and eat. They have whisky for breakfast, whisky for lunch, whisky for dinner. You would think they were tourists.' Now, even those who thought Ally was simply out of his depth knew that this was a total fabrication. Through the complexities of the translations of different languages, perhaps Chetali did not mean exactly that, or it had simply been concocted by the foreign reporters. But the printing of it made it true. That's what mattered. A defeat and ill-founded rumours – these could have been handled with some intelligence, awkward though they were. But there was also a bonus-money wrangle in the background which suddenly became public. This was never satisfactorily dealt with, and it left a lingering sense of grievance among the squad.

But it was the next blow that put paid to any chance of redemption for the entire party. Willie Johnston and Kenny Dalglish had been chosen for a drug test in the stadium in Cordoba after that Peru match. The others had trundled up to Alta Gracia, leaving behind a hidden bombshell. Around lunchtime the following day I received a phone call from the BBC office in Buenos Aires hinting that something 'fishy' was going on between FIFA and the Scotland camp. That was all. They alerted me to the fact that some kind of storm was brewing. I was in my room trying to imagine what the fuss might be about when I had a call from Buenos Aires saying that Willie Johnston had failed his drugs test. Ally told me later that no official from the SFA International Committee was in the hotel when the telegram came from FIFA informing them of this. He went straight to the SFA medical man Dr Fitzsimmons' room to find out the medical background to the reported use of a banned substance. He walked straight in on the Celtic doctor, who as a devoutly religious man was deep in prayer. Ally admitted that all he found himself saying was, 'You'd better say one for me, Doc. Look what I've got here!' I was as incredulous then as I was in later years in Seoul when I got the same kind of call in the early hours of the morning, this time to tell me that Ben Johnson, the winner of the Blue Riband event, the 100 metres, was on his way home from the Olympics after failing his test. Those of us in the hotel in Cordoba, though, were sceptical. We felt it was just another hare being let loose by the irresponsible tabloids. So many stories had been circulated and had bitten the dust, even though the smears remained to tarnish the image.

As it happened, we had all been invited that very day to the Sierras Hotel jointly by the SFA and the Minister of Sport, Dennis Howell, for one of those mind-numbing receptions during which nothing much is said or done and the choice is stark: remain bored or reach out for the drinks tray like one of those mechanical arms in a car assembly line. The latter choice was popular. But this was no small-talk occasion. Virtually every journalist of any note went up there with the zeal of those who had been commanded, 'Sink the Bismarck!' Their sole target was Johnston.

Trying to be both polite and ruthless in pursuit of a quarry at the same time could have called on many skills. The one chosen was frontal assault. We, the BBC, followed the trail with an electronic camera at the ready, and plunged amongst the sedate guests looking for Johnston. It seemed a thousand others were trying to do exactly the same thing. Reception etiquette 'went oot the windae', as they would say in Glasgow. We were suddenly faced by an irate Ally, incandescent with rage. He pounced in particular on the unsuspecting Trevor MacDonald, who, as you would expect from a skilled journalist, was trying to wrench the facts from Johnston. MacLeod pushed at the cameraman, and ITN's distinguished presenter had to beat a hasty retreat as the Scottish manager's frustration erupted. When it became clear that Johnston could become the centre of an undignified scrum, the SFA decided to secrete him out of the reception, and the inevitable decision was made to send him homewards. Ernie Walker, who had only been in his secretarial office for a year, delivered that verdict to the press a couple of days later. 'Explaining [that] to the world's press was the most humiliating experience of my life,' he told me. But he also added, 'The way Willie

Johnston played that day, you would have thought it was a sleeping pill he had taken. The drug certainly did not enhance his performance.' As he spoke to the press, a proud and dignified man looked shamed and saddened, as if any more negative news would break him. Walker wanted to be able to look his counterparts from other countries in the eye and retain their personal respect. He was to rise from the indignities of that period to become an influential officer of both UEFA and FIFA, and was effectively the man who selected the USA for the 1994 World Cup, which sadly he missed through illness.

The drug Johnston had taken was Reactivan. It is hardly a performance-enhancing pill. Dr Alan Cooper, medical director of the British subsidiary of Merck, the company that manufactured it, said shortly afterwards, 'Nobody has ever recommended Reactivan for use by sportsmen and it has never been tested for prevention of that kind of physical fatigue. It is a tonic – rather an old-fashioned concept. It is often used by doctors for patients who are a pest and frankly don't need anything.'

Johnston had turned out to be more of a malignant than a pest. For he had lied. Even supposing that Reactivan was no more effective than taking Smarties – and that anyway the pills, he claimed, were handed out liberally at his club, West Bromwich Albion – he had told Dr Fitzsimmons before the Peru game that he had taken nothing out of the ordinary. I think this was more the act of a simpleton than a charlatan, but the effect was catastrophic. Johnston was driven through the night to the Argentine capital and flown home before any journalist could waylay him. As he lay on his back on the floor of the Mercedes, accompanied by assistant secretary Peter Donald, sweeping through the gates to avoid the view of the press, he uttered the plaintive cry, 'Why does this always have to happen to me?' It was as if he felt hard done by, that he was a victim rather than a perpetrator, that people did not understand him. It was a compound of stupidity and ignorance.

The rest of us had to stay on, clinging to the wreckage. We might have gone completely under had we known that another Scottish player, Don Masson, had approached the manager and told him that he had taken Reactivan as well, since he had felt convinced by Johnston that such a thing was commonplace. Johnston's room-mate Tom Forsyth told people that after listening to the stern lecture from the doctor on banned substances before the tournament started 'I was scared to brush my teeth', but that apprehension obviously had not rubbed off on others. To the manager's amazement, Masson then denied he had taken the drug and that he was trying merely to take the 'heat off' Johnston. If that wasn't confusing enough, the SFA then decided to decline Ally's demand that Masson be sent packing immediately. It is clear the manager did not believe in Masson's volte-face. He wanted him out of the country, away from the rest of the squad, suspecting he was a destabilising influence and a troublemaker. In fact there were others prepared to vie for that dubious honour, for during a candid confrontation with the rest of the squad, others owned up to having Reactivan as well. Ally and the doctor trawled through the hotel again, and pocketed over a couple of dozen of such tablets from different rooms. Many years later I approached MacLeod to name the players who had admitted to having the pills in their possession. He kept his silence on that. I suppose one reason for that is that he could not extract from any of them confessions that they had actually used the drug. But such widespread possession, in this case, brings you nine-tenths of the way to believing that others must have been swallowing them as well.

According to Ally, Masson made an astonishing retort when he was informed that because of the trouble he had caused he would not play in the remainder of the World Cup, and that if the manager had his way he would never play for his country again. The key reason, the manager pointed out, was lack of loyalty, to which Masson replied, 'There is no such thing in football. You are kidding yourself on if you think there is.' There was enough in that remark to suggest the true stature of the manager in the eyes of some players, as Allan Rough confirmed. 'The Anglos thought Ally was just a hick. They didn't take him seriously. They thought he didn't really know anything about the game. He was a lovely man in many ways and he really did want to be friendly. He didn't want to fall out with anybody. Most of the Anglos considered that to be just a weakness. After that first defeat they started to put the boot in.'

With the Reactivan now flushed down various toilets, Scotland prepared to take on a nation of whose footballing prowess, or lack of it, we knew scarcely anything. Iran was seen as a possible antidote to the depression that existed amongst the Scots players, and, by now, the media. A win would help ease the pain. I travelled with ITV's Martin Tyler, who was to become Sky's distinguished commentator, to a training ground outside Cordoba to have a look at the Iranians in training. Tyler said to me, 'They look as if they should be out herding cattle.' They were tall, dark men who looked awkward on the ball and gave the impression they had learnt their football by correspondence course. It was a stumbling, uncoordinated session, and although such training exercises can be very deceptive, we left their camp believing that nothing could have come better for Scotland in their time of need than these gauchos from the Middle East. But we had overlooked one important aspect: they were big and strong. And we should have paid closer attention to their recent record: they had drawn with Yugoslavia and Bulgaria and lost only 0–1 against Wales. We wrote them off on the basis of a 3–0 thrashing by Holland in their first match.

On 7 June Scotland and Iran came to the wide-open, poorly designed stadium in Cordoba where the dug-outs were something like 30 yards from the touchline. From the commentary positions, another 50 yards further back, the players looked like Subbuteo pieces. Distance, on this occasion, did not lend enchantment. It was as if, in the whole history of mental torture devised by man to inflict pain on his fellow creatures, one hellish trick remained to be tried, and that was being forced to watch Scotland try to play football against a team of World Cup novices. It would have made one develop a fondness for the thumbscrew.

CHAPTER EIGHT

ALL THE GUILTY MEN

The central problem was the disintegration of Ally. He disappeared. He locked himself in his room. When leadership was required he was not around. The players could not find him. When he returned to Scotland and gave his post-tournament report to the SFA, he described his participation and involvement at the height of the problems in such glowing terms that even the taciturn Ernie Walker was struck dumb by it. It was utterly contradictory to what had happened.

Scots football supporters, suffering the inconsistencies for which they were certainly not mentally prepared, proved on 7 June 1978 that you do not need a full moon to be turned into baying werewolves. At first the couple of hundred or so of them were forcibly merry amid a thin crowd of 7,938. The thought persisted in that gaunt, sparsely filled stadium that perhaps even the local population had concluded that the Scottish team now had a leprous quality, given the nature and quantity of the publicity that had been heaped upon them, and had decided to shun them. It was the poorest attendance of all the World Cup matches.

Those absent missed a slow, nightmarish slide towards humiliation. Scotland were without the exiled Johnston, the disgraced Masson and the injured captain Rioch. They brought in Sandy Jardine and Willie Donachie of Manchester City and started with the substitutes from the opening game, Lou Macari (Manchester United) and Archie Gemmill, as captain. The changes made little difference to the overall impression of a group of men who had lost their way. The principal quality of the Iranians was their refusal to be pushed around. Their strength and running power became evident in the early stages of the game as Scotland were mispassing in such a manner that you felt, despite assertions that they had put their misfortunes behind them, they were in fact being weighed down by events. Even when, two minutes before half-time Eskandarian, the Iranian centre-back, was so harassed by Jordan that he was pressurised into attempting a back-pass to his goalkeeper but succeeded only in sending it 15 yards into his own net for

Scotland to go one up, the comical aspect of that goal was not treated with a belly laugh, but almost as if it were a sick joke.

I and my colleague Allan Herron from the *Sunday Mail*, sitting alongside me in the commentary position, had enough experience of Scottish failure to sense we could be heading for a fall, so inept were Scotland in the second half. It was a man called Danaifar who pushed Scotland over the edge with half an hour remaining. With the Iranians increasing in confidence and creating movements of which we did not think they were capable, this speedy forward dispossessed Gemmill, swept round Jardine and beat Rough with a shot from an acute angle. Seconds later Rough made a superb save from another forward, Ghasempour. In a mood of desperation, Ally sent on Joe Harper of Aberdeen to replace Kenny Dalglish with 15 minutes left. Harper had not played international football for three years and was about to play his last game for Scotland; Derek Johnstone, with recent scoring form, remained on the bench. It simply did not make sense. But then so many bizarre events had happened prior to this match that nothing was any longer surprising.

At the final whistle, with the score 1–1, Ally dipped his head down into his hands as if all he had left was the hemlock to sip. Throughout the last 20 minutes in particular the BBC producer had decided to focus in on close-ups of the Scotland manager. It was cruel and almost vindictive, because we saw a portrait of a sensitive man in mental turmoil. They would not leave him alone. He would occasionally place his face into his cupped hands like a child would do in a cinema hiding from a particularly gruesome scene in a horror film. When it surfaced again you could see it was etched in the pain of incomprehension. He bobbed up and down like that innumerable times, and the BBC did not miss a moment of the agony. Later that week BBC producer John McNicholas, at heart a friendly man, was ordered to put together a montage of the aftermath of that game with particular emphasis on Ally's reaction. His editing colleagues back in Buenos Aires helped him with a degree of sadism that was clearly calculated to highlight the folly of the Scots, as personified by one man. They contrasted the joyful pre-World Cup Ally with the miserable wretch sitting in a foreign dug-out, tortured by events unfolding. They also cut into this montage the reaction of a bunch of Scotland supporters who from their antics would have torn the manager apart had they got their hands on him. You could see them literally spitting with fury and chanting, 'Resign, resign!' This was the same mob who only a couple of weeks earlier had been hailing Ally as a demi-god. Their ugliness was curiously a kind of antidote to the immediate criticisms of Ally, for you had to feel sorry for a man at the mercy of an unthinking, hypocritical crew of people who had dwelt in fantasy land far too long. By some quirk of fate, about an hour after the game, the team bus was unable to move for 20 minutes inside the stadium perimeter, trapped because of a security arrangement. I watched as Scottish supporters gathered round the bus and unleashed on players and manager their pent-up fury. It was ugly, and it presented another image to be exploited.

BBC London knew what they were doing. It was payback time – for the Wembley antics, for England not being there – and they unleashed what by any account was an assassination job. The raw material of failure was there to be plundered, of course, but the pictures contained elements of poisonous ridicule which I felt were even racial in their tone. I only saw the montage several days later, and I suppose I was so drugged by the funereal atmosphere surrounding the camp that my critical faculties were somewhat numbed. It was only months later when I saw it replayed that the full force of its vindictiveness impacted on me.

The day after the game, in Buenos Aires, a journalist went to interview Rod Stewart for his reaction. Before the tournament the singer had asked me to lay some of my commentaries on the World Cup record he had made, including that famous game at Anfield, which I was delighted to do, thinking I would be in the money, as Stewart was truly a global star. He had chosen a samba-like beat for the song. In his hotel room all Stewart could do, in response to the journalist's questions as to how he now felt, was kick a nearby suitcase and snarl with disgust, 'That record will never make it to number one now!' Our embryonic partnership in the world of pop was shattered.

As Stewart was kicking his suitcase, we were all assembled again on the hill overlooking the hotel, waiting to attend to Ally and his inquest. He looked pale and distraught as he plumped himself down on his cane chair without the usual cheery preambles. Then, as he was about to speak, a dog (not the reincarnated Pedro, who was still out there motionless on the road) came ambling up and began to nuzzle into Ally's thigh. He put his hand round the neck of the dog and declared, 'Well, at least I have one friend here today.' We might have succumbed to the syrupy sentiment induced by Lassie in days gone by, but this moment hardly worked that way. This was not a lump-in-throat time. It was in fact crushingly embarrassing, entirely the wrong opening gambit for a media who were certainly after his blood but would have paid more respect to a man feeling less sorry for himself and displaying some fight. He had none of that in him now. He was broken. There was still one game to go, but you felt that he was now beyond repair as a manager. This perception was endorsed by a highly placed SFA official who told me in unambiguous terms years later, 'I could put it this way. After the drugs fiasco and the Iran result, Ally hid under the bed. He locked himself in his room. We never saw him, and neither did the players much. The team were utterly rudderless. He shirked his responsibilities. When the going was rough he did not want to know, he just disappeared. That was a major part of our downfall.' Allan Rough vouched for Ally's lack of presence. 'He became a lonely, broken-looking man. You would wander round the hotel and you would suddenly come across him sitting on his own in a quiet corner staring into space. This was his own choice. Nobody was trying to avoid him. He just cut himself off.'

Not from some painful questioning by the media he didn't. He always believed that part of the hostility directed towards him was because an article had appeared in the *Scottish Daily Express* as an 'exclusive' interview during the first week they had been in Argentina. He claimed he'd been offered £25,000 for that exclusivity but had turned it down because he wanted a non-exclusive relationship with the press, for obvious political reasons. But in fact the paper ran it as an 'exclusive', which incensed some of their rivals who in turn, as Ally maintained, wanted to take it out on him for selling himself to one paper. At the time they didn't believe a word of his explanation. But that did not wholly account for the grilling he got that day, which centred principally on the possibility of his resignation. He parried those questions by stressing that there was one game to go and that Scotland, arithmetically, still had a chance of qualifying. Now we were beginning to see him cutting a sad, squirming figure who needed bailing out from this inquisition by somebody. There were no volunteers for such a task coming from the ranks of SFA officials. Nobody was really intervening. He had cut himself off from others so he could now stew in his own juice, they seemed to be saying. They had in effect written him off. The press in particular had undergone a metamorphosis. Men who normally had good personal relationships with him were prepared to write as scathingly as they ever had about anybody. Signs were given by certain players, particularly Don Masson, that they would be prepared to sell stories to the highest bidder.

After that, the Holland game was as comforting a thought as staring a pampas bull in the eye. For that match we all decamped to Mendoza, which was some 500 miles away from Cordoba. It was a town completely unknown to us at the time, but the name can now be seen scattered throughout supermarkets on the labels of some of the best wine in the world. The media were well disposed to it, although the discovery of a hidden gem such as Mendoza wine could induce only temporary bliss. It did not affect predictions on what the morrow might bring. The Dutch were unassailable. We wondered how this bedraggled bunch called a Scottish squad were faring in their new quarters, a smaller hotel on the outskirts of the town. They felt more at ease. As Lou Macari said to me afterwards, 'Alcatraz would have been better than the hotel in Alta Gracia.'

The change might act as a tonic, but that was the last thought on our minds as we approached the Estadio San Martin on 11 June. It was as if a gigantic ladle had scooped out a segment of the Andes into a bowl that acted like a paddling pool for some mythical giant from the mountains. It was arguably the most dramatically sited stadium I had ever been in, hemmed in as it was by a string of towering peaks. It was to be a game with a Wagnerian backdrop, and a goal that could have been set to the thrum of the Ride of the Valkyries.

As any player who ever sat in a dressing-room with him would tell you, Ally was no tactical genius. He was a motivator above all else. But at that level you need more than a touch of sagacity in man-management and the deployment of resources. We had been puzzled by his team selections, but then what manager in the middle of the world's greatest football tournament is not beset by outsiders who think they know best? Even the Dutch coach, the Austrian Ernst Happel, had gone into a huff with the Dutch media – which admittedly is not a hard thing to achieve with them, given the constant niggling and bickering that goes on within their fold. Like Ally, Happel had cut himself off from others and remained a dour, isolated figure as he let his players argue amongst themselves about money and bonuses, which the Dutch do customarily with the panache of Wall Street brokers. With him, though, it had worked, despite having come to Argentina without Cruyff, Peters, Kist, Geels and, above all, the man who had put Celtic to the sword in the San Siro in 1970, Wim van Hanegem. The latter had astonishingly turned up at Schipol Airport suitably garbed in his World Cup uniform, ready for the outward flight, given a television interview about the team's prospects, then hailed a taxi and headed back home. But what Happel was left with were not the dregs. He still had nine players from the highly successful 1974 World Cup squad, who had blown the final against West Germany because, as Jock Stein famously said in his analysis of the match, 'They were the better team. But they were fighting the Second World War all over again. They wanted to humiliate instead of just going out to win.' With that core, they still were a formidable force.

In the post-Argentina inquest, some tedious and useless analysis was attempted on the various selections made by Ally for the three games. You could have gone on endlessly about the possible permutations that might have been used in any of the three games. Two over-arching facts remain predominant features, though. In the first game an elderly team, who as we had anticipated had peaked the previous season and had been selected largely out of loyalty, had been caught mid-stream by the unexpected strength of current, and had floundered. Then, in that final, memorable game against Holland, the élan and boundless effort the Scots players clearly exhibited came from the simple fact, in my view, that they were demob happy. They wanted out of there. They could see the light at the end of the tunnel that would take them away from the horrors. Of course they would have been deeply indignant about the criticism they had received, and that would have acted as part of the spur. Their pride had been hurt. But in reality there was not a single player in the squad who really believed they could beat the runners-up from the previous World Cup by three clear goals, which is what the situation demanded for their continued participation in the tournament. The Dutch could only fail to qualify were they to lose the game by the same three-goal margin. The prospect of that only provoked chuckles among our television corps, in between slurping the superb Mendozan wine. One of their key players, Johannes Neeskens, was extremely doubtful, but the Dutch do not like to lose at any time, and certainly not by a heavy score. So I have never believed the Scottish players were driven by the need for national redemption, but rather by the thought that soon they would have one-way air tickets in their possession.

This 'don't-give-a damn-now' attitude meant less tension in their play.

Perhaps those of us waiting for the Scots to appear might have interpreted their relative lateness in coming on to the field of play as the opposite – a reluctance to appear at all. But this was down to some odd belief by Ally that getting out too soon and having his players hang around would be psychologically deflating. He refused to answer the first call to action and ordered the dressing-room door to be shut. They only emerged after the third request by a FIFA official, with the stern warning that if they didn't get out there forthwith 'official action' would be taken against them. Creating a crisis before facing another potential crisis might have some esoteric justification as a way of coming to the aid of the needy, by making them stand up for their rights. But you have to lie down flat on a leather couch to work that one out. In fact the players thought this was merely Ally being obsessed by minutiae. When they did appear, this was the team: Rough, Kennedy, Donachie, Buchan, Forsyth, Gemmill, Rioch, Souness, Hartford, Dalglish and Jordan. Nowadays you look back on these names not merely with nostalgia but with deepening respect for the innate and abundant talent that existed then, compared to recent times. However, the team selection for this game really emerged from heated discussions with players who by that time had decided to call a spade a spade. Ally had to listen.

Note the name of Souness, playing in his first ever World Cup game at the beginning of a distinguished international career. Ally had reservations about him until, of course, he saw him operate in this game with such maturity and self-confidence that it merely exposed the shallowness of thinking and planning that had preceded this whole venture. Jardine, Burns, Macari and John Robertson all stood down, which meant that no recognised winger would be fielded. I recall at the time sitting in the commentary position with my co-commentator Allan Herron and jointly coming to the conclusion that Scotland were simply out to avoid annihilation and humiliation by crowding out the Dutch in midfield. But the game flowed surprisingly freely, both sets of players giving the impression they were actually enjoying what was, in comparison with the flatness of the Iran game, an exhilarating romp. When Rioch, back in the side as captain, headed a Souness cross against the angle of post and bar with only five minutes played, it seemed almost audacious to do that to the Dutch. The adventurous bounce in the steps of the Scottish players seemed out of character to the Argentine dourness that had beset them on and off the field. Back in the London studio, watching this as the principal analyst was Jock Stein, ready to give his half-time and post-match analysis. Years later, during his stint as Scottish team manager when he was preparing for his first World Cup in Spain at Sotogrande near Gibraltar, he recalled for me how he had responded to my and Allan's commentary. 'It was an amazing transformation. At first you both sounded as if you were at a funeral. Then you got slightly more enthusiastic. Then you both sounded as if you were at a wedding. And at the end you were almost back to your funeral again!'

The mood indeed scaled from the funereal to the hysterical. The game unravelled before our eyes like a heavily wrapped present from which you despondently peel off layer after layer until something like a gold watch reveals itself. Even the largely local crowd of 35,130 was in tune with the game and responded to some of the skirmishes with voices that were clearly in favour of the Scots. And when Neeskens, of immense value to the Dutch, had to be taken off with further damage to his ribs after a reckless challenge on Rioch, the tide was flowing towards the Dutch goal almost constantly. When Dalglish put the ball in the net only to see the goal disallowed for a preceding Jordan foul, something stirred inwardly amongst those of us who had been so downbeat about this game. At least they were going out fighting. Then Stuart Kennedy botched a clearance, stumbled over the ball and, in trying to retrieve the situation, sandwiched Johnny Rep between himself and Alan Rough. A penalty was awarded and you felt that nothing could possibly go right.

In a way it was an historic moment, for Rensenbrink stepped forward to take it and he scored the 1,000th goal in the history of the World Cup finals. Not that we knew that at the time. What we did know was that it had not depressed this Scottish side. They went after the Dutch almost as if they were enraged. They besieged their goal, and only one minute before half-time Jordan headed down a cross for Dalglish to hook in the equaliser. Drawing with the Dutch at half-time seemed as if it was going to be the peak of Scotland's achievement in Argentina. But astonishingly another possibility arose when Souness, playing superbly, with that arrogance that had been so lacking within the team in the other games, was bundled off the ball in the box by Willy Van Der Kerkhof, one of the Dutch twins playing in that game. Dalglish scored from the penalty, and after only two minutes of the second half the Scots were ahead. There was a degree of incredulity in witnessing this. It was difficult to appreciate how these down-and-outs were getting the upper hand against the Dutch aristocracy.

Then came the 66th minute. When this moment is mentioned to me, as it has so often been, I visualise it rather like recalling puberty and that first sexual fumble which aroused feelings that made you believe life really did have something worth living for. For it came with that suddenness which simply enhanced the surge of clashing disbelief and wonderment. We watched a goal that made men of us again, after the whimpering wimps we had been throughout that sojourn. It was scored, of course, by Archie Gemmill. It was a goal with a narrative – a beginning, a middle and an end.

Firstly, the little man collects the ball, looks at goal and starts to move. The commentating voice in unison with that is neutral. He swerves one way and then the other until he is almost impossibly through the entire Dutch defence. As he pokes the ball almost insolently between the legs of the hitherto impassable Ruud Krol, the voice rises a pitch. It can't be, can it? Jongbloed, the Dutch keeper, is a big, gangly man who you think could stem a breach of the Boulder Dam. Yet with a delicate coolness Gemmill flicks the ball past him, leaving Jongbloed a flailing wreck.

The reaction in the commentary area was quite unprecedented. Both of us had risen as the run reached its climax, and then exploded. I looked along the line of commentators, and to a man they were on their feet, about 20 or so of them, as if to a hypnotist's command. I have never experienced that again anywhere in the world. It was the greatest goal ever scored. It was to us then, and it still is. Of course that contention raised objections and ridicule from around the globe, and I had cited to me examples of magical goals of sheer genius, goals that came from bewildering inter-passing, goals from stunning distances, goals of cunning and stealth, and so on. I accept all of that. But the impact of a goal is about both its quality and, above all, its context. The Gemmill goal was scored against the background of national humiliation which foreigners had not been slow to remind us of. His, for that one brief, shining moment, was an antidote to depression pharmacists might have envied as they handed pills out to the melancholy. Somehow or other he had battled his way through the pain of insult and produced something so naturally that you felt it was proof of the genuine article of Scottish football. After all, as a teacher I used to watch boys in playgrounds scoring goals like that at playtime. It was a throw-back to the simplicity of football. Its skill, its timing, its audacity permeated even the thickest skin of the thickest of their critics. It was the greatest goal ever scored.

Then came Johnny Rep three minutes later. At 3–1 Scotland knew they needed only one more goal to stay in the competition, but the fair-haired midfielder thrust his way down the centre of the field and unleashed a raging drive from 25 yards which Rough had no chance of stopping. And that, as you would say, was that. We knew then the illusion of qualifying had effectively been shattered. The Rep goal encouraged the belief, fostered mostly by English commentators, that the Dutch had really toyed with Scotland and that they could have scored any time they liked. I put that belief to the test in 1998 when I worked alongside Rep during the World Cup in France. 'I just shut my eyes and hit out,' he explained when I asked him about that goal. 'Sure, I have scored goals something like that before, but I don't think any as well hit. I suppose it could have gone anywhere. But the idea that we planned it that way is complete nonsense. If you know anything about football you know that it isn't often you can find yourself behind and then catch up. The game runs away from you. We were genuinely concerned about losing the game by a big margin. I thought Scotland were genuinely unlucky not to make it on that last game.' I doubt if he was being patronising as he comes from a tradition that does not indulge much in flannel.

Even so, from many sources there was only a very grudging acceptance of the overall performance, with the exception of the Gemmill goal, which was genuinely praised. In Mendoza's airport lounge the following day, while waiting for hours for the fog to clear and our flight to Buenos Aires to take off, Alan Sharp, the Scottish novelist, pronounced to me from beneath his wide-brimmed hat, 'We've just discovered a new way of losing!' I had an odd, hangover-ish feeling at the time accentuated by the fact that I had just had to bribe a goon with a gun at the gate of the Scottish party hotel to allow me to sneak in and ask Ally about the rumour that had swept the press corps that he was to announce his resignation that very day. 'Rubbish' was the only word he spoke to me before stamping off.

The rumour persisted. Alex Montgomery, writing for *The Sun* at the time and ghosting Lou Macari's column for the paper, heard that Lou had broken off from the Scottish squad and headed for Cordoba. Unable ,like the rest of us, to fly, Montgomery hired a taxi driver to go the whole 500 miles or so, so desperate was he to listen to Macari 'spilling the beans', but after the ramshackle vehicle had six mechanical breakdowns and four punctures, Montgomery snapped, the driver took flight, and there in the middle of the vast pampas were two minute figures, one intent on beating the stuffing out of the other, and that other fleeing for his life, all in pursuit of a story. Two more casualties of the Argentina expedition. When he eventually caught up with Macari, all the little forward would say was that the SFA had made errors in such matters as accommodation and travel arrangements. There was nothing sensational in that. It was Mr Grumpy we were reading, not the great revealer. Although he did say that Ally had told him he was going to resign – something that angered the manager, as he felt it was a distortion of a conversation they had had before the Holland match, and that others were fuelling the rumour. So this was not entirely a shocking revelation, although made to appear so by the paper. When Macari spoke to the *Observer* (11 June) he again uttered what many of us had concluded anyway, though coming from the mouth of a player it did carry a certain weight. 'If clever people had been in charge,' he was reported as saying, 'they would have taken the pressure off by telling us we were coming to play against the best players in the world. Instead, we were bombarded with crap about beating the rest of the world … Tunisia and Iran are better prepared than we are.'

In his final press conference before he made his escape, Ally sounded bullish. Only goal difference had prevented Scotland from qualifying, he stressed, as they had finished on three points in the group along with Holland but just behind them, Peru having topped the table. He talked about how as a small nation we had done well just to be there. That was rather different from the pre-tournament bombast. English sportswriter Frank McGhee, responding to Ally's assertion that by beating the Dutch his players had shown the world the real Scotland, wrote, 'This is like losing the world war and then inventing the atom-bomb.' In the *Daily Mirror* of 9 June, just two days before the Holland match, James Sanderson aired the dissatisfaction coming from 'the top brass of the SFA', as he put it, one claim being that they had pleaded with Ally to go and see the opposition but he had refused as he felt it would be all right on the day. The report then quoted the chairman of the International Committee, Tom Lauchlan, as saying, 'We handed everything to him – money, resources, everything. Now we [the SFA] are being caned.' Also trying to wash his hands of responsibility was Tom Younger, the SFA vice-president, who was also quoted in that same report as saying, 'The meeting of the selection committee can't come quickly enough.' Ally, it seemed, was heading for a brutal slaying. But others, like me, could reasonably conclude that the SFA were complicit in the downfall, not innocent bystanders. Had they really investigated the cramped, monastic conditions of the hotel and the training ground an hour away from Alta Gracia? It was so bad that one of the players claimed not even the cows would eat the grass there.

However, when Ally did sit down with SFA officials back in Scotland to make his report on the tournament, the SFA secretary Ernie Walker's chin dropped in amazement and almost hit the long committee table. For what he was listening to was Ally portraying himself as a gallant leader who had led from the front when the squad was in crisis, going from room to room encouraging, sympathising, consoling. That was in fact the opposite of what had happened. Ally palpably was not a leader. He had ducked too many responsibilities to be called that. Even those, like me, who basically liked the man and ended up with great sympathy for the personal grief he felt, knew he was not what he purported to be. A vote was taken at that meeting on his continued employment which ended in a tie, 3–3, with chairman Tom Lauchlan casting a vote in favour of the manager. He should have gone then and there, but he was now a terminal case.

It was one thing for Ally's bosses and the media to take him to task. It was quite another when the public in general seemed to turn against him. When the stragglers from the Scottish party arrived at Glasgow Airport after having parted with the Anglo contingent at Gatwick, there were about 200 fans there to acknowledge their return as opposed to the 30,000 who had seen them off at Hampden. Not that they saw much of them, for they were smuggled out of the airport by security officials. 'Home by the Backdoor' was the *Daily Record* headline of 16 June. It was a cameo that reflected the jaundiced mood of the nation. Andy Cameron's record 'Ally's Tartan Army' had suddenly stopped selling the day after the Iran game. In Dundee a shopkeeper offered them for sale at a penny each, with the free offer of a hammer to smash them to pieces. The bitter faces of hatred I had seen among the support in Cordoba were mirrored in others whenever you mentioned Ally's name in public in Scotland for a long period after the debacle. It was as if he were being criminalised. That he did not deserve. We had all helped put him on the pedestal, and now he was being torn down like one of those political statues in eastern Europe, reflecting an outraged awakening. The pandemic of adulation that had swept through the land and given us such outlandish expectations was really self-induced, although Ally had certainly helped foment it like a circus barker. We didn't seem to have any mechanism to halt the fever and read the true underlying feeling, which was that of a nation grasping for any symbol of identity, however fanciful.

There were no doubts in most of the political world that football matches thousands of miles away could alter the mood of a nation and affect voting intentions. The politician who disregarded the fact that football was part of a resurgent national cultural identity – with writing, theatre and the arts at the time also reflecting a burgeoning self-confidence in a country where many thought independence was on the horizon – would have been extremely naïve. Donald Dewar, the newly elected Labour MP for Garscadden, who was to become Scotland's First Minister in the future Executive, was heard to say on the eve of the Scotland–Peru game, 'We can afford to win in Argentina now the SNP is on the run,' the SNP's Margo MacDonald having been beaten by Labour's George Robertson in the 31 May by-election at Hamilton. Clearly Dewar felt that a surging SNP and a victorious Scotland team would be detrimental to the Labour Party in Scotland. There is little doubt that nationalism would have received an enormous boost from such a footballing success, given their tendency to milk any gratuitous quirk of fortune that suggested Scottish self-reliance. Margo MacDonald took part in a television documentary years later in which she lamented the effect the traumas of Argentina had had on the outcome of the devolution debate and referendum vote, which took place eventually on 1 March 1979 and produced sharp divisions, with one third of the population for devolution, one third against, and a third abstaining. She felt the World Cup debacle had helped damage that feeling of self-reliance which had begun to snowball in the early 1970s. It might seem far-fetched to link a Dutchman, with eyes closed, scoring a goal from 25 yards in Mendoza – the moment that underlined Scotland's failure – to a constitutional impasse and devolution being delayed for another two decades, but it certainly did not act as a tonic. Jim Sillars, Margo's husband and SNP apostate from the Labour Party, also lamented what he felt might have been a tremendous boost for the political independence he now avidly sought for Scotland when he spoke in the same documentary of the ultimate embarrassment. 'It certainly transmitted itself to the political field,' he said. 'It was a case of "Here we go again. Are we ever going to be able to do anything right ourselves?"'

But, perhaps not surprisingly, it was Ally himself who provided the most bizarre postscript. It was sounded 16 years later during the Maradona drug scandal at the World Cup in the USA. In the 1 July issue of the Sun, after being asked how he had been affected by the drug scandal of Argentina, Ally replied in these astounding terms: 'Everyone thought if we beat Holland by three goals in our last game – and we were three-one up at one stage – we'd have gone through. What they did not know was that FIFA had told us they'd deduct two points from us because Willie Johnston took the banned drug. We [presumably the SFA officials and Ally] decided it was best to keep that news from the rest of the players.'

So had we all been living the ultimate fantasy of getting excited about a possibility of qualification that simply did not exist? Was there something essentially fraudulent about that match, rendered effectively null and void when historically it has remained one of the most colourful matches in the history of Scottish football? The plot thickens when you take into account the reply Ernie Walker sent to my researcher Pat Woods, who sought confirmation of the gist of Ally's assertion shortly after he made it. It is dated 5 August 1994.

Dear Mr Woods,

My recollection is that FIFA did indeed deduct two points from Scotland because of Willie Johnston's indiscretion, but there was never any question of keeping this information from the players. It is a long time ago now, of course, but I clearly remember that we were all hopping around with excitement during the match with Holland when it looked as though, despite everything, we still had a chance of going through. The news about the deduction of points presumably came to us after the match. In any case, to suggest that there was some kind of plot to keep the players in the dark is rubbish.

Like you, I was rather surprised that there was no mention of a deduction of points from Argentina [in the Maradona case], but I must confess that all of my instincts are to try to forget the awful memories of the 1978 World Cup!

Best wishes . . .

The fact of the matter is that FIFA deducted no points. The only penalty Scotland suffered was that Johnston was banned for a year from international football, although in fact he never played for his country again. It remains a mystery why Ally suddenly surfaced again with this fantasy, all those years later. It is even more intriguing that a man wholly on top of his job, as Ernie Walker always was, gave this notion considerable credence in that reply. The deduction of points never happened; there is no record of anything like this in FIFA files. One of the commonest outcomes of mental trauma is amnesia. The wounds of Argentina had obviously produced that other alternative – hallucination.

That was a condition that never applied to two special men who during the period of the Argentine fiasco had made decisions back in Scotland that would transform the domestic game.

CHAPTER NINE

GIANTS

Working in the media during the era of Jock Stein and Willie Waddell was like being caught in a vice of mutual animosity. Two Protestants from Lanarkshire have a better than even chance of binding together even in the worst of times. But Stein had forsaken his childhood fancies, which included an almost idolatrous respect for Waddell, the great player in light blue, and had become the most virulent and successful opponent of Rangers in their entire history. Waddell was steeped to such an extent in Rangers' tradition that at times he sounded more like a southern senator in the States, steadfastly segregationist but knowing at the same time he could not hold those beliefs in a rapidly changing world for too much longer. 'We are not Glasgow Rangers,' he would say. 'We are *the* Rangers. I don't want that word Glasgow in front of us.' I have always believed that Waddell, on the basis of the number of conversations I had with him, felt that what Stein achieved after his dramatic conversion to green and white was nothing short of treachery. This view might have been confirmed by Rangers' earlier efforts to 'tap' Stein and offer him the possibility of the job at Ibrox, not just on the basis of his ability but because he was truly 'one of us', as they would put it. Those secretive initiatives came to nothing, of course.

These two men jousted in a way that made Scottish football seem like a parody of the global Cold War which locked together two other great forces during that period. The tug of both men was so powerful, in different ways, that they had radar capabilities which could identify the source of any private criticisms of their clubs in an almost eerie way. The media scene was populated by more spies and informers than you could have found on either side of Checkpoint Charlie at the time. This was not just football that was being played out; it was a basic power struggle over the territorial imperative. Stein had turned the world upside down with his boldness and shrewdness. Waddell came to Ibrox intent on seizing it back. But now, at the end of May 1978, they were both gone from the dug-out, Stein with bitterness in his heart over the insensitive manner in which the board had handled his recent departure, Waddell with alacrity some six years earlier, in June 1972, for with a hop, skip and a jump he had engineered an elevation to general manager of the club, promoting his coach Jock Wallace as his successor. I suspect that had a general manager been appointed over Stein, he would have ended up doing nothing other than choosing carpets for the executive lounge. Stein was an absolutist who really could not have worked in an environment in which he did not have a say over everything at Celtic Park. Waddell was of the same ilk, in terms of his wish to subjugate and persecute if necessary. But it panned out so dramatically differently for the two great rivals.

News came through to us in Argentina of two managerial changes: on 24 May John Greig took over the reins at Ibrox from Wallace, and four days later Billy McNeill was confirmed as the new Celtic manager. It was difficult to accept that Stein was gone. He had towered over the panorama for so long that, like Etna, he could never be extinct. But even as I heard that news I knew that he would not allow himself to expire slowly and sadly into oblivion, as his great friend Bill Shankly had. Before that month was out I felt that Ally MacLeod was being stalked by an invisible force greater than anything he had had to face during the World Cup, and that Stein was simply biding his time. He certainly had that 44-day sojourn at Leeds before moving to the post he really wanted, Scotland manager, on 4 October 1978. The appointment of Billy McNeill, who would not have returned to Celtic Park to replace Stein had his former manager not taken the trouble to coax him to do so, seemed suggestive of a long-term strategy worked out mutually between himself and Celtic. That, of course, was not so, since McNeill would have remained contentedly in Aberdeen as their manager, and to this day, for a variety of reasons, he regrets the move. But on the surface it seemed as if all the Celtic board were doing was ratifying an apostolic succession. It was treated that way by the media, who felt that McNeill, as a Lisbon Lion and with already impressive managerial credentials at Pittodrie, could hardly have been overlooked for the job. However, the Greig appointment, although it did not cause immediate scepticism, gave rise to a question which seemed fundamental and obvious even then: can you jump directly from the dressing-room into the managerial seat? In more recent times that factor has become an irrelevance as finances above all else initiated the era of the player-manager. Graeme Souness himself was to come to Ibrox in that mould in later years. But the difference was that Waddell was still there. If anybody felt that Greig would be flying solo, they might have us believe that Concorde could have been piloted by the chief steward. Waddell told journalist Ian Peebles at the time, 'People say football management is a young man's game nowadays. They really mean coaching is a young man's game. Management needs worldliness. There's a lot more to a club like Rangers than 90 minutes on a Saturday afternoon.'

You wouldn't need to convince anybody about that in this day and age. It was an initiative that certainly made a lot of sense, but also gave rise to mutterings in the media that all Waddell had been doing in 1972 was stepping out of the line of fire. Stein was getting too hot to handle. That thought arose mainly because an elevation to general manager at that time was unique. Waddell could have offered solid reasons for awarding himself that promotion, given the burden he had carried for so long, which was tragically to take its toll on him in later years. He was so steeped in the ways of the club that at times he carried himself like the curator of a museum, ensuring that nothing could interfere with the artefacts of the past. He was schooled in that by Bill Struth, the great Rangers manager of the 1920s to early 1950s period, who presented a face to the world of stern puritanical authority which brought success even though he never dirtied his feet on a training ground nor spoke a word about tactics in his life. But his rule was absolute. On match days during Struth's reign, Waddell and his colleagues had to sit around in their jock-straps and vests until two minutes before kick-off, when up would come pants and jerseys so immaculately laundered that the shorts would have a crease in them. Cleanliness being next to godliness, the ploy seemed to work most times, even though some of their opponents felt that that adage did not apply to the way Rangers played on the park. This military-like attention to detail made Rangers feel superior, a cut above the rest, which from a distance might seem preposterously self-regarding and almost comical, were it not for the fact that Rangers were the dominant force in the game under Struth. Journalist Hugh Taylor wrote of Rangers that they 'could be the Scots Guards of football in this country'. So what worked well off the park had an effect on it. That was something Waddell never forgot, both to the benefit and, in some ways, to the detriment of the club. But even when he was not on the touchline he was still the backbone of the club. He had proved that beyond question by facing up to recurring adversity.

Although 'Deedle', as he was better known amongst punters up front and the media behind his back, had become a manager with Kilmarnock in 1957, he never lost sight of his beloved Rangers and some time later, as a journalist, poured scorn on some of their efforts to keep pace with Jock Stein. He tasted success, though, in the dug-out. I recall describing the scene as he rushed on to the pitch at the end of the game against Hearts when the Ayrshire side won the league title at Tynecastle on 24 April 1965, to hug his captain Frank Beattie in an explosion of emotion which was quite uncharacteristic. I saw him in the throes of victory on occasions after that day, but all he would display was a puckering of the lips which hovered between a smile and a scowl, and a nodding of the head as if in assent at some declaration. Occasionally there was a brief clenched fist too. He was as far removed from the modern touchline prancers as the minuet is from pole-dancing. In public he was largely an undemonstrative man who could appear terrifyingly dour. You knew trouble was brewing with him when he lowered his specs to a point on his nose where they teetered precariously like a ski-jumper at the top of the slope, dipped his head towards you with his eyebrows converging, and gave you a pre-emptive stare that left you only seconds to decide whether to stay put and brave it out or leave by the nearest window. He could bully, cajole and inspire, and ultimately was the spiritual leader of a club that debatably might have collapsed under the weight of the problems which through various misfortunes were heaped upon them.

Davie White was sacked as Rangers manager on Thursday, 27 November 1969. The following Wednesday Waddell was appointed the new manager, just days after doing the proverbial hatchet article in his newspaper, the *Scottish Daily Express*, headed 'The Boy David Must Go'. It remains one of the seminal headlines of that era. Waddell had just issued his manifesto and would go on to become one of the strongest and most influential managers in the history of the game.

It is true that whatever changes he had in mind he would find it difficult to win society over as a whole to his fresh outlook, considering that Rangers' unwritten but tangible sectarian policy still left him vulnerable to the charge that his club was deeply, morally flawed. It is also true that he tentatively made this a public issue with his supporters when on 12 August 1972, as the new general manager of the club, he walked to the centre circle at Ibrox and made a pre-match announcement that sectarianism would play no part in the future of the club. It did not materially alter the conditions within the club. There was no stampede of Catholics to the marble entrance hall of Ibrox to offer their services, nor was there an exodus of the faithful fearing a contamination. Nothing much happened in fact, and he was open to criticism of window-dressing on this issue, but given that he came from the stern Presbyterian tradition of Struth, and from a world which those people in charge thought would never change, his daring to raise the issue at all was at least an unprecedented venture into uncharted waters for the club. The promise to sign a Catholic if the right one turned up would, however, hang in the air with the tenacity of a soap-bubble.

Before John Greig became manager, Waddell had, of course, worked the principle of a combined managerial force closely with Jock Wallace, who had come to Ibrox in 1969 as coach. When Wallace was appointed manager in 1972 with Waddell as his overlord, it made Ibrox seem innovative, Celtic conventional. But it did nothing to alter the balance of power. To start with, who was really in charge at Ibrox now? There was a feeling that Waddell, the power behind the throne, would influence everything his new manager did. That was uppermost on our minds as Wallace set out on his first full season as a manager in 1972/73.

We knew Wallace, the former miner and jungle fighter from the Malaysian insurrection of the 1950s, to be a tall, strong man who could lift you up with one hand and consequently could only possibly be cowed by an onrushing express train. So it seemed on the surface. Derek Johnstone, that versatile Rangers player, was impressed. 'Every morning he used to go into the gym and do a couple of hundred arm-pulls with the weights. He was fanatical about that. He never ran because he had bad knees. But every day he would start the procedure in the gym by doing it himself and never flinched. He was one of the fittest men I have ever met.' So it seemed Rangers would be picking up the Spartan ethic to combat Stein with a devotion to fitness that preceded anything else on the football field. When Wallace took his players to the sand mountains of Gullane beach to run up and down like inmates of a boot camp, he was trading on that image precisely, not only for pre-season training but also as some kind of reassurance policy for the supporters, who were clearly being informed that Rangers would stop at nothing to get ready for the affray.

But this wasn't a completely true picture of Wallace. It was surprising the number of players I came across who believed that underneath the armour-plating he was, as Derek Johnstone described it to me, 'a big cuddly bear'. Anybody who had any dealings with him outside Ibrox found him gentle, jocular and approachable. Unless he had ordered you to heave on to your back a rucksack full of stones and run up the terracing steps ten times, which from reputation you felt was what he might bark out to any pallid, puny person who crossed his path, you could not fail to warm to the man for being the opposite of what people largely imagined him to be. One evening in his own home I saw him phoning his son in the USA, where he was studying horticulture, with tears in his eyes simply because he hadn't seen the lad for some time. It was unsettling at first to see this side of him. But I was to witness enough of this man privately to be aware that the cruder image of him was a distortion. In that sense I felt that the projection of toughness was an effort to balance the fact that underneath all the chatter about rivalry in the media he suspected he was a match neither for Stein nor for Waddell in the internal battles he ultimately had to fight at Ibrox.

Before he took the step of elevating Wallace to the managerial post, Waddell had first to prove that the pair could bring success. As a journalist, not long before accepting the Rangers managerial position, Waddell had gone to Tynecastle to profile the man who was then a coach with Hearts but who had made himself famous as the man who had inspired Berwick Rangers to defeat Glasgow Rangers in a famous Scottish Cup tie in January 1967. He was impressed by Wallace, filed the name away in his mind, and when he was appointed Rangers manager on 3 December 1969 he brought him to Ibrox as coach. At first the reaction was positive and Rangers went 11 matches without defeat. At that time I interviewed Stein, who seemed more than piqued that so much attention was now being paid to the Ibrox renaissance. 'Have you forgotten about us then?' he said with that effective dry sarcasm of his. 'Are you sure you can spare us the time?' But the Rangers momentum petered out, and I suspect Stein thought it would too: in their last ten matches Rangers won only two and finished the league 12 points behind Celtic. The following season their league form was disastrous. They suffered a total of nine defeats and managed only 16 wins, which was their lowest total since league reconstruction in 1955/56, as was their goal tally of only 58 goals. There seemed to be a growing feeling that Rangers were actually being guided by yesterday's men, that the terracing icon of the 1940s and 1950s could not necessarily transpose the Struth ascendancy into a modern era. Waddell was past it, it seemed.

However, a form of redemption was on hand, and it came on a wet Saturday afternoon, 24 October 1970, in front of 106,263 spectators. The previous Saturday Rangers had been humiliated at Ibrox by Aberdeen and had lost 2–0. Now they had to face Celtic again in the Scottish League Cup final, which was beginning to seem to Rangers players like being sent to the master's study for an inevitable caning. The day before the final a 16-year-old, minding his own business as it were, saw his name on the Rangers squad sheet in the dressing room. Derek Johnstone did not think much about it until later that morning when Waddell took him into the boot room. 'He told me he was giving me complimentary tickets for the game and that I was to make sure that all my family came to the match. I wondered what this was all about, and then he said it: "You're playing tomorrow." I didn't sleep that night, but I dreamed I would score the winner. I suppose any young lad told he was playing in the final at my age would have dreamed the same. All those hours before kick-off passed in a haze.'

No haze existed for the lad when five minutes from the end of the first half he rose just inside the penalty area above the Celtic captain Billy McNeill and with a distinct nod of the head – which one of his team-mates called the 'good morning nod', like the one you might give the neighbour – scored the only goal of the game from a cross by Willie Johnston. 'To be honest,' said Johnstone, 'that victory did not register with me until days after. Deedle actually was full of smiles, and although many people didn't like him, because of his manner, he was like a father to me. He regarded me from that moment on as somebody that had done him a real favour.

For instance, a couple of days later I went to Iceland to play in a Scotland U-19 game when I met Graeme Souness for the first time. I showed him the medal I had won because the goal scored by the youngest ever player in a final had become so well publicised. Unfortunately I left that precious medal behind in the hotel room in Reykjavik, and when I got back to Ibrox I was terrified of having to tell the boss that I had lost something as significant as that, because I felt he might have thought I was just not serious enough about what had happened. I prepared myself for a bawling out. But all he did was get the name of the hotel, lift the phone, and it was sent back from Iceland the following day. He was fatherly like that.'

That victory resonated throughout the rest of the season in the Ibrox community and acted as a kind of vaccination against the feeling of capitulation to Stein's continuing mastery in the league, but its effects had worn off by the end of season 1971/72, despite the European triumph in Barcelona in May. It was time for another shot in the arm. It was at the end of Wallace's first season in charge that they achieved one of the notable victories in the club's history – notable not only because it was in the club's centenary year, and not only because it was the cup final of the SFA's 100th year, but because had they not won the match Wallace's first season as a manager would have ended in humiliation. This was the game after which I witnessed for the first time the fractious nature of his relationship with Waddell, which was brutally exposed as that of master and slave. It was the Scottish Cup final of 1973 against Celtic. It was also called the 'royal' final because Princess Alexandra was invited to lend credence to the existence of a royal box at Hampden. Unwittingly she would turn out to be partly responsible for what might be called a one-sided rupturing of the delicate Waddell–Wallace relationship.

Rangers had made a bad start to the season and had lost three of their first five matches. But after making new signings like Tom Forsyth from Motherwell, Quinton Young from Ayr and Joe Mason from Morton, from early December 1972 the club went on a self-perpetuating run of 25 league and cup matches unbeaten which certainly caused Stein some apprehension for the first time in years. But it wasn't to be enough. On 28 April 1973, the last day of the league season, Celtic got the points they wanted from their match with Hibernian in Edinburgh when Dixie Deans scored after only two minutes to relieve the tension and pave the way for a 3–0 victory. That same day Rangers were comfortable winners against East Fife, 2–0. But Celtic had taken the league for the eighth consecutive time, this time by a single point. And since Rangers had been scalped 1–0 by Hibernian in the semi-final of the Scottish League Cup earlier in the season, a game they had had to play without the injured John Greig, it looked as if Rangers were simply acting out that now well-rehearsed part of understudy to the main lead.

If there were any fears about the gradual erosion of faith in winning the league amongst the Ibrox support, after eight 'yomping' years trailing after Celtic and waiting for the divine intervention they felt was due to them, they would be dispelled by an examination of the attendances at Ibrox for the latter part of the league season. Only on two occasions did crowds rise over 20,000 before the Celtic visit on 6 January 1973. It was not until the run-in with six games to go, when they were very much in contention for the title, that they mustered crowds more representative of their potential, when Hibernian visited and drew 51,000. It was Stein who said off-camera to me at Seamill in preparation for the Scottish Cup final, 'The Rangers crowd turn up when it matters.' He was referring to the ticket sales for the game which showed that the slightly greater preponderance was for the Rangers support. It was another version of what he would later say to me about that club's massive following: 'With the poor results they get, it's got to be about more than football for them.' Well, he knew what it meant, since he had been steeped in it as a boy. It was also an acknowledgement from a man whose senses were as fine-tuned as any before a vital match that something special was brewing.

On 5 May 1973 Hampden Park was continually sluiced down by blustery rain. It drove straight into our commentary position, which at Hampden at that time was low down in the south enclosure, our eye level not far above the players' boots, from which vantage point you could barely discern any sense of pattern about the play. It was from this very worm's-eye view that the BBC had in 1965 one of its nights of calamitous failure with coverage of a game Monty Python at their most inventive could not have bettered. All it lacked was the dead parrot. In a League Cup semi-final that ended 6–4 for Rangers against Kilmarnock, there were so many camera-jams, so many canisters of film being dropped in the dingy surrounds as they tried to change the reels, so many fumblings and so many sorting things out in the gloom that we managed to film only two goals. According to our version, courageously transmitted later that night, the game had been drawn 1–1. In between those two goals, from what we salvaged, only an X-ray machine could have identified either players or ball. In later years I bumped into the young trainee assistant cameraman working alongside me that shambolic night, when he popped up in the aisle of the transatlantic aircraft we were on. He was making his way to Hollywood to direct a film with Robin Williams, and his name was Bill Forsyth, who had become famous for *Gregory's Girl*. After thanking him for his hospitality,

I added, recalling that night at Hampden when we invented 'Spot the Ball', 'At least we saw the ball in *Gregory's Girl*!'

So we were far from comfortable. The position was too low and the rain was attacking the camera lenses. Beside me in the commentary position was Billy Connolly, ardent Celtic follower, who was just beginning his rise to stardom and was loved by the *Grandstand* audiences when we used him to comment about Scottish football for the UK in his inimitable style. His Glaswegian patter illumined pre-match chat on a grey day on which you felt that for Princess Alexandra to understand what was going on the palace would have had to send her to a series of tutorials on Irish history and the Troubles. The banners flew and the songs of mutual recrimination were hurled rather than sung from end to end. Even after only about five minutes the princess might have decided that the concept of a 'united' kingdom was a dodgy one.

As expected from the favourites Celtic, they flowed into action with the verve that can only come from a side sporting players like Dalglish, Johnstone and Connelly. It was Celtic's leading goalscorer, Dalglish, recording his 21st goal of the season, who put Celtic in front with a typical flourish. With 24 minutes gone at that stage the game seemed to be fitting the accustomed pattern – Rangers fussing and working hard, Celtic scoring. However, the inevitability of more to follow from Celtic was disturbed eleven minutes before half-time when MacDonald drew George Connelly wide on the left before bursting past him and sending a neat chip towards Derek Parlane, who scored with his head. It was about then that we noticed the change on the field. Rangers were not being outplayed. In fact they were the dominant ones. I remember at half-time Connolly telling us he didn't need a sandwich as he had just eaten all his fingernails. He bit more furiously only 20 seconds into the second half when Rangers scored in a manner that caused just a fractional second of incredulity before the crowd became aware that the ball was in the back of the net, so quickly had the goal come after kick-off. Young stabbed a ball in the direction of Parlane, who then swept it forward to Alfie Conn. The man who was to sign for Celtic in future years beat goalkeeper Ally Hunter in the race for the ball and poked it into the net. Stunning. Goals like that shouldn't happen so quickly.

Rangers, now in the lead, were brought back to earth by a Celtic equaliser in the 54th minute when John Greig handled a shot heading for the net and Connelly coolly slotted home from the spot. Six minutes later it was all over with a goal that even now prompts you to imagine it as the comical sort a minister is allowed to score at a Sunday School picnic five-a-side. The scorer, though, was no man of the cloth. He was the uncompromising Tom Forsyth, some of whose tackles ended up high on the Richter scale. He had come up for a Tommy McLean free-kick and watched almost as a spectator, it seemed to me, as Derek Johnstone headed against the post and the ball trundled slowly along the line to where, quite uncovered, Forsyth stood, almost transfixed, as if it were a landmine sliding his way. I recall vividly his first attempt from no more than half an inch from the goal-line to make contact with the ball, his body leaning back at entirely the wrong angle, his leg stretched out too far and the ball getting trapped between a leg not in control of itself and mother earth. He seemed then to let his foot roll past the ball as if he had lost coordination. And then somehow his studs made proper contact and he squeezed it over the line slowly, giving the ball an almost disbelieving look to verify that it had indeed crossed the line (which it had by about ten inches) before running off to be congratulated for this extraordinary display of originality. It seemed as if he had taken a quarter of an hour to get the ball over the line, and Stein in the dug-out must have felt anguish at the dereliction of his defence. Thereafter Rangers never looked like conceding another.

Stein offered Jock Wallace a handsome tribute at the end by going straight to him with congratulations. Like all the great managers I have known, Stein was a 'crabbit' loser, but he genuinely liked Wallace as a man, although he had little time for Waddell, and in a way he must have known what that victory meant to somebody who was under the cosh at Ibrox. If anybody had any doubts about the extra pressure on Wallace they should have witnessed the scene about half an hour after the final whistle when we invited the winning manager to our position to be interviewed live for *Grandstand*. We placed him in a position facing the pitch and track, and me with my back to it. He was never the most loquacious of men and his sentences about football were peppered with the word 'character'. That was used to sum up his philosophy on footballing attitudes, but it did become rather repetitive. But that day he was inevitably cheery, and he joked about Celtic with Billy Connolly, who took it in good part although obviously hiding the pain deep in his heart.

But as the interview progressed I noticed a change coming over Wallace. He seemed not to be paying attention any longer to the questions, but was staring past me out on to the pitch. From the look on his face I could see he was perturbed, and he did mumble eventually that he had to stop and go. So we wrapped up the interview. Intrigued, I turned round to see what had caught his attention. And there was Waddell, out on the track just in front of the tunnel, incandescent with rage. You could lip-read the obscenities coming from him. He was pointing, in quick motions, firstly to Wallace then to the ground just in front of his own feet, like a dog-owner telling the pet to come to heel. Apparently he had been doing that throughout the interview. Wallace humbly walked towards him, and another tirade was directed at him before they both disappeared up the tunnel. They had just won their first domestic trophy in nearly three years after wandering in the wilderness, yet the general manager was behaving as if Wallace was no more than the hamper-boy. It was done so publicly that I have always felt Waddell was making a gesture to all the media that when all was said and done, he was still the boss. Princess Alexandra had asked to speak to the winning manager, so Waddell then came out to escort his manager into the royal presence.

The subservient or dignified way, depending on your interpretation, in which Wallace accepted such treatment received an almost poignant underscoring two days later, when in an interview with the *Glasgow Herald* of 7 May, speaking of his days in his home village of Wallyford in the east of Scotland, Wallace recalled, 'When I was eight or nine I would hang about at Wallyford waiting for the Rangers bus, going up to people and saying, "Mister, will you give us a lift?" Sometimes they took me, sometimes they didn't. I had this friend, and together we had a ball. He stood on the wing crossing them. He was Waddell. I stood and headed them in. I was Waddell.' His boyhood hero had now become his nemesis. Perhaps his tolerance sprang from that ancient admiration. On one occasion, sitting in the marble hall at Ibrox waiting to interview a player, I heard the clatter of voices, like cymbals being struck, coming from the top of the stairs. It was Waddell and Wallace screaming at each other on the landing above. It was a verbal clash that seemed to include every Anglo-Saxon obscenity in the vocabulary. It went on spectacularly for about ten minutes before I heard a door being slammed. Of course harsh words are often exchanged inside clubs as part of the emotional framework of football, so that single incident, while stormy, could be passed over easily enough. But it was not isolated. Every Friday players who passed Waddell's office at the head of the marble staircase could hear the glass panel on the door shaking with the vibrations of screaming coming from within, as the two men clashed over team matters. While I pay due credit to Waddell as the only leader who could have guided Rangers through their horrendous crises, I pay much less to him for generally spurning the milk of human kindness.

But over the next few years Wallace, with Waddell behind him as vice-chairman of the club, began to gain the success the supporters badly desired. The sensitivities of each individual within an organisation are of little consequence when you are running up success. By 6 May 1978, when Rangers won the Scottish Cup 2–1 against Aberdeen, Wallace had become the first Rangers manager to win two trebles. Their other clean sweep had come two years earlier, the season after they broke the Stein stranglehold on the league by winning the title for the first time in ten years.

Despite that unprecedented triumph, Wallace left Ibrox a couple of weeks later with the praises of the legions of supporters still ringing in his ears. It came as a shock to some, but not to his family, who despite his toughness had known he had had to endure endless tirades at the hands of Waddell. He gave another explanation which might have been a factor in tipping him over the edge, as Derek Johnstone recounted. 'I went to see him for I heard he was leaving. I was surprised with all these trophies we now had. And remember, he was Rangers daft. He loved the club. It was his boyhood dream to go there and he had a terrific bond with the supporters. So I was shocked when I heard it. But when I saw him that Thursday he just said to me, "Deedle won't pay me any more money. He just refuses an increase, and I know many managers in the game down south are getting much more than me, so I'm getting out and that's where I'm heading." It was then I put my foot right in my mouth when I said to him, "For God's sake don't take the Leicester job. It's been knocked back by at least five English managers." You can imagine how I felt when I heard on the following Monday he was the new Leicester manager!'

So the era was ending with the demise of a decent man who would return for a briefer and less successful spell to Ibrox, and the handing over of power to a new Old Firm generation. The managerial faces in the summer of 1978 might have been new, but they still wore the warriors' masks of an ancient tribal feud.

CHAPTER TEN

THE TRIBES GO TO WAR

Standing at the tunnel-mouth in front of the main enclosure, Chief Superintendent Hamish MacBean, Commander 'F' Division of the City of Glasgow Police and regular match commander at Hampden Park, was beginning to relax after the normal tensions surrounding a cup final involving the Old Firm. It was 10 May 1980. The sun was out. The world seemed a great place for one section of the crowd, but a hellish aggravation for the other. The match he was responsible for supervising had just reached its conclusion after extra-time. Not in a superbly dramatic style, for the football that day was fraught with nerves, and most of the players had been affected by the extremes of tension which come from the torrents of abuse hurled from one end of the terracings to the other. The game had suffered consequently from the fear of losing. Fanatical support can sometimes depress as well as inspire. Make a mistake and you let an entire community down, a community that regards its superiority as being confirmed by triumph. In the 107th minute a stabbed shot by the Celtic captain Danny McGrain was deflected by a leg stuck out more in hope than anything else; the sudden deflection sent the tall, lanky Rangers goalkeeper Peter McCloy in the wrong direction, and the cup was won. The leg in question belonged to George McCluskey of Celtic. They thought it was all over. It wasn't.

As McGrain ran with his team towards the Celtic end of Hampden Park to show off the trophy after the presentation, something instinctively made Chief Superintendent MacBean turn away from the scene of jubilation to look at the area just below the royal box in the main stand. What he saw sent a chill through even his experienced veins. For there, in the most expensive seats, reserved for the more affluent of the Old Firm support, punches were being thrown and necks being wrung. Men in '£500 crombie-coats were battering hell out of each other', as MacBean described the scene. Bodies were clashing and faces were being pummelled as vitriolic anger tipped over into outright violence. He was at first taken aback, and then, when Inspector Willie McMaster beside him also expressed astonishment at this spectacle, MacBean, turning back to the pitch, stiffened at the sight of what he now saw. All he could say to his companion was, 'Never mind what's happening in the stand. Look what's going on out there!'

Although we did not realise it at the time, that one innocent celebratory gesture by the Celtic players was to catapult Scottish football into a new dimension. We watched as rejoicing youths in green and white suddenly leapt on to the pitch and made for the players to join them in choruses of triumph. It all seemed so simple then. But there is nothing simple or innocent in enjoying the fruits of labour in an Old Firm match. There was an unexpected response. Suddenly, Saturday came alive. The final had not driven one comatose, because they never do; there is always something on final day that causes part of you to twitch now and again. But neither had it prompted power surges through the body. It had been ordinary. Yet here, now, were the surges that did excite interest. They came from both ends. The sight has never been expunged from the memory of the now retired MacBean. 'It was kids who came on at first from the Celtic end, over the safety fence. Now, when you get one side winning in an Old Firm final, the supporters of the losing side normally head for the exits as quickly as they can, leaving the stadium to the victors. But I will never forget what I saw at the other end. The Rangers supporters had been heading out and most of them were halfway up the terracing. But I always remember the sudden change of direction. For when they saw what was happening at the other end, with bodies coming over the fence, they suddenly stopped, turned en masse, headed downwards again and swept on to the pitch. They were then joined by reinforcements from other Celtic supporters, and in no time the field was covered.'

The Celtic and Rangers players had sensed the danger and had raced for the shelter of the stand before the main throngs descended on the halfway line. The Celtic supporters, minus their players on the pitch, were beginning to taunt the other end. Sitting high above the pitch in the commentary gantry, having gone through the normal ritual of hosannas about the winners, I confess I found this initially fascinating and, to be honest, exciting. I perked up. The waves of rushing bodies swept towards each other. Initially, from that height, it was like watching armies of conflicting ants about to scrap for a morsel of food left on the halfway line. For whatever then ensued, I can vouch for the fact that there was no unarmed combat. The lines never actually crossed. Whatever else was to happen, they remained apart. The inflated descriptions of the battle from some quarters suggested bodies clashing, thrashing limbs and messy scrapping. It was not like that. The only bodies clashing were in the front stand where the laundry bills for blood-stained Armanis would have been considerable.

From my vantage point there seemed to be a few seconds of phoney war when nothing seemed to be happening, a sort of hands-off situation, until somebody lobbed a bottle towards the enemy. After that, the deluge. I know not from which side it originally came. Nor does MacBean. That did not seem to matter. The heavens rained down bottles. Then something occurred to me, and it was at that moment that I uttered a fairly obvious comment to the live television audience, whom I imagined were calling for non-football lovers to rush to the set and witness this astonishing spectacle, which looked as if it might turn out to be more compelling than the beach battle in the film *El Cid*. I asked rhetorically, 'Where are the police?' Joe Black, who was then the spokesman for the Police Federation, remembers that remark in the commentary distinctly, for he knew that something had gone seriously wrong. 'Normally the tactic was to flood the track with police just before the final whistle,' he said. 'A decision was made to alter that for some reason. And you see what resulted.'

MacBean offered a valid explanation for what the police had concerns about. 'The big flashpoints for us were always outside the stadium. The worst was the area just behind the old North Stand where the supporters could clash as they left the ground. Now, because the match was on a knife-edge throughout and there was no clear-cut decision and it went into extra-time, it meant that hardly anybody left the stadium until close to the final whistle. Now, if you have a clear-cut winner then many of the defeated side leave and there is less potential for clashing outside the ground. But in this case we knew that the exodus of the Rangers support, which started with about ten minutes to go, might cause some problems of mixing in the street to the north of the ground, so we had deployed our forces outside. It's always a knife's edge at the game. You hold back your resources for as long as you can inside the ground and then, because of what could happen outside, you have to release as many as is necessary to go to the well-known potential flashpoints. There is no way we could relinquish our responsibility for that. So when the first rush came over the fence I realised our mounted resources were on the other side of the North Stand outside the ground, and that we had a problem.'

His explanation certainly suggests that there was no last-minute change of tactic, but that their deployment strategy had been well worked out in advance. Indeed I can attest to the fact that the worst trouble I ever saw after any Old Firm match, in and around any of the Glasgow stadiums, was in that notorious zone just behind the North Stand which both sets of supporters would use as a route over the hill towards the city centre. Cup final Saturdays were a living hell for the residents in that area, so it seemed at least common sense to have that heavily policed. But the bottles were inside the ground. 'They were coming down like rain,' MacBean admitted. 'I went out there and you had to have one eye on the sky at the same time as trying to organise the resources. As you rightly identified, there was no actual fighting. They never crossed into each other's territory. The only danger was that somebody might produce a knife, step forward, a quick flash and somebody is stabbed to death, and things then really would get worse. The only actual fighting was when one or two of my officers foolishly tried to make arrests and ended up struggling with people but could achieve absolutely nothing doing that. Indeed that was one of the changes I instigated afterwards, that you never try to make an arrest in those situations. You firstly try to get control of the crowd, and be on top of it before you arrest. But remember, my officers were in a really difficult situation with bottles indiscriminately being thrown.'

Then, just when it seemed like they might turn and wreck Hampden Park itself, the scene changed. From off-stage, suddenly appearing in a blur of whiteness like angels of mercy, the horses appeared. The mounted police emerging from one end of the stadium charged and drew their long riot batons for the first time in Glasgow since the 1926 General Strike. My own impression was that they did not lash out indiscriminately, but that their very presence and the intimidating way in which they launched themselves forward were enough to scare the wits out of people who in sectarian mode are very hard to scare indeed.

Meanwhile, I recall that my voice had lapsed into a kind of Martin-Bell-war-correspondent tone, and I delivered a brief homily on the iniquities of sectarianism. It was to the effect that here were two tribes who simply hated each other, and that they had clearly seen this as an opportunity to have it out once and for all. I remember a colleague saying to me on the platform, 'Let them batter themselves to bits. It will do us all good.' Undoubtedly, in the arcane world of that special animosity many of them would attempt that and then, on the Monday morning, share a workbench or an adjoining desk with somebody they had been lobbing a bottle at that afternoon. Riots there were a-plenty in other parts of the footballing world, but this was different. Jock Stein always insisted that this fixture was a safety valve, that it channelled the putrescent bitterness for a limited period into 90 minutes, which then defused lingering feelings. He was in a unique position to lend his analysis to the phenomenon, having crossed the barriers imposed by tradition. Stein was also a pragmatist who disliked what he heard and saw in the main but felt it was unavoidable, and therefore in that sense the fixture's usefulness was in discharging the potential for more violence across the sectarian divide outside football. He believed that without this fixture, in the West of Scotland in particular, people would look for ways to become more like Northern Ireland, and that methods of expressing hatred would become more sinister and dangerous.

It was only one view among many. Historians and sociologists have long studied the causes and suggested possible remedies for it all. In 2004, the Scottish Executive established the policy of making religious hatred an offence against the law, which although commendable in many ways raised the obvious problems of application and seemed to many to be ducking several issues. For Scotland was divided by sectarian mind-set, not just by the choice of song you bawled at anybody else as a provocation. The crowd that assembled that day at Hampden brought with them perverted beliefs in their own identities. Although the vast majority came from in and around Glasgow, they had travelled from all parts of the country. Buses of supporters, for example, came from a small community in the village of Glenboig in North Lanarkshire, a county ridden with sectarian sensitivities. I knew this village well at that time. It had two schools for the different faiths and the focal point for social life was the large pub in the main street. That establishment had two doors – one for Catholics, the other for Protestants. You dared not go in the wrong door. It is not that a beating awaited you if you did. Stigma would apply though, and stigma in that setting was difficult to live with. You went to your own side of the bar as well. But there was never any trouble. The banter was crisp and genial across it, even among the Old Firm supporters in for a pint that very day before setting off for that 1980 final. So people used to boast to me about how peaceful, benign and worthy of praise this arrangement was. But this always seemed to me to be even more sinister than the screaming of abuse at each other. For it suffered from that most robust of all factors in sectarianism, acquiescence. It was tradition. The two-door policy is a mental state that carries right through our society.

It is encouraging to note that at least in some areas people are not only questioning this but taking steps to lessen the divide. In practical economic terms, North Lanarkshire Council over the period 2002–04 decided to build seven common-campus schools serving the two traditions, which would have been a significant step towards possible integration. They had a model to work on. A common-campus school had been set up in the new town of Cumbernauld which served both Catholic and non-Catholic pupils. It was a decision that struck a note of harmony in the community among parents and teachers of both persuasions. They were certainly divided in terms of classwork, but they shared playgrounds, dining-rooms and a common reception area for visitors. They had a teachers' staff-room which had a sliding partition door to be closed if necessary to divide the two groups of teachers. They even provided separate cookers and microwaves for both sets. But in the couple of years of its existence that partition had never been closed, nor had there been any need to utilise the separate cooking facilities. There were utensils there quite untouched in that time. And to crown this achievement they had one football team to serve both parts of the school. Catholics and Protestants sharing football jerseys, ostensibly from the same school, was unprecedented in that area and a triumph of common sense.

But, sadly, this did not apply in other areas of North Lanarkshire. The Church authorities of the diocese of Motherwell mounted a vigorous opposition to any such integration and insisted on quite separate staff-rooms and different reception areas, and even went so far as to ask for separate gates for entry to the schools for the different faiths, which was rejected by the council as going a step too far. The rigid division of staff-rooms for the respective teachers, who were not consulted, added £650,000 to an already overstretched budget. If anybody has any doubts about the intensity of the opposition to the Cumbernauld model in this sectarian-ridden area, they can be dispelled by the experience of Councillor Tom Curley, a former Celtic player and a Catholic in support of these steps towards integration, who came out of a meeting one evening and discovered that someone had thrown acid over his car. Whether with a piece of chalk in your hand or a glass of lager, Scotland's two-door tradition seems unassailable. The chief photographer of the *Daily Record*, Eric Craig, needed a brain operation after being struck by a bottle that day at Hampden. But radical surgery still awaits the system of educational separation which, whatever else it does, identifies and validates tribal dissension.

So this 'riot' had deep roots. Billy McNeill and John Greig, the respective managers that day, had grown up with them in their separate ways. They knew all about it. Like most of us they accepted it and got on with their jobs. The news of their takeovers was greeted by those of us in South America as if a political upheaval had taken place in our absence. Greig, apprehensive though he might have been about moving directly from dressing room to manager's office, truly wanted the post. McNeill was deeply reluctant about taking on his. When he brought Aberdeen down to play Rangers in the Scottish Cup final of 6 May 1978, only a few weeks away from leaving the Dons, he stood with me, just outside the tunnel, surveying the crowds beginning to assemble on the terracings. 'Look at that,' he said, sweeping his hand in the direction of the Ibrox masses on the west terracing of Hampden. 'That's their big advantage. When you've got that sort of crowd your players get a right lift. I hadn't realised what it was like to have that Old Firm support until now. Now I can see it from a different angle. We can't compete with that kind of backing. When players come out and see that, it puts them in the right mood. In my dressing-room I've got Bobby Clark, one of my most experienced players, and yet I can tell he's a bundle of nerves. Can you believe that? It's not helping anybody, that. He shouldn't be, but he is. I've got to do in there what Jock Wallace doesn't need to do, and that's to try to lift them.' That could have been interpreted before an important final as defeatist talk (Aberdeen lost 2–1), but he and his family loved Aberdeen and were glad to put much of the sectarianism of the West of Scotland behind them. Only one man could have persuaded him to return, and that was Jock Stein.

At Ibrox, meanwhile, the old order persisted. Greig was hampered by the religious embargo, made even more problematical by McNeill plundering the Protestant market. Only a couple of months after taking on his job, on 18 September, McNeill signed winger Davie Provan from

Kilmarnock for a then Scottish record fee of £120,000. At the beginning of November he went to Dumbarton and brought back midfielder Murdo MacLeod for £100,000. These were two lads who could and would have gone to Rangers had that club taken up their interest in them more quickly. They were both from families orientated to Ibrox. Neither of them blinked before signing on, as Provan, now a distinguished commentator with Sky, put it bluntly to me. 'Not a problem. As soon as I signed that form for Celtic the switch went off. Any affection for Rangers went out the window. If you asked Kenny Dalglish, Danny McGrain or Murdo MacLeod, who all came from the same background as me, they would say the same. What Rangers did was their own business, but we had grown up probably desensitised to their religious stance, and I suppose everybody accepted it as a natural part of our game. Even as Celtic players Rangers were simply the team that could prevent you getting your win bonus or winning a championship. That was all. They were simply the enemy. And, of course, they were certainly disadvantaged by their position, and I agree with the Stein view in his time that Rangers changing that policy would have been the last thing Celtic wanted. But it was never at the front of our minds.'

To lend some further insight into the web in which Rangers had become entangled, it is only necessary to speak to certain players who came into contact with their vetting system. One such was Frank McGarvey, a forward whose career extended to English football as well and who signed for Celtic from Liverpool on 11 March 1980 for a then club record fee of £250,000. 'Jock Wallace tried to get me for Rangers first,' he recalled. 'I got a message saying he was really interested in signing me. I was playing junior football at Kilsyth Rangers at the time. Now, somebody at Ibrox thought I was a Protestant and it looked like they were going ahead. But then they discovered I wasn't, and although I was told, though I can't prove it, that the idea of my signing still went to board level, when they heard about my background that put an end to it. That's why I went to St Mirren. For when the guy I talked to heard what school I went to and that made it impossible for Rangers, they got on the phone to Sir Alex Ferguson who was manager at Love Street at the time, and told him I was a good young player and that he could have me now, because they couldn't. I know that sounds a bit unreal now, but that's what went on in those days.'

That phrase 'in those days' should remind us that he was referring not to the age of Copernicus but to a mere three decades ago. But they were learning. I recall Greig talking to me about the restrictions he had to work within, not in terms of an outright rejection of what his club's footballing policy was, but more as a sort of grumble that you might hear from a man who doesn't have enough money to work with. He knew, I knew, everybody knew that since the talent in Scotland was not as prolific as it once had been – in fact it was beginning to shrink – his choice of players from within the tradition was becoming more restricted. In that sense Greig could be seen as the manager who represented that transitional phase in Rangers history which brought them closer to the inevitable catharsis of revolutionary change.

He was initially successful as a manager, and that insulated him for a while against the mounting effects of the social realities closing in on the club. But I believe his career entered its terminal stage on 21 May 1979. It was an evening after which, in my view, he was never the same man. Ironically, this fateful encounter should have taken place in January, but was postponed because of one of the severest winters in years. Celtic were unable to play a league match between 23 December 1978 and March 1979. So this fixture was squeezed in at the end of the log-jam of fixtures. It was Celtic's last game of the season, while Rangers would have two more to play. If Celtic won, the title would be theirs. A Rangers victory would have acted as the springboard for them to go on and win the title with their two games in hand. It was essentially the league decider. Greig was also tantalisingly on the verge of a treble: the Scottish League Cup was already his, and a second replay with Hibernian in the Scottish Cup final beckoned, with Rangers still favourites to win that.

Davie Provan admitted that the outcome of that Monday-evening match arose from that most powerful of all motivations in sport, the refusal to accept defeat. 'I have been in much better Celtic teams than the one that played that night,' he said. 'But if you recall that season there were other times when we were down to ten men and we just wouldn't lie down and accept that. I know it sounds like a cliché, but the truth is we just had wonderful team spirit. You can judge that when you know that you enjoyed coming to work every morning. Billy [McNeill] was the mainspring for that. He had the dressing-room in the palm of his hand and we would have gone through brick walls for him.'

The brick wall that night was created by the sending-off of John Doyle ten minutes after half-time when Celtic were already one down to

Rangers. Doyle and Alex MacDonald had engaged in a running personal battle up till then. As MacDonald, who had scored the opening goal after only nine minutes, jokingly told me about that incident, 'The pair of us spent most of the time trying to kick lumps out of each other.' Doyle decided to take some retribution and he lashed out at the Rangers player as he lay on the turf after a tackle by Conroy. Such a rash act might seem inexplicable even now, unless you are prepared to accept that in this particular fixture the tribalism developed on the Glasgow streets from boyhood translated with ease to the minds of some of the men who played in these fixtures. The body language of both Doyle and MacDonald was about street values, about how they were brought up. It was fuelled by hatred for what each thought the other stood for. This Proddy-Tim primitive side of the game, served up as a personal duel, was the honest representation of what either end of the sectarian spectrum thought of each other, and both players were judged to be doing what comes naturally. They were warrior heroes. Even without Doyle Celtic fought back. They won 4–2 and lifted the title against the odds.

Davie Provan identified one of the principal factors of that night. 'Rangers still had the core of the side which was so successful under Jock Wallace, but they were an ageing team. They had done everything. They had won their medals. They were faced by a young Celtic side who had little to show for their efforts at that time. So they were desperate for medals, against a Rangers team which I think was just beginning to go on the slide.' At the time that did not occur to MacDonald, but it did eventually. 'When I think of it, we were all getting to the stage where we were sitting around in the dressing-room after the replay against Hibs in the Scottish Cup final wondering who was going to be the first to leave the club. We had been around for a while and we knew changes were on the way. So that was unsettling. I think Greigy actually got rid of me too early to Hearts because I played for another seven years. But it was difficult for us and the manager, knowing we were on the verge of transition.'

McNeill, too, was having his problems, centred around his continual disputes with club chairman Desmond White, a situation that would culminate in his first departure in June 1983. In one instance, after a game in the Bernabeu in March 1980 when Celtic were knocked out of the European Cup, beaten 3–0 by Real Madrid after having won 2–0 at home in the first leg, the Celtic players over-indulged in the bar of the hotel, and when I returned there after the commentary there was glass strewn everywhere. Three days later McNeill phoned me to see if I could verify the fact that John Doyle had been at the centre of this disturbance. I had no knowledge of this, but it was clear McNeill was targeting this player. It turned out that Doyle was a favourite of the chairman who believed he personified the spirit ideally desired around the club. On the other hand, it was reported that McNeill had said that if Celtic had not won that famous game against Rangers and had blown their chance of the title because Doyle had been sent off, Doyle would never have played for Celtic again. So there was a tension there between the manager and chairman, which eventually became unbearable.

On that cup final day in May 1980, though, the future for both young managers looked reasonably promising, whatever the result. Hemmed in their respective dressing rooms, in directly contrasting moods, they knew the football itself would be overshadowed by other events even though they were oblivious to much of what was occurring outside. The rioters eventually retreated in a mass scurry to the terracings like frightened mice when the police horses began to make their presence felt. The pitch was left to the police and the stewards, but now it resembled the biggest litter-bin in Scotland. Out of a crowd of 70,000 that day, the casualty list was 100, including four policemen. Fifty fans were taken to hospital, and there were 210 arrests, 160 of them inside the ground.

Immediately after the game MacBean and his officers sat down to prepare a report which they knew would have to be presented before the following Monday when questions were being prepared to be answered in Parliament. The *Glasgow Herald* of 12 May reported, 'For two hours yesterday the Chief Constable and his top aides met to discuss the riot. Later it was stated that the possibility of a ban on all future Old Firm games had been discussed, but that would be up to the regional council.' There was as much chance of Glasgow City Council, packed as it was with Old Firm followers, proposing an abolition of the fixture as of them rendering all Glasgow pubs non-alcoholic. MacBean certainly made it clear to me that his hands had been tied. 'What was not reported so widely is that I was affected by another very important factor,' he said. 'In 1979 the police had been awarded large wage increases. The cost of policing of all football grounds soared. Clubs were facing larger bills and wanted us to cut back on the numbers we sent to grounds. The police authorities themselves began to think that perhaps they did not need to resource football with such numbers. They were thinking that because there had been no trouble within football grounds for a long while before this. And that was simply because football was hugely and effectively policed. Now there were to be cut-backs. That day at Hampden Park I did not have the resources I would have ideally liked.'

But there were others who strongly dispute the police analysis of the day, amongst whom was the most vociferous, the secretary of the SFA Ernie Walker. 'Despite what Patrick Hamill, the chief superintendent, said in defence of the Strathclyde force, a major blunder had been committed. So what was the upshot? At the next game at Hampden, which was a British Championship match against Wales on 21 May, they poured police into the stadium. There was only a crowd of about 30,000 at that match, but even had there been a much bigger crowd, who in their right senses would ever have believed there would be any trouble at a game against the Welsh? It was almost embarrassing to see the heavy police presence there, standing in their hundreds staring into a crowd that was only a third of what the place could hold. After the blunder of the previous game, this was overkill.'

The Executive and General Purposes Committee of the Scottish Football Association produced a report on 26 June. After making it clear that they felt the police tactic of leaving only a token force inside the stadium was a blunder, they went on to fine both clubs £20,000 each, to be paid by 15 July, and asked for a meeting of both chairmen at a later date. At that meeting they were asked to renounce all forms of sectarianism. Celtic assured the committee that they would co-operate in any way. Rangers declared that their current club policy was in association with the SFA's wishes. The committee made it clear that they were not satisfied with the latter's assertion. But there they drew the line. They were powerless to act on what they believed to be Rangers' sectarian agenda and could only deliver a slap on the wrist. The momentous changes were still to come in that establishment.

But what would the consequences be? We simply were not sure as we wound our different ways home that night. Something had to give. The McElhone Report on Scottish football, produced by Glaswegian MP Frank McElhone two and a half years earlier, had lain collecting dust. It needed the kiss of life. Paradoxically, it received it that day, for within it was the proposal to ban alcohol from all Scottish football grounds. It was given legislative force by the 1980 Criminal Justice Act (Scotland), which went even further in enforcing a ban on alcohol from trains and coaches carrying spectators to grounds for games. Typical sights thereafter were football buses being stopped outside any town, the passengers being asked to alight and the interiors being searched for alcohol. For some it was hard to take, considering the culture of indiscriminate drinking which surrounded football, and some supporters expressed to me during that period the feeling that they were being treated like cattle by the police, herded about as if they were potential criminals.

You have to wonder, though, that if the Celtic players had not run – in all innocence, I have to stress – towards their supporters that day and sparked off the chain of events we might have waited many more years for the necessary draconian measures to deal with an environment of alcohol-fuelled fanaticism. In an odd way they did the country a service by stepping, quite inadvertently, out of line. The transformation that took place fulfilled a social need to move football on from the age in which the recreational pleasures of the least advantaged in society were greatly alcohol-dependent. The working man's sport had been mired in the habitual practice of stoking the senses to make football more meaningful. The 'cairry-oot' from the pub was as vital to the average supporter as an oxygen-pack was to the space-walker. Prohibition has bred a different kind of supporter.

It was a visit to Hampden a year later that brought the effect of the radical change home to Ernie Walker, who was responsible for all cup final arrangements. 'It was a quiet Sunday morning,' he recalled. 'I took my two girls to Hampden to have a look around. It was the day after the Scottish Cup final between Rangers and Dundee United, which I had attended. The place, of course, was deserted. We firstly went down to the end where the Dundee United supporters would have been and climbed into the terracing. Now, normally on a Sunday morning after a game like that you wouldn't have been able to walk anywhere for thousand of bottles lying around. It was so devoid of them that I told my girls, "I'll give you a pound for every bottle you can find." About twenty minutes later one of them came back with a single Coca-Cola can which had been flattened underfoot. That was all. Then we went down to the Rangers end where the bulk of the crowd would have been. We could not fill a single shopping bag with what had been left. In all the previous years we would come and see ten huge industrial skips being filled with bottles and cans. Now, I had been cynical about this legislation and felt the habits were so ingrained in the fans that they would still bring the bevvy to the games regardless. But I was astonished. It worked. It was the most spectacularly successful piece of legislation I have ever known. This was an historic watershed in our game. I'll always remember that single, squashed Coca-Cola can. It told the whole story.'

Men can be trampled underfoot just as easily as Coca-Cola cans. This is what the cup final managers John Greig and Billy McNeill might have felt as they faced their own difficulties in this new era of terracing sobriety. Leaving aside their own problems arising internally, there was one man challenging them who had already that year made his philosophy clear to anybody who came within his reach – namely that he would crush anything or anybody standing in his way.

CHAPTER ELEVEN
BLOOD-LETTING

It was Alex Ferguson's *Forrest Gump* moment. It was just before 4.45 p.m. on an afternoon during which the sun was bouncing sharply off the crags of Arthur's Seat in Edinburgh, lending a lofty, noble background of vividly green grass and hawkish-looking rock to an elevating moment in Scottish football life. All this was spread out in front of me like a pageant we never really believed we would see. The date was 3 May 1980, the Saturday before the infamous Celtic–Rangers Scottish Cup final, and Easter Road Stadium had just witnessed something of a massacre. Aberdeen had routed Hibernian 5–0. Even so, we were unsure of the significance of that game until information from a match on the other side of the country rendered the result historic.

At my back lay the Firth of Forth, from which winter winds of brutal intensity could attack you and make you curse Auld Reekie's very existence. To my front lay Fergie's future. For that benign spring day changed our perception of him from being a rollicking, reckless, infuriating, irascible charmer who might possibly be remembered eventually as something of a talented rebel consigned perpetually to a second tier of influence, into that of a lustful winner. For suddenly he erupted. There was that hiatus when the final whistle went, when nobody was sure how another result at another ground was going to affect the day, and then, as if he had been attacked by a swarm of invisible wasps, he took off. Word had come: Celtic had drawn 0–0 with St Mirren, Fergie's former club, and Aberdeen were now league champions for only the second time in their history. It was his first major football prize.

In 1999, in a cinema watching the eponymous hero of the Hollywood film *Forrest Gump* starting an uninhibited run that would end up with him simply disappearing out of the stadium, I thought of Fergie that day 19 years earlier. He was at full pelt. He gave the impression he didn't mind if he ended up on the beach at Portobello. The Aberdeen supporters were certainly at that end of Easter Road, but it was not a skipping-for-joy run towards them, it was a sprint, without any sense of direction. Here, in full view of our cameras, was a man utterly beside himself with joy. He had broken the mould. In Glasgow he had been seen merely as a pest by the Old Firm, but now he would put the fear of death into them until the day he departed for Manchester United. The run ended when he enveloped a player in an ecstatic bear-hug. It was the kind of embrace he would give me on the pitch of the Ullevi Stadium in Gothenburg three years later.

What made the scene so startling was the fact that Aberdeen had torn up the script we had been writing over the previous two months about the destination of the league title. Celtic had led the championship by eight points on 1 March and were fully ten points ahead of Aberdeen, who admittedly had two games in hand. But in the run-in, the Dons beat Celtic twice at Celtic Park, 2–1 on 5 April and 3–1 on 23 April. The very fact that the presence of almost 100,000 Celtic supporters over the two games did nothing to intimidate the Aberdeen players hinted at a sea-change taking place in the power base of Scottish football, but nothing more than that. It was one thing to indicate great potential, it was quite another to achieve it. And not until those seconds immediately after the game at Easter Road could we bring ourselves to accept Aberdeen as capable of winning the major prize. For, with the honourable exception of Billy McNeill who, had he not left the club prematurely and indeed reluctantly to go back south, would surely have brought them some form of success, Fergie emerged head and shoulders above a long series of managerial strugglers at Pittodrie.

Eddie Turnbull and Ally MacLeod had certainly brought them a measure of cup success, the Scottish Cup in 1970 and the League Cup in 1976 respectively. But over the longer distance, in the league, they rarely seemed to have the staying power or the self-confidence to match the Old Firm. Playing in Glasgow was almost inevitably a sobering process for the club when at times, particularly under Turnbull, they seemed on the verge of making a league-winning breakthrough. Turnbull, with his acidic, ruthless manner and his brilliant coaching abilities, had given them a harder edge, a greater self-belief. He did not suffer fools gladly. During one training session at Pittodrie which we were recording before the 1970 Scottish Cup final against Celtic, a joiner in the stand was repairing a seat and his hammering was disturbing our sound-recordist. We asked Turnbull politely if he could ask the man to desist. He walked the full length of the pitch then lacerated the man with a string of obscenities that could not have been exceeded by an RSM in front of a dumb squaddie. It was simply his nature. At Hampden after the Drybrough Cup final of August 1972 when he was Hibernian's manager, we wired him up for an interview after his triumph over Celtic. Seconds before we went on the air a sudden thought obviously shot through his mind. 'How much am I getting for this?' he asked. Off-hand I had no idea, and told him so. 'Then eff off,' he retorted. He ripped the mike off his jacket and stalked off up the tunnel. Not even Stein would have done that. That hardness did Aberdeen no harm. They needed it. Ally MacLeod gave them bounce and attractiveness, won them a cup, but also nearly got them relegated. MacLeod's personality was too mercurial to give Aberdeen the long-term edge over the Old Firm.

Then Fergie came. I visited Pittodrie after that initial championship win and sat with him in his office and in the boot room, where he launched into analyses of players and teams, made verbal assaults on the reputations of certain members of the media, denounced the West of Scotland bias against his team and cracked jokes, particularly about Jim McLean, Dundee United's manager. He was a man who combined restlessness with self-assuredness. His conversation was astonishingly frank at times. One day he suddenly said to me in his office, 'Greigy is in real shit. I don't see him lasting.' There was nothing startlingly new in what he was saying, because everyone knew that John Greig, the Rangers manager, was going through hell in failing to deliver for the Rangers multitudes. At first I took it to be a remark simply out of sympathy for a former team-mate for whom he had the greatest admiration as a player. At a later date he was to add to that comment in a more startling way, as we shall see. But the man Fergie had really been aggravating during that period was Billy McNeill.

The Celtic manager had been enjoying a measure of success, especially at the expense of their great rivals, but he was not a completely happy man. While Fergie was forging a healthy and productive relationship with the inestimable chairman of Aberdeen, Dick Donald, one based on the latter's utter respect for the manager and his unwavering support for him, McNeill had to deal with Desmond White. White had eventually developed an intense dislike for Jock Stein, too, whom he had eventually outmanoeuvred and left with no option but to refuse a derisory offer of a role 'selling lottery tickets', as Stein put it, once he had stood aside for McNeill in 1978. He had not liked Stein's barely disguised contempt for directors on the board whom he regarded merely as hangers-on with little input to the benefit of the club. As Stein had built up a reputation that allowed him great independence of action, especially under the former chairman Sir Robert Kelly, it was almost inevitable that McNeill would be more constrained from the outset than his predecessor. He knew what he was letting himself in for and had been warned by Dick Donald, in so many words, when he left Aberdeen – that he would never be as happy at Celtic Park as he had been at Pittodrie. As in so many other matters, Donald's perception was crystal clear.

What McNeill brought to the role, of course, was complete devotion to the club he loved. But such affection had its limits, especially when it came to money. Here, White was unflinching. This lay at the core of the eventual disaffection between the pair. Or, in another sense, it was used as a means of levering McNeill out of the club. The public were not to know of this until it was too late. The Celtic legions saw McNeill only as a hero. He had snatched the league title against the odds with a young team in 1979, and by 1983 he had won three Premier Division titles and both the Scottish and League Cup once each. With such a formidable record you might feel a manager would have been insulated from any fate outside bubonic plague. But, as at Ibrox, the Celtic mentality is affected by ambitions that at times border on the ludicrous. Celtic had won the Scottish Cup in 1980, but to have been so far in front of Aberdeen in the league and yet to have failed to capture the title flawed his record in the eyes of some. The game that saw an unprecedented collapse of his team was at Dens Park, Dundee, on 19 April when, after Roy Aitken had given them a seventh-minute lead, Celtic were thrashed 5–1. McNeill talked about that game afterwards as one of his biggest ever embarrassments in football. He also knew that coming up fast on the outside lane was the flamboyant Fergie.

But McNeill's personality was also something that clearly bothered White. An ebullient character, and always animated in company, the Celtic manager was involved in an incident in September 1980 with journalist Gerry McNee en route to Hungary for a game: he threw a punch at the writer. Much publicity was given to this, which inevitably the Celtic board could hardly ignore. They subsequently fined him £500, which at that time was a considerable sum of money. When McNeill refused to speak to journalists the following month after a league game at Paisley against St Mirren, because McNee was in attendance, another rebuke came from the board and White issued a statement to the press: 'You can rest assured that Mr McNee will be accorded all the normal press facilities in future.' You do not need to be ridden with cynicism to see this not just as promoting clarity but as an anti-McNeill riposte. It must have been excruciating for McNeill to know he was being publicly keel-hauled. The relationship was now layered in a Siberian frost. How else could it have been?

A couple of years later, in October 1982, McNeill was sent to the stand for complaining about the refereeing after Aberdeen's third goal in a game they won at Celtic Park 3–1. He had eyeballed referee Andrew Waddell on the touchline, an incident that produced the *Daily Record* headline 'Silly Billy'. He was fined £200 by the SFA and rebuked by his own board. But there was one factor that gave him sustenance: he was loved by the supporters and his players. It was something of the relationship that Stein had established before him. It was said at the time, and has been subsequently repeated about that period, that White and his board were laying great stress on the importance of maintaining the club's good name, which had to be represented with dignity by any Celtic official. Historically they represented values which they felt transcended the footballing norm. But that view conveniently forgets that under the chairmanship of Bob Kelly, later to be Sir Robert, Stein had indulged in outbursts that were like missile hits on referees, opposing managers and players, officials of all ranks, and cowering journalists. Nothing was really said about that by his superiors as he ploughed his way to the top, dragging Celtic with him. That was the real world for him – success for the club. Kelly knew how to handle that. White did not. That does not exonerate any particular McNeill conduct, but it does place in context the astonishing spectacle of the men in charge at Celtic Park eventually manoeuvring a successful manager out of the door. Celtic were making a needless blunder.

Superficially, it was made to appear to be about money. For although he was a players' manager, that is not to say that he did not have his problems with them, as he had to toe the line on budgetary matters. This is something that in retrospect Davie Provan appreciates. 'Billy's pressures stemmed from being squeezed between the demands of players for more money and the obduracy of a board, completely dominated by Desmond White. I had a major fall-out with Billy in the early 1980s just before we went on a trip to New York. There really was bad feeling between us over money. And of course this was ridiculous. For we knew that he had his hands tied. That didn't mean we couldn't go and demand what we thought we deserved. But here was a man whose living was dependent on him keeping good relations with players. It would be the success of players which would keep him in a job. Yet he had to fall out with them from time to time. The situation was hopeless. Billy should have been completely separate from the negotiations. But actually overall he did a great job for us. Remember, wages were rock bottom when Jock Stein was at the club. Even the Lisbon Lions were on just £60 a week. Now, when I joined the club it was double that. Then, after about two years, he had got us up to about £250 to £300. So, although he had to be hard with us, he actually achieved a lot in improving our lot.'

But that was not enough. Stein had suffered from lack of proper investment by the club after the Lisbon triumph but had not complained publicly; McNeill had no such inhibitions. He told the *Daily Record* on 6 August 1982, 'I am looking to the chairman, and the board in general, to back me in my bid to strengthen and improve Celtic Football Club.' It sounded like a *cri de coeur* which he knew would fall on deaf ears. On 28 June 1983 the same newspaper's front page was headlined 'Shattered! Amazing Slap for Billy McNeill'. It was their reaction to McNeill being told by the board that if he did not like his own personal terms he could go. The board added in a terse statement, 'Mr McNeill requested a contract and a wage increase. This was unanimously rejected by the [six-man] board.' And just like that, McNeill left and signed on as Manchester City manager, to the astonishment of the broad spectrum of Scottish football.

A letter was written to the *Glasgow Herald* on 7 July that year which reflected sympathy for McNeill: 'The atmosphere of family has been destroyed, loyalty has been discarded and our spirit of tolerance and charity has been dissipated into a meanness of spirit and servility to money that is deeply abhorrent. This cordiality, this special relationship between club and supporters, what is left of it? No doubt success will come the way of Celtic FC again – success in the playing sense, that is. For one has the feeling that though there may well be a return to a degree of normality, the awareness is that, as with any sound relationship, things may achieve a plateau of tolerance. But they will never be quite the same again. This is the legacy bequeathed us by Mr White and the directors of Celtic FC.' The apocalyptic nature of that epistle revealed just how shocked the Celtic supporters were.

This contrasted with the strident chant from supporters at Ibrox a couple of months later, on Saturday, 17 September 1983, of 'Greig must go! Greig must go!' For on the other side of the city McNeill's erstwhile rival was suffering in a dramatically different way. In the season of the infamous 1980 Scottish Cup final, Rangers had finished fifth in the league, eleven points behind the new champions Aberdeen. The following season they had finished third, twelve points behind Celtic, but had won the Scottish Cup. In season 1981/82 they again trailed Celtic by twelve points, but managed to beat Dundee United in the final of the League Cup. In 1982/83 they won nothing and finished fourth in the league. Ibrox managers do not survive on such statistics; they merely provide a route map out of the marbled front entrance. The beginning of that 1983/84 season saw a sad ending to a career that had promised so much which set in train the whirligig of events that would eventually bring Graeme Souness to Ibrox.

For on that Saturday in September, Fergie took Aberdeen to Ibrox and proceeded to trounce Rangers. Their two goals by Mark McGhee were certainly scored late in the game, the 71st and 79th minutes, but that barely reflected the Dons' utter superiority throughout the match. But it is what then happened which provided a more dramatic focus on the malaise at Ibrox. For the Rangers supporters turned tail. They stood virtually en masse in the new Copland Road Stand and headed for the exits. You could even have said that it looked like some were trying to push people out of the way to get out first, having no stomach for any more of what they were seeing. Our cameras focused on that, and although I cannot recall my precise words, it was to the effect that the supporters were entitled to vote with their feet and that it was not before time they had demonstrated their disgust, for Rangers seemed to be blind to their own inadequacies. It was hardly an endorsement of the management. As we will consider in a later era, just before Fergus McCann took over at Celtic, we could conclude that disloyalty is a more potent force for change than the undying loyalty of Celtic supporters who did not desert their club in such huge numbers but whose very unswerving devotion led only to a protracted time in the wilderness.

I knew that Greig had listened to and watched that broadcast. The following week, when Rangers played St Johnstone, I went inside the pavilion to the corridor where I was normally given the team selections for the day. I was met by a Rangers steward who was obviously waiting for me. He simply said, 'You are not allowed in this area any longer and you won't be allowed to talk to any of the players again.' When I asked him who had imposed this, he said simply, 'Mr Greig.' I was both surprised and disappointed that he had not confronted me himself. I knew I was not dealing with a tyrant but with one of the most genial men in Scottish football, a sociable, witty man who could be the best of company on foreign trips where his gregariousness made him a great favourite of the media. He was not one for confrontations. I had seen a glimpse of this prior to the League Cup final against Celtic in December 1982 when we attended a training session to film the preparations. One particular sequence of moves they were practising continually broke down around one player, Ian Redford, who had signed for the club from Dundee in 1980. Greig was heaping some scorn on him for not controlling the ball properly and finishing the move with a shot at goal. Several times he did this, when to the astonishment of the camera team Redford turned and swore at the manager crisply and effectively. Equally astonishing was the fact that Greig simply turned away as if he had not heard this. Remember, the image of Greig as a player was still firmly etched in the public mind. He was one of the great battlers of all time. He shirked nothing. He lifted Rangers on the field on countless occasions when they looked on the point of collapse. He was the most inspirational captain of his generation simply because he had to haul mediocre teams to success and shouldered responsibilities even greater than McNeill, who quite simply played in better teams around that generation. On that basis, you could hardly argue with those who in later years voted him The Greatest Ever Ranger. But as a manager we were seeing the slow descent into failure of a man who was discovering for himself that he was not adequate to the task he had been handed by Waddell.

'He lost the dressing room,' Alex MacDonald, his colleague for years at Ibrox, said simply to me as he recollected those days. That phrase can be either one of the most damning verdicts in football or something almost poignant, as in this case. For MacDonald said it with regret. Like others, he was utterly determined to help Greig be a successful manager. It is true that MacDonald was so dedicated to Ibrox he would have joined forces with Auld Nick himself to make the club triumphant, but in this case he knew he was talking about a decent man who was infinitely softer in his outlook than the image he had portrayed on the field to a wider public. 'He had absolutely no man-management skills, absolutely zero,' MacDonald added, again with a tinge of sympathy which reflected the view he should never have been given the job in the first place. 'You wanted Greigy on the park beside you. When he wasn't there you missed him. Off the park his influence wasn't the same.' It was noted by his back-room staff that he would change his mind frequently about team decisions, and in one classic case he attempted a ploy that could be interpreted as reckless and desperate or as daringly imaginative.

In December 1982 he recalled former Rangers player Gordon Smith, then with Brighton on a month's loan, to play in the League Cup final against Celtic. 'It was a call I got from Tommy McLean, not John Greig, asking me to come [back] for a period,' Smith said. 'I had still been angry with John because of the way I had been forced out of Ibrox in 1980 after the Scottish Cup final only a couple of months into a five-year contract. He had given me all kinds of warnings about what would happen to me if I didn't leave, so I was muscled out effectively. So I was surprised by this call to come back. I eventually phoned him. That was the Wednesday. I accepted verbally, but then when I said I would see him on the Monday after the cup final, he said, "What do you mean, Monday? I want you back to play in the final." I could hardly believe that. I went back to speak to my wife about it and I felt I was making a mistake, because I felt that if we didn't win I could end up as the scapegoat. I consulted Jimmy Melia, who was Brighton's manager at the time, who told me to go and play in the final and if it didn't work out he would take me back, because he wasn't going to be manager much longer, as he expected to be sacked. That in itself took me aback. I agreed to return to Ibrox.

'But as soon as I went back into the dressing room I felt, right away, that the place was a disaster. It was the worst atmosphere ever. When I had been there in my first spell the team spirit was great, the dressing room was bubbly. It was nothing like that on my return. I was also slaughtered by the media as they blamed Rangers for bringing back players who were past their sell-by date. I was only 27 though. Think of Alex Rae in 2004 coming back to Ibrox at the age of 34, without too much of a fuss. But we were a beaten team even before we went out and lost 2–1 to Celtic. I had hoped to play well, win, and then perhaps be asked back on a longer-term basis. But I hadn't appreciated how bad things really were. John didn't talk to me again after the final, until just before the loan was up, when he told me he would not extend it and I replied that I wouldn't want it anyway given what the spirit was like. To my astonishment, he agreed. He said, "I know, there's a terrible atmosphere down there in the dressing room." I couldn't avoid saying, "Well, whose fault is that, then?" He just said, "I know," as if acknowledging his own failure. For although he was a good coach and tactician, he knew nothing about man-management.'

Smith returned to Brighton and went on to play at Wembley in the FA Cup final the following spring, thus becoming the only player to have played in two cup finals in the same season in different countries. It was an episode that smacked of desperation, and it weakened an already vulnerable Greig. His life had become a misery, and it was affecting his health. He resigned on 28 October 1983. During his period of management Rangers had played 189 league matches, winning 81, drawing 52 and losing 56. He had won both the Scottish Cup and the League Cup twice, but his best league performance was in his first season when the club finished second. It was a failure in management, set against the context of a club emerging through a traumatic period of disaster and stadium change that would have taxed the skills and spirit of almost anyone in that position. In many ways he had much to thank his mentor Waddell for in his career. But it had been a mistake to appoint him.

Not that anyone within Ibrox would have dared utter a word of criticism about that. Everybody was terrified of Waddell, who was still a presence and influence at Ibrox during Greig's tenure. A former director, the late Jimmy Robinson, once told me that at board meetings the different chairmen of the club would not open their mouths until they were effectively given the nod by Waddell. He had gone from manager to general manager and then to managing director; finally, as his star was waning, he was put on a consultancy basis. At the peak of his powers he would sit down-table from the chairman but would effectively chair the meetings with a sullen determination that intimidated all into silence whenever he pontificated. Not a move was made by Rangers FC but that it required his imprimatur. In a way that was just as well, because in terms of football acumen he was head and shoulders above everybody else there. His greatest triumph was in holding the club together in times of deep crisis and providing the vision that made them leaders of stadium development in the UK. This was appreciated even by people within Ibrox who came to dislike him intensely.

Back in December 1970 Tommy Craig, the physiotherapist at the club at the time, had been asked by Waddell to think about stadium development for the future, as from time to time Craig embarked on special tasks for the manager. Craig looked around the stadium and sketched some thoughts on the back of a Christmas card. 'I still have that card,' he admitted. 'I sketched a few details but I did come back to tell Deedle that I thought the stadium was a death-trap. He was a bit taken aback by that, but told me that would be considered in the near future, after the next Old Firm game on 2 January 1971. Of course, sadly, that was the game of the Ibrox disaster, when 66 people died on stairway 13 at the stadium. An awful, awful event. Waddell and I agreed afterwards that it would be better if we never mentioned that the subject had ever arisen in our conversations.'

The images of that disastrous night, principally the bodies laid out in a line at the stadium, will never leave me. Nor will the role played by Waddell, who assumed command rather like that lieutenant who took over from Captain Queeg in the film *The Caine Mutiny* to save the ship from inevitable disaster. As Craig admitted, 'Waddell was the only one there who could handle that. For the others around him ran for cover, ducked out of the way, made themselves scarce. He was brilliant. He dealt with the police, the insurance people, the press, getting players to the hospitals to visit the survivors. I don't think he slept for weeks. That's what it seemed like.'

One of the closest witnesses to this was the man put in charge of the original investigation, Joe Beattie, a chief superintendent of the Glasgow police, stationed at Govan at the time. When he went into the Ibrox boardroom a few hours after the tragedy he found the directors in disarray. According to him they were going around like headless chickens, cracking the occasional joke and generally giving the impression that they simply could not comprehend the magnitude of what had occurred. Beattie was appalled. It was not until Waddell appeared in front of him that he felt a sure hand would be put on the helm. He brushed aside all the uncertainties of the men around him and took charge from then on. His public statements, and his gathering of the Rangers clan to close ranks and put the club on an even keel in the wake of the appalling calamity, gained him enormous respect with various public authorities which I believe has been greatly underestimated, except by those who were close to him at the time.

But it took a tremendous toll on him. Many of us witnessed his decline in the early 1970s with alarm. Those close to him suffered. Frank King, the club secretary, was so intimidated by Waddell that one morning he snapped, crawled under his bed and refused to come out. The nervous breakdown came as no surprise to those who knew what was going on. Craig confessed that he suffered too, after having been the blue-eyed boy for so long. 'Waddell was really an out-and-out bully,' he said. 'On one occasion I was offered the possibility of helping Frank King as a kind of part-time assistant. I think he just wanted rid of the man and had me in mind to help oust him. I turned that down. Then one afternoon in 1974 I was called up to Waddell's office where he informed me that Campbell Ogilvie from the Scottish League office was to be appointed the new club secretary, and I'll never forget Waddell's words to me: "You had your chance, boy, you blew it, now you can fuck off!" From that moment on I never had a single conversation with him again, until I left the club. But, as everybody knew, even though great efforts were made to keep quiet about his angry ways, the board of directors were scared shit of him.'

The problem was that his personal problems were affecting his judgements. He was drinking heavily. Perhaps that more than anything else accounted for the astonishing way in which he had not only tried to intimidate Jock Wallace throughout, but finally, and effectively, had seemed to shun him, as if he were some hick who had stumbled on Ibrox by mistake. 'Even at the time of winning trebles under Jock Wallace he would come into the dressing-room and shake hands with everybody and ignore Jock completely before walking out again,' Craig said. 'And I'll always recall the time he was in the Motherwell boardroom for a game at Fir Park and, having imbibed a lot, turned on their directors for having brought Jock back from Leicester to be their manager. There he was, drunkenly berating them for appointing a manager who in his words was "an effing clown". He was talking about the man he had brought to Rangers in the first place, and in front of guests and the like. He was forced to write a letter of apology to the Motherwell chairman.'

The erratic conduct worsened from around 1974 onwards. Just before his outstanding work on developing a new stadium was going to be revealed with the opening of the Copland Road Stand, I visited him in company with a London producer of *Sportsnight*, Scotsman Jim Reside, and a camera crew to gain access and particularly point out to a UK audience, with a certain degree of pride, the initiative being taken by a Scottish club in reforming the whole manner of watching football. Yet there was Waddell in his office, shouting obscenities at us, in his alcoholic haze barely able to prevent his elbow from continually slithering off the edge of his desk. His condition at half-past two in the afternoon was itself an indication of just how seriously he was being affected. Jim and I beat a hasty retreat, feeling only saddened that a man's great qualities had been snared by an addiction. He was dissolving into a furtive drinker with whom coherent business could not be done at any time after mid-morning.

Lawrie McMenemy spoke to me once about Brian Clough's battle with the bottle, and felt that it was too easy to pour scorn on men like that. Like Waddell, Clough's weakness derived greatly from the stress he undoubtedly suffered through fronting his club's successes. It was sympathy and help they needed. Waddell's inbuilt truculence, compared to Clough's apparent relatively cheery disposition, made that almost impossible. It is significant that he gave up his consultancy when things were going against Greig in 1983. But he was always around on match days, even when Wallace returned to the club for a second spell in 1983, which could not have been easy for Waddell's first ever appointee. Greig's demons did not pursue him into private life, for he made it clear he was renouncing football management when he left Ibrox, saying, 'I am finished with the game!' He went on to develop a successful broadcasting career and, eventually, did PR work with the very club he had left.

So 1983 was the most vivid, moulting year of all that decade. Gradually the old coats were shorn and new colours emerged, with personalities coming and going as the managerial game seemed to be in a state of flux around Glasgow. Waddell, Greig and McNeill, who had been intertwined as personalities for over two decades, were now gone. Waddell slipped towards the back of the pecking order, merely a sniper, as news of Wallace returning to the club reached his ears. David Hay slipped into the managerial seat with Celtic. A seismic shift was taking place. That's why Fergie made his famous run that day in May 1980. He had seen the promised land. He had been preparing, long and weary, for the breakthrough. And to think that I first saw the clearest evidence of his dedication in the unlikeliest of settings.

CHAPTER TWELVE

ENTER FERGIE

His face stood out amongst the thousands of Celtic supporters entombed in the claustrophobic interior of Malpensa airport, just outside Milan, while flights were being cancelled left, right and centre, chaos was reigning and the monsoon outside would have defied even a latter-day Captain Oates of the Antarctic to utter bravely, 'I am just going outside and I may be some time.' It was hellish, both inside and out, the depressing atmosphere compounded by the aftermath of an unexpected defeat. The former Rangers player sat stoically among the people he had always wished to heap embarrassment upon, his face largely expressionless. Every now and then somebody would recognise him and he would become more animated and indulge in some friendly banter with Celtic supporters who thought he had lost his marbles, being where he was, or else he had, as one of them cheerily shouted at him, 'seen the effin' light!'

Alex Ferguson could have stayed at home, put his feet up and watched Celtic play Feyenoord in the European Cup final of 1970 on television, as most of Europe had. He chose instead to be there. I was surprised to see him, and since there was so much time on our hands as the foul weather had caused mayhem with the flight schedules and left thousands stranded for hours, we had time to talk. 'What are you doing here?' I asked, for although he had recently become a Falkirk player he was still a Ranger in the eyes of the public, in the tradition of 'once a blue-nose, always a blue-nose'. I recall that he just smiled and quickly hid his face with a cupped hand in a mock effort to try to remain anonymous. After that we talked for a few moments, simply about the game, which he discussed dispassionately, feeling that Celtic could have won the cup with their early chances though Feyenoord looked the better footballing side overall.

It was the first time I had spoken to him since shortly after the Rangers–Celtic Scottish Cup final a year earlier when, given the task of marking the Celtic captain Billy McNeill at corner-kicks against Rangers, he suffered the indignity of watching the same man climb, unchallenged, to head Celtic into the lead after only two minutes. The cup was lost from that moment, and Ferguson shouldered much of the responsibility for the defeat. A loser's medal from that game was all he ever had to show for his time at Ibrox, and so hurt was he by that day that he eventually threw the medal away in disgust. Around the start of the following season I confess I felt that the future was dim for this man. Now here he was, so remote from any suggestion of pursuing a coaching or managerial career that the significance of his presence was utterly lost on me. I certainly thought it odd that he had travelled to Italy because he was Rangers to his toenails, although once he had attained some status in the game in later life he castigated them for their policies. It is easy enough in retrospect to understand that the man simply found the game of football and the nature of this particular event so compulsive that he was drawn to it like the proverbial moth to the flame. He was obviously ambitious in a way we could not have understood at the time: he had few credentials to allow us such an interpretation. Between the impassive face of the intruder in Malpensa airport waiting to leave his very first European final, to being the central figure that night in Barcelona in May 1999 with the very trophy in his hand that had just eluded Celtic, lay a trail pursued with a fanaticism that sometimes seemed beyond comprehension.

Without Aberdeen Football Club, that career may never have got off the ground. Mind games were not invented in the granite city, but Ferguson, one of the greatest exponents of such, was domiciled in that clean environment between the years 1978 and 1986. He stepped into a club mired in decent orthodoxy and shook it to the foundations with the bravura of a street-fighter who wanted the world to know he would take on anybody. Those who thought that football management was a case of picking players in certain positions for the club and then sending them out of an afternoon in the hope that it would somehow work out needed only to spend ten minutes deep in the small manager's office or the tiny boot room at Pittodrie with Ferguson in the early weeks of his first season to realise that he was adding a very special dimension to the club which it had sought for years but could not clearly define for itself. It was about attitude. Ferguson was providing them with a simple and stark philosophy. Although the comparison would probably be painful to a supporter of left-wing causes, and to the former trade unionist that

Ferguson is, the bible-thumping, fundamentalist utterance of George W. Bush, 'Either you are for us, or you are against us,' reminded me of the stance taken by the new Aberdeen manager when he faced the world then, to which dictum he has subsequently adhered. For his first step was to foment the view that anybody living south-west of Perth was a potential threat to the club. He associated most of the West of Scotland press with a virus worthy of reference to the World Health Organisation. He earmarked particular individuals for special contempt, and encouraged his players to do likewise. If Aberdeen did not take on this bias head on, it would not survive, suggested his frequently aired body language. It was a carbon copy of how Stein had initiated his new charges at Celtic Park in the benefits of storing up grievances against a hostile press. Old Trafford has been the beneficiary of that Ferguson mind-set. He took it south with him when he eventually left.

Of course there was an historical belief before he arrived that the club did not get its fair share of attention, nor respect, from the national newspapers, based primarily in Glasgow. And to a great extent that was true. Rangers and Celtic sold newspapers in greater numbers than any other club; television audiences were greater for games involving the Old Firm. In the commercial world, these facts dictated terms to editors and proprietors. The fact, too, that journalists of these outlets could park themselves within minutes of their offices outside Ibrox and Parkhead added greatly to the ease with which column inches could be produced or interviews slapped on the screen. All this, seen from the north-east, looked like an institutionally ingrained cold shoulder for the club. Some people within Pittodrie did let this resentment surface from time to time. But it was a tiny bubbling spring compared to the volcanic outburst that erupted with Ferguson's coming. Even their most abrasive manager up till then, Eddie Turnbull, could hardly be described as brazen and bold in his mission to provoke his players into resentment about all of this. And these were some of the kinder descriptions used about Ferguson as he presented an invariably fulminating face to the world in taking on the task of lifting a benign club into full military mode.

Ferguson I had known previously as a player with Rangers and as a manager at St Mirren, but you could tell he had quickly and effectively dropped into the north-east political mould. On top of that the volatility of his nature was immediately evident to the players. Willie Miller, who was to be one of the greatest club captains of all time, described his entrance to the club as 'like a bull into a china shop'. That was at dressing-room level. At another level he was more cautious. This resulted from the aftermath of his dispute with St Mirren, who had sacked him in May 1978. The industrial tribunal to which he took the club for unfair dismissal adjudicated in the harshest of terms, reporting that: 'It shows him as one possessing, neither by experience nor talent, any managerial ability at all.' Think of an ancient scribe noting of the teenage Alexander the Great that he 'will never be able to mount a saddle' and it might give you an idea of the scale of misjudgement that report contained.

So Ferguson applied himself to the job by coming to a sound relationship with the chairman Dick Donald, he of the constant brown trilby and the gentle smile for virtually everybody in his presence, and the erudite director and former player Chris Anderson, secretary of Robert Gordon's College who, on the basis of the industrial tribunal report, might have concluded that the former St Mirren manager was not fit for a job cleaning the players' boots. The latter actually described Ferguson to others, quite freely at times, as behaving like a megalomaniac, but he had to turn a blind eye to it since he was bringing the club the kind of success they had only dreamed about. That said, there seemed to be perfect cohesion between dressing room and boardroom, which was only upset when Anderson tragically developed motor neurone disease. I had become particularly friendly with Chris and his wife Pat, and to watch him quickly succumb to the disease and see the commiserative but encouraging tone Ferguson developed whenever Anderson was wheeled into the club and had to be assisted to eat and drink, was to see the manager's deeply sensitive nature.

They had certainly, however, taken a gamble with this man from the west, although they had consulted with the oracle himself, Jock Stein, who was unhesitating in his encouragement of Ferguson, knowing that the club needed somebody to transplant the bone-marrow of a club which had crumbled too easily in times past. For all that stories mounted about the bawlings that went on in the dressing-room, most of the visitors allowed near the dressing-room area, and amongst whom I was fortunate to be included for a period, found one of the wittiest and most genial of men. He would crack jokes, tell us of the tricks he would play on folk, particularly in his personal rivalry with Jim McLean at Dundee United, and gave you the impression that life was not worth living if you could not josh around for some of the time. In contrast, we also began to hear about his classic tantrums, and in my naïvety in those first three years of his reign there I suppose I felt that I would never be on the receiving end of one. In fact, it was not until much later that I learnt what it was like to cross him.

There was another initial problem – the legacy of Billy McNeill. The man who had moved to Celtic had recently stabilised the club after the emotional swings and roundabouts of Ally MacLeod. In his first game at Pittodrie in 1977, McNeill, adorned in a glorious red shirt, which must have been a culture shock to his many remaining admirers in and around Glasgow, beat Rangers 3–1. That helped get his feet under the table in a big way. Then from December that year his side had gone 23 games without defeat and were only pipped by Rangers for the title on the last day of the 1977/78 season. A week later they lost the Scottish Cup final to Rangers 2–1. But McNeill had built a fine foundation, and even more importantly had developed a superb rapport with his board and support. It was going to be a difficult act to follow. But at 35 years of age the Govan boy was up for it.

Willie Miller was there from the start. 'Right from the beginning it was all a bit confrontational,' he recalled. 'Alex was not the refined man you see now. He was young and a bit rough round the edges, but you could tell he knew what he wanted. He knew the kind of people he wanted around him that he could trust. I thought at that time I was a kind of senior player, because I was captain and had been playing since 1974. I had lifted the League Cup in 1976 under Ally and we had taken Rangers all the way in the league just before Alex came. So, although there was nothing dramatically hostile in it, we did have our differences. It used to get up my nose, for example, when he kept on and on at first about how his captain at St Mirren, Jackie Copland, used to set up his line for the set-pieces. I couldn't take it any longer, and I told him I couldn't give a bugger about what anybody else did, and I would do it my own way. It was small things like that which I had to get sorted out with him. But confrontation was always in the air. You never knew how he would react. There was a fine line he walked between being normal and cracking up. We were quite alike in that respect, because the only thing we wanted for the club was success. If that meant kicking a few arses or throwing some tea cups around the dressing-room from time to time, then so be it. But although that happened with nose-to-nose arguments, kicking doors, kicking the radiator, he used to stand in front of us for the team-talk and

1967. Building the QE2 on the Clyde had to take its turn as the national obsession for football was at its zenith.

ABOVE: Cathkin Park. Former home of Third Lanark. Its dereliction became a symbol for Scottish football's lack of foresight. Later it was gentrified into a play park.

RIGHT: Jimmy Mason, Third Lanark and Scotland, one of the greatest exponents of traditional Scottish inside-forward play, posing as a Harry Lauder look-alike before a Scotland game at Wembley in 1949.

The one that got away. Celtic Park 1972. The first ever penalty shoot-out in Glasgow in the Celtic v. Inter Milan match, and the first ever miss. Dixie Deans did not ask for the match-ball as a souvenir.

Lisbon 1967. Who pinched his shirt as a souvenir? The face in the crowd is Billy McNeill's. The tune they were playing in the background at that time was another British triumph of that year, Sandie Shaw's 'Puppet on a String'.

Barcelona 1972. The Agony and the Ecstasy for John Greig before the real battle took place on the pitch.

How did he miss? It was cried in unison by the nation over Billy Bremner's lapsed chance in Frankfurt 1974 against Brazil in the World Cup. He never did come up with the right explanation.

Giants. The duels between Willie Waddell and Jock Stein in the 1970s were hardly conducted according to the rules of ancient chivalry. Instead they owed much to sumo wrestling.

Optimism and showmanship prior to the World Cup of 1978. Ally MacLeod's magic carpet ran out of stardust somewhere over the Andes.

Cordoba 1978. A classic Scottish 'sair heid'. Ally MacLeod only surfaced for air after the referee blew his whistle at the end of the 1-1 Scotland-Iran match.

Mendoza 1978. Scotland v Holland. The World Cup came alive for one brief shining moment as Archie Gemmill netted the greatest goal ever scored anywhere in the universe.

ABOVE Sir Alex, when he was just a plain old winner of the Scottish League Championship in 1980 for Aberdeen. He was good at hugging, and very proficient at bawling.

LEFT Who did cross the ball for John Hewitt to score the winner in the Cup Winners' Cup Final for Aberdeen in Gothenburg against Real Madrid in 1983? Curiously different versions survive.

Jim McLean smiling. No more Mr Scrooge. If you have just won the Scottish Premier League Championship in 1983 with Dundee United then it is worth presenting a new face to the world.

Thugs. They were also called Uruguayans. Paul Sturrock barely survives a mugging as the South Americans battle their way to a no-scoring draw with Scotland in the Neza in Mexico City in 1986.

More like a meeting of Rotary International than revolutionaries. But Scottish football exploded into a new era when Graeme Souness, David Holmes and Terry Butcher got together to revive Rangers in 1986.

People power 1990s. Not since the sans culottes *of Paris became the foot soldiers of the French Revolution have we seen such a popular force as that from the streets around Celtic Park helping to oust an old regime.*

The Saviour. Or was he? Fergus McCann, with mike, being assailed by critical supporters in 1998 who did not like his stewardship of the club, even though he had apparently rescued it from oblivion.

Building for the future. Manager Dick Advocaat and chairman David Murray of Rangers view a magnificent new training complex completed in 2001 which was also a significant signpost to an enormous debt burden.

The Hop, Step and Jump Competition won at Celtic Park by Martin O'Neill after watching another Celtic triumph. Seven trophies he won before his sad departure.

Alex McLeish, Rangers manager who gave birth to silver triplets in season 2002/3. He was expected to be as fertile every season by a demanding support.

Fraternisation is just one of the skills of the Tartan Army whose reputation soared in Spain and was augmented in France in 1998 as they left the bad old days behind and became an ambassadorial force.

Walter Smith, Scotland's manager in San Siro in 2005. Taking over from the Pied Piper from Germany would be no easy task for the avuncular ex-Rangers manager.

he wasn't like that all the time. And I think it's a bit of a myth that has got around, that it was a constant war in the dressing room under him.'

The transition from McNeill to Ferguson and all that that meant in terms of a more aggressive approach inevitably led to resentment amongst some other players. Joe Harper, for instance, was a folk hero in the north-east when Ferguson arrived. He converted his rotund physique and lack of height into positive assets and tore into defences, becoming the highest goalscorer in Aberdeen's history with 199 goals in just 308 games. But he was also a stirrer of people. It was acknowledged that he was not slow to voice opinions. His 32 goals scored in Ferguson's first season there could not insulate him from the manager's wrath. Harper told me some years later that at a team-talk, where views were being sought by the manager on the way things were going, he had voiced dissent about playing on his own up front in the new 4–5–1 formation. He felt that it was right to speak his mind, as the manager had recommended. But he ended up in Ferguson's office afterwards, in the privacy of which he took a tongue-lashing and was warned never to question tactics again.

Then there was Steve Archibald. The good old Scots word 'thrawn' comes to mind when I think of Archibald. Perhaps other words come to Ferguson's mind. Of all the players I had to deal with personally, Archibald seemed to live in a self-regarding and impenetrable cocoon. He was elusive to us at the BBC when we wanted him for interview in those days, unlike others who would come gladly to the cameras. Several times I tried, and while I would have preferred the Greta Garbo 'I want to be alone' rejection, I had instead to make do with hearing 'eff off' a couple of times. Then one day, when there was much talk about Tottenham Hotspur's interest in him, I got word from *Grandstand* in BBC London that the great man had deigned to be interviewed. Up I went to Aberdeen, where I was met by a player who looked as if he had been converted by St Paul himself. Archibald could not have been more co-operative. We were actually invited into his home, where he talked about the great team spirit within Pittodrie and the confidence he had for the club in the future. All this was for the birds though. He was already at loggerheads with his manager on several counts, and on one occasion had actually taken a football, opened his manager's door and kicked it hard into the room where it rattled off all four walls, with Ferguson sitting there transfixed. The fact that he was not shown the door after that act of flagrant disrespect showed that he was too important to the manager to be instantly quelled. But now Archibald felt it was time to be seen up front, because of the transfer talk surrounding him. *Grandstand* had forked up the cash to entice him to take part, as he was known to be then, and continued to be long afterwards, one of the coolest mercenaries in the business. He was transferred shortly after that to Spurs for £1 million. But he left with a reputation. 'The Man Who Stood Up to Fergie' would surely be an apposite epitaph to his career.

His leaving did not create a vacuum, for the appetite for the task that Ferguson developed over his period at Pittodrie stemmed not from successes but also from failures and his response to them. One such came early in his career there and gave rise to serious doubts about his fitness for the job. Ferguson took Aberdeen to Hampden Park on 31 March 1979, only ten months after taking over, to play Rangers in the Scottish League Cup final. It was a battle. Derek Johnstone fouled Steve Archibald in the first minute, which effectively neutered him, and Doug Rougvie, the mountainous Aberdeen defender, was judged by the referee to have badly fouled Johnstone with only six minutes remaining and the score at 1–1, and thus became only the second man in the history of major finals at Hampden to be sent off (the first was Jock Buchanan of Rangers in the Scottish Cup final of 1929). This is the incident, which so enflamed Ferguson, that you might say prompted the complete and absolute spiritual break with his first love. It's not that he had not wanted to beat them from the outset. But he felt, as he saw it, that a man wearing the colours he had worn himself with pride had cheated to get one of his players sent off. The gloves were now off with Rangers for the rest of his stay at Pittodrie. Four minutes into injury-time Rangers scored the winner through Colin Jackson. John Greig had just won his first trophy, and Derek Johnstone, the subject of Ferguson's wrath, had picked up his first prize as captain. The formal interview I had with Ferguson after the game revealed a man suppressing, with great difficulty, a rage that had been building up since the first tackle on Archibald. Off-camera he was certainly less restrained, and blitzed Johnstone for having got his man sent off. But his public restraint was noted by Alex Cameron of the *Daily Record*, who wrote in the 3 April issue about his 'complete restraint after the final whistle and his refusal to say anything against anyone, especially the referee. Ferguson and his directors conducted themselves in exemplary fashion despite their deep disappointment.'

What Cameron overlooked was that Ferguson was on his last warning from the SFA, having been ordered not to speak to referees for two years after an incident in February 1977 with referee Ian Foote at Motherwell when he was the St Mirren manager. That might have been a factor in his reluctance to say anything publicly about the final. However, on 19 April 1979 Ferguson became the first Scottish manager to be banned from the touchline for breaking that injunction twice. The fine of £100 on top of that was a considerable amount in those days. He would have to sit out matches until December of that year. I did feel, though, that in some of the remarks he made to me about the tackling in that Rangers game he was licking his lips over the prospect of the next confrontation between the two teams. Ferguson, with ease, had vaulted over his formerly great affection for Rangers to become a predator after their blood. The origin of the now apparently self-sustaining animosity between the two clubs is said to have occurred in October 1988 after an incident between Neil Simpson of Aberdeen and Ian Durrant of Rangers, but I would contend that it was born that day at Hampden. As we all know, some of us to our regret, Ferguson never forgets. His pre-match build-up to games against the Old Firm would from now on be like a call to the storming of the Bastille.

It worked a treat, too, for in the following season (1979/80) Aberdeen beat both members of the Old Firm home and away in the League Cup, although they threw the prize away when it was in their grasp. In the Scottish League Cup final at Hampden on 8 December 1979 Aberdeen simply defeated themselves. On a miserably wet and cold day, only 27,173 turned up expecting to see an automatic win for the favourites against the largely unfancied Dundee United side. It was quite unusual for Aberdeen to be favourites for a final in Glasgow, and they played as if they had been handed a new role but not the proper stage directions. They had much of the ball, but were bereft of the final touch, and as I sat there the feeling grew that, since United were lacklustre themselves, this was a turkey of a game. It went to extra-time, in which nothing much happened again, and the game ended goalless. I certainly was not looking forward all that much to the replay, to be held at Dens Park, Dundee, on 12 December. But the evening game under floodlights was a revelation in all kinds of ways. Firstly, Ferguson was outwitted by Jim McLean, manager of Dundee United, his great 'local' rival (their duels I will consider later). Instead of featuring as the underdog, United were more aggressive and utilised the talents they had more effectively, and they looked like winners from the start. This did not go down well with some of the Aberdeen support.

The commentary position at Dens Park was suspended above an enclosure which for that game was packed with Aberdeen followers. In general their support is one of the best behaved anywhere, even to the point of docility, too often. But an element within it had been developing over several years which certainly did not take its cue from the teachings of Mahatma Gandhi. They could be highly abusive, and they were that night. At half-time, with Dundee United leading 1–0 thanks to a Willie Pettigrew goal, they started to throw anything they could get their hands on at the television gantry. Well protected though we were, bottles were smashing just under our feet, and we were witnessing the bizarre sight of the smashed remnants raining down on the heads of those who had thrown them in the first place. This went on for several minutes before anyone realised we were insulated, and that they were inflicting damage on themselves. Afterwards I told Aberdeen director Chris Anderson about the incident. I had the greatest admiration for this man, but he had difficulty accepting that their support could do such a thing. I always believed thereafter that Aberdeen occasionally turned a blind eye to some of their more unruly element, continually citing the fact that the Old Firm legions were infinitely worse. In the second half, the Aberdeen fans were drifting away long before the final whistle as United added another two goals to take the cup.

Was this conduct worth addressing? I think it was, in the sense that Ferguson had developed a culture of expectation on a higher and more excitable level than previous managers, not just in terms of achievement but in the manner in which he projected himself to the public. His volatility was reflected in the antics of some of the support, although he described the home support once as so benign you could hear them rustling their sweetie papers. Roy Keane, with his prawn-cocktails remarks about some self-indulgent Manchester United supporters not letting their presences be felt at Old Trafford, might have been reading from the same script.

This was a black night for Ferguson, debatably one of the lowest points in his career. He was not on the bench for the game but in the stand, still sitting out his suspension, and he had decided to go for the same selection as the previous Saturday. United had made two crucial changes. He admitted his selection mistakes almost immediately afterwards. But the bitterness of the Aberdeen support over the defeat was reflected in the graffiti that suddenly appeared on a wall just outside Pittodrie: 'You have let us down again'. With the amazing series of games after that which brought them the league title against all the odds, and produced that delirious Ferguson run at Easter Road, he and his team redeemed themselves. The graffiti of the future would take on a rosier hue.

CHAPTER THIRTEEN
THE LAST TIRADE

It was midnight. Two men bedecked in red and white made their tentative way towards a spot just outside the city of Aberdeen. They were making the first-known pilgrimage in the north-east of Scotland. The area, not being overloaded with places of reverence, was now recognising the reality that one had been established on 3 May 1980, the day the title had been won by a club outwith the Old Firm for the first time in 15 years. Their destination was a bungalow in the village of Cults which had been transformed by events into a target for the faithful. Inside, Ferguson was still awake but certainly not expecting visitors. When the two strangers eventually had the door opened to them, Aberdeen's manager realised what he had let himself in for. For in his post-match television interview with me, after he had recovered from his run down the pitch, he had inadvertently thrown out an invitation to all and sundry by saying in so many words that he would be holding an 'open house' that night for celebrations. A couple of supporters had taken that literally, and turned up at his house. They could have been sent packing, but instead were invited in to watch the BBC's recorded highlights of the historic event. They were his people. They were now absolutely won over. He knew the strength that that would give him in times of crisis.

That was just one side of him that day. The other was just as typical of his ambivalent personality. For even as he watched his side destroy Hibernian 5–0, he was, nevertheless, eventually fined £250 by the SFA and banned from the touchline for a year for 'foul and abusive language' to the referee at half-time. His flock loved him the more for it. That day at Easter Road would burn in strange ways into their psyche. As journalist and Aberdeen aficionado Jack Webster wrote in the *Scottish Daily Express*, 'The coincidences began to dawn. It was 15 years to the day that Bobby Clark, Aberdeen's most capped player [to that date], had signed for the Dons. It had seemed the prize would elude him. Willie Miller's mother was recalling the amazing fact that he had been born exactly twenty-five years ago – his birthday was the previous day – just as Aberdeen had been celebrating their only previous league championship in 1955.' The suggestion seemed to be that all this had been ordained by some higher power, which had decided it was now Aberdeen's turn.

Aberdeen took to the mantle of winners as to the manor born. They were in it now for the long haul. They finished second to Celtic the following season, 1980/81, and, although they were beaten to the post by the same club again on the last day of the season in 1982, it did nothing to deter them from travelling to Glasgow for the Scottish Cup final against Rangers with proven players who had tasted success, some of whom, such as Willie Miller and Alex McLeish, were now the backbone of the Scotland side under Jock Stein. They had beaten Celtic in a previous round and were to face an ageing Rangers side struggling under John Greig. Some of these Rangers players were about to wear the blue jerseys for the last time. Sandy Jardine, Colin Jackson and Tommy McLean all knew they were on the way out as players, although McLean was to be appointed assistant manager to Greig. They were in no fit state to meet a team on heat. In a curious way, it looked also as if it was merely a set-up for an anti-climax like the one Aberdeen had suffered at Hampden against Dundee United two and a half years earlier. But this was a more mature side now and they overran Rangers 4–1 in extra-time. I recollect being lyrical over McLeish's equalising goal, which he scored ten minutes before half-time with a delicate chip from the edge of the penalty area, and which he probably never again emulated. Although curiously he had scored a similar type of goal in the training camp at Cruden Bay in the days before the final, one which had elicited from one of his colleagues the remark, 'You'll never do that again!' The defender's coolness summarised the condition Aberdeen were in – controlled self-confidence.

That effective balance was not suddenly to evaporate in the European arena, even though history told them a sorry tale. For by the beginning of their most famous season, 1982/83, their record of failing in eleven attempts since 1967 to reach even the quarter-finals of a European competition marred their overall statistical record. Ferguson, though, had been astutely preparing for another assault. Even though he had lost a player of the quality of Steve Archibald, in May 1981 he made one of the most important acquisitions during his time at the club by signing

Peter Weir from St Mirren for a then Scottish record transfer fee of £300,000. That single fact alone reminds us now of the financial status of Aberdeen at that time. It was unprecedented for a club outside the Old Firm to pay such a sum. It also indicated that Ferguson was alive to the potential of certain players to fit into his game plan in the longer term, an instinct that subsequently showed itself even more dramatically in England. Weir knew the kind of man he was joining. 'Fergie actually signed me for St Mirren when I was a lad and playing as an amateur,' he said. 'When I went in to see him with my father to sign on, I asked for a £500 signing-on fee. He offered £100 and wouldn't budge, no matter what we said to him. After I had this checked out with some other clubs, I accepted. But I was young and I never trained under him before he left for the north. I had heard so many stories about him from other people that I kind of braced myself for this [at Aberdeen]. But he was tremendous. He made us winners. He knew how to get the winning mentality into us. He could go crazy at times. We were scared of him, absolutely scared. I'm a man of 47 now, but I remember just how terrified we were when I think back. The whole team was terrified, not just me. But it gave us the will to win. And he made me as a player. I would like to thank others in the game for what they did for me, but it was Fergie who brought out the best in me.'

You can tell when a team is on a roll. I sensed it with Celtic in 1967, with Rangers in 1972, and in the early stages of Aberdeen's European Cup Winners' Cup campaign in 1982/83. Willie Miller had settled contractual grievances with the club, and in the process had turned down a greatly publicised bid by John Greig to bring him to Ibrox. With him as captain again, they disposed of Sion of Switzerland with ease, scoring seven against them in Aberdeen in the first round. A John Hewitt goal was the only one over two legs against Dinamo Tirana in the second round, where they had to play in 95 degrees' heat. Then, in a politically disturbed Poland Doug Bell scored the only goal of the game against Lech Poznan (where the bread riots were taking place) to add to the two they had scored at Pittodrie. They were in the quarter-finals. And drawn against Bayern Munich.

I recall the speculation surrounding that game because we had to wait two months, until March 1983, for the game to be played. Franz Beckenbauer, retired as a player but much in demand as a newspaper and TV pundit, haughtily stated to the *Aberdeen Press & Journal* just before the tie, 'As soon as the Scots step outside their own country they are only half as good as they are at home.' So the Dons' performance in the Olympic Stadium in Munich on 2 March should have worried him. From my distant commentary position that night in a stadium that is often soulless, and from which Bayern in 2005 made their escape to a new home, the players looked to be the size of Subbuteo pieces, but I never felt Ferguson's side were going to succumb. They achieved a no-score draw with an accomplished defensive performance and enough promise in attack to hint at something special in the return leg. Weir in particular had a splendid chance but had to strike the ball with the weaker of his two feet, the right, and missed the opportunity. Something special did occur at Pittodrie. Aberdeen went 2–1 down in that second leg, but I felt I was joining in the hysteria of the crowd towards the end of the game as first Alex McLeish headed home a Strachan free-kick after some deceptive 'dummying' over the ball, like a Tommy Cooper trick, which bamboozled the German defence, and then, only one minute later, Hewitt squeezed the ball through the keeper's legs to take the Dons into the semi-final.

They disposed of Waterschei, the little-known Belgian side, 5–2 on aggregate in that semi-final and for the first time in their history they were in a European final – albeit against Real Madrid, the huge favourites to lift the trophy. I remember the rain in Gothenburg on 11 May 1983. It was mocking the whole ethos of cup final day. It never seemed to relent, although because of the nature of the events that transpired it could have rained albino frogs for all we cared, or indeed noticed. But the grey day, and the fact that Aberdeen had housed themselves in a small village well outside the city and thus we would not see much of them before the game, added to the sense of separation from this major event. It was not until the players turned up and walked on to the pitch of the Ullevi Stadium to test its damp surface that I felt the stirrings of something important about to begin.

I was there on that occasion to report for BBC news in London, and to work with Jeremy Paxman and Jill Dando as a presenter for breakfast television. I was to try to grab Ferguson for an interview as soon as possible after the game, win or lose. As I watched the players walk about in tiny groups, appearing to be cheery and confident, or pretending to be so, I had this sudden sense of foreboding, that my instincts had got this wrong and that for 15,000 Dons supporters in the ground it might all end in a dreadful anti-climax. They had done almost outrageously well already. But Real Madrid? I had watched these white shirts on a gloriously sunny evening at Hampden in 1960 – along with 127,261 others, the biggest-ever attendance at a European final – thrashing Eintracht Frankfurt 7–3 with one of the greatest attacking performances of all time, and I had retained a naïve belief in their invincibility. The very mention of their name seemed to afflict Aberdeen with dwarfism in the eyes of many. But not so for their assistant manager Archie Knox, as Peter Weir recalled. 'I remember Archie coming back from training one day well before the final and suddenly going very strong about our chances. "They are not the team they used to be," he rammed into us. He was so convincing about it as he analysed them for us. He really did instil the belief that we could win.'

Knox, of course, was correct. Real were not a team that had inherited the greatness of the past. This tone of believable self-confidence was reinforced by Ferguson, as Willie Miller noted. 'He was exceptionally calm. Normally he had this nervous cough when the stress was on, particularly before big games. You could hear him approaching before you saw him because of that sharp cough. Sometimes it was so intense you felt he was going to vomit. But curiously, that night, he wasn't like that. He just seemed to be enjoying the whole idea of being there.' John Hewitt, surely outside of Aberdeen one of the most underrated footballers of his age, also noticed the sense of accomplishment the manager was exuding, before a ball was kicked. 'He just told us to enjoy ourselves. We were privileged to have reached the final, so just go out and play your normal game. Forget what they are like, just be normal.'

It is here that I am reminded of the calm, studied and unflurried attitude of Stein in the Lisbon dressing-room in the last few minutes before the European Cup final in 1967. I am convinced that Ferguson drew on that template. He had grown closer to Stein, who was, in fact, an honoured guest of Aberdeen that evening. He had been staying with the team at the hotel, and although Ferguson knew what he was doing tactically, without any help from anyone, the very presence of the man he considered 'the master' and a word or two of advice and encouragement here and there must have been invaluable.

The relaxed atmosphere produced an electrifying performance. Aberdeen were the better side throughout. Real were not the prancing, elegant artists who had so often entranced the eye. They were a chasing side, demented at times by the swift-passing movements of their opponents who were dealing better than them with the gluey surface. Aberdeen went into the lead when Eric Black scored after seven minutes. They looked confident and clearly dominant. But Real equalised after Alex McLeish miscued a back-pass and Leighton's desperate dive and collision with Isidro was judged by the referee to be a foul. Juanito scored from the penalty spot. The game went into extra-time, and with only four minutes left came the goal that is, of course, the most famous in the club's history. It is indelibly etched on the minds of every Aberdeen supporter.

Or is it? My abiding memory of the cross that came from the left wing is that the Spanish goalkeeper looked a certainty to reach the ball before anybody else. But he didn't. From nowhere, John Hewitt, who had come on for the tiring Eric Black and had already been nicknamed 'Supersub', propelled himself in a diving straight line, touching the ball with his head even as it seemed to find the fist of the keeper, and redirecting the ball into the net. Despite the rain, delirium ensued. But who put the ball across? Peter Weir takes up the strange corollary to that great moment. 'I wish I had a pound for every time I have been introduced in public as the man who made the cross for the goal in the final. Even when I've gone recently to presentations at schools it happens. I went to one of those, and a man who ran the schools football stood up and said, "Here's Peter Weir, the man who crossed the ball for the winning goal in Gothenburg," and I am standing there embarrassed. I say nothing. It's simply because nine times out of ten I was on the left wing, swinging balls across for the rest. That was my forte. But it was Mark McGhee, in fact. I was deep in midfield, went past a couple of players and slipped the ball out to the left wing where McGhee was. He sent in a picture of a cross, and that was that.' Not quite. For the goal that won the cup did not escape the technical scrutiny of Ferguson. 'He talked to me after the game,' said Hewitt, 'and explained that I had made the wrong kind of run for the ball. He had always told us to make diagonal runs into the box. If a ball was coming across, like the one Mark put in, I should have moved towards the near post. I had made a beeline over the penalty spot. I had broken one of his commandments. When he told me that after the game, I think he was joking. I think!'

With only a few minutes left I had to leave the stadium and race round the outside to get to the other entrance and on to the pitchside where we had a camera prepared to take interviews. As I ran round, with the rain still coming down, I did not know what was happening inside. I could hear the Aberdeen supporters singing, but I knew it was not over and I feared Real might equalise. Indeed, just before I left my seat they had taken a free-kick which had just slid past the Aberdeen post. It had to be retaken, and they almost scored again. It was as if I was being sent to relieve a besieged fortress. Would I make it in time before the insurgents broke the defences? That fear of anti-climax surfaced again. By the time I had overcome an officious gateman and gained entry I could see Ferguson, tense and attentive, looking at the referee. Then the final whistle went. His entry to the pitch was slightly less demented than his famous run at Easter Road; I recall him slipping in one of the puddles. Then he turned and saw me making my way towards him. He picked up his pace and threw his arms round me, and I lifted him off his feet.

They came back to a city that embraced the players lovingly and enjoyed such celebrations as to destroy the myth of Aberdonian dourness. They were entitled to think they were on the edge of a fruitful era, one that would consolidate this club as a major force for decades to come. During the subsequent depressing years of failure, those memories still warmed the hearts of those people who could not, and cannot, come to terms with the financial harshness of the modern game that has effectively neutered this great club.

My abiding memory of that evening is the bear hug we both enjoyed, not only because of a much less amicable moment to come in our relationship, but also because the elated interview he gave me that night was in stark contrast to the astonishing one he offered ten days later when Aberdeen took on Rangers at Hampden in the Scottish Cup final. An Eric Black goal in the 112th minute of a game that had dragged remorselessly on into extra-time won the cup for Aberdeen, so I expected a buoyant Ferguson. In fact, he recorded one of the interviews you might label as 'unique'. I recall him saying, as the players paraded the cup, 'It was a disgraceful performance!' At first I thought he was talking about Rangers, which would not have surprised me as he would sound off about them at the drop of a hat. But as he proceeded I gradually became aware that he meant no such thing. With increasing incredulity I realised he was talking about the players who had just won him two cups in ten days. He lacerated them, although he went out of his way to exonerate Miller and McLeish, who had, he said, 'won the cup for us, as they played Rangers by themselves'. The *Glasgow Herald* of 23 May recorded him as adding, 'If the Aberdeen players think I am going to accept that standard then I will be looking for new players next season.'

Weir distinctly remembers the ensuing moments in the Aberdeen dressing room. 'We were all celebrating in the dressing room and the champagne was popping. We weren't aware of what he had said on camera. We were all dancing about, and then in he came. He went crazy. He shouted for us all to sit down and then went ballistic, saying things you couldn't repeat now. We couldn't believe it. He put a dampener on the whole evening. We went back to a St Andrews hotel on our return to Aberdeen, supposedly to celebrate, but some of the players left and went back to their families, they were so disappointed in what he had said. He did apologise to us all the day after, but by that time it was too much for some of the players, and I know a few I could name who never ever spoke to him again after that.' It is something he probably now regrets, and he explained afterwards, in mitigation, that he had hardly had a proper night's sleep since the triumph in Gothenburg. I spoke to him again shortly after that Hampden outburst and he was back to his ebullient best, knowing, of course, that he was now one of the most discussed men in British football. I still revelled in the fact that he spoke to me candidly and forthrightly any time we were together.

But my time was to come for an entirely different kind of reckoning. Perhaps I should have known better than to think I would be treated any differently to anybody else who apparently crossed him. For he had become the master of the tirade. You heard many stories about rages which, if you were to believe the tales, could scatter whole herds of cattle in the Cairngorms. For those of statistical bent, we should record here that the first publicly recorded instance of cup-throwing in the Aberdeen dressing room was in a foreign part, namely Pitesti in Romania, to where the Dons had travelled on UEFA Cup business in November 1981 and looked like squandering a three-goal lead. Gordon Strachan, who had shouted back to his manager during the game, 'Away and shut your face!', was the target of the aerial attack. We do not have a note of how many cups sailed through the air, but thankfully Strachan was as elusive in a dressing room as he was on the pitch, and they all missed. It might have been a scene straight out of the Mad Hatter's tea party, but it worked: Aberdeen came through and qualified for the next stage. On one occasion I heard a door being kicked when I was standing just inside the pavilion at Pittodrie, and the sounds coming from the Aberdeen dressing room were akin to a bull having been let loose inside. I also knew he had invaded someone's house once, after Joe Harper was seen to be eating a dish of haggis and neeps – an affront to the manager's dietary rules which caused Ferguson to lift the plate and throw it down the sink in a tantrum. He thought his player was already overweight. But all this came second-hand to me. It would have been better had it stayed that way.

By the mid-1980s BBC Television was more often at Pittodrie than at the two Old Firm clubs put together. At least for some Aberdeen people this dispelled the myth, fondly nurtured in the north-east, that we had an unassailable Glasgow bias. Ferguson was appreciative of this. One day late in April 1984 he phoned and invited me up to Aberdeen to attend the official supporters rally in the Beach Pavilion, just beside the stadium. I had no idea why he had bothered to do so until I was surprised by the chairman of the association who presented me with a large glass bowl for having been at most of the club's triumphs over the past couple of seasons, and for having heaped genuine praise on the team's performances. It was Ferguson who had engineered that for me. During that spell he and his charming wife Cathy had dined with my wife and me several times. On one occasion, after dinner, he stayed until the wee sma' hours talking football to me, and although it is easy enough in retrospect to say so now, I thought it would be difficult for Aberdeen to hold on to him, as he exhibited all the traits of a man who had much bigger ideas in mind. It is risky to get close to a manager as you might be thought to be at their behest; you might also have to offend when the time comes to be critical. But at that stage I was as close to him as I had ever been to anybody in club football. In the autumn of 1983, when it was not yet public knowledge that he had been approached by Rangers to take over from John Greig, he confided that to me in his office at Pittodrie, and added, 'How could I go back and not sign Catholics? What would I tell my friends who are Catholics? "You lot aren't good enough for us!" I just couldn't do that.' In Mexico in 1986, during the World Cup finals (which I will deal with in detail later), he unburdened himself to me from time to time about the problems he was having as an international manager.

But my early-detection radar system should have been in operation a lot sooner, one night in May 1983 at an end-of-season football dinner at the Normandy Hotel near Glasgow Airport. Ferguson had been the life and soul of our group, but when we went into the toilet he suddenly turned to me with a much more grave demeanour and said, 'I've got to get something off my chest. It's been building up in me for a while.' He then quoted me something I had said about Aberdeen's performance in a game much earlier in the season. It was said earnestly, without any great rancour, but his mood had changed, and it stayed like that for the rest of the night. Incidents obviously lay fallow in his mind, even over lengthy periods, until some weird chemical reaction took place and it all came out. Such a bone of contention needed thrashing out more dramatically a few years later.

On 15 October 1986 I travelled to Dublin to commentate on the Republic of Ireland against Scotland match in a European Championship qualifier. It ended 0–0. During the game I made several references to what I perceived to be weaknesses in Jim Leighton's performance in goal. I thought no more of it until I turned up at Easter Road the following Saturday. I walked in about an hour before the game and I could see Ferguson standing with his assistant manager Archie Knox and some others, chatting with some Hibernian officials. When he saw me, he turned, and I expected the normal cheery welcome. Many will recall watching *The Incredible Hulk* on television and in the cinema, how his chest expanded, his clothes were torn asunder and his muscles bulged in concert with a change in personality, from the benign to the monstrous. It was something like that I saw in Ferguson that day. His first words were the gentlest of all, but they were hurled like missiles: 'What the eff do you know about goalkeeping?' At first I was taken aback and wasn't sure what he was on about. A few seconds later, as he poured out his abuse, I knew it was my comments about Leighton which had irked him to the verge of GBH. Knox, who is no blushing violet himself, was quiet witness to the fact that, instead of lying down to this, I attacked myself. It was road-rage brought indoors – although, as he probably perceived it, my Mini against his Rolls. We did not exchange blows, but our saliva crossed paths like tracer bullets as nose to nose we entered that subterranean world where tantrums leave all other senses behind. Had it lasted any longer we would have been drenched in each other's body fluids. But, eventually, from somewhere I became aware of a uniformed arm worming its way between us, and in a gentle but persuasive way I heard a voice saying, 'Gentlemen, I think we should stop this or else I will have to take action.' It was a policeman of superintendent rank, I suppose, judging by his uniform. And by the look on his face, he was deadly serious. I walked through the vestibule, along the tunnel and out on to the edge of the pitch. I was shaken, as anybody would have been, not simply by the act itself but by the sudden change from what I thought was a genuine friendship into hysterical animosity. It was the end of the affair.

So he was well equipped to leave Aberdeen and head for United the following month. He was now a Machiavelli inside a Sherman tank. Such a man was certain to survive in that English jungle, where he was bound to run into greater flak than he ever had north of the border. He would roll over his nearest and dearest if that was what was needed in pursuit of whatever his ideals were. That armour-plating has been his biggest asset of all. Scottish football owes him an enormous debt for the realignment of power that took place in the 1980s, at a time when it seemed the Old Firm mould could not be broken. Under Ferguson, who as a player had won nothing in his career, Aberdeen became the first team other than Rangers to win the Scottish Cup three years in succession, 1982–84. They also won the Premier Division in two consecutive years, 1984 and 1985 (to add to the 1980 breakthrough), and the Scottish League Cup in 1985. Of the 25 trophies contested during his tenure at Pittodrie, Aberdeen won eight, Celtic and Rangers seven each and Dundee United three. He brought back to Scotland the Cup Winners' Cup and, uniquely, the Super Cup. And during that time his influence spread to the international sphere with 12 of his men pulling on the Scotland jersey.

He had enacted the dream of achieving what at first seems impossible, but he was not alone in bearding the Old Firm lion in its den. By the mid-1980s there was an even more incredible story to be told, about a man who looked at times as if only a local anaesthetic applied to the cheeks would induce a smile. Ferguson always referred to him, almost affectionately, as 'Wee Jim'.

CHAPTER FOURTEEN
THE CORNER SHOP

He raised the cup to his lips, paused for a moment as he finessed a look at the television camera, then said, 'Close your eyes, mother!' before bending his lips guiltily towards the champagne and taking a sip so tiny it would not have made a ladybird tipsy. If Jock Stein was Scotland's king of teetotallers, Jim McLean, manager of Dundee United, was its prince regent. He was not one predisposed to sipping champagne from ladies' slippers, but one who preferred a slug of Barrs Irn Bru out of a plastic cup. Indeed, as McLean said himself, 'Jock and I used to sit down with a cup of tea and a digestive biscuit when we were together with the Scottish team. That was the strongest we ever took at night.'

Two tea-jennies sipping Earl Grey together is such a twee image that it collides with the reality of their being two of the most ruthless operators ever to put the fear of death into footballers. In 2005, McLean made an admission to me that would sound strange to anyone who regarded him as fearsome at the height of his career. 'To be honest,' he said, 'I was dead scared of Jock. I really was frightened I would say something that would offend him at any time.' Some of McLean's players would find it hard to believe he was scared of anything, but there is no doubt that he felt in awe of Stein at times, perhaps too much. On the other hand, Stein regarded McLean firstly as an irritant as a managerial opponent, and then with great respect for his achievements and tactical know-how. It was that tiny sip, one afternoon, that reminded me that they had more than abstinence in common.

The cup he had taken his minimalist sip from was not plastic but of the best silver, and large enough to hold a jeroboam of the stuff. It was the Scottish League Championship trophy of 1982/83. This was not a private occasion, of course. He was sipping in front of the millions who were watching on the box, on *Grandstand*, as he and his team were being enthroned as the best in the land. For on that spring day in 1983, playing away from home but only yards from his own ground at the other end of

Tannadice Street, Dundee United became league champions for the first time in their history. Not only had McLean broken the habit of a lifetime by touching the dreaded alcohol, so had the club itself by usurping Scottish football's law of natural selection, which decreed that Dundee United could never rise above dowdy provincialism.

As I dared him to drink from the cup on that showery spring day, he had initially given me a quick stare which suggested he might tell me where to stick the cup, in one of those characteristic outbursts that stemmed from his deep-rooted suspicion of anybody in the media. But it was live television, and despite his almost conscious effort not to allow himself to be seen enjoying life, there really was little option for him but to throw off the Ebenezer Scrooge image and join the revelry. But with caution. There was to be no sudden transformation into the playboy of the western world. The players actually hoisted him on to their shoulders with the trophy so that he could be seen as the master of all he surveyed. He contrived to look both satisfied and uncomfortable, all in one.

It is integral to the Dundee United story, as it unfolded, that some of those same players had to acknowledge their indebtedness to the manager in this way, with their teeth clenched. For you cannot study the impact this historically unfashionable club made during its rise to the top without also examining the complexity of the McLean personality. There are those who would have had him keel-hauled under Captain Scott's ship the *Discovery*, which is berthed on the River Tay in the city, for conduct that shocked and scared them to their core. To them, this phase of Scottish football could have been entitled 'Fear and Loathing in Dundee', given the animosity ranged against McLean, instead of his own self-deprecating characterisation of the period as a fight between 'The Corner Shop' and the supermarket giants. The fact that I chose McLean's words as a more than adequate tag for this era makes it clear I am fascinated as to how the strengths and flaws of his personality culminated in the end-product for the club – unimaginable success. The former Southampton manager and TV pundit Lawrie McMenemy, talking to me years after McLean had removed himself from the dug-out to the boardroom, used a comparison with Brian Clough to explain how he rated McLean: 'Nottingham Forest and Dundee United were one-manager clubs. When Clough and McLean went their different ways the two clubs lost their special power. It was the strong personalities of these men which made the clubs. And they will never be the same again without them.' He was proved right.

If McLean had a common bond with anybody as he and his players started to command attention, it was with Alex Ferguson. In fact, according to McLean, Ferguson had skipped part of his honeymoon to share a room with him at the Inverclyde Sports Centre when they were both doing their coaching courses. They might have been rivals, but they needed each other. Life was not always deadly serious, though. Ferguson particularly liked to pull fast ones on McLean. He heard at one stage that the United manager was looking for a new scout for the Glasgow area, so he phoned McLean to tell him he had found one and gave him the man's telephone number and name. When McLean made the call and asked to speak to a Mr Lyon, he discovered he was phoning Calderpark Zoo, and then realised it was 1 April. But they were certainly joined at the hip in believing the world was 'agin' them. Like Stein during his initial phase at Celtic Park, they perceived their jobs to be more than just preparing men for a match, and placed emphasis on the bias they faced, especially from what they believed were the despots in the press who would like to see them crushed underfoot.

Indeed, the first time I encountered McLean his assertiveness almost took the breath away, being so unexpected. It happened in the corridor outside the Dundee United dressing-room at Ibrox in April 1973. I knocked politely on the door and asked if I could have his team selection for the day, as we had to do in those days. He opened it himself; perhaps nobody had dared move to do so ahead of him. The small but sturdy man who appeared in front of me gave me short shrift. 'If you can give me Jock Wallace's selection, I'll give you mine. Not until then. If I give you mine all you'll do is go and tell them our team. And anyway, I heard what you said about us on the box the other night. I thought it was rubbish.' Bang. Door shut again. Oh yes, I remember it well. 'Who is this cheeky upstart?' I recall thinking. But I had to admit he had left his mark. I would not forget him. He was the first manager since Stein to deal with me as if I was an intruder, and it was clear he was going to kow-tow to no one. He and Ferguson were setting out their stalls as men obsessed by their own belief that despite the obvious handicaps that had weighed down Aberdeen and Dundee United in the past they could overcome them by dint of shrewd management, sheer hard work and terrorising. Indeed, during McLean's first full pre-season training regime in the summer of 1972, Walter Smith, then a United player and now Scotland's national manager, wanted to present his new boss with a bill for the clothes he had been forced to alter, because he had lost a full stone in weight. From first to last, despite the justified praise for tactical know-how, McLean, as his players will testify, based his philosophy on absolute fitness. If you lagged, you suffered. To watch United at their best was to watch a side that simply never stopped running.

He had not applied for the vacant United post when it became available on the resignation of Jerry Kerr in November 1971. At the time he was assistant coach at the club down the street from Tannadice, Dundee FC. He had to be asked, and he accepted on 3 December that year. So he had a considerable head start on Ferguson in trying to establish his personal credentials and achieving credibility for the club. But he had a more difficult task. Aberdeen's solid fan base looked good on paper, and their average attendances were healthy and solid before and after the renovation of Pittodrie (in 1980 it became the first fully seated stadium in the UK). Even though I very often felt that in the stadium the supporters made as much sound as the cod being landed at the nearby harbour and were too often obliterated by the noise emanating from the smaller number of visitors, they were nevertheless substantial and loyal. Dundee United did not enjoy that foundation. Within the city of Dundee itself they had always been considered the lesser of the two clubs, with a much smaller support base. So McLean was starting with the task of convincing the city itself that the club could prosper.

Even more problematical for him was the easily expressed scepticism beyond the city boundaries. Tom Hart, Hibernian's gruff chairman, told me in 1973 that when clubs were contemplating league reconstruction the one club they did not want in the elite league was Dundee United, and that view was shared throughout the land. Their attendances were appallingly low, barely rising above 4,000. But in the mad dash of season 1974/75 to finish in the top ten to qualify for the new Premier Division, one man on the field was giving them a battling chance. His name, Andy Gray. As he caught the eye with courageous performances, verging on the reckless at times, shirking nothing that came his way (and sustaining long-term injuries as a result), it became clear he was a striker born in heaven. He was joint top scorer, with Willie Pettigrew of Motherwell, that last year of the old league with 20 goals. Yet even his performances could not rouse the majority of the city. Seven days before United went off to play the 1974 Scottish Cup final against Celtic, the club's first final since 1940, they attracted only 3,800 at home. In the previous game, against Partick Thistle, it had been 2,700. McLean was in deep despair about that. Dundee's *Sporting Post* had warned as early as 1973, after Gray scored four goals in a 6–0 win over Dumbarton watched by only 3,500, 'What a tragedy it would be for United if such attendances force them to sell Andy Gray.' In September 1975, Andy Gray was sold to Villa. The fee was said to be about £110,000. Five years later Gray was sold on to Wolves for £1,469,000. He had been 'stolen' by the English in a way which amplified the feeling that Dundee United were indeed, despite their Premier Division status, small fry. And there is little doubt that nobody outside their own community would have batted an eyelid had United simply disappeared into the fold of Forfarshire junior football.

But one UEFA Cup final, a European Cup semi-final and three European quarter-finals later, McLean and United could justifiably claim to represent one of the most astonishing transformations in European football history. Sometimes, even yet, you feel it defies logical explanation, and in many ways it has become obscured by other events and the passing of time, particularly as United slid into serious decline.

It was an evening in 1979 that had brought them much more serious appreciation, though they had in fact been sending out warnings before that. In November 1978, ten days after a Lion Rampant had been hoisted over Tannadice in celebration of Dave Narey becoming the first United player to be capped in the club's 69-year history, they played Rangers and recorded only their second win over them in nine years with a 3–0 victory, their first goals scored against that club at home in seven attempts in the new Premier Division. It was the nature of the win I recall. It was as near to a rout as you could get against the Old Firm. The *Sporting Post* commented, '15,247 saw a game that Tannadice fans will retell to their grandchildren.' Narey himself scored with a penalty. There were the stirrings of something special happening, although it was still difficult to appreciate. When on 28 April 1979 they lost 2–1 at Celtic Park, McLean's admission that 'we just aren't good enough, yet, to win the league' was like throwing in the towel, but the word 'yet' suggested he had attached a coda saying that there was more to come. This candour, allied to the facts that he had retained only one player (the goalkeeper

Hamish McAlpine) from the side he inherited from the previous manager, that five of the team were under 21, and that the three players he had bought (Hegarty, Fleming and Phillip) had cost only £65,000 in total, might in themselves have epitomised how this club would achieve success against brutal odds. It was eventually accomplished through enforced frugality, the almost ruthless development and retention of young players, and a manager who believed in shock-and-awe tactics.

How many of the journalists and supporters who travelled to the Olympic Stadium in Rome on 25 April 1984 to watch this club's efforts to gain a place in the European Cup final itself could have recalled the day a mere eight years earlier, during the first season of the Premier Division, when a parochial Domesday scenario was being written within the city of Dundee as one of its two clubs faced relegation? United had to travel to Ibrox on 4 May 1976. If they gained a draw they would be saved and their neighbours Dundee would go down. McLean himself, fanatically superstitious, recalled one of the most harrowing moments in his life. 'It was horrendous. A good friend of mine was sitting beside me in the dug-out but he didn't appear for the second half when the score was still nothing each. I gave instructions to get him back, and drag him if necessary, for I am very superstitious and I needed to have everybody sitting in exactly the same seat throughout the game. We got him back, but he spent the rest of the second half looking at his shoes. He couldn't bear it. Then we got a penalty. It was taken by Hamish McAlpine, our goalkeeper. He was taking them all at that time. We had a drill then that two of the least-booked players in the team would run in on the keeper from different angles and pressurise him just in case Hamish missed any time and had to run back up the field to get into goal again. And you know, he hit the post with this one. That made it worse. But he made a mad dash back and we held out for the draw. It would have been disastrous for us to be relegated. It was a terrible experience. But we became all the stronger for it. For the next season we won our first five games in a row, beat everybody and were top of the league. And although we just survived at Ibrox, we ended up in fourth place at the end of next season. And from then on we were never less than fifth in the Premier [Division], and in 18 years out of the 22 that I was manager, we qualified for Europe.'

Rome eight years after that scramble, in a European Cup semi-final in front of 80,000? To have predicted such a thing that day at Ibrox would have made you eligible for sickness benefit under the Mental Health Act. But the progress was steady. On 8 December 1979, Hampden Park housed a miserably low crowd of 27,173 for the Scottish League Cup final between Aberdeen and Dundee United. The incessant rain, the standard of play and the non-Old Firm nature of the tie constituted a drab afternoon that left you with a sinking heart at the prospect of having to face up to it again, after a goalless draw. It was a game Aberdeen ought to have won on pressure alone. At Dens Park the following Wednesday, history was made. Ferguson named the same players, McLean tinkered with his side. But the emphasis was on the positive nature of United's play: they threw off the shackles of the underdogs to become a set of players who had miraculously grown up inside a few days. They riddled Aberdeen with swift attacks and blunted their efforts to score with composed defending. This was a side maturing towards potent self-belief. Willie Pettigrew scored the first two goals, and Paul Sturrock, after a 40-yard run and a deflection off Willie Miller's legs which sent Bobby Clark in goal to the wrong corner, made the final score 3–0. It was the first trophy in the club's 70-year history. There was something in keeping with the sobriety the manager demonstrated himself in that walk back down to their own ground with the cup. They assembled in the boardroom for a celebration of sorts, but it was low-key and disciplined, so ill-versed were they in the ritual of success.

It was to become a habit, though. A year later they reached the final of the same competition. Although the odds against it happening were incredible, it was to be contested by the two Dundee clubs. As ground reconstruction was taking place at Dens Park, the venue chosen wisely for this special occasion, the crowd was limited to 24,700 when in fact double that figure wanted to attend. Several days before that game I travelled to interview both managers, McLean and Tommy Gemmell, and to film some of the training. The contrast could not have been greater. McLean was central to a session concentrating on sprints, exhorting his players as if he was watching a favourite horse coming up the home stretch. It was an extraordinary display of commitment on a wet, miserable day which called for some special devotion to the sport, even to venture outside. Gemmell, on the other hand, was presiding over a carefree five-a-side session in the indoor gym. It would perhaps be unfair to compare one session with the other, but it was the atmosphere at each ground that I found so distinct: McLean obsessive, fretting; Gemmell laid-back, as friendly as ever. I sensed a clear winner even before a ball had been kicked. On 6 December 1980, on a ground that had just been cleared of snow but which retained inches of frost, United proved me right by overwhelming their hosts Dundee. The second trophy in their history had been added to their cabinet by a score, again, of 3–0.

McLean had now been with the club for the best part of a decade, and gradually he was seeing the benefit of what he considered to be the core value of his management style, namely the development and retention of young players and the incentives he established to make the entire range of his players perform to his satisfaction. It was this that was setting him apart from others in football. Young lads could be on long-term contracts of up to eight years, if option clauses in contracts were utilised. As always in contractual matters with clubs, there was another side to this coin. Some players who were middle-ranking in the club and not regarded as one of the established first-team players wanted to be released from what, after several years there, seemed more like a sentence than a contract. Thus, on the back of that came the depiction of McLean as captain of a press-ganged crew, not a football club. One player, Alex Taylor, simply refused to carry on, and his father went all the way to Tannadice to have a violent confrontation with McLean about this, thus gaining the manager and the club publicity they could have done without.

McLean remains utterly unrepentant about following a course he felt was the only one for such a club. 'There is no doubt at all I was ruthless about keeping players,' he admitted. 'The club paid me to bring them success, and that's what I was after in retaining and developing young players. And that was to our benefit. That was my first and only task in life – to get them, if I could, to the top. The first way for us to compete with the bigger and richer clubs was in rearing our own talent and holding on to them as long as we could. When I first came to the club there was no youth policy. There were only two S forms [young school kids] on the books. I then spent all my Sundays going round the public parks in the area just looking at players and trying to pick youngsters who we could make into players. Then, when we got them in, we knew we would have to develop them properly. That meant we had to retain them as long as we could. We looked after them and coached them, made sure they had the right diet and training, and kept them to a good lifestyle as far as we could manage. It was only ever our intention to do well by them. I spent hours on the pitch with Andy Gray, crossing bad balls to him. It was no use plying him with good balls for he scored too easily. It was the bad balls that helped him. His right side was not nearly as strong as his left side. We helped him develop that.' Andy Gray is certainly not one to contradict that. 'I had two years with Jim,' he said, 'and I could not have had a better coach. I used to think he was bullying me. He used to bring me back for training in the afternoon, on my own. "Why me? The swine!" I used to think. But it's only afterwards you realise he was making you a better player.'

Then there were the bonuses. McLean's brother, Tommy, playing for Rangers around the time of McLean's first successes, was earning roughly £600 a week. But the bonus at Ibrox was only £28. At United, according to McLean, there was a basic of £300 but a bonus of up to £300 on top of that for a win. But you had to be playing, and you had to be winning. It was a great incentive for the players, and over the years it worked handsomely. But for those who were not playing regularly and not gaining the bonuses it caused tensions, leading to the desire of some to break free from their contracts. Still, although the players themselves would admit they were trained to a superb level of fitness, reflected in their avoidance of serious injury – astonishingly, McLean used a hard core of only 12 players throughout the title-winning 1982/83 season – you have to feel that the bonus system was just as beneficial to the health of the squad as a Mediterranean diet or daily press-ups.

That squad, with all these different McLean layers of authority placed upon them, certainly played that championship season with an exhilaration that lent no impression of oppressive authority. Quite the reverse, in fact. They were fine players after all. McAlpine in goal and a defensive set-up in front of him which almost invariably featured Richard Gough, Dave Narey, Paul Hegarty and Maurice Malpas (all of them internationals) evokes memories of a disciplined, athletic barrier. Players such as Davie Dodds, Derek Stark, Billy Kirkwood and John Holt always made you think they were pure McLean inventions who would probably not have made it elsewhere, so integral were they to the overall structure without being outstandingly brilliant. Then there was the searing pace of Paul Sturrock, Eamonn Bannon and Ralph Milne up front, which made United renowned for their counter-attacking. They really were inferior to nobody, although they had to fight all the way for their title.

As if to underline these important elements in his side, McLean himself pointed to the game which he felt tilted the championship their way. It was on 20 April 1983 at Celtic Park, two weeks after United had lost there 2–0 in a league clash. 'I think Billy McNeill definitely made a mistake that day in being so attack-minded,' he said. 'We went one up through Paul Hegarty, then Charlie Nicholas equalised, and in the second half we went down to ten men when Richard Gough was sent off. But Celtic just kept coming at us, attacking, and that left them exposed to the pace we had with Milne, Bannon and Sturrock. It was right up our street. We ended up winning 3–2, and we felt that if we just kept winning every game from then on we could win the league. The players believed they could, and they did go on and win every single game.' Billy McNeill, it has to be said, left Celtic a couple of months later, for in the three-horse race between his own club, United and Aberdeen, the Parkhead men had faltered in a terminal way for his management during the closest race in the history of Premier Division football up to that year.

On 14 May United needed a win at Dens Park against their city rivals to clinch the league title for the first time in their history, whatever Celtic did in their last game at Ibrox against Rangers or whatever Aberdeen would achieve at home against Hibernian. Nagging at them was the thought that if they drew 0–0 and Celtic won 2–0 in Glasgow, the two clubs with identical records would have to play off for the title. Surprisingly, by modern standards of crowd control, it was not an all-ticket game. The official attendance was 29,106, although unofficially it was nearer 30,000, as some locals feel entry was made in mysterious ways. On a rain-sodden pitch which referee George Smith had requested to be forked in places to aid drainage, all the elements fell into place at the right time for United. In the fourth minute Ralph Milne chipped a delicate first goal when he saw the Dundee keeper Colin Kelly off his line; this was followed seven minutes later by a Bannon penalty-kick, which rebounded back to him off Kelly for him to net and put what seemed like the seal on the game. But then, midway through the first half, a sudden tension developed when Iain Ferguson scored in a breakaway for Dundee. McLean, fairly low-key until that moment, then began his customary dug-out stridency, shouting his way through the rest of a match whose outcome, despite the narrowness of the ultimate score (2–1), was never really in doubt. They were now the champions.

Not that the press outside Dundee then took the club to its heart, because they still had to contend with a manager who simply felt, by his own admission, that dealing with the media was something of a necessary evil. So he did not go out of his way to cultivate relationships or to court popularity as some other managers did. Sometimes McLean would come to the interview spot or into the press room almost spoiling for a verbal fight, so aggressive did he seem at times. He trusted few in the media. An obscene comment was once scrawled on one of his suitcases during a foreign trip, and he blamed one of the press corps for it and banned him from Tannadice. But it was a jape by Ferguson again. Even though the Aberdeen manager owned up to it when he heard about the journalist's ban, McLean did not lift it. He felt he had to be forthright to compensate for what he felt were his own vulnerabilities. 'Everybody felt I was a supremely confident man,' he said. 'I wasn't. Of course, I expressed strong views from time to time when I was asked for my opinion, but in fact I was very insecure. I know that sounds strange given my reputation. But I honestly never felt confident in other people's company.' Indeed, by that stage he was now so accustomed to having his dour expression commented upon that he adopted it, very wittily at times, as his trademark.

But there were other factors, of course, which helped the club remain the focus of attention outside the Old Firm, and which along with Aberdeen had them renamed as the New Firm. I never thought we were into a permanent switch of power in Scottish football, nor did either Ferguson or McLean. It was in Europe that I think I appreciated United more than anything else. They simply were a delight to watch, either through the tactical variations they employed or the sheer audacity of their goals. Paul Sturrock recognised McLean at his best on those occasions. 'He was a tactical genius,' he said. 'He could tinker with positions during a game, switch us or make substitutions which altered the course of the match. He had always done his homework, of course, but it was the improvisations he came up with which we came to utterly trust and respect, and which made all the difference. He changed my game from being a running striker to a linking striker and made me a better player. And the things he was doing then were well ahead of their time. Everybody thought we normally played 4–4–2. But in fact it wasn't quite like that. Most people talk in the Premiership [where Sturrock was working at the time] about playing 4–5–1. Well, McLean was using that system with us all that time ago. I was the fulcrum at the top of it, and we had so many late runners coming from midfield that many teams couldn't handle us.'

One such unstoppable evening came on 3 November 1981 when, having lost 2–0 in the UEFA Cup away to Borussia Mönchengladbach in October, they trounced the Germans in the Tannadice return 5–0. This included a run from the halfway line by Bannon, who left four Germans in his wake before slipping the ball into the net. The calibre of the team performance and the signature contributions by individuals made us aware that they could go far that year. Of that match McLean recently told me, 'That was the game that made all the difference to us in Europe. After that we had great self-belief. Up to that time we were a small club making up the numbers. Maybe it was my fault in allowing that thought to arise. From that game onwards we really believed we could be in the latter stages of all the European competitions.'

After having beaten Radnicki Nis 2–0 in the home leg of the quarter-final, they looked certainties for the semi-final. On 17 March 1982 we all travelled into the hill city that would be bombed to shreds in the 1990s during the Balkans War, and saw there such flagrantly biased refereeing that you had to see it to believe it. The night before the game, in a rather dull, spartan hotel where the menu was the size of the Magna Carta but which in fact had nothing on it available to eat, we had seen a man with directors of the home club being wined and dined with great flourishes and with sustenance they could not muster for us. They apparently had a special reserve of food for special people. He was the referee, who lived only 25 miles away across the border in Bulgaria. It showed, sadly, throughout the game. In the first couple of minutes, Paul Sturrock, right in front of us (with the referee almost at his side), was blatantly kicked. The referee's blind eye on that occasion set the tone for allowing Radnicki every advantage. United lost 3–0 and were out.

But if they thought that was bad, it was but an innocuous aperitif compared to the 1983/84 season when they played magnificently to reach the semi-final of the European Cup and were drawn against AS Roma. 'That was the worst experience in my life,' McLean admitted. 'We beat them 2–0 at Tannadice and we really hassled them out of their usual rhythm and won deservedly. The Italians had claimed that we must have been on drugs the way our players performed. I honestly thought they were joking. So when I heard that, I just made a quip, saying that whatever drugs my players were on I hoped they would be on them on Saturday again. Well, the Italian press picked that up and they slaughtered me for treating this lightly. All I was doing was making a joke. The return leg was the worst atmosphere of any football match I have ever attended, and that includes any Rangers and Celtic game.'

I can vouch for that. On 25 April 1984, even though I was sitting high above the Olympic Stadium in the commentary position, I could sense the seething hatred emanating from the packed terracings. We had already seen various missiles being thrown at the United bus as it arrived for the game. It had been claimed by the Italians that McLean had been shouting 'Italian bastards!' at them from the dug-out at Tannadice, so the welcome he personally received fell only a few security guards short of a lynch mob. It is true that the president of Roma, Giuseppe Viola, had retracted his ridiculous accusations of drug-taking by telexing UEFA just before the game. But what McLean did not know at the time – he still had no inkling of it until I brought it to his attention years later – was that an attempt had been made in the background to nobble the referee, the experienced Michel Vautrot of France. Viola had been approached by two people who claimed they could 'fix' the referee. It is said that 100 million lire (about £50,000 at the time) passed hands as Viola agreed to the attempt. But Vautrot was entirely incorruptible, and the two conspirators, knowing this, never approached him, although the president thought they had. The two pocketed the money and headed for the good life, just as United walked out to face a Roman crowd who had lost nothing of the vitriol and lust for blood which Nero had bequeathed them.

The day before the game I attended a press conference held by McLean. He was brutally frank in admitting that 'The Corner Shop' was in many ways out of its place in such a situation, that the size of the club should have determined a less distinguished ranking, and that by rights they really should not be only one game away from the European Cup final. You could hardly disagree with him. He was being almost disarmingly honest. What they had achieved was nothing short of miraculous. But his attitude was downbeat, too much so in my opinion. There was just a hint of defeatism in it, although that was not what he intended.

Whatever their mood on the day, they fell flat. But they had a glimpse of almost delirious possibilities, which also passed through McLean's mind as a potential for real trouble. 'Ralph Milne missed a sitter early in the game,' he recalled. 'If he had scored, and I had hoped he would, then I doubt if I would have got out of that stadium alive.' Milne shot weakly over the bar from close in after a cut-back from Bannon. He had frozen. The Italians then netted two in the first half through Roberto Pruzzo to bring the aggregate score level, but had Milne done better with his chance, Roma would have had to net four to progress to the final. It perhaps ranks as one of the most expensive misses by any Scottish club in Europe. What McLean had feared about his own safety almost came to pass since he was attacked by four Roma players as he made his way to the stand after the 3–0 defeat. He was saved by his two coaches, Walter Smith and John Gardiner, who had to fend off his assailants. McLean never doubted the probity of Vautrot and insisted the defeat was because all the players had fallen short of form, with the exception of the youngest in the side, Maurice Malpas. Meanwhile, Giuseppe Viola was enjoying what he thought had been his significant part in United's downfall, though the bribe money, unknown to him, was at that time being spent lavishly in the best hotels by two crooks.

It was not until three years later that all that experience helped United reach the final of the UEFA Cup. This was to be the ultimate vindication of the management style of McLean and the dedication of his players. They had beaten the Terry Venables-managed Barcelona twice, 1–0 at Tannadice on 4 March 1987 and 2–1 in the Camp Nou two weeks later. I will long remember being vastly excited by the sheer audacity of that second victory, and then walking down the stairs from the high commentary position to encounter the entire United board standing expressionless on a landing, almost as if they were waiting for a cue from the manager as to how to react. He was there, phlegmatic and constrained, simply being himself. On the journey back to the hotel on the team bus the English journalists with us remarked afterwards how astonished they were at the low-key mood of the party. They simply did not understand the McLean ethos. Hootenannies were not in their psyche. But as McLean recently said to me, 'I just wish I had let my hair down and enjoyed some of these victories with the players.'

Onwards they went, dourly off the field and brilliantly on it, into the final, but with the strength ebbing from them. In those final two games with IFK Gothenburg in May, the factor that beat them more than anything else was the number of games they had had to play throughout the season – some 70 matches. They lost 1–0 in Gothenburg in the first leg and then had to play a Scottish Cup final against St Mirren on the Saturday before the second leg. They were on their knees, as McLean admitted. 'This was without doubt the worst Scottish Cup final ever,' he said. 'We were awful. Even Eamonn Bannon, in the 69th game of the season, was absolutely knackered, and he was one who was always up front and eager to get on. But, like the rest of the players, he was struggling. We lost 1–0 after extra-time and I knew we would be up against it on the Wednesday against the Swedes at Tannadice.'

They were. Lennart Nilsson scored for Gothenburg midway through the first half on the evening of 20 May, and although the mighty frame of John Clark popped up to score an equaliser on the hour with a fierce drive, that was all they could give. They had run out of steam. Before the second leg UEFA had delivered the trophy to the United boardroom for safe keeping for the eventual winners. True to his superstitious nature, McLean had refused to touch the cup throughout the whole week before the match. 'I now wish I had had my photograph taken with it, because it was the nearest I ever got to it,' he admitted to me years later with a laugh. They were proud of their achievements, but perhaps then he must have realised that this was a turning point and that things would never be the same again. The best was past. Many years later, when he was asked in a Grampian television interview if United could ever repeat that feat of getting to a European final, he offered an abrupt and emphatic 'No!' The answer was as uncompromising as he has always been.

He does admit, though, as we have seen, to being superstitious, which some of his players felt was a fatal weakness when considering the five separate occasions when he took his players off to contest a Scottish Cup final and insisted on taking a different route and stopping off at a different hotel each time so that the bad luck of the previous final would not apply. It did not work, for they lost each time. Thus the feeling arose that he was either jinxed at Hampden or that he was simply too defeatist in his approach. However, if you study the games United played there – and I commentated on all of them – they suffered severe bad luck at times. In 1981 I recall Willie Pettigrew missing one of the easiest chances of the season in the extra-time final when it was 0–0. That would have won the cup. In the League Cup final of that year against Rangers Paul Sturrock scored with a stunning 20-yard drive in the second half which would have put them 2–0 up. It was disallowed because Holt was judged to be offside when he was certainly not influencing play, and they lost again to Rangers. In the 1985 Scottish Cup final against Celtic they were outstanding, and were leading 1–0 until Celtic's Davie Provan took a free-kick 13 minutes from the end of the game. As he prepared himself to take the kick, these were my exact words: 'Only twice in the history of the Scottish Cup have goals been scored from a free-kick in a final. Is this a bit of history? . . . It is! Davie Provan – the equaliser! Thirty-two minutes of the second half gone and only the third direct free-kick scored in the history of this competition!' After that Frank McGarvey stuck his head improbably into a shot-cum-cross six minutes from time and United had lost the cup. In my view, in terms of percentage of play and scoring opportunities, they ought also to have won the finals they played against St Mirren in 1987 and Motherwell in 1991. Such sequences of defeat might lend validity to a theory that they were jinxed at Hampden, but only in their first final, against Celtic in 1974, did I see a 'defeatist' United. They simply were not good enough then.

Whatever statistics you might use to sum up this man and his contribution to Scottish football, you cannot separate the McLean personality from the United record book. It would not have existed at all without him. But was it so necessary to present a hostile face to the world, to enrage players, to hound journalists he disapproved of, to give the impression of a man chewing himself up needlessly, so often, in the aftermath of games, and to have such an obsession with the task he set himself that it is entirely probable it contributed to his heart problems, which eventually required surgery? Again he is uncompromising. 'I certainly could not have done it any other way,' he said. 'I had to give my whole being to getting success. I'm proud of the fact that if I didn't like something I said it clearly and loudly. Do you know that if we lost on a Saturday, Doris, my wife, wouldn't be able to talk to me until the Monday? Even sometimes when we won, she still couldn't talk to me. Of course, I regret many things. I regret having missed the bringing up of my kids, especially my older boy. I was too often a stranger to him. Alex Ferguson once said to me, "How can you bring up kids and be a football manager?" I remember saying, "We don't bring up kids, the wives do it," and it hit me 100 per cent then what I was missing.'

Certainly none of his players could visualise him pushing a pram.

They experienced the full extent of his commitment to their success, and the venom sometimes spat at them. None of them doubted his abilities, though, and they see his rages in better perspective now. For they contributed to a bonding from which United benefited enormously, as Maurice Malpas pointed out. 'We linked up against him in a way. We wanted to protect each other, and the only way we could be shielded from his anger was to go out and play for each other and win. He might even have known that that was a good psychological ploy for him. It certainly worked.'

Some players, however, did make their views known. Hamish McAlpine, the goalkeeper, was fined frequently for stepping out of line. His most significant clash came on 5 January 1980 at Celtic Park. Ten minutes before the interval he challenged Roy Aitken for a ball in the penalty area and the referee awarded a penalty for Celtic. 'I went in at half-time and Jim went for me,' McAlpine recalled. 'He virtually accused me of throwing the game. That was enough for me. I took off my boots and my strip, told him he could take over if he wanted and that I wasn't going back out till he apologised, and then I jumped into the bath and just lay there. The other players kept shouting at me to come back out. I told them I would come back out when he apologised. It kept going on right through half-time until the referee knocked on the door to tell us to come back out. I just lay there. He knocked about four times and I was still lying there, telling all and sundry I wasn't coming out until he apologised. Then some of the players came in and grabbed me and started to shove on my gear while I struggled with them. Eventually I gave up and ran out on to Celtic Park soaking wet and without the apology I knew I would never get anyway. But I had made my point. Now I have a laugh and a chat with him over these times whenever I meet him.'

Years after this incident Hazel Irvine of the BBC fronted a fly-on-the-wall documentary on McLean during which he came over as refreshingly frank about his life and managerial style. There is a moment when he is seen in action in his office shouting instructions, by remote control, to his coaches about the game. Eamonn Bannon was the subject of one of those calls. 'I had been ill before this game but he had persuaded me to play,' Bannon recalled. 'I was playing badly because of that. I had no strength. But during the documentary he was heard shouting to the dug-out, several times, "Get Bannon aff! Get Bannon aff!" When it was eventually shown on the box I had the embarrassing experience of hearing people shout at me in the street for weeks after that, "Get Bannon aff!" I had become suddenly notorious for Wee Jim wanting me off a football pitch. And that was a game I had gone out of my way to play through illness. It was the only time he came to me and apologised about anything.'

McLean was drugged by the game. Had he not been, he would have won more friends, but fewer trophies. When he was recovering from his heart operation, Ferguson phoned him and simply said, 'There is no bloody way they could ever have found a heart in you!' It was a jest. Others might not have seen the funny side of that. That is the equation which puts him amongst the most remarkable phenomena in football management, and why one day in 1983 he and Jock Stein were sitting in a car in the Hampden car-park. McLean was stopping off for advice on his way to Ibrox to be interviewed for the Rangers job. It was a crucial, career-defining moment which McLean talks about even now almost like a political historian referring to the Tony Blair and Gordon Brown meeting at the Granita restaurant in Islington. 'Jock said to me, "Who won the league last season?" I replied, "We did." "Will you win it next year?" he asked. "I don't think we'll win the league," I said, "but I think we've a good chance of winning a cup." "Then you are a failure," he said. He was desperate for me to take the Rangers job. Absolutely desperate. For my sake, not for Rangers' sake. Stein was God to me.'

Stein always claimed to me that McLean, when he left his car that day, had decided to become the new Rangers manager, but McLean disputes that. He still had to make up his mind, he told me. When he got to Ibrox he put it bluntly to the board that he needed to be able to sign anybody he liked, and that, of course, included any Catholic players. As he said, 'Not a single Rangers director objected to that.' The job was his for the taking. But he spurned it and returned to Dundee, and now it bothers him. 'I deeply regret I did not accept that at the time,' he said.

Perhaps part of the reason for the regret is that he returned to United to become involved in the part ownership of the club and, in the long run, an internecine dispute within the shareholding group that would require Tolstoyan length and insight to understand. But it did not diminish him in the eyes of Stein, who a year earlier, in 1982, had felt when taking his Scotland squad to Spain for the World Cup finals that he needed 'The Corner Shop' owner at his elbow.

CHAPTER SEVEN

SUNBURNT

The topless German girl who lay sprawling at the poolside just outside Puerto Banus near Marbella did not seem to mind that 007 was occasionally sneaking a glance at her. We all were. Except that Sean Connery's wife was sitting beside him as well, feeding her poodle and muttering incessantly in French. It was as well the poodle was a distraction because we noticed she was unaware of Connery pointedly eyeing the scenery.

We were in Tony Dalli's restaurant being fed by the restaurateur himself; he sang arias as he plied us with pasta. Billy McNeill had accompanied me to interview the great man and record his views on what he had seen, so far, of the 1982 World Cup finals in Spain. Connery, in punter's mode, was as concerned as any of us. 'Are we going to shoot ourselves in the foot again?' he asked McNeill anxiously, not long after sitting down with him. He had watched the first match on 15 June from the Estadio La Rosaleda in Malaga, against New Zealand. McNeill, who has a talent in diplomacy and PR that had been shockingly underused by Celtic, had struck up a good rapport immediately by telling Connery that he was the greatest of all the 007s and that Roger Moore was but a pale imitation of the real thing. The big man, who at that stage was going through a quieter phase in his film career, was mightily impressed, in his own quiet way, and flowed into conversation, but obviously, like all of us, he was now carrying renewed doubts about the Scottish team's temperament.

To talk to the most famous Scot since the beginning of time seemed the perfect way to illustrate the nagging thought we believed had been exorcised from our mentality but which still persisted: give us the right stage and self-destruct we will. We had just suffered a panic attack. Think of a sag suddenly appearing in the middle of a newly built bridge, and you might sense the flush of terror beginning to rise from our toes. Disaster seemed imminent. I had been to New Zealand with Jock Stein to see the All Whites, as the national football team there called themselves, and regarded them as little more than enthusiasts with designer boots. Stein had reminded me of Iran in Argentina when I expressed that view. Surely not again, one had to think? When New Zealand suddenly scored two goals in the Estadio La Roselada in the space of two minutes to pull Scotland back to a narrow 3–2 lead, a creepy feeling of *déjà vu* seeped into our media positions, and commentators and journalists alike who carried the scars of Argentina sought words that would convey only a modicum of concern, without revealing the first stirrings of blind panic.

There was a recovery, of course, to win 5–2, but still we wanted to talk to Connery about our vulnerability, our lapses, our intoxication with football that sometimes blinds us to realities. He is no philosopher, but he is blunt and emotional about the national side, seeing it as one of the most important vehicles of our culture. And as Edinburgh journalist Craigie Veitch always points out, 'Here's a man who can make off with the most beautiful women in the world. But he's missed out. If he had stuck to professional football with Hibernian, he could have owned a pub in Easter Road by now.' It is doubtful if Connery suffered much sense of loss in not going down the traditional football trail, even if he was a promising youngster. But he represented a body of views that had to be listened to. And throughout our interview he was more than slightly nervous about Scotland's prospects after watching that first match. Scotland had won, but it had left us all with doubts.

And it had all seemed so promising. Jock Stein was in charge, and from the moment he took over as Scotland manager in 1978 the mood relating to international football changed. Ally MacLeod had been a salesman; Stein was an insurance man. The former Celtic manager made it clear to many of us that he wanted to take the 'fiery cross' element out of the Scottish game and make it less dependent on emotion and more focused on planned, deliberate football. He did not want to douse the game in theory, but craved achievement of the right balance between our own natural instincts and the need to keep them in check at the same time. It was a tall order. He was an ageing man who certainly did not have the same hunger for the chase as he had when he took over at Celtic Park. And he was more vulnerable now in his SFA role. With the Celtic job came power and privilege; few, on the outside, would dare challenge his authority as a result. His superb club record insulated him as well. But now the media could speak their minds about things without having to face up to his wrath during the Sunday-morning inquests at Parkhead.

It is not that he had suddenly taken a vow of silence, though. After a 1–0 Home International defeat at the hands of Northern Ireland in Belfast on 16 May 1980, two years into his role, which I covered with Laurie McMenemy as my co-commentator, he asked to see me down at the Seamill Hotel on the Ayrshire coast where he was based with the Scotland squad prior to the next match against Wales. This was his old Celtic haunt, and where he had planned his first ever cup victory with Dunfermline in 1961. I had expected some bonhomie. Instead I was interrogated about every word I had uttered in that commentary, which certainly had been critical of the way Scotland had played. He referred to McMenemy as 'that bloody Englishman', even though he was talking about his closest friend south of the border. In a way I was glad to recognise the Stein of old, who could not care less about social friendships when it came to defending his players.

But by the time he arrived in Spain there was a rising scepticism surrounding his ability to pull it off for Scotland. He had endured press comment you would never have associated with Stein in his heyday with Celtic. After the 1–0 defeat by England at Hampden on 29 May 1982, for which Stein had excluded key players such as Aberdeen's Willie Miller, Alex McLeish and Gordon Strachan for what was, after all, fundamentally a final warm-up game before the World Cup finals, he was denounced in the press. On 31 May Alex Cameron in the *Daily Record* wrote, 'Only the pipers played well, and they selected themselves … Scotland were a yard slow on the ball and this included Kenny Dalglish and Graeme Souness.' Hugh Taylor in the *Glasgow Evening Times* on the same day offered the scathing comment, 'Robbery! If this was just a warm-up practice game for Spain, how about giving the long-suffering fans at least some of their money back?' This talk sounded sacrilegious compared to the reverence that had been shown him when he was Celtic's manager. When you look at the non-selection of the Aberdeen players you have to take into account the likelihood that the well had run dry for them after an arduous, and ultimately disappointing, league season and an extra-time Scottish Cup final against Rangers just a week before this international. Stein read that situation properly, and rested the players. His critics did not, although at the time I confess to feeling short-changed myself as I watched a deliberately weakened Scotland team take on the English. He wanted to win. He always did. But he also wanted to put the emphasis on the World Cup. The last thing we needed, he felt, was a trumpeted victory over the English to inflame optimism. He had seen how counter-productive that had been prior to the World Cup in West Germany in 1974.

I had witnessed how well he understood the psychology of preparation for such events five months prior to that England match, at the draw for the finals, in Madrid, in December 1981. He sat near the front of the stage, and I saw him discreetly slip on spectacles for the first time ever – something he would never do anywhere near a football stadium. It was a minor physical flaw he was obviously too proud to make public and could hide more readily than his constant limp. What he saw through his specs initially was a shambles, and I hoped not an omen for worse to come in the finals themselves. But in a curious way it was to provide the wily Stein with a psychological exit strategy, if things were to go amiss.

In World Cup draws, although it seems initially complicated, with various patterns of possibilities, you can work out in advance, after the first and second levels are out in the open, what might come next. Halfway through the draw, I confidently predicted to our live audience that when the next ball came down the long plastic chute they were using, Scotland would be drawn to play Brazil. In fact it was Argentina's group that was selected. My producer was fuming with anxiety at my having made such a blunder, and I was struggling to find the right words to work myself out of this (but was rapidly feeling like fleeing), when after a few minutes everything came to a halt. Officials began to rush about the stage as if a fire alarm had sounded. Then, as blandly as if they had just been performing a rehearsal, which they most certainly were not, they announced that the draw would have to be redone. Somebody had messed up the rolling of the balls down the plastic tubes. FIFA had blundered. We were off the hook, and indeed it was Brazil's group Scotland ended up in, along with New Zealand and the Soviet Union, who were described in the colloquial way as 'Russians'. But when we travelled the following day to select hotels along the Costa Del Sol, where two of the games would be played, Stein did say to me in the hotel in Benalmadena, 'I wish it had been that Argentina group.' He then repeated that to others to emphasise the scale of the task confronting him in Brazil's group. He did not say it in so many words, but you could easily infer from his comments that we should write that game off, even then, in December. This was the hardest group of all, he kept saying. 'If only they had stuck to the original draw' was the rather jocular theme he pursued, although at the same time playing up the anticipated joy of meeting up with Brazilian football. He was of course talking to the Scottish supporters. Whether rightly or wrongly, it was a shrewd defensive theme he maintained up to and throughout the competition.

It was the Algarve that Scotland chose for their build-up. They stayed beside the Henry Cotton-designed Penina golf course where the heat could have skinned a cat. The noticeable factor for many of us, though, was the distinct chilliness that existed between Kenny Dalglish and his manager. They clearly were not getting on. Dalglish and he had not really parted on gloriously amicable terms when the player left Celtic Park, and there might have been a residue of that left in their relationship. Moreover, Dalglish had not been at his best. He was left out of one of the friendly matches they had arranged against an amateur Portuguese side, and I recall him, that evening, sitting on the sidelines of the small park they were in looking as if he would rather have been back home tending the east-end Glasgow pub he had bought. Dalglish never liked sitting out a football match of any sort. That did not augur well for the finals. The player was still looked upon as a sort of talisman by the Scotland support, yet here he was appearing to be out of sorts, and out of favour.

When they reached Spain the squad was based at Sotogrande, close to the rock of Gibraltar. Stein's first private comment to me after the first press conference was not about football at all. 'How could that rock be British?' he said. 'Look at it. No wonder the Spaniards want it. It's part of their country.' He was obviously as enamoured of British imperialism as he was of some of the media following the team. For he was sliding into a suspicious vein of mind, given the unprecedented criticism he had had to experience as national manager, and spent much of the time I had with him trying to extract from me what other journalists were saying about him. Early on they were not saying much. At that stage the jury was still out.

It did ease the tension with the media when he announced his selection for that opening New Zealand game, for they noted he had included Dalglish. It was hardly remarkable when, after only 32 minutes of the match, Scotland were three up, with a goal by Dalglish and two from John Wark. But then came those ten minutes of confusion midway through the second half when the All Whites pulled the score back to 3–2 through a combination of Scottish complacency and the sheer athletic ability of the New Zealanders to keep running in the damnable heat. Across from the commentary position I noticed that the Scottish flags and banners had been stilled, as if by command. Mass stupefaction was about to set in. You could sense it. Then, in a fit of simple assertion of superior ability, John Robertson and Steve Archibald, the latter on as a substitute for the hapless Alan Brazil, scored two in the last 17 minutes to pull the team back from the slippery slope. There was no real jubilation in that victory. Even Stein had had a scare, and used words such as 'self-inflicted wounds' that would be eerily prescient. 'We are the greatest nation in the world for punishing ourselves at every turn,' he said. Cue 007.

Connery came out, a few days later in our interview, with that nostrum to which we resort when all else fails in trying to understand what makes us tick. 'We always do better against the bigger teams,' he said. 'I think we could do well against the likes of Brazil.' This is something of a myth, for Scotland had been clobbered by the mighty as well as the meek in the past. But we knew where he was coming from: that the Scots could occasionally turn adversity into glory. Although our most famous Scot ever made it sound like received wisdom.

It was as well thinking that way as the days sped by and Seville and the Brazilians beckoned. In preparation for that trip, my co-commentator Billy McNeill and I were summoned to meet Jimmy Hill, then the leading pundit and guru of BBC television, to fill him in on what was happening inside the Scottish camp and bring him up to speed with team news. We repaired to a fish restaurant in Torremolinos, ostensibly to discuss the possibilities of this match. In fact Hill, who is a likeable and charming man socially, tends to hold court on these occasions and made it clear he loved his relationship with Scotland's supporters, even though one of the banners they used to hold up for the cameras, 'Jimmy Hill's a Poof!', was one of the more kindly expressions of views. His talk was mainly patronising about the Scottish team, and little did we know then that he would provoke one of the biggest breaches of relationship between Stein and the BBC, to whom the manager had become quite attached before Spain. After much alcohol had been taken, and with McNeill sending up Hill by promising to support him in his bid for a knighthood after he had just missed out on the recent honours awards, we headed next day for Seville.

It is a deeply religious city of pilgrimage and devotion. Appropriately, therefore, it was the place where the Scottish support underwent a conversion that has lasted ever since. Ally's Army had been a phenomenon of stupid, unrealistic triumphalism. That night in Seville the transition to Tartan Army began to take place. On 18 June, the city surrendered to hordes in carnival mood, many of whom, in the carousing that went on, gave the impression they had forgotten what they had come for in the first place. The longest dancing conga line ever seen on the planet, comprising men and women from places of great cultural similarity such as Auchterarder and São Paulo, swung its way around the city centre like a multi-coloured thread in search of a tapestry. The canary yellow of Brazil merged with the tartan in an almost tropical profusion of colour. As Seville's heat induces skimpiness of dress, there were acres of flesh on show as well. Melanoma was on nobody's mind. The dark days of Wembley and medieval crowd misbehaviour were now being cleansed from the system of Scottish supporters. That evening heralded a new era of Scottish crowd conduct. The grim and serious nature of supporting the national side could be held in reserve for a quiet corner and not necessarily exhibited by smashing in the nearest convenient pub window. All this, of course, coincided with a time when English supporters were seriously mimicking the Visigoths. The message was clear.

It seemed even hotter inside the stadium than outside, although it was bad enough there. You felt from the start that the Scots could not possibly compete in such an atmosphere. Brazil had not won the World Cup for 12 years, but their name still kindled the notion of greatness. This was the tournament in which their own self-regard and strutting would bring their eventual downfall against the Italians, but that night, in that sultry atmosphere, with the sweat dripping from the nose, you felt the girl from Ipanema would have taken on the Scots and won.

Stein made four changes from the New Zealand match. Allan Rough kept his place to achieve his 50th cap, a figure reached by only six Scots prior to that date. Willie Miller took over from Allan Evans of Aston Villa, who was then to disappear from international football. Dalglish and Brazil were dropped in favour of Asa Hartford and Steve Archibald as a lone striker, which was an indication of the caution being expressed by the manager. And then there was David Narey. He was the first Dundee United player ever to be capped for Scotland, and I saw him make his debut against Portugal in the Stadium of Light in Lisbon on 29

November 1978, Stein's first overseas game in charge and one never seen by the public because half an hour before kick-off the television cameras were dismantled in front of our eyes and the local TV company was thrown out of the stadium by Benfica officials for not having paid their contractual dues. Viewers missed an accomplished marking performance by Narey on the gloved Portuguese playmaker Alves. He received modest reviews for that performance, but nothing compared to what was in store for him after this one.

For in the 18th minute Souness, who was the most dominant of the midfield players in that first half, swung over a cross for Wark to head into the path of Narey. He let fly with the outside of his right foot and the ball soared majestically into the roof of the net. A mirage? There was no time to pinch yourself to see if you were dreaming because you could see the Brazilians instantly bristling with indignity at this audacity. I knew, immediately, that this goal could be a provocation. However, up on the roof of a tall apartment building just outside the ground, Jimmy Hill, watching the game on a monitor, had decided on words to describe this moment, when his time came. At the interval, after Zico had equalised with a superb free-kick 12 minutes from the end of the half, Hill called Narey's goal a 'toe-poke'. 'A what?' I asked Billy McNeill beside me, for confirmation. He buried his head in his hands. Hill insisted afterwards that it was a well-meaning phrase, inferring no slight. But to other ears, including Stein's after the game, it was like describing Henry Cooper's left-hook on Muhammad Ali, which put him on the canvas, as a 'tickle'.

Like Ali, Brazil got up off the canvas and made sure normal service was resumed. The heat became even more oppressive, and Scotland did not help themselves by conceding a goal only three minutes after the restart, when Oscar, ludicrously unmarked, was allowed to head in from a corner-kick by Junior. Zico, who had never quite won over even his own public as the inheritor of the Pele skills, was still exciting to watch at times. But as the Scots continually viewed him as the greatest threat, the Brazilians constructed a goal from a completely different source when Eder, coming from a wide position 25 minutes from the end, floated the ball over the advancing Rough to put any thought of revival out of our heads. Then, four minutes from time, with Dalglish on for Strachan and McLeish for Hartford, came the fourth Brazilian goal, which was like kicking a man when he is down. The fair-haired Falcão, who looked more Nordic than South American, took a pass from the left, strode through midfield and sent a low, wickedly undeviating shot through the defence into the net. For its beautiful execution it was worthy of a hallelujah from our commentary position. Our exclamations were uttered in that spirit which you have to maintain when playing this country, namely that you are never beaten by them, you are only educated. That lesson was not lost on Stein after the game, who stated the obvious. He told the *Daily Record* of 19 June, 'Losing to Brazilians carries no disgrace.'

He found stern words for Hill's appraisal of the Narey goal, however, and was looking for blood. It was also a useful way to deflect the fire from those who might have accepted the Brazilian defeat as inevitable but who were now concerned that having conceded two late goals to the New Zealanders, and now having to face a Russian team that needed only a draw to go through, Scotland were on the brink again. It was a similar situation to 1974 in West Germany when Yugoslavia required only a draw to progress, and duly got one in Frankfurt. This hardly seemed an appetising prospect. So Hill was a convenient *bête noire*. I have no knowledge of Stein and he ever meeting up in Spain before the end of the tournament. Had they done so it would have been worth witnessing.

To show Jim McLean and Andy Roxburgh, his two assistants, that he was quite relaxed about meeting the Russians, Stein pulled a fast one on them by asking them to help him out by writing down the team each of them would select to play that game. After they had cogitated for some considerable time and written them down painstakingly, Stein took their lists and without even looking at the names tore up the slips of paper, saying, 'Ach, I'll just pick the team myself.' It was a fatherly joke rather than a reminder of who was boss. But it is interesting to note what McLean himself said later about his association with the Scottish squad. 'I'm still ashamed today of the way I did that job, and ashamed I may have let Jock Stein down after he had shown a great deal of faith in me and in my ability as a coach. Quite honestly, I was a disgrace as an assistant manager.' He said that because he did not realise until it was too late that he had not spoken up when he should have about tactics and selection. He was too much in awe of the man to take issue with him, and because of his utter domination at Tannadice he simply did not know how to handle being a subsidiary. Stein, though, was partly comforted by the fact that both the Brazil and New Zealand coaches predicted a Scottish victory over the Soviet Union, even though Eder's late winning goal for the South Americans against the Russians had inflicted on them their first defeat in 23 games.

It is worthwhile noting the names of the men Stein chose for his last ever World Cup finals game: A. Rough (Partick Thistle), D. Narey (Dundee United), F. Gray (Leeds United), G. Souness (Liverpool, captain), A. Hansen (Liverpool), W. Miller (Aberdeen), G. Strachan (Aberdeen), S. Archibald (Tottenham Hotspur), J. Jordan (AC Milan), J. Wark (Ipswich Town) and J. Robertson (Nottingham Forest).

Malaga on the evening of 22 June was cooler than Seville had been, but not by much. We were all nervous. As a commentator, you must of course try to remain as objective as you can, but sometimes it is impossible to repress the feeling that you would like to find words that might actually alleviate what is happening in front of you. It is a ridiculous notion, but it does enter the mind. As a result, in trying to prevent that, I was sometimes accused of going to the other extreme and being too harsh on Scotland from time to time – an uncomfortable position that was to affect my position with the BBC eventually. This game taxed that ambivalence to the extreme. There was one name added to the team from the Brazil match: Joe Jordan replaced Asa Hartford. Jordan is one of the players Stein felt represented the more impulsive, less thoughtful approach to the game which he thought only encouraged the cavalry charges he deplored and stunted Scotland's development in the modern game. Yet here he was resorting to the very style he thought he had successfully discarded, and with Archibald, who had looked a lonely and isolated figure against Brazil, beside him Jordan was going to spearhead an aggressive, less sophisticated approach. Stein had known all along that this game would be the decider, and he agonised over the simple fact that had Scotland defended better against the All Whites they would have gone into this game needing only a draw. By contrast, it was now the Russians who required that.

It was Souness's finest hour. There was something in the way he commanded midfield that suggested he owed us all something, for being unable to release the positive side of his talents until then. He passed and probed in a way that prompted a surge of freshness throughout the Scottish side, which we had feared might wilt in the heat again. They did not. Inspired by their captain, Scotland took the lead after only 15 minutes. Archibald and Jordan both challenged Chivadze, the Russian sweeper, and as the ball broke kindly to the Spurs player he nudged it forward to his partner who had a straight run in on the goalkeeper, Desaev. The man who had scored World Cup goals in 1974 and 1978 kept admirable control in his long run, and with a skill that frankly few of us thought he had, he slotted it between the goalkeeper and the near post for the first goal. After that Scotland looked assured. Miller at the back was immense. Strachan was a darting firefly of a player, illuminating midfield with incredible energy. Souness was tackling with ferocity, intent on sending some of his opponents to rest homes in the Urals to recuperate. It was going well.

Then, after a scramble 15 minutes into the second half inside the Scottish penalty area which my good friend from Scottish Television Arthur Montford would have characterised as a 'stramash' as the ball seemed to bounce and ricochet from player to player, the Russians equalised. Their scorer was Chivadze, no less, which gives an indication of how they were now attacking desperately. He miscued his shot, but Rough was off his line for reasons that were not entirely clear to me at the time, and the ball sailed over his shoulder weakly into the net. A Russian spectator just in front of our commentary position then proceeded to block our view by waving his arms about like a madman. To get him to desist, and I must confess in a pique of anger at having watched a ludicrously conceded goal, I punched him on the back. He stood up from his seat and was all of six feet eight inches. I decided not to punch him again.

There was still a chance of survival, until that fateful moment six minutes from time. It was a collision in the good old silent-film tradition created by Mack Sennett, developed by Laurel and Hardy, refined by Abbot and Costello and gloriously revamped by Tom and Jerry. The pair involved were Alan Hansen and Willie Miller, the latter of whom always played better with his Aberdeen partner Alex McLeish beside him. Up till then he had been impeccable. Hansen and he rushed for a ball just below us on the touchline. They seemed to merge into a helpless tangle of arms and legs with the ball slipping past them like a dog breaking from a leash, and Shengelia, the Russian striker, was after it like a flash with only Rough to beat, which he did with ease. Two-one down with six minutes left. Old, old story, but you are still never prepared for it. Souness did score a cleverly conceived goal two minutes from time, but it was too late.

'It's always too bloody late,' said Ernie Walker, the secretary of the SFA, as he walked down the stairs of the Malaga stadium on that beautifully balmy evening after the game, wearing the expression of a man who had just been forced to endure an enema made of iron filings. His slow gait was unsteady and stiff, his stare towards some distant horizon wherein might lie an escape from the consequences of the sudden fit of madness he had just witnessed. As he arrived at my side, he stopped for a moment and in a few words the rest of the world might have considered gibberish but which between fellow Scots conveyed a profundity of meaning, he added to the comment, 'Only we could have done it that way!' In my interview with Stein afterwards, I saw a man who was struggling to find the right tone and words. Ian Archer, writing in the *Sunday Standard* of 27 June, wrote of Stein's reaction to this hugely disappointing result, 'Even while engaging in polite conversation his eyes were fixed in the middle distance. He had been in the same dark places as Willie Ormond and Ally MacLeod. Defeat hurt.'

Walker and Stein had set great store by their partnership, believing that given their mutual respect and backing it would be different this time. In many ways it was. He had developed a disciplined side whose behaviour on and off the field was impeccable. Stein had handled the press with dignity and without false promises. Gordon Strachan was voted, by the Spanish press, the outstanding player of Group 6, ahead even of the best of the Brazilians. You could, in retrospect, have queried Stein's assertion that the group was the toughest of all because neither Brazil nor the Soviet Union reached even the semi-finals. But we all knew his warnings had been part of his strategy of dampening expectation. Another journalist, Ian Peebles, attempting to scrape the barrel and find some solace, described 1982 in his *SFA Football Annual* as 'the year Scotland became the half-time champions of the world'. The fact that Scotland had been winning or drawing at half-time in all three games, and had scored first in all of them, was enough to inspire this weirdly creative attempt to pan for gold in a dried-up creek. But it was mere quack medicine for the legions who had gone to Spain with so much hope. There were no major protests, as there had been after Argentina. They had grasped the reality that the lapses in the first game had cost Scotland heavily and that essentially the squad had given as much as they could, but had been subject to unexpected and cruelly surfacing fragilities.

I did not meet up with Connery again until 1998 in Paris, curiously on the eve of another Scotland–Brazil match, of which more later. Of Stein I certainly saw much more over the next three years, as he geared up a newer generation of players for another World Cup. The last time I spoke to him was the day before he died in Cardiff on 10 September 1985. The profound sense of loss that spread that evening through the entire Scottish football family lingered strongly. It was still there with us when, months later, we surrounded the Scottish squad, posing for photographs in front of constructions that dated back to AD 700. It was June 1986, the country was Mexico, the site was the ancient city of Teotihuacan, and the constructions were the enormous pyramids that towered over the area near the Scottish team's dowdy hotel. But given the tragedy of Stein's passing the year before, the cruel strokes of fortune that had dogged Scottish teams in World Cups in the past, and the creepily developed sense of superstition on the back of all that, we kept quiet about the fact that the broad ancient road that stretched into the Aztec city behind the squad was called 'The Avenue of the Dead'.

CHAPTER SIXTEEN
MONTEZUMA'S REVENGE

'Scum of the earth' is what he said, and you could tell by the look on his face that the sentiment was the product of careful calculation, not a spur-of-the-moment comment. Normally, Ernie Walker was the soul of discretion whenever he pronounced in public. Off the record he had one of the wittiest and sometimes most cutting of tongues, slagging folk with tiny verbal knock-outs. This time there was no compunction about airing his feelings publicly in the aftermath of a game played amid the slums of Mexico City which was to scar the record of the World Cup finals in 1986. It was as serious a slur as you can throw at anybody. Walker was a genuine supporter, not just an apparatchik. He had been wounded yet again. So had all of us on that 13th day of June in the Nezahualcoyotl area of Mexico's capital, or Neza for short. And in a way he was manufacturing words we could shelter behind, almost as if acting as the battering ram for the general feeling of disgust the media felt and would have to express in some way. But here was somebody putting words in their mouths for them so that they themselves could not be accused of the usual knee-jerk reaction. This was our top official wading in like a tabloid journalist. 'Good on you, Ernie,' was the initial reaction in the fetid atmosphere of the Estadio Neza press room. Then you had to wonder what FIFA might have to say about the outburst.

To gain some understanding of why a fastidious man like Walker would clearly break the protocol of retaining a tight-lipped silence, even under provocation, you have to consider the context of the Mexican campaign into which he had been thrust. In the first place he was missing Stein. He had built up a relationship with him which was the closest Stein had ever had with any official at any level of football, with the possible exception of the late Sir Robert Kelly, the former Celtic chairman, for I do believe that his association with Walker was, on a social level, much closer. Now the secretary had to deal with a man whose outlook had run counter to the authority of the organisation he represented. Alex Ferguson had taken over from Stein as Scotland team manager, on a temporary basis. There had been talk about his accepting a full-time position, had he been granted overall control of the entire Scottish football development. But I never saw that as a possibility, considering his rocky relationship with officialdom. He had been carpeted several times by the SFA during Walker's period of office and had been banned twice from the touchline. And while this is something both could easily have laid aside as irrelevant, the relationship was certainly not as harmonious as it had been with Stein.

After the first group game against Denmark, for example, Walker banned all television units from the Scottish hotel, partly as a reprisal against what he perceived to be distorted stories being put about by some broadcasters about the accommodation there, which certainly did not conform to the ideal set by the widely travelled and rather pampered professional players. In truth, the hotel was a cross between a sacked monastery and a dog's home, if you were to take the word of the team. That was the point of the ban. The SFA, continually haunted by the legacy of Argentina, did not want to reveal the same irritations that had bedevilled that expedition. There were no permanent phone lines in the hotel, so the players rightly had a complaint to make about lack of communications. Indeed, a television reporter had given a temporary line, set up by his company, to one of the players inside the hotel. He had grabbed the phone eagerly, spilled the beans as it were to his family and to journalists in Mexico City, and the news had therefore got out about the rough conditions, as described by the players. Then the phone had been handed to a queue of his mates who, unknown to the reporter, spent literally hours on the line talking to loved ones back in the UK, thus running up a bill for the television company greater than had ET made a call back home. The broadcaster speedily dismantled the line after that, much to the delight of the SFA. But the damage had been done. They were being accused of another piece of lack of proper planning in putting our brave lads into a doss house.

What was not taken into consideration by anybody attempting to pillory the SFA was the fact that they had been latecomers. Until they had played Australia in Melbourne on 4 December 1985 in the second leg of the play-off for the finals they were far from certain of qualifying for Mexico. Scotland had won the first game at Hampden on 20 November and looked favourites to go through, but it was not until the goalless draw in the return game that they could really take any initiative. So they were last in the queue for accommodation. This is what brought them to the Aztec City and its pyramids, and to a dispute that was blossoming stupidly into a major issue. For Ferguson was so much in disagreement with the television ban that he circumvented it by deliberately walking out to the barrier at the front gate to be interviewed by me, in the full knowledge that everybody would know he was defying his employer (this was a few months before our monumental bust-up, remember). 'That bloody man won't stop me from talking,' was his first comment before we started the cameras rolling.

Ferguson had the advantage in the sense that he had other plans in mind for the future. His was a distinctly temporary position. He had no desire to take on a job that Stein, in a fit of candour to me after Spain, had admitted was 'impossible'. Walker knew that as well, so there was no need for Ferguson to be concerned about long-term consequences. But from bitter experience we knew that even the tiniest scrap of conflict within a camp can influence events, so there was general worry about the mood, and in retrospect one wonders whether it might have affected Ferguson's judgement on matters, given that he must have known as the tournament progressed that Walker and he were not intimates. Ferguson, at that time, enjoyed a fruitful relationship with his chairman at Aberdeen, Dick Donald, who nurtured and tolerated him with genuine fondness and sagacity. Now, here in Mexico, he was out on a limb, putting his reputation on the line without, apparently, the backing he was accustomed to.

This did not affect his working practices or his relationships with the players, though. Roy Aitken, then the Celtic captain, played in all three games in Mexico. 'Fergie was brilliant,' Aitken told me. 'He seemed to do everything right. He had built up a great background team. Andy Roxburgh, Craig Brown, Archie Knox – they all knitted well. The variety he brought to the training methods, the way he talked to the players, the sense of fun he introduced – all that added to a great atmosphere. When we had that long spell of altitude training in Santa Fe we felt we could not have been better prepared for the finals.' They were preparing to play Denmark, West Germany and Uruguay in Group E, which when drawn was considered by the most objective reporter to deserve the label 'Group of Death'. The South Americans and the Germans had won the World Cup four times between them. And Denmark had the strongest team in their history, including the marvellous Michael Laudrup.

Two weeks before the tournament we took up residence in a palatial hotel on a small hill just outside the New Mexico town of Santa Fe, and only 45 minutes by car from where the first atomic bomb had been exploded at Los Alamos. The desert air and the luxuriousness of the hotel induced a sense of well-being that fitted the desire to prepare well, but in a relaxed manner, considering the harrowing season most of the players had come through. But there was a certain unease underlying the relative calm. This centred on three names – Graeme Souness, Kenny Dalglish and Alan Hansen. The latter two were not present; Souness was. You could hardly miss him as he rarely threw off the bearing of consummate self-belief. Without apparently trying, he seemed set apart from the other players. There might have been another reason why we thought so: he was the newly appointed manager of Rangers. Whatever the strength of conviction he had, it is difficult to imagine that a man who had just taken on one of the most important managerial jobs in British football, with a club that was floundering and whose support, one of the biggest in world football, were demanding instant success, was not preoccupied with, if not significantly distracted by, the task at hand. He was also getting on in years, having already turned 33.

The Rangers manager was to provide Ferguson with a major headache, which added to the pressure brought on by Kenny Dalglish, then the Liverpool player-manager. Ferguson was infuriated by what he regarded as a snub – Dalglish simply turning his back on the finals. Dalglish had gone out of his way to persuade Ferguson to include his Liverpool team-mate Alan Hansen in the squad. Ferguson ignored that. When the squad was eventually announced, Dalglish pointedly took a bottle of champagne round to Hansen's house to console him. It is true that many of my English broadcasting colleagues could not believe that Hansen was not preferred to what they considered was the lanky awkwardness of Alex McLeish, and thought that it was sheer favouritism on Ferguson's part to pick his own players from Aberdeen. But the McLeish–Miller partnership had worked like a dream in European football under him. And still vivid in our minds was the occasion at Ninian Park, Cardiff on 19 May 1979 when John Toshack ripped Hansen apart and scored all three goals in Wales's victory over Scotland. The comical collision with Miller in Malaga in 1982 was also difficult to ignore as an example of how the two could not combine well. Hansen had also been deemed unreliable by Stein, and had pulled out of several games that demanded his presence. It lent the impression, whether rightly or wrongly, of a lack of commitment. Somehow or other, Hansen could not quite translate his brilliant Liverpool form into the Scottish blue. Because it was clear that Dalglish had not got his way over Hansen, many interpreted his decision not to travel to Mexico as a deliberate snub. In fact, the surgeon dealing with Dalglish's knee ligament problem had advised him against playing. Whatever interpretation could be put on it, Ferguson was far from pleased. We are told they eventually made up, but, knowing them, it is hard to imagine.

What we could not possibly have imagined was the impact the Neza neighbourhood of Mexico City would make on us as we travelled there for the first game on 4 June. It was a stinking slum area which we were told had a population of about one million. There were beggars everywhere. Ragged bundles in the streets would turn out, on closer inspection, to be mothers with kids wrapped together to shelter from the frequent monsoons that hit the city at that time of the year. The appalling and obvious misery of those people underscored the disgrace of bringing a World Cup to a country so burdened by unrelenting poverty. In fact, the peso plunged during the tournament. If you combine that with the persistently clammy heat and the altitude problems of that country, it would seem something of a mystery that Mexico had been chosen at all. It was no mystery, though. The competition had been thrust on the largely downtrodden Mexican population in a shady deal between Televisa, the Mexican television company, and the disreputable João Havelange of Brazil, the then FIFA president, who had a commercial interest in that company. At the meeting to decide the matter, in Stockholm in May 1983, not even the presence of Henry Kissinger – formerly adviser to President Nixon and advocate of the hardline policy that caused the trampling-over of countries in south-east Asia, now its born-again peaceful football ambassador – could divert Havelange in the pursuit of his goal. Four years later Ernie Walker, fully aware of what had happened and by then the most influential of the FIFA triumvirate to decide the venue of the 1994 World Cup, ensured it would go to the country to which it should have been sent in 1986 – the USA.

The stadium itself was neat and compact and certainly did not reflect the misery that existed on the other side of its walls. But misery is transportable, or so it proved that day, as the game swept away the pre-match Scottish confidence. The Scottish side included only four players from outside the domestic league: Souness of Sampdoria, Nicholas of Arsenal, Strachan of Manchester United and Nichol of Liverpool. But it was the home-bred Celtic captain, Roy Aitken, who had the most to feel disappointed about. The Danes had gone into the lead in the 57th minute when a cross-ball rebounded from Miller's legs and fell to the feet of Preben Elkjaer, who scored the only goal of the game with that favourite left foot of his. It was another goal though, the goal that never was, which so irked Aitken. 'It was 1–0 to them but I felt we still had a great chance,' he said. 'So when I sent in this volley just towards the end of the game which crashed behind the goalkeeper, I thought that was it. I felt the momentum would shift our way. Then, somebody pointed out the linesman on the far side had his flag up, for offside against Charlie Nicholas. I couldn't believe it. Charlie was on the touchline, nowhere near the goal. In no way was he influencing play. Nowadays that goal would have stood. It didn't then, though, and that dumped us.' The result could certainly have gone either way and there was no reason for morale to be shattered. But Scotland had not created the much-hoped-for bridgehead to take into the game against West Germany in the sweltering town of Queretaro, three hours north of Mexico City.

Just as, inevitably, the sniping started on the back of the first result, it was heartening to relate that the Scots were not the only group suffering a persecution complex. For we took a camera crew to the German team hotel the day before the game and saw their manager Franz Beckenbauer in action. Understanding not a word of German did not preclude me from grasping the drift of the Kaiser's address to his own press corps. It was not so much a bawling match, more a lecture peppered with sizzling contempt. He took no questions, but rose majestically at the end of his speech and walked out. Luckily he walked through the ranks towards us, for he had agreed to be interviewed about the match the following day and true to his word he made directly for a small room where we had set up the cameras for him. When he slumped down on a squashy leather couch, he actually sighed, as if in relief. It transpired that a German newspaper had accused some of his squad of introducing prostitutes into their training camp in the weeks before the finals. 'What can you do when you have so many vultures surrounding you?' he said after explaining what the problem was. 'They just print lies, you know. Do they really want us to win?' It could have been a Scottish official speaking in Argentina. Beckenbauer, whom I had got to know through various interviews I had conducted with him over the years, spoke impeccable English and proceeded to decant some of his frustration and anger on to us. It was almost refreshing to know that this cool figure who cut his footballing style almost to a design by Armani could be revealing a susceptibility to pressure from the outside.

When I returned to base I wondered if such matters could influence events, but at the same time I felt I was merely clutching at straws. I mentioned this to Ferguson on the phone, but the skilled exponent of mind games merely laughed. He knew that the factors of German quality, searing heat, dehydration and a defeat already behind his team would be more influential than rumours about the recreational pursuits of German players. There was also something more important on his mind – Graeme Souness. Alan Davidson of the *Glasgow Evening Times* wrote a perceptive piece on 5 June, after the Denmark match, that said, 'Fine player and dominant figure that he is, Souness tends to overawe the rest of the team and I believe that others should take on more responsibility.' I could find no disagreement with that, and could only amplify it by recording that even so he was not the influential player he should have been. He was a problem. He had almost iconic status and an uplifting personality, yet he was clearly not delivering as we might have expected. Ferguson was obviously wrestling with this. But there he was, chosen again for the game in the Estadio Corregidora in Queretaro on 8 June.

Ferguson made three changes: Eamonn Bannon, who could run like a gazelle, was brought in, David Narey replaced Alex McLeish in defence, and Steve Archibald, his old rebel from Aberdeen (now with Barcelona), took the place of Charlie Nicholas, put out of the reckoning after a brutal challenge by Denmark's Klaus Berggreen in the first match. The BBC immediately hired Charlie to sit alongside me for the game to help introduce the programme from the stadium, much to the chagrin of Jimmy Hill, whose normal role that was. Indeed, so offended was he by being usurped for this one decidedly Scottish occasion that my producer said that Hill had immediately contacted his agent in London to find out if it was a breach of contract.

The only breaching that mattered to us was that of the German defence in the 18th minute when Strachan, with a neat spin and a quick dash, swept the ball past Harald Schumacher from close in. He went straight off to acknowledge the sun- and tequila-soaked Scottish support behind the goal, though the wee man sensibly stopped short of vaulting the high advertising hoarding. It was too cripplingly hot to feel any great exhilaration, but I did begin to hope the German newspapers had been right, that prostitutes had been secreted into the team hotel and that, like a flock of Delilahs, they had shorn the players of their strengths. But it was not to be. With indecent haste, Rudi Voller equalised for West Germany, only four minutes later. As Nicholas and I drank seemingly gallons of water for the rest of the game to keep us going, you could not help but marvel at how some of the players managed to sustain the pace. Of course it slowed down, but some were slower than others. We noticed towards the end of the first half Pierre Littbarski, no slouch he, leaving Souness behind in a short spurt that made the Scotland captain's legs look like they had been cemented to the ground. That was ominous. Four minutes into the second half Klaus Allofs scored for West Germany and Scotland now seemed to be faced by giants of men who, far from looking like roués having a rest from hotel pranks, seemed as if they had come straight from a health farm. A single-goal lead in such torrid heat lent that impression, and although Strachan's industry and guile were immense, and throwing on Davie Cooper, the left-footed magician of the touchline, for only the last 15 minutes sparked some life into the side, there was really no way back. By the end Souness was virtually at a stand-still, utterly bereft of the towering strength he normally manifested. It was so noticeable that I asked Nicholas the question, as the players crawled from the field with the Germans victorious, 'Is it conceivable that Fergie will drop Graeme for the last game? He doesn't look fit.' Nicholas, who has now learnt through his television experience to be refreshingly candid, was much more diplomatic then. 'Graeme's a great player,' he replied. 'How do you drop great players?' That was the dilemma staring Ferguson in the face. But the conditions in Queretaro were so severe that it might have occurred to him that they had taken a special toll on Souness, and that he could recover.

Littbarski and Strachan were kept behind for the statutory drug test, and given the aftermath of the Willie Johnston affair in Argentina we stayed on for the result, just in case. As an illustration of the torturous dehydration everybody suffered that day, even though they drank water constantly, bottle after bottle, neither of them could pee for nearly an hour and a half. In what I am sure was a breach of every regulation in the book, we ended up joining them at a table, somebody produced a pack of cards from somewhere, and into a game of brag we went as we waited for nature to come to the aid of two little men who off the field looked like choirboys who had just sneaked away from evensong. Strachan managed to pee first. 'Scotland one, West Germany nil,' he said as he exited the test room, punching the air.

But it was time for every Scot to take pause and reflect. In the Zona Rosa area of Mexico City two nights later, the Soho of the city, in a restaurant to which the famous film director Luis Buñuel used to repair every day for lunch, a spectrum of Scottish media men growled their way through a long meal. In essence we were preparing for the obsequies we felt would inevitably follow the last game against Uruguay, even though their surprising thrashing by Denmark 6–1 had given Ferguson's men a lifeline. A win would see Scotland through, but pessimism abounded. There were three strands to the thinking. Firstly, there was the blunt and basic one that Scotland were simply not good enough for this level of football. Secondly, that Ferguson, as a part-time manager, could not be up to the task. Thirdly, Souness was finished as an international player, and, as a corollary to that, he had too much on his mind, for it would have been stupid to think he was not already planning how to cope as the manager of Rangers. There was a heated debate about that. The manager must play him against Uruguay, some thought. He would give it something special, in perhaps his last ever game for his country. Others felt he was well past his sell-by date. In that discussion you could predict that Ferguson would be damned if he did select him, damned if he didn't, depending on the result. Over and above that, we knew that all was not well within the Scottish camp, with Ferguson and Walker hardly bosom buddies. The situation contained all the elements of imminent disaster. The conclusion, quite simply, was that Scotland would do well to retreat from Mexico by avoiding another humiliation. As I recollect it, no one that night amongst several of the most prominent British journalists and broadcasters could boldly forecast a Scottish victory, even though they had to feed the masses the usual hyperbolic optimism.

Then we learnt of something that had never happened to Souness in his entire footballing career: he had been dropped for the first time. The new Rangers manager, though, has always respected Ferguson for coming to the cubby-hole called a hotel room to inform him personally about that and assure him it was one of the most difficult decisions he had ever had to make. Souness, who had taken an aversion to Mexican food and had existed on Mars Bars and glucose and water drinks, and in addition had much on his mind about the future, had lost almost two stones in weight during his time there and agreed that the manager had made the right decision. Not everybody thought that on the afternoon of 13 June in the Estadio Neza, however, for a Scottish team without Souness, even though his form had been poor, was like dispensing with your true leader. With the benefit of hindsight I think those of us who thought it correct were proved wrong. Scotland that day needed a ruthless hard man in the side. Within the camp Walter Smith had argued for Souness's inclusion – unsurprisingly, because he was about to join the man as his assistant manager at Ibrox – but Craig Brown and the other coaches backed the manager. Nor had Ferguson included the fiery Steve Archibald, who let his strong feelings about that be known to the manager. Alex McLeish was still recovering from flu, but had always felt he was not selected because Ferguson was becoming sensitive to criticism over playing his own club players. It was surely one of the unhappiest team selections Ferguson would make in his entire career. But for Paul Sturrock, the Dundee United striker who had been dropped for the game against the Germans but was brought back for the last match, it was another factor altogether that influenced the outcome. 'It wouldn't have mattered who we fielded,' he said. 'We got the shit kicked out of us anyway.'

That was not the language used in the ultimate FIFA tactical breakdown of the game, but Uruguay did seem to have borrowed techniques from Thai boxing or alligator wrestling. They targeted one man in particular – Gordon Strachan. After only 40 seconds the Uruguayan midfielder Jose Batista, with complete indifference to the fact that much of the civilised world would be looking in, took aim at Strachan and sunk his boot into the midfielder's leg. He went down. Would he get back up? That was the first thought, so vicious was the challenge. The French referee Quiniou, whom we knew could be tactfully blind to some incidents on the field if it suited him career-wise, could do nothing other than send him off. I felt, and I am sure others did at that moment, a sudden rush of adrenaline passing through me. How could ten men survive for all of 89 minutes at this level, with Scotland aware that a win would see them through? It seemed we were on the verge of a real breakthrough, but the Uruguayans combined their ruthless, crude aggression with a work rate and astutely defensive tactics which rendered Scotland inept. Roy Aitken felt they just could not get going properly. 'I'll always remember about that game how they fell down, feigning injury, lying as if dead at times, sometimes rolling over and over; taking their time with the so-called injuries, kicking the ball out of the field; dwelling over goal-kicks and free-kicks; clipping our heels, punching us off the ball, pulling our hair from the back, spitting on us. A lot of crudeness. But it was the starting and stopping so much that spoiled the rhythm of the game. If you look back at the records of that match I think you would find that the ball was only in actual play a third of the time. It was a charade.'

It was more than a charade. It was the usual World Cup *danse macabre*. It was tripping over your own feet. It was airport time again. The feeling was like the sickliness ordinary tourists might feel when Montezuma's Revenge takes toll on the intestines. Hence the scenes at the end, when Walker vented his cold, calculated fury on the South Americans. He was to receive a rebuke from FIFA for his remarks and has never liked being reminded of the words he used that day. He was only being human, though, and the supporters could sympathise with a man who simply expressed the views held by most people who watched that game. Of course, with the benefit of hindsight Ferguson had to face up to the inevitable criticism for not playing Souness, who would, on reflection, have acted like Robocop in the face of the cynically brutal Uruguayans, and conceivably might not have seen out the 90 minutes. But the awareness of having no real intimidating physical power against the thugs added to the notion that a selection blunder had been made. Ferguson did admit to people that he had made a mistake, but it was behind him now. His thoughts were now on his own future, with various English clubs closing in on him. He had had enough of the task of trying to convert the humdrum into the exceptional.

Although we did not realise it at the time, these two men were about to cause a convulsion in Scottish football. I watched Souness leave the stadium that day. He did not seem unduly perturbed. If anything he might have looked smug. Did he really appreciate what he had let himself in for by going to Glasgow? He did look like a cool gambler about to play for high stakes. But in his first words to me about Rangers he had sounded more like a prophet about to come down from the mount.

CHAPTER SEVENTEEN

SOUNESS AT BAY

Graeme Souness's first declaration of intent was made beside our camera on a hill overlooking Santa Fe on a day in May 1986 on which the New Mexico prairie that stretched beyond us was bleaching in the sun. The trouble was, the camera wasn't rolling. He would not go on the record about his new role as Rangers manager; he would only talk to us as captain of the Scottish side heading for the World Cup in Mexico. Protocol demanded such, he informed us. So as we lounged at poolside he had no objection to letting me know privately how he would go about his quest to be the greatest Rangers manager of all time. It is not that he made that arrogant claim in so many words. When he got to the sentence he really wanted to emphasise, you could sense a steely determination in his voice, as if he wished to validate his uniqueness for this job. 'There will be no holding me back from signing a Catholic at any time,' he said. And then added, for good measure, 'And I don't care if Celtic beat us four times in the league, so long as we win the championship. We have to get rid of this traditional mind-set. People will have to change.'

The earth did not move under our feet, nor did the birds stop singing. But there was something epochal about his words that signified the world had slipped into a new orbit. You could tell he was deadly serious, but hearing these words in the context of the historically ice-bound football culture of the city of Glasgow was like hearing somebody boasting about heading for the Arctic wastes garbed only in a loincloth. That day he made his objective seem ridiculously simple, without completely dissuading us that he was being a trifle naïve. It seemed then that whatever he had in mind when he got to Ibrox, he would distance himself from the lunacies of the tribal warfare within the Old Firm tradition. But after a swift learning experience, the man who wanted to rise above it all insisted eventually on having portraits of the Queen hung up in the Rangers dressing room at Celtic Park, any time they went there, to 'counteract all the greenness surrounding us', as his captain Terry Butcher once explained to me. 'You're playing for her,' Souness once told the players, lending a nod to the sovereign, before they ran out to face their deadly rivals. Then there was the reality check he thought he was offering in the Santa Fe sun, that losing four times in a season to Celtic was of no relevance so long as his supporters watched Rangers winning the title. After his very first Old Firm game, a Glasgow Charity Cup match in which he played and in which Ally McCoist became the first Rangers player in history to score a hat-trick against Celtic on two occasions, he ditched that idea as being as unrealistic as asking the *Titanic* survivors to endorse the joys of lifeboat travel. One game in, and already he knew that tolerance of such defeats is not a virtue in Glasgow. And, rapidly, this man, for all his experience and urbanity, his snappy dress sense and the sleekness of the cosmopolitan traveller, came to realise in his first few weeks at Ibrox that he was not leading a football club but heading a mission to save an institution whose rigidly conformist past conflicted heavily with the demands of the modern world.

Rangers had been in a mess for several years. They had, debatably, the best modern stadium in British football, virtually completed in 1981 to seat 42,000 (and thereafter increased in capacity to 52,000), but as a barometer of their real worth, when they played their first official game amid the new, sumptuous surroundings on 19 September that year they were beaten 2–0 by Celtic. In the eyes of their supporters such events devalued the club considerably, and by the time John Greig resigned in the autumn of 1983 crowds had slumped to as low as 7,000. Their search for a man to take over from him was initially fruitless. But just outside Glasgow at Motherwell, a man was desperate to take up the cause. Spiritually, Jock Wallace had never left Ibrox. He had had a spell in England with Leicester after leaving Rangers, then had moved to the Lanarkshire club. When the press furore increased over the managerial situation in October 1983, with speculation mounting about Greig's future and making his departure inevitable, Wallace phoned me and asked if I could contact John Paton, the Rangers chairman, to tell him that he was ready, willing and able to take it on again. 'Why don't they effing well come for me?' he asked me. 'I can still do it for them.' Out of courtesy to Wallace, for I liked the man, I did make 'accidental' contact with Paton one evening and dropped the Motherwell manager's name to him in a jocular way. Nothing really registered and I pursued it no further since frankly I did not think Wallace was the right choice for Rangers at that stage. Then, one evening, I received a call at home. When

I answered it a man was singing. The song was 'The Sash My Father Wore', the anthem of the more committed Rangers supporters. I recognised the voice as Wallace's. After singing a line or two *con brio* he stopped and said, 'I've got it! I'm going back.' He was indeed. The fact that he knew he had been only the third choice of the Rangers directors behind Jim McLean and Alex Ferguson, both of whom had rejected the job, did not perturb him in the slightest.

Even in the manner by which he had informed me, in song, I knew it was a retrograde step for the club. Wallace's trumpeting of his Protestantism always seemed to me to have a strong element of theatricality to it, suggesting that he played to the gallery. In his personal relations with people he was the very opposite, as his Catholic assistant manager at Motherwell, the ex-Celtic player Frank Connor, could confirm. Wallace was in fact a warm-hearted, genuinely kindly man, lumbered by the traditions he adhered to without a shred of bitterness as a result of the intense bigotry he supposedly espoused. But though he had displayed great personal courage in his life, especially in the jungles of Malaya during the communist insurrection, there was one bold step he could not bring himself to take: a complete split from the old ways. It is that which led to his downfall in 1986.

On 22 March that year, Rangers played a league game against Celtic at Ibrox. It ended, remarkably, 4–4 on a day of incessant rain. What made it even more exceptional was that the visitors played for virtually a whole hour with ten men after Willie McStay had been sent off for a foul on Ted McMinn. Long after the match, when the Celtic directors had gone, Wallace came into the Ibrox boardroom in jubilant mood. He punched the air and resorted to another chorus of 'The Sash'. The mood did not match Rangers' current status then, for they had only drawn the match and were still rooted in fifth place in the league, hopelessly out of touch in the title race. There was one director there who was appalled by Wallace's resorting to populist type. His name was David Holmes. He was not a Rangers man in the traditional sense; in fact he was a supporter of Falkirk. But he was on the board specifically to represent the business interests of the owner of the club, Lawrence Marlborough, who had inherited the huge family construction firm of his grandfather, the previous owner and chairman John Lawrence, and who was now resident in Lake Tahoe in the USA. After hearing that day a manager expressing joy after drawing at home against their greatest rivals, who had played the majority of the match with only ten men, Holmes felt he had to act. He left Ibrox that night, went straight home, lifted the phone, dialled Lake Tahoe and told Marlborough that he had had enough and wanted to give up his Rangers directorship because the club was living in a dream world.

Holmes could see that Wallace and most of his fellow directors were mired in fantasy and had no intention of changing their ways. On his first day as a director, for example, he had gone to Ibrox for a Hibernian match and had been initiated into a curious ritual. Before every game the directors would hold a sweep, for a fiver each, to see who could guess the size of the crowd that day. On his slip Holmes dutifully wrote '40,000'. At the end of the afternoon when they examined the slips it was revealed that the chairman, John Paton, had won with '13,300', only a few hundred short of the actual figure. Paton laughed when he showed the figure Holmes had put down. It was mocked. 'I couldn't believe it,' he told me. 'Here we had a stadium with over 40,000 seats and there was the chairman amused by me thinking we could fill it. They had lapsed into a mind-set which accepted all the jokes of the day, like how the architect should have built the seats facing away from the pitch. And I would watch crowds of about 7,000 turning up and I was hearing nothing coming from my fellow directors which suggested they could reverse this situation and put bums on all of those seats.'

His attitude certainly did not commend itself to the directors, but he found a strange ally in the figure of Willie Waddell, who no longer had any official connection with the club but who was in an honorary position and never missed a game, although heavily indebted to the bottle at that stage in his life. He could appear to be simply a curmudgeonly passenger who attended the drinks cabinet far too often, but he still possessed a degree of gravitas that the directors would not ignore. His backing of Holmes was odd, though, in the sense that Waddell had always been suspicious of outsiders. He obviously recognised something in this new man that would benefit the club. Without Waddell standing full square with him and publicly going out of his way to make him feel at home, Holmes's task, difficult enough though it was going to be, might have been intolerable.

The answer Marlborough gave Holmes that day was to change the course of Scottish football history. For the exile in the States asked him what it would take to keep him on the board, since he knew that Rangers were in a slump and had not won the league for eight years, and even he was running out of patience. Holmes told him that to stay he would want full control of Rangers Football Club. Marlborough agreed. Thus began the era that was, from whichever angle it is viewed by either friends or foes of the club, to transform, or disfigure, or regenerate, or unbalance the footballing landscape. The trend was set which sent Scottish football into a version of the Roaring Twenties. Holmes, whose clarity of purpose got up some journalists' noses, was dubbed by journalist Jim Blair of the *Daily Record* 'The Joiner from Falkirk, who would be the Carpenter from Nazareth'. It is something that never bothered Holmes as he set in train a process that revolutionised the Scottish game.

It started in Paris, as Holmes recalled. 'Lawrence Marlborough was a tax exile, so we had to have the whole Lawrence Group meeting in Paris, and that, of course, included Rangers Football Club, which was losing money hand over fist with the stadium only quarter-filled every week. I spelled out what needed to be done, which certainly did not go down well with the Rangers chairman at the time, John Paton, who was present. But I was given the reins as the new chief executive and after coming to terms with a few directors for their removal and meeting Jock Wallace in a car park in Strathclyde Park and coming to an amicable agreement with him about his removal, I decided that I had to project this club to a wider world. One man was in my mind – Graeme Souness, who was known throughout Europe. We needed to have somebody who could project the club's image internationally, and would be widely known throughout the game. I contacted him through the good offices of journalist Ken Gallacher and promised him an exclusive on the story if anything happened. I think in doing that I incurred the enmity of other colleagues of his in the business. But it did happen, and my whole life was then turned upside down.'

Holmes had one major bargaining tool which is occasionally forgotten. English clubs were banned from European competition during that post-Heysel period. Rangers offered to anybody, almost inevitably every season, participation in these tournaments. Holmes played this card strongly with the Sampdoria player, who in turn used it as an inducement to wade in with the chequebook south of the border. The first major step was to acquire English international defender Terry Butcher, who had been put on the transfer list by Ipswich to help them fund a new stand and get in more season tickets. Of course goalkeeper

Chris Woods had already been signed from Norwich, but it was Butcher the gigantic defender who stirred the imagination of the media and the support. Although people at the time thought he had chosen Rangers out of many alternatives, Souness was the first man actually to approach him. So he had little option but to meet up with Rangers, and although it was understandable he had certain reservations about coming north of the border to an environment he knew little about, his wife had absolutely none, and after his £750,000 transfer they both settled in as if to the manor born. The Englishman became even more of a Ranger than a boy born and brought up in the shadow of the stadium. 'The English press came up in force to watch me play my first Old Firm game at Ibrox in August of that year,' Butcher recalled, 'and we happened to win 1–0, when Davie Cooper slipped a ball to Ian Durrant to score. After the game I told them that's why I had come here. Big crowds, tremendous atmosphere, playing in cup finals – all of that. I just felt caught up in the whole Rangers thing.'

Holmes almost immediately suffered a trauma. It came, unexpectedly, on 9 August, as he sat in the stand at Easter Road and watched his expensively acquired player-manager walking from the field after being sent off by the referee in the first league game of the season. Souness had tackled George McCluskey in a manner he later regretted. The Hibernian player was carried off, but only after mayhem had ensued in the middle of the field. All 21 of the players were involved in the punch-up, and all were booked. Rangers, with ten men, lost 1–0. Holmes went home that night seriously wondering if he had made the mistake of his life. He went to a restaurant and for the first time admitted to his wife that he was uncomfortable, even embarrassed, to be seen in public as the Rangers chief executive. After all, he had put his neck on the line by having to go to the bank to borrow money to bring Souness and the rest of the players to Ibrox, for in Holmes's own words 'Rangers were skint when I got there'. Indeed, one Sunday only a few months into his tenure he discovered that there was no money left in the coffers to pay wages, which they normally did on a two-weekly basis. He had to go back to the bank again to borrow more just to cover that. When you are engaged in that sort of financial Indian rope-trick you want to see fairly rapid returns on your investment. But there he was that day in Edinburgh watching an implosion. He kept his nerve, however, and on the Monday morning addressed the whole squad, warning them that as he was the paymaster he would countenance no such disorder again, whatever the provocation. To be sure there were no mass brawls after that, but it did nothing to dampen the ethos Souness had immediately established.

Before he arrived Wallace had fed the masses the belief that he and he alone could produce the animus to take on the arduous task of overtaking Celtic. The results in his second spell at Ibrox showed that to be a myth. Souness converted the myth into reality. Of course Holmes had spelled out to him that he had been brought there simply to win, and especially to win the league in the first season, and that he would bankroll him to do so. So Souness conveyed that target to his staff, not by simulating commando courses, like Wallace, but by developing mental attitudes akin to a hungry wolf-pack hunting for prey in Siberia. Anybody who has any doubts about that will find that code of conduct more than hinted at in the words of Terry Butcher. 'It was fierce even in training sessions,' he said. 'On Fridays we would have England against Scotland matches. Us Englishmen in the squad hated losing to the Scots. They were hard battles. But that was transferred into our spirit on a Saturday. And in particular it developed us for the Old Firm match. I got caught up in that atmosphere far too much. My wife said I went from one extreme to the other, from being a naïve Englishman not knowing anything about it into becoming someone sucked into the hatreds too much. I ended up with an immense hatred for Celtic, not on religious grounds, but just as our greatest rivals. Your hackles would flare up whenever you saw a Celtic jersey. My wife said in that respect I had become not a very nice person. I had ended up like a supporter. You just didn't like being at Celtic Park surrounded by all that lime-green colour. You just wanted out of the place as soon as you could. It became a habit to walk into Celtic Park and make sure everybody wiped our feet on the Celtic crest which lay on the floor there. We weren't instructed to do it. It just happened because you could feel the animosity as soon as you walked in there, and that was our way of dealing with it. And in general we bonded well in working up the belief that everybody was against us, so to hell with them, just beat them!'

It was this new purpose to his life that helped Butcher captain Rangers to the winning of the Skol (League) Cup on 26 October against Celtic – the first trophy of Souness's managerial career. But again it was tainted by controversy: Maurice Johnston of Celtic was sent off and crossed himself as he left the field, not out of a fit of religious remorse but as a nifty bit of tribal identification which would be recalled by some strident loyalists amongst the Rangers support some three years later. As I commentated on the late Davie Cooper walking up calmly to score the winning penalty which gave Rangers that cup 2–1, I sensed that Rangers now had a backbone which had been significantly missing for years. Butcher lifted the trophy that day as if he had been born in Govan. An English import leading a Scottish club in that deeply committed manner no longer seemed a freakish phenomenon, simply a piece of good business by the joiner from Falkirk.

But in that first season alone Holmes knew he was dealing with a maverick spirit within the ranks, and that it would be difficult to keep Souness off the front, never mind the back, page. On the second last day of the first season at Pittodrie, on 2 May 1987, with the ground crammed full and Rangers supporters massed outside without tickets, Souness was sent off again after an incident with the Aberdeen defender Brian Irvine. This lent an ugly side to a day that should have been one purely of triumph, for Butcher's headed goal helped the club to a 1–1 draw which earned them their first league title in nine years, as Celtic had been beaten by Holmes's beloved Falkirk that same afternoon. In the celebrations that followed Holmes came to the same *modus vivendi* as that agreeable Aberdeen chairman Dick Donald had with Alex Ferguson, that control of such personalities had to be balanced against the results achieved.

This fine judgement had to be applied the following season, for on 29 August at Parkhead Souness was sent off for the third time in 12 months, for a tackle on Billy Stark of Celtic, and received a five-match ban from the SFA. But it was an incident after the match that had a nocturnal aftermath. After the game the chief executive dived for the cover of his Falkirk residence to avoid any of the normal press intrusions following in Souness's wake. He thought he would not see the manager again until the following Monday, but late that Saturday night the player-manager appeared on his doorstep in a disturbed mood and was asked inside. Holmes's account of the conversation that followed revealed a man in turmoil. 'Graeme came in and told me he had met the referee, David Syme, outside Celtic Park. "I had a go at him," he admitted to me. "I called him a big effing poof. It'll be in the papers tomorrow. And in any case I've had enough. I'm resigning."' Holmes knew that the SFA would not regard his manager's remarks to the referee as idle badinage, but he adopted a positive stance. 'All I said back to him was, "OK, if that's what you want." I think he was a bit taken aback by that, and said, "Is that all you have to say?" I just told him that if he didn't want it, then so be it, and that I had an insurance policy in his assistant Walter Smith who was perfectly capable of taking on the job. I then told him I wasn't going to offer a shoulder for him to cry on, nor was I going to listen to him saying he couldn't take the pressure. I also reminded him that I had done deals in the past to keep his name out of the papers on more than one occasion, and now if he felt he had to go then that was up to him. But he had to remember what I had done for him. I said we could shake on that there and then and he could leave the club. He asked me if he could think about it. I told him he would have to tell me before he left the house that night. He did shake hands, but only after telling me he would stay on.'

There is a suggestion in Holmes's stance that night, although he certainly would not interpret it this way himself, that he had been driven to the limits and was torn between welcoming the possibility of relieving himself of the burden of unnecessary controversy and his absolute belief that Souness was the best man for the job. That Holmes had indulged in brinkmanship himself and had offered to open the door for his exit, only for Souness to relent, paid handsome dividends for the club in the years to follow but certainly did not turn his player-manager into a Trappist monk, nor did it convert his players into buttercup-picking Brownies.

That was made clear in Souness's dealings with the press. He had his favourites amongst the media, as all managers do, so there was nothing unusual about that. What was different was his truculence at the very existence of the Fourth Estate. If the *Guinness Book of Records* took account of press conferences, one of them at Ibrox would have been timed as the shortest in footballing history. We awaited Souness's post-match presence in a room on the ground floor of the stadium, adjoining the marble entrance hall. He opened the door, entered, made a kind of Nureyev pirouette, and left, slamming the door behind him. That was the press conference. He was conforming to the contractual requirements of the league to make an appearance, which he had done with grand contempt for all those present. From Stein to Ferguson, and throughout McLean's period, I had watched them all wrestling with or massaging the media whenever it suited their purpose, and all three could manipulate them brilliantly. But too often Souness treated them as if they carried a communicable disease. It did not seem wise to me at the time. Nor did it particularly help that he had a column ghosted for one particular tabloid, thus inviting the enmity of competitors. At the time I recall talking to him about that, since he rarely spurned the television cameras, and asked him if it really was necessary to be so openly belligerent. He simply said, 'I hate some of these bastards. I don't need them.' That is the point. He did need them, for if ever a man wished to project a positive image, it was Graeme Souness.

He and Holmes most certainly did not need some of the headlines they generated. Allan Herron penned an article for the *Sunday Mail* on 21 February 1988 headed 'Ibrox £6 Million Flops' after Rangers had been knocked out of the Scottish Cup by Dunfermline. We should first of all observe that a sub-editor, not Herron, created the headline. But note it. It is contemptuous. It is a 'reprisal' headline offering not a jot of sympathy. It is a payback headline. It highlights the folly of big spending. They were queuing up, then, to get back at Souness for his treatment of them. Don Morrison wrote in the same newspaper, after an incident Souness had with journalist Gerry McNee when the player-manager threatened physical violence during an argument on an aircraft returning from Bucharest, 'David Holmes has done a magnificent job in putting Rangers into the big time since he took over and appointed Graeme Souness. But now he has to get their behind-the-scenes public relations act together and restore some dignity to a great club.' Alex Cameron of the *Daily Record* had written a few months earlier, 'How sad that the brave and costly enterprise of Rangers is being sabotaged by their own indiscipline . . . Rangers are so far ahead of the game in almost every aspect it is depressing that they regularly trip themselves up on the pitch.' When 'Candid', as he was nicknamed, was crossed in any way by anybody in football, he could suddenly turn into the Grim Reaper, his fingers tapping out the Death March from *Saul* on his typewriter. Since he had been treated brusquely by Souness he positively glowed when he had to rebuke him in public. That sort of reporting neither wins nor loses games, but it builds up needless tensions and aggravations, and the warring with the media from first to last, however much he might deny it, got through to Souness. He was self-immolating, while at the same time putting bums on seats, as Holmes had demanded. Ibrox was bursting at the seams, and paradoxically the more the media laid into the management the more the ranks closed amongst the support.

The reason for that was not simply growing success for the team, but the parade of names brought to Ibrox during his reign. As the chorus of rebukes about big spending soared amongst other managers who simply could not compete on that level, Souness always insisted that he never spent more than £1.7 million on any one player. But he could spend, apparently at will, backed by a man who was willing to be his Goldfinger. Butcher and Woods came for less than £1.3 million, Jimmy Nicholl cost £70,000, and Graham Roberts signed for £450,000. Combined with other less prominent signings, he spent £2,275,000 in his first season – breathtakingly huge for the Scottish game at that time. Richard Gough then became Scotland's first £1 million signing when he returned from Spurs. Defender Gary Stevens also came for £1 million, and Kevin Drinkell and Mel Sterland for £500,000 each. Trevor Steven then popped up for £1.5 million. Souness also picked up, relatively cheaply, men who made useful contributions, such as Trevor Francis and Ray Wilkins. It is calculated that in all he spent £15.5 million on signings during his management. His philosophy was to buy and discard, not to develop or nurture. If you could not hack it at first, you went. Of the 37 players he bought, 17 were moved on after varying periods. Richard Gough said once, 'It is like a revolving door. Sometimes you wondered just who would be in the dressing room when you arrived for training in the morning.' So, the criticism of lack of judgement can be levelled at Souness for the merry-go-round he created. But there is another way of looking at it. After years of languishing in a trough of mediocrity, Rangers wanted instant success. A ghostly-looking Ibrox on match day was intolerable given the potential they had. Any businessman would have come to that conclusion. So you marry the impulsive nature of the man to the impetus of the quick fix and the tolerance of mounting debt, underwritten by the market value placed on the stadium, and you get the revolving door and success. The rest of Scottish football, especially Celtic, looked on with a mixture of bewilderment, envy and increasing unease at the imbalance being created. It is hardly taxing the intelligence to understand that Rangers greatly preferred that situation to the ridicule being heaped upon them before Holmes arrived. They were now providing the comedians with less ammunition.

One arena they hoped would increase respect was European football. It was never to be achieved in the way Souness would have hoped. A summary of his feelings about that situation was made to me briefly in

Belgrade Airport at the end of October 1990 after his side had been trounced 3–0 by Red Star in an era when countries were limited to only two foreign imports. 'How can I win a European trophy with 11 Jocks?' he barked as he swept past me. He was uttering a truism that was bearing down heavily on him. He couldn't buy success in Europe for that simple reason. He did not have the patience, and neither did the supporters, to create something along the lines developed by Jim McLean at Dundee United over several seasons. Their appetites had been whetted by the triumph over the formidable Dinamo Kiev side early in his second season. They had been beaten 1–0 in Kiev on 16 September 1987, and when I walked out on to the pitch prior to the return leg at Ibrox two weeks later, I could barely believe my eyes. It was as if it had developed anorexia. The sidelines had been sucked into the very limit of the accepted dimensions. The nearest touchline seemed curiously distant from the edge of the pitch. It was legal, but was it sporting? Corinthian values were something belonging to the hansom-cab age. This was brutally effective business being done. Oleg Blokhin, one of the best players ever to come out of the former USSR, did not like it, for on the left side he liked width from which he could create chaos, with his speed and bewildering changes of direction. He was effectively corralled that night by the narrowness of the pitch. Amid intense passion Rangers triumphed 2–0 with goals by Falco and McCoist. Souness's detractors, and there were now many, called it a cynical ploy; in many of the taverns of Glasgow he was a hero. But you can't cart narrow pitches around with you, and eventually Rangers were shown to be not good enough for the European stage, even as they steadily progressed towards outright strangulation of the domestic game.

Steadily, but not entirely smoothly. They finished third in the league at the end of 1987/88, 12 points behind Celtic, but won the Scottish League Cup. The following season Souness won his second championship, the 39th in the history of the club, and claimed the Scottish League Cup for the third successive season, for the first time in Rangers' history. During that 1988/89 season a good friend of Souness's, a businessman originally from Ayr who had won the Scottish Young Businessman of the Year Award in 1984 through his successful running of a massive steel group, and who had interests in a basketball team in Livingston, expressed an interest to Souness in buying Rangers. That interest had grown because

Rangers were again strapped and melting into serious debt through having to cope with huge wage bills.

I met David Murray for the first time before he became the owner of the club, when Souness and I went to Livingston to help out in a charity basketball shoot and watch the great American player Alton Bird in action. Murray was sitting at the side of the court throughout these proceedings, and when he talked, you listened. I knew little about him, but he was the sort of man who commanded attention. He had experienced incredible misfortune: in 1981 he was involved in a horrendous car crash which necessitated the amputation of both legs, and afterwards he suffered the intense pain of watching his young wife die of cancer. It might have put an end to most men, but not Murray. Backed by personal wealth and attributes of character that demonstrated incredible courage and vision, his overtures to Lawrence Marlborough were successful, since the exile believed he would be placing Rangers in safe hands. Murray acquired a 76 per cent stake in the club at a cost of £6 million and agreed to take on the existing debt, which various sources put between £4 million and £7 million. In addition, Souness himself became a shareholder and director with a 7 per cent share valued at £600,000. Everything had been put in place by 22 November 1988.

Suddenly, with the temerity and timing of a Caribbean pirate attacking a gold-laden galleon, Robert Maxwell, newspaper magnate and proponent of keeping the tradition of megalomania alive, swept on to the scene with an outrageous bid to upstage Murray. David Holmes, still in position as chief executive but knowing that his time would soon be up, was lunching with the editor of the *Sunday Mail*, Endell Laird, in the newspaper's offices at about that time when in walked the abrasive Maxwell. The lunch had been arranged merely to soothe some of the passions Laird's newspaper had aroused within Ibrox, so Holmes was not prepared for the entry of the proprietor of the paper, who came to the table all guns blazing on the subject of buying Rangers. Maxwell was an unrepentant bully, but he met his match in Holmes. The chief executive might initially have given the impression to some, with his white hair swept nobly back from his brow, that he was of angelic stock. He is not. He is from Falkirk. In an exchange of barrack-room language between the two, Holmes made it clear he would not be intimidated by Maxwell's bombast, and sent him packing. The familiar Ibrox cry of 'No surrender!' was transcribed that day into 'No sale!'

So Marlborough bowed out and Murray entered. The first aspect, which is still debated, is how good a deal it was for the entrepreneur. At that time he was reckoned to be the 107th richest man in the UK with a personal fortune of £35 million. So £6 million for Ibrox seemed, even then to people in the know, a steal. Perhaps the debt Rangers carried at the time might have made the prospect untenable to others, but the fact that Maxwell had come crashing on to the scene suggests that the debt was wholly manageable and that the commercial potential was enormous. The other aspect was the role of Holmes. He left the club having played a part which has almost been airbrushed out of the Ibrox story. Although he had spells as chairman of Falkirk and Dundee to help their commercial survival, he disappeared from much of the limelight to which he had become accustomed, and although you could hardly describe it as a cuckolding when Murray took over, there is little doubt that not much credit was going to be pushed in Holmes's direction in later years, when the spoils of victory under the new leadership were being dispensed. He could not have undertaken that role without making enemies, and there is little doubt that he sometimes rubbed people up the wrong way. But he did kick-start the whole rigmarole of buying and spending which heralded the beginning of what you could label, without particularly endorsing the trend, the modern era of Scottish football. His involvement could never be described as anything other than seminal, even though it seemed to pale into insignificance compared to what followed.

We were about to enter an era of wheeling and dealing and legislative change accompanied by incredible sums of money and a rise in the prominence of agents. It would creep up on the Scottish game like a silent killer. Murray and Souness, bonded tightly in a commercial love affair, were to overwhelm their detractors in various ways, but perhaps most notably by taking a fancy to a small, red-haired player who, given his public displays of affection for his origins, seemed to conform to that sometimes derogatorily expressed mantra 'once a Catholic, always a Catholic'.

CHAPTER EIGHTEEN

THE WORLD TURNED
UPSIDE DOWN

It started as the kind of rumour you would place in the 'Elvis is alive and well and living in a timeshare in Tenerife' category. It did not quite reach the feverish intensity of the sort of gossip known in the best circles as 'the talk of the steamie', but it is true that little whispers were doing the rounds in media quarters that something improbable was about to happen. I heard them myself at the time, but in all honesty I dismissed them as part of the chaff that afflicts our business in the silly season. After all, it was July 1989, and much of the sports media was lazing about on beaches by the Med or in Florida.

That is why Iain Scott, now sports news editor of the *Daily Record* but then deputy to the sports editor of the *Scottish Sun*, suddenly found himself thrust into a situation that produced the scoop to dream of. Irritated by the constant queries he was receiving about this specific rumour, on Sunday, 9 July he approached the editor of his paper, Jack Irvine, with news reporter Isabel Murray, who had heard the same whispers, and put to him the question that sparked Scott off on a quest that was to end, astonishingly, on a mountain top in Italy the following day. 'The editor knew Graeme Souness well, so we went in to see Jack,' Scott recalled. 'We were lucky he was in on this particular Sunday or else what happened might not have landed in our laps. We asked him to telephone the Rangers manager and ask him once and for all, "Have you signed Maurice Johnston, or are you ever going to sign him?"'

Unsurprisingly, Irvine expressed some incredulity about such a question, for only two months earlier Billy McNeill, manager of Celtic, had convened a press conference at which Johnston, then with Nantes in the French league, was paraded, proudly flaunting a Celtic jersey and posing at a desk with pen in hand, simulating a signing. It has since been reported that at the time somebody had jokingly remarked to McNeill that he'd better get him registered there and then, but McNeill had not taken such a remark seriously, as Johnston's immediate future seemed a formality. The prodigal son was returning to the fold. Who could have blamed McNeill for making that simple assumption? For coming when it did, the news of Johnston's imminent signing for Celtic arguably produced such an electrifying effect throughout the entire Celtic community that it helped them prevent Rangers from winning the treble that season, for McNeill's team won the Scottish Cup final on 20 May 1989 with a goal by Joe Miller. Still, Irvine made the call to Souness.

What followed then might have been taken from the Watergate text-book on how Woodward and Bernstein of the *Washington Post* skilfully used subtle telephoning interviews with reluctant subjects to get them to imply, if not exactly openly admit, certain matters. Firstly, Irvine asked Souness outright if Johnston had been signed, or was about to be signed. Scott, who had the tape of this interview played to him immediately afterwards for his consideration, remembers that opening gambit above all. 'It was then that I discovered what the phrase "pregnant pause" really meant,' he said. 'There was a silence. Souness was in his car heading back to Edinburgh. He asked Irvine to call him back when he got there, which he did. We listened again to the conversation. Jack asked him several times different questions in different sorts of ways, and although he never at any time said yes or no we could feel something was on. "I think he's signed him," I said. Jack agreed we should rip out what was being prepared for the paper and immediately devote a whole 16 pages to debatably the biggest story we had ever had, even though we had received not a single piece of encouragement from Souness. It was just the fact that he hadn't denied it that prompted us to believe we were on to something big. He could still have been stringing us along, of course. But we took an almighty gamble.'

They knew that the Rangers squad had already left for pre-season training in Italy, and that if anything were to happen it might take place out there in the mountains of north Tuscany. So Scott was dispatched to find the first available plane and get out to Il Ciocco, the magnificent hotel and training complex just above the village of Barga, the birthplace of many Italian restaurateurs in the West of Scotland, even though he was going purely on the basis of Souness failing to deny the rumour. To try to keep his movements and suspicions secret, Scott could not even tell his wife why he was asking her to pack an overnight bag and have it and his passport sent out to him by taxi, just in case somebody intercepted the call and blew the whole enterprise. 'To be honest, we [Scott and his photographer] were terrified,' he said. 'Supposing Souness was just stringing us along? Suppose we had misinterpreted what he had said? We could end up looking like the biggest fools in newspaper history because of the 16 pages we were now committed to running on this. If this was right then, good God, we were winning a prize. If we were wrong, I could be out of a job, and who would touch me after that? I arrived in Italy not having seen what the newspaper had run on the Monday morning because they had all been sold out by the time I got up to the airport hotel, and there wasn't a word about Johnston in any of the other papers. That made me even more worried. And we couldn't ask any questions or discuss it in public in case we were overheard. It was getting like a spy movie.'

During Scott's flight, unknown to him, Rangers had called a press conference that Monday morning at Ibrox. I was in Scotland at home at about 9.15 a.m., at just about the time Scott was landing, when I took a call from my son. 'The *Sun* is running a story that Maurice Johnston has signed for Rangers,' he said. 'All my workmates are crowded round the phone waiting for you to give them an answer. Is this really true?' I remember my answer distinctly: 'Tell them there is more chance of the Pope signing for Rangers than Mo Johnston.' I think, afterwards, he would have had a hard job convincing his mates that the BBC's principal football commentator really did have his finger on the pulse of Scottish football. But I was not alone in being utterly wrong-footed. Half an hour later the BBC phoned to confirm that there was indeed an Ibrox press conference but with no mention of the subject of it. Still, I had to get there, pronto. 'Surely not?' I kept thinking as I drove across the city. When I got there, later than I had intended, the photographers were already coming down the marble staircase. 'Is he there?' I asked one. He just nodded. In Italy, a few moments earlier, Scott had taken a call from one of his colleagues who told him that he was constantly being ridiculed by other journalists from rival newspapers, as they assembled in the stately Blue Room at Ibrox, for creating a monumental fuck-up (as they put it) by running such a preposterous story. Then the door had opened and in had stepped Souness with his new signing.

When I first saw Maurice Johnston in his blue Rangers blazer sitting beside Souness the first shock waves of his appearance before the press had already subsided, but there was still an air of incomprehension hanging over the throng. He sat there, not like an iconic 'First Ever Catholic' – yes, others from that faith had slipped under the Ibrox radar unknowingly, but this was the accepted historic breakthrough for which many had waited generations, a fact underlined by the reaction to Johnston's appearance – but more like a bewildered wee boy on his first visit to a museum. The fact that the blazer was two sizes too big for him accentuated the feeling that this was not real, but some kind of charade. I had been born and brought up to believe that water could never flow upwards. It was like watching a fundamental law of physics being turned upside down. I suppose you had to have been inured from the cradle to the immutable principles which set the mould of the relationship between religion and the two clubs in our native city to truly appreciate what was happening.

They ushered him out, eventually, to an uncertain future. Outside the stadium some supporters amongst a crowd of about 300 or so asked me, in sullen disbelief, if it was true. Yes, I replied, it had happened. To be fair, nobody spoke out of line in the crowd, which nevertheless seemed to be clinging together in incredulity.

Historically it is of no importance which newspaper scooped any other with this episode, other than in the narrow professional sense. The simple fact that Irvine and Scott were prepared to take a terrible gamble on their own professional reputations demonstrates powerfully just how cataclysmic this signing was. You have to wonder, though, why no others pursued the rumour with such diligence. Scott's narrative does suggest that their instincts were driving them on more confidently than they perhaps realised at the time. It certainly negates the publicly accepted belief that the story was handed on a plate to his newspaper by the Rangers manager, for Scott heard every word that passed between his editor and Souness.

Now everybody braced themselves for aftershocks. Of course there were negative reactions. Indeed, when Johnston belatedly arrived at the training camp in Italy, he was excluded from talking to Scott and could only wave cheekily at him from the training ground, as if he had done no more than sign up for a new health club. It was an early intimation that

Rangers had signed a man with a personality able to sustain the flak which he knew would be coming his way in different forms. Scott ran into another problem, for although photographs of the new player were permitted by Souness, the home Scots in the squad were at first reluctant to be seen in his company in public. They had greeted him warmly enough, but privately. Ian Durrant, playing cards with Johnston, told Scott it would be embarrassing to have to face up to the lads in his local Rangers pub if he were to be seen sitting down beside this 'ex-Celt', and shied away from having a snap taken. In short, the native-born Scots, brought up in the orthodox manner, did not know how to cope with the situation, although they soon learnt. Stories that Rangers supporters burned their scarves and tore up season tickets abounded, but were greatly exaggerated. Some of that certainly occurred, but other tales are pure mythology. Some supporters were actually paid to stand and burn scarves for the benefit of certain cameras. News even filtered through that the loyalist stronghold of the Shankhill in Belfast was on the edge of revolt. But the reality was that apart from the actions of a few delinquents, life, curiously enough, went on as normal. And that was the point. Once it had happened, you simply had to wonder why it hadn't happened before. For I detected only a sense of suspension of judgement, not hostility, among the crowds that turned up to watch Johnston in action, aside from a few cranks who certainly will go to their graves worrying about papist conspiracies in the Teletubbies. Ibrox still filled itself to capacity. That was what mattered more than anything to Souness.

This tolerance was not born of a new-found ecumenical spirit, but largely because the crowd perceived Souness to have cuckolded, shafted, humiliated and indeed destabilised the great rivals, and with such audacity that any deep sense of loss at ditching an old tradition was made to seem, at least to the vast majority, long overdue and worth it. Archbishop Winning, on behalf of the Catholic community, issued a statement of endorsement that ended 'hope the signing will help overcome the religious bigotry which has divided Glasgow for decades', but Celtic were seething. This was no historic breakthrough to a more enlightened age; this was treachery and sabotage. McNeill was not only incensed and embarrassed but worried about the overall effect this would have on Rangers' playing status, given what now appeared to be their new 'open-door' policy. He was right to be concerned.

Johnston had treated his former club miserably. He was the catalyst that led to Rangers inflicting on their rivals one of the most wretched eras in their history. Had they signed him instead of Rangers I am convinced Celtic would have won the league title that season, but instead he crossed the city and gave a boost to the historic nine-titles-in-a-row run of the Ibrox club. Leaving aside the social issues, this is how this crucial acquisition tilted the balance of power so heavily in Rangers' favour. Johnston's agent, Bill McMurdo, an ardent supporter of Northern Ireland loyalist groups whose home just outside Glasgow was festooned in all things red, white and blue but who nevertheless did business with Celtic for both Johnston and his other Parkhead client, Frank McAvennie, put the blame for this squarely on the shoulders of the Celtic board. The *Scottish Sun* of 10 December 1994 reported him as saying, 'I didn't want Mo to sign for Rangers, you know. But in the end he opted for Rangers and I knew he would handle Ibrox all right because he gives 100 per cent to whoever he is with. The furore over his "move" to Celtic beforehand was down solely to the Celtic directors who, bluntly, tried to save face by blaming me for it all. But the truth is they knew what was happening. Anyway, around that time none of them understood the workings of freedom of contract.' Dumb Celtic board versus sharp operator is how that reads. Everything was legit, though, and the sounds of Celtic claiming the moral high ground and crying foul were quickly drowned in the press, if not amongst their support.

When Johnston scored the only goal of the game against his former club at Ibrox on 4 November 1989 and ran towards the crowd like a born-again Bluenose, he was seen to be effectively sealing a pact with the devil, or courageously helping shunt Rangers into a new era, depending from which side of the sectarian divide you viewed it. Anybody knowing Johnston, who had been sent off to reside in Edinburgh with a certain amount of security surrounding him, would tell you that he bore no stamp of an historic symbol but went about life almost blissfully unaware of the controversy he had caused. He has been written up subsequently as a gallant rebel who flew in the face of fortune to help end an iniquity. He was in fact a likeable, roguish wee Glasgow fella who liked a good night out, was great company and knew more about the train stations around Europe than the Stations of the Cross. With the greatest respect to him, he wouldn't have known a moral cause had it been gift-wrapped and handed to him as a Christmas present. It was the Rangers cash that got through to him.

You sensed, underneath any conversation you had with him at the time, that Souness was purring with contentment, as you would do if you had your opponents on the run. He had learnt a salient lesson as Rangers manager: hatred ran deep and was accentuated against him personally for the changes he had wrought. When he was banned from the touchline and had to sit in the directors' box at Celtic Park, many supporters in and around that 'respectable' area spent as much time turned away from the game shouting abuse at him as watching it. Many of his reactions stemmed from not being able to cope with that. Above all, there were those who simply did not want Rangers to change from their inflexibly sectarian ways. It suited them to have Rangers increasingly weakened by their refusal to flow with the tide. Celtic were the first to worry about that. Souness's chutzpah, backed by Murray's relentless drive for success, which caused him to say to me on one occasion 'I'll buy the league!', thus indicating he would stop at nothing, had changed the historical agenda once and for all. It was to take another nine long years for Celtic to find the solution to the new opposition.

Not that Souness had a more peaceful life as a result. When they returned a year later to Il Ciocco, their training camp in Italy, Johnston was involved in an unseemly row with the England striker Mark Hateley and had to be sent home. He arrived back in Glasgow with bruises on his face, accompanied by the excuse that he had flopped rather heavily down on the bare springs of a bed. Whether true or not, it was as believable to the tabloids as a sighting of the Loch Ness monster in the Broomielaw. But in a sense his joining Rangers had not turned him into a Trappist monk. He was what he was, a footballer who liked a good time and drank too much at times. This certainly did not deter Souness from being his cheerleader. He was, after all, a striker of quality who blossomed through playing in the same team as Hateley. In two seasons in a row he ended up as Rangers' leading goalscorer with a total of 40 goals. Nor did it dampen Souness's sense of adventure, for when he signed Mark Walters for £500,000 from Aston Villa in 1989 he introduced Rangers to their first black player in 50 years. Sadly, in Walters' first game at Celtic Park the first thing I noticed when he approached the famous 'Jungle' underneath our commentary position was that bananas were being thrown at him and jungle noises chanted. Equally sadly, not too much was written about that immediately afterwards, as if amid the sectarian bitterness the throwing of bananas was a mere jest. The outrage about that only surfaced once he had been subjected to the same treatment from Hearts supporters in a later game.

The aggravations, as Souness saw them, piled up. A major one was his row with Scottish Television. During a game played at Ibrox on 17 February 1990 against Hearts, the STV cameras picked up something unusual. Cameraman Norrie Walters, positioned just above the tunnel at Ibrox, saw a head appear just at the point of exit. It was Souness. It just so happened he ought not to have been there. He was banned from the pitchside by the SFA, so this constituted an offence. Walters, though, as any professional would have, considered it worthy to be picked up, for in television it is useful to have such footage for editing purposes. He had no idea what he was setting in train. For in the final *Scotsport* edit the following Sunday afternoon the brief shot of Souness was publicly shown on the box. By Tuesday the *Daily Record* had shown a blurred but blown-up picture of the Rangers manager, taken directly from the television, which pinpointed his offence, perhaps more graphically. All hell broke loose. The SFA demanded an explanation from Ibrox, as Souness did from STV. Murray demanded an apology before he would allow their cameras back in. He thought somebody within the station was out to get his manager.

It is here that a subtext comes into play which demonstrates the mind-set of the sectarian ethos. Souness learnt from within STV that two men deeply involved in their output were Celtic sympathisers – the director of the game that day, Dermot McQuarrie, and the producer of home programmes, Dennis Mooney. They had 'suspicious names', as it was put to me at the time. Souness smelled conspiracy. Mooney then became involved in a personal dispute with Souness which had a curious aftermath, years later, as Mooney recalled. 'Dermot and I went to see him, after we had been informed that we were banned from carrying out any more interviews at Ibrox. To say he was annoyed was an understatement. We tried to explain that the shot of him at the tunnel was an integral part of the coverage of the match, and had not been "painted" in deliberately. He couldn't accept that. Eventually because of the ban we decided not to cover any of Rangers' home games, which caused some concern amongst advertisers who were paying handsomely for television presence. We got our presenter Jim White to read out a statement on one of our programmes, which indicated no malice on our part. David Murray considered that that fell far short of an apology, which of course we were not prepared to offer, and the dispute dragged on until it all petered out eventually. But Graeme could not be convinced that we were innocent and always believed we had set out to get him. When I retired in 2001 and my colleagues made a video of all my friends' views on me, they asked Souness for a contribution when he was manager at Blackburn. He did so, very graciously complimenting me on my hard work and professionalism. But when they turned the cameras off he snapped out, "That little c— stitched me up, you know."'

It was actually the SFA who stitched him up, to the tune of another fine of £5,000 and an extension of his touchline ban for another two seasons. Soon after that, despite a ban on interviews, Terry Butcher inadvertently gave one to STV just outside Ibrox, and coming on top of Butcher's non-appearance at the Skol (League) Cup semi-final against Aberdeen in September 1990 (after being left out of the side) it caused such strain on his relationship with Souness that Butcher left Rangers to move south again, to become Coventry's player-manager, much to the distress of his flock of admirers. This single-mindedness of Souness, in dropping an icon from an important game and eventually not standing in his way when he sought new horizons, had already been demonstrated when after a dressing-room dispute with Graham Roberts (another cult hero) he shunned him completely and forced him out of the club.

So despite Rangers' continuing triumphs, their manager seemed to be getting no nearer to achieving a *modus vivendi* with the Scottish game. Indeed he was taking a scunner to it, as many had done to him. In October 1990 he introduced to Ibrox the splendid Oleg Kuznetsov, an ex-Dinamo Kiev player of renown. It is interesting to note that after both the away and home legs against Rangers in the European Cup in September 1987, David Holmes noticed that the Kiev player had appeared on crutches, with his knee obviously bandaged beneath his trousers. When Souness approached him at that time to ask permission to sign Kuznetsov, his chairman refused, saying that it looked as if he had something wrong with his knees. It was David Murray who eventually sanctioned the signing three years later. The Ukrainian lasted 93 minutes in total before collapsing. I saw him twist and fall at St Johnstone on 20 October after a not especially heavy tackle and did not realise how serious it was until I saw Souness, a full half an hour after the game, walking slowly around the ground as if to calm himself. He had just learnt that a cruciate ligament would put his new signing out for the foreseeable future. He then went on to brand the opposition as 'hammer-throwers' in the press room. It seemed an unnecessary and unfair slur. He did not like Perth, for in a subsequent visit to the same ground he had an unseemly altercation with a tea lady called Aggie which left him in a mood of what was turning out to be terminal bitterness. The headlines that appeared the following morning must have exacerbated that feeling. A new heroine had emerged in Scottish life, Aggie, who after standing up to Souness and publicly giving him some of her sharp lip was now being praised as the Boadicea of the tea cup. It was demeaning.

On the back of these incidents, and the emergence of some evidence of Souness's frustration, he had to issue a denial in the *Rangers News* that he had any intention of leaving Ibrox, prompting Alex Cameron to write in the *Daily Record* on 28 February 1991 that the statement 'refutes finally any lingering doubt about him moving back to Liverpool to replace retired Anfield boss Kenny Dalglish'. But barely six weeks later that is precisely what he did do, after two defeats against Celtic (in the space of eight days) in the latter of which three Rangers players were sent off along with Peter Grant of Celtic. His final press conference was not held in the Blue Room but in a hospitality suite on the other side of the stadium, and it was a perfunctory affair, with Murray trying hard to show that business would go on as usual but scarcely able to hide the fact that he was unhappy. Souness spoke briefly, then, without taking questions, turned on his heel and walked out of the room and out of Scottish football with the same straight-backed, chest-jutting style he adopted for all his sendings-off.

His enemies had a field day. In the *Glasgow Evening Times* of 16 April, Alan Davidson wrote, 'The news that Liverpool will almost certainly be allowed to return to that [European] arena next season probably sealed his decision to leave.' Ian Archer went for the jugular in the same edition and called Souness's departure 'an act of betrayal'. He also labelled him contemptuously as 'a product of the yuppie Thatcherite world'. That struck a chord with some later chroniclers of that era. Indeed one lengthy tome took that as its whole theme, identifying Souness, rather ingenuously, as Thatcher's man. In fact he was more a Mississippian Rhett Butler than a Carlton Club Sir Keith Joseph. He was essentially a gambler who had arrived at the gambler's paradisiacal ideal of being able to use other people's money for his enterprises – or follies, if you will. It is not as if he had landed as a free-marketeer amongst a coven of socialists at Ibrox, glued together in their admiration of Keir Hardie. The boardroom had always been dominated by self-made, small-time businessmen dragged along in the wake of John Lawrence and his building empire, and deeply involved in local Tory politics. But they couldn't run a whelk-stall. Holmes had put in place better business practices, and with the coming of Murray, the institution was attempting to accomplish what they felt was their true destiny – to dominate Scottish football, or 'buy the league' in the new owner's choice language, and in so doing almost put Celtic out of business. Wasn't that what they had always wanted to do, way back before free-market guru Milton Friedman could put two and two together? Holmes, Souness and Murray had simply shown them how to do it. In the process Souness had won three championships, put Rangers on course to win a fourth, and lifted four Scottish League Cups (though he never won the Scottish Cup). But the real legacy was to establish the vigorous but ultimately self-defeating commercial ethos of a sport which had previously been within the provenance of amateurs who loved the game but who were economically illiterate. It is not that the game as a whole was about to go down the fruitful path of regeneration – far from it. But it was all going to be so different now.

But it has to be said that neither Holmes nor Murray were the trailblazers. It was another man who had elbowed his way into the business who could truly claim that. In 1981 Wallace Mercer had become the principal shareholder of Heart of Midlothian after a boardroom struggle which saw him defeat the other protagonist, Kenny Waugh, a bookmaker and well-known Hibernian supporter, 3–2 in the voting. He was a property developer who came to the assistance of Hearts, mainly at the behest of ex-player Donald Ford, and parted with about £350,000 of his own money to save the club from possible liquidation. But he was seen by the media and the public in general as a man with a gift for public relations, which had never been seen before in Scottish football. With his substantial girth, Falstaffian cheeriness and penchant for sharing a glass or two with anybody within touching distance, he became immensely popular with the media. But more than that, he gave such uplift to Hearts, not just in terms of the money that pulled them back from the brink but in his bouncy optimism, accessibility and outspokenness which were godsends to the press and inspiration to his supporters. He was a friend, some might even have said a clone, of David Murray. They certainly came from the same political stable. He was almost immediately disliked by Hibernian supporters, which in a sense indicated that Hearts had perhaps gained a winner.

In the 12 years he was at the club he took it to the brink of wiping out the sneer, laid constantly against them, 'always the bridesmaid, never the bride'. Season 1985/86 could have been called 'Hearts Year', even though they had nothing to show for it eventually. After a poor start to that season they went on a 31-game unbeaten run which took them to within touching distance of the title. In the last game of the season, on 3 May 1986, they played Dundee at Dens Park as league leaders, needing only one point to win the flag. Celtic were at Love Street playing St Mirren, needing to win by a considerable margin to stand a chance of a surprise catch-up.

Alex MacDonald had become the first player-manager in Scotland when appointed by Mercer in 1982, and there is still sadness in his voice when he recalls that day. 'There had been a virus going about and we knew some clubs had been affected by this,' he said. 'We had managed to avoid it. Then, that week, it struck us. One of our key players, Craig Levein, went down with it on the Friday, and that, for a start, upset all our plans. We had two men at Paisley to phone us if there was any scoring going on. Well, eventually they stopped phoning us because Celtic had gone three, then four up and we were still at nothing each. Then Albert Kidd scored for Dundee.' That was seven minutes from the end of the game, and as I described the goal I knew that was the end for Hearts. Kidd scored again shortly after that to inflict even more pain. The mass of Hearts supporters behind the east goal resembled a funeral party. 'At Dens Park there is a long walk to the pavilion,' MacDonald continued, 'and that is the worst walk I have ever taken in my life when the game was finished and we knew Celtic had won 5–0. I was watching the supporters lying on the terracing weeping, and then I went inside and had almost everybody in the team weeping, so I couldn't hold it back and I started myself and had to go into the toilet to compose myself. It took me a long while before I could come out.' The former Rangers player Sandy Jardine was then with Hearts as player and assistant manager, and he is blunt about how the day went. 'St Mirren had a lot of Celtic-minded players in their team,' he observed, 'and nobody is going to convince me other than that some of them didn't give of their best in that match.'

As the scenes of grieving unfolded in front of our cameras, I made the remark that you could only feel deep sympathy for supporters who had been a mere seven minutes away from winning only the fifth league title in their history. The former Lord Provost of Glasgow, Michael Kelly, of Celtic association (and later a Celtic director), went on a BBC programme the following week and criticised me for departing from the norms of journalistic objectivity. He was never renowned for objectivity himself so we paid little attention to his remarks.

Mercer was also getting frustrated at the financial weakness of both Edinburgh clubs, and in 1990 he initiated an audacious and quite unprecedented takeover bid of his city rivals from which he was never to recover credibility. Hearts and Hibs were in desperate straits. The latter had just come off a disastrous share-issue. Mercer announced that he intended to buy a 51 per cent share in Hibernian and merge the two clubs into one called, curiously enough, Heart of Midlothian. Any outsider looking at the record of those two clubs in the city, with dwindling attendances and weakening in comparison to the Old Firm, might have seen that as a sensible commercial venture, to secure for the capital city one 'super-club' able to withstand the financial uncertainties of the future and to compete on a more level playing field with the Glasgow clubs. Locally he had simply put his head on a chopping block. He was pilloried by both sets of supporters. Mercer, essentially, was an outsider himself, with Rangers sympathies in earlier days. He totally misread the depth of feeling for both clubs. The loss of a focal point of identity was certainly too much for the large Hibernian support, who echoed the chant which even some Hearts supporters were to use of Mercer eventually, 'Fat Tory bastard!'

The 1980s had changed into the 1990s with a new breed of man entering the scene. Stein, the giant who represented the old-style dressing-room entrepreneur, was gone. Waddell, decidedly one of the great men of Scottish football, had died, a lonely man, gradually weakened by his personal demons and the huge physical effort involved in reconstructing Ibrox and fending off the hostilities. Jock Wallace had sadly lapsed into Parkinson's, and before he died I witnessed the chilling opaqueness of the disease in his profound silence when you spoke to him. New men for a new age seemed appropriate, even though it was the banks who pulled the strings. They still do. But there seemed to be no preoccupation about where the money came from as the new decade dawned. The public were not concerned about spend, spend, spend. What was debt to a football club after all? Who would possibly have the temerity to terminate any of these focal points of community life in Scotland? Well, one bank was deadly serious about exactly that, and it was targeting the east end of Glasgow.

CHAPTER NINETEEN

PARADISE REGAINED

Postscripts to periods of history can sometimes be couched in language both pithy and imaginative. 'There's an end of an auld sang,' said the Earl of Seafield about the death of the Scottish Parliament in January 1707. British Foreign Secretary Edward Grey said, as war broke out in 1914, 'The lamps are going out all over Europe; we shall not see them lit again in our time.' And from Winston Churchill, in 1940, came that halfway house between overture and finale, striking a tone of defiance against increasing odds: 'This is not the end. It is not even the beginning of the end. But it is, perhaps, the end of the beginning.' You can detect something of a flavour of the times in just a few words.

In similar vein, Bill Shankly's remark to Jock Stein after the winning of the European Cup in 1967, 'John, you are immortal now', stands out in terms of Celtic Football Club history as an attribution of greatness, a beacon that is forever pointing to an age of mastery. Recall it and you can define a period distinctly from just that one throwaway line. But there are others to consider in the club's history, especially from the early 1990s. Of the many things said to me of that period, two statements stand out. They have to be placed against each other in order to sample a whiff of an era of confusion, conflict, blood-letting, hypocrisy, lying, deceitfulness and eventually triumph. They were uttered to me in absolute sincerity. The first is stark: 'Fergus McCann took away the heart and soul of Celtic and replaced it with a cash register.' The second, by comparison, is almost redemptive: 'McCann is almost certainly the most important Celt since Jock Stein.' These polarised views about the man who was to change the course of history for the club reflect those turbulent few years in the 1990s which started with the arrival of a small, bald, bespectacled figure from the other side of the Atlantic with a plan for the redevelopment of Celtic Football Club, which at the time seemed as feasible as offering a timeshare on the Sea of Tranquillity.

We will come to the two men who uttered these statements eventually, but first it is necessary to recall the plight of the club as the new decade unfolded. By 1994 they were slowly becoming a laughing stock and were apparently on the verge of bankruptcy. They had gone heavily into debt for the first time in their history with the reconstruction of their main stand in 1988. On the playing side they were simply chasing, but showing no signs of catching, Rangers, who through the finances of the Murray empire were now spending as if they were sponsored by the International Monetary Fund. Celtic were having to borrow heavily to stay in the race. They had been humiliated by the sudden conversion of Maurice Johnston to Rangers, succumbing, as Souness and Murray must have anticipated, to a feeling of vulnerability as their great rivals seemed to have entered the real world. Moreover, Rangers had modernised their stadium. Celtic's was big and safe; it conformed to the conventional standards, and even more so to the acceptance of a social view which presupposed people demanded the modernisation of everything in life, such as shopping malls and new cinema complexes, with the exception of football stadia. Within Celtic Park that view had been given credence by the chairman and secretary Desmond White, who had told the *Sunday Post* on 28 October 1984, in response to what was happening elsewhere in stadia development, 'But our supporters have illustrated they don't want our stadium to be all-seated.' This was either a noble endorsement of people power – which, as we will see, the Celtic board of the future was much less susceptible to – or, as even Celtic supporters would tell me at the time, just a convenient excuse not to spend money. Five years after that statement, there was Hillsborough and the subsequent report of 1990 under Lord Justice Taylor which led to all-seated stadia. Now the club had to change. But it has to be noted that on the Parkhead board there were no real entrepreneurs, no real risk-takers, like Murray. They were all dedicated to the club, but they gave the impression of being in a befuddled state, clinging to the romantic belief that Celtic had values that set them above the ordinary and that only they could truly preserve the heritage.

To that end, five prominent directors had formed a 'pact', thus erecting a barricade around their shareholding which would not allow any significant entry into their domain. That aroused firstly suspicion, and then, when they were failing to produce the goods, outright hostility, especially amongst Celtic-loving businessmen desperate for financial input and, ultimately, influence. On the field, Celtic teams were inadequate. Since winning the double in their centenary year of 1988, they had never risen above third place in the league as Rangers ploughed on, raising the horrifying spectre for Celtic crowds of their outdoing the great Stein. By 1994, ten in a row seemed more credible than anyone would have anticipated six years earlier. An enfeebled Celtic, or one going out of business altogether, as Rangers marched on, was untenable. Time to act. Protests mounted and the effect of people power began to be felt through the demonstrations of such as the 'Celts for Change' movement.

As the saga neared its conclusion I hosted our weekly discussion programme *Sport in Question* for Scottish Television in front of a Celtic-slanted and potentially hostile studio audience who sat there like a phalanx of sprinters on their blocks, tensely awaiting the starter's pistol. When the signature music finished and the red light blinked on above the camera, I could sense that all eyes were immovably fixed gravely on two cousins sitting beside me on the panel as our guests. Even as I calmly read the introductions on the autocue, I thought of the words of Bette Davis in the film *All About Eve* when she crisply anticipated some acrimony at a cocktail party with the comment, 'Fasten your safety-belts, we're in for a bumpy night!' The turbulence was not slow in coming, for the invited audience turned this programme into an inquisitorial roughing-up of these cousins in a manner Torquemada would have envied.

They were Kevin and Michael Kelly, directors of Celtic Football Club, which at that time looked as if its very existence was imperilled. It was now public knowledge that Celtic were in dire financial straits, and the unthinkable prospect of a closure of their business was on the agenda. As the questions were hurled at these two men, who at least had had the courage to come out and face up to their accusers, they looked curiously mystified, as if their attitudes and policies were being grossly misunderstood. I then asked Kevin Kelly, the chairman of the club, outright if he would ever sell his shares and relinquish ownership of the club. His reply was specific and significant: 'I would need to know the person and need to know if his motives were right for the club.' Michael Kelly compounded this astonishing admission with the comment that the club would be prepared 'to listen to any decent offer'. The audience at that point took a moment to realise the implication of what had just been uttered, then broke out into applause. For it was the first sighting of a chink in their armour. They were admitting for the first time in public that selling up was an option after all. But was this just a smokescreen to allow them to get out of the studio that night alive?

They were about to be put to the test, for a transcript of those remarks was soon being studied by a man on the other side of the Atlantic. He was interpreting them, mistakenly as it turned out, as a come-on. It was about then that even the non-Celtic public were beginning to prick up their ears at the presence and sound of Fergus McCann, who was about to prove that image means nothing if you have a ruthlessly singular concept in mind. For in truth he did not cut the Napoleonic figure the terracing critics of the board, who were now organising public meetings of protest and planning boycotts of games, might have imagined was needed. He was certainly a 'Celtic' man in the sense that in his teens he had been social convenor, no less, of the Croy Celtic Supporters Club near Kilsyth in Stirlingshire, and had fought for the right of women to travel in their hired buses, for the first time. It is said he told his parents he was leaving for Canada only the night before he emigrated. These were early signs of a cussedness which he exported to North America. Clearly he was a self-centred individual who possessed the qualities to succeed in the harsh business climate of the market there. And he made his fortune, in the travel business. Now, appearing on various television screens in Scotland, spouting his beliefs on the future of Celtic with his bunnet propped on his head and with a slight squint which reminded you more of the silent-screen's Ben Turpin than Wall Street's Gordon Gekko, people had to work hard to take him seriously.

That, of course, is quite unfair to the man, but truly his image was one of the first difficulties he had to face in becoming a credible public figure. After one game he came to the back of the Celtic Park Stand, not far away from the directors' box, to be interviewed by me on Radio Clyde about his project. He spoke impressively, with clarity and determination, but there were tinges of contempt in his voice as I questioned the credibility of all this, as if I had some ulterior motive in mind. I could tell he was no pushover. And he was causing annoyance to the people he was gunning for. A couple of weeks later my colleague, journalist and broadcaster Hugh Keevins, nowadays of the *Daily Record*, was about to interview him for the same radio station in that same position at Celtic Park when stewards appeared on the scene and informed both of them, just as they were going on air, that the board had instructed them to leave the stadium forthwith. Keevins and McCann were escorted outside to the car park where the interview was conducted in the radio van. It made for a great news story which reflected badly on the board. The appearance of trying to stifle McCann lent him more credibility, not less. I doubt if even an Alastair Campbell could have helped the Celtic board out at that stage. So nothing was going to come of that television studio revelation by the directors. It looked indeed as if all we had got was a smokescreen. This made McCann more determined, and the board infinitely more vulnerable. As he continued to speak out, publicising his prospectus on ground re-development and his plans for the club, people started to respond. Battle lines began to be drawn, but it has to be said they changed from time to time with such bewildering complexity that it is best now to draw attention to the two men who made those conflicting statements mentioned earlier, to clarify as best we can the biggest ever power struggle in Scottish football history.

Of those two men, Brian Dempsey was clearly the most articulate opponent of the board. Of Dempsey I could say I 'kent his faither'. Jimmy Dempsey was the Labour MP for Airdrie and Coatbridge in the 1940s and 1950s. I had helped him get elected once, when I was a young teacher, and I had always taken an interest in how his offspring fared. In the early 1990s I noticed that his son Brian was always referred to in the media as a 'millionaire property developer'. He had done well out of life. But he has, 11 years after this major upheaval in his life, concluded that McCann destroyed the ethos of a family club and replaced it with ruthless and uncaring commercial values. Then there is the other view represented by financial consultant David Low, who identifies McCann with Messianic qualities, someone without whom Celtic would now be regarded as hopeless romantics squandering their potential as they headed either for oblivion or mediocrity. We are left to wonder which is the more telling postscript. Or do they, in fact, dovetail neatly? Certainly both men were in the thick of the plotting and counter-plotting, as Dempsey vividly recalled.

'I was watching football until very late one Wednesday night in late February 1994 when I got a phone call,' Dempsey told me. 'It was just before midnight. It was from Kevin Kelly, who is a nice man without an ounce of malice in him. He said, "We've got a wee problem. Could I see you tomorrow morning, but strictly in private?" I asked him to tell me what the problem was. His reply silenced me for a moment: "If we don't have a million pounds in the bank by tomorrow, the club will be put into receivership. And I have already spoken to Noble Grossart [a prominent merchant banking firm from whom help was being sought] about who would be the best receiver." I remember saying to Kevin, "That's a wee problem?"' Aghast, Dempsey tried to control events through his bankers and accountants and assured Kelly eventually that all would be well and that the £1 million could be guaranteed.

That is how serious the situation was. People, even today, do not appreciate how close the club was to vanishing and having to apply for re-registration for membership of Scottish football, perhaps under a new name, as Airdrieonians had to do in 2002 to become Airdrie United. This was just one of the possibilities, and certainly no fantasy.

On learning that the bank had given Celtic until noon on 4 March or else it would lapse into the serious situation of receivership, Fergus McCann, who was at the time in Phoenix, Arizona, took off hot-foot, landed back in Glasgow, got the necessary papers sorted out, and with the clock hand turning to the witching hour – at precisely 11.52 a.m. – lodged the required amount. The impression is very strongly given here that he was the only man prepared to show the colour of his money. He was now firmly in the driving seat, although with many speed traps awaiting him.

If that sounds intriguing, it was only the culmination to such a twisting of events and alliances that it is no wonder supporters were baffled by what was going on and worried by the lack of material progress to get rid of the now much-hated board, who had been saved for the time being but were still highly vulnerable. One such frustrated man was Willie Haughey. Haughey is a completely above-board Celtic supporter who would have crawled through the Panmunjon minefields to see his team play in North Korea, and who had built up his wealth through a very successful refrigeration business. In alliance with another businessman, Gerald Weisfeld, he had got so fed up with some of the inconsequential meetings that were taking place with the board that he had blurted out at an EGM in 1993 that he would be prepared to buy heavily into the club. This led to another kind of brinkmanship, as he can never forget. 'We believed the board were going to sell out to us,' he said. 'We went to a lawyers' office in Edinburgh to meet them and to finalise the buying of shares, as agreed. We thought, this is it. At last this club is going to change. But they did not turn up. We were left stranded.'

Why did the board act as they did? How could serious businessmen take rebuffs like this and still fight on? Why were men swapping alliances in the debate about the future of the club with the alacrity of acrobats? One thing has to be stressed: they all loved and were devoted to the club. In a crucial sense their fight over the ownership of Celtic, to prevent either the embarrassment of foreclosure or the more remote possibility of it going out of business altogether, was essentially different from the crisis that had enveloped Rangers in the 1980s, when they lapsed into a financial morass and looked like being deserted by their following. These Celtic men were fighting to retain identity; Rangers had wanted simply to be better than they actually were, knowing that they had the potential wealth and support to be so. Celtic FC was, on the other hand, the dramatically outward expression of the robustness and growing strength of the Catholic community over the previous decades and its burgeoning success in all walks of life, particularly through the entrepreneurial and professional classes, many of whom had surmounted historical intolerance to gain footholds in niches that were virtually the monopoly of the Protestant middle class in the earlier part of the century. Allowing the club to disappear, or letting it subside into perpetual subservience to Rangers, would have been like disowning their own genetic make-up and taking away the vital beacon of that identity every week. The green and white hoops seemed to lend legitimacy to what they had achieved in life, and would continue to do so.

But there the homogeneity ceased. For the differences in how to achieve the permanency of the club were so diverse and acute that it begat enmities and a bitterness that will be taken to the grave by many of the principals involved. And, of course, to be a Celtic director was to have status within that community which was not too far short of holding office in the Church. It is not surprising, therefore, that even among the 'rebels' there would be infighting to try to achieve a position on the board. Four years prior to the takeover Dempsey had been appointed as a Celtic director, along with the ex-Lord Provost of Glasgow Michael Kelly, to form what was described at the time as a 'dream team'. Dempsey recalled that on the day they were photographed together as the new men Kelly, surveying the surrounds to which he was now attached, said, 'I've waited all my life for this. Nobody is going to take it away from me.' Destiny seemed to have pervaded the precincts. A mere five months later the same Kelly conspired with others to turf Dempsey out, famously only 48 hours before the eventful Skol (League) Cup final with Rangers. Whether the well-publicised blood-letting affected the performance of the players is hard to say, but it certainly did not help, as the team went down 2–1. His boardroom enemies wanted him out because he was a strong and articulate personality and had been vigorously pursuing the policy, and receiving great publicity and support from strong quarters, of removing Celtic Park from Parkhead to a site further north-east, Robroyston, on the fringe of the city. Curiously, that was not all that far away from Springburn on the north side of Glasgow, to where the club had considered re-siting Celtic Park in 1892 before opting to cross Janefield Street to the present ground. Now Kelly and Dempsey were bitter rivals.

On Friday, 4 March 1994, with a scheme to move the club to Cambuslang collapsing and the board feeling the combined heat of the 'rebels' and supporters (notably the Celts for Change movement), not to mention the pressure from the Bank of Scotland, one by one the directors of Celtic Football Club caved in. But Michael Kelly was the last man standing. He would not budge until he got the price he wanted. When McCann heard about this he exploded. Kelly was holding out even though McCann had vowed, in the transatlantic vernacular, that they would not get a dime. Under the influence of Dempsey, McCann relented, against his best instincts, and Kelly was not left empty-handed. The old board were out. But not without a last-gasp effort to wrench control away from the McCann group. For around that time, late at night, Haughey received a telephone call. It came from David Smith, Celtic chairman and financial director. 'It was astonishing,' he said. 'He offered me and associates, there and then, 52 per cent of the shares and ownership of the club. We didn't act on that because we didn't trust them any longer.' This could only have indicated the desperation the board felt at the club falling into the hands of what they deemed to be the 'wrong' people. To no avail, though, for Dempsey and McCann were to go outside, on to the entrance steps of Celtic Park, on separate occasions, where the man who had been usurped by Kelly as a director almost four years earlier could announce with obvious pleasure to a cheering crowd of several hundred, 'The game is over. The rebels have won!'

Victory did not bring the unity the crowd outside, and the general public, assumed would naturally spring from their achievement. The relationship between Dempsey and McCann was becoming acrimonious. On one occasion, when Dempsey invited McCann to his home for dinner – and after finding him later on rather eccentrically lying on his back doing floor exercises – he made an objectionable remark that forced Dempsey to ask him to leave the house immediately. Then, in the immediate aftermath of the ousting of the old board, Dempsey refused a directorship, and Celtic Football Club was now in the hands of a man who would run the club with an iron fist. It was a culture change of dramatic proportions from what had preceded it. There is an echo of what Celtic had now left behind in Michael Kelly's feisty defence of himself and others in his 1994 treatise *Paradise Lost*. He wrote of that fateful evening that saw the handing over of power, 'I could hear the crowd outside chanting "Michael Kelly's on the dole" before they made their way back to their peripheral houses. McCann greeted them at about 10.45 and they dispersed tooting their horns, uncaring that they had seen the last of the real Celtic.' Those many thousands who from their 'peripheral houses' followed Celtic to Seville for the 2003 UEFA Cup final might conclude that his last sentiment, 'the last of the real Celtic', has simply not stood the test of time.

Throughout all of this, the footballers in the green and white shirts had to go on playing as if they were immune to the intrigue in the background. That was never going to be easy. They were in the managerial hands of Lou Macari. The little man who had had the pluck, or gall, to stand up to Jock Stein as a young player was in every sense a free spirit who, although of similar independent mind to McCann, saw his job in an entirely different vein from the executive who was introducing American-style business methods, even to the men in tracksuits. Macari regrets that he did not react quickly enough when he became aware he was not wanted. 'The first game after they took over we had to play St Johnstone,' he said, 'and I got a call from Ken Gallacher [*Sun* journalist] to inform me that he had heard McCann was coming to see me that day. He made it clear he thought that McCann was going to tell me he didn't want me as manager. Ken was close to Brian Dempsey, so I knew there was something in this. Well, McCann came into the dressing room about an hour before kick-off. He didn't know me from Adam, and I could see him looking round the lads, as if he was wanting to see who the manager was. He did introduce himself eventually but never said a word about the future. But I knew this was not healthy, for I never really met him. We didn't talk for weeks. The first real contact was by memo. He was only a few yards away from me in his office, but he kept sending memos to me, and this first one was to ask me to attend eight o'clock management meetings every Monday morning, with the catering manager, the groundsman and others. I'm not being big-headed, but the Celtic manager sitting in at what he called a departmental heads meeting with all these others was just plain daft. I can understand now he was bringing his North American business practices to the job. But it wasn't for me, nor should it have been for any Celtic manager. So I just sent a deputy.'

Macari was doomed, and he knew it. His stomach curdled one day when, after negotiating at length and arranging terms for the contracting of a promising young player, Simon Donnelly, who many thought might be the new Kenny Dalglish, he had to sit and watch the paper being torn up and thrown in the bin after only a cursory glance at it by his new boss. That summer Macari wanted to travel to the USA to take in the World Cup finals, as many managers do on these big occasions. He was not banned from doing so, but McCann wanted the manager to fly to and fro across the Atlantic between games. Macari was determined to set out and stay for the duration, as is the norm. At Manchester Airport he phoned McCann to leave him his hotel numbers, but the new chief executive told him that he would only be allowed to travel on his terms. Macari refused, saying such a suggestion was ludicrous. He was told he would be sacked if he went. The manager told him to go ahead and do that. It was the end of four months of utter disaffection between the two men.

Macari later sued for wrongful dismissal in a civil case in the Court of Session Edinburgh. He lost, and was left to pick up huge legal bills. A case was skilfully built up against him focusing on lack of diligence in the post, accusing him of hardly ever being there when he was needed and spending much of his time in England. To this day Macari claims this was a distorted picture and that his time in England was spent watching games, hunting talent. It did not wash with the judge, Lady Cosgrove, who nevertheless in her 82-page summation said of McCann, 'He was frequently reluctant to answer the precise question asked and I formed the impression of a rather devious individual.'

Results on the pitch under Macari had been poor, though. And Rangers were marching on. Celtic needed inspiration and credibility. They sought it in Ayrshire. The problem was that the object of McCann's desire, ex-Celt Tommy Burns, was already contracted to Kilmarnock as manager. What then followed was executed either through ignorance of the conventions of Scottish football or simply a ruthless disregard for them. When you consider the labyrinthine efforts that were undertaken to 'tap' Burns quite illegally, you can only conclude that McCann was riding roughshod over accepted practice. It is not that tapping did not, and does not, go on in football; it was in the aftermath, during which Celtic were taken to task for what they did, that you can see how accurate an analogy was Haughey's description of McCann's pursuit of his aims: 'Like a dog with a bone – he would never let up'. Burns flew back, on request, from holiday in Tenerife to meet McCann in a hotel in Manchester. It was indiscreet to be seen in the same hotel, even in England, but that did not seem to matter. They talked for hours. They went to extraordinary lengths to maintain the notion that he was still in Tenerife so that negotiations could still go on. Back in Scotland, still secretly, Burns, a devout Catholic, was taken to mass in a church in Viewpark, North Lanarkshire, with a baseball cap tugged over his face to avoid detection. Some altar boys recognised him but did not put two and two together. To all intents and purposes he was still in Tenerife. On 12 July, Burns quit Kilmarnock to join Celtic.

The Scottish League imposed a fine of £100,000 on Celtic for improper dealings, and in May 1995 the SFA ordered that a sum of £200,000 be paid to Kilmarnock after a tribunal hearing, which the Ayrshire club had preferred rather than go to law. The fact that neither of these payments was made in good time was perhaps either an indication that McCann felt he had done nothing wrong or that he was simply a bad loser. But there were certain consequences that affected the relationship between manager and owner. For in the tribunal hearing they had offered contradictory evidence. When asked twice if he had approached Burns to offer him the job, both times McCann had replied, 'No.' When asked the same question, the new Celtic manager had replied, 'Yes.' This did not sit well with McCann. He was angered and embarrassed. It did not help matters when in November 1994, in one of the biggest upsets in their history, Celtic were beaten in the Scottish League Cup final by lower-division Raith Rovers on penalties after extra-time. This result added to the awful publicity over Burns. McCann summoned directors to a meeting at Celtic Park where he recommended that Burns be sacked. One of the reasons given was the manager's testimony at the tribunal. One of the directors present could only conclude that McCann was looking for support to sack a man for telling the truth. That was untenable, and in some dismay at such a suggestion the meeting broke up in disarray. For the time being, Burns was safe.

Doggedness again comes to mind about McCann. It is here we can understand, in retrospect, how valuable it was to Celtic, in the long run, to have had a man in charge who seemed quite invulnerable to adversity. For McCann was pushing on with his ground redevelopment at Celtic Park, while Celtic played their home games at Hampden Park. He was also preparing for a shares issue, with the opportunity for the public to buy into the club. It sounded more exciting in prospect than their future football status, for Celtic were still unable to dent Rangers' supremacy. In season 1994/95 Celtic finished in fourth position, 18 points behind the Ibrox men. Motherwell and Hibernian both finished above Celtic, who drew half of their games. McCann had only been in the job for just over a year, but he was stirring the pot. And he wasn't totally insulated from criticism either by his financial backers, some of whom were still arguing with him about the sums of money each should contribute, or by the media, who in reflecting supporters' concerns put the emphasis on player purchases, not ground re-development. Only a thrawn individual could have survived all of this.

But his relationship with Burns was coming apart at the seams because of irreconcilable differences of which the manager was ultimately to say, 'I needed to buy and sell players quickly, but Mr McCann was always searching for a logic within that. Unfortunately, within football there is very little logic. Mr McCann wasn't a football person. He didn't understand the psychology of the game. He didn't like the emotion, the passion, the competitiveness attached to the game – anything like that. Basically that's what keeps the game going.' Winning the Scottish Cup in May 1995 against Airdrie by the narrowest of margins (1–0) simply led to a well-publicised fall-out with Burns. The public were certainly on the manager's side, as it seemed to be emerging that McCann was even more stingy with the cash than the previously discredited board. Rangers were still seen to be buying players of a higher class because they obviously could afford to. By the end of season 1996/97 they had won nine titles in a row. Ten beckoned, in a way that raised the storm cones around the country's Celtic supporters. The sniping grew around McCann as a result. Even so, he had the resolution to take on the SFA in the shape of their secretary Jim Farry, whom he accused of deliberately mismanaging the registration of the Portuguese player Jorge Cadete, to the disadvantage of the club, in a bitter, almost personal dispute that lasted two years. He also pushed Willie Haughey off the board. If troubles brew, don't hide behind the parapet but get out there and seek more – this seemed to be McCann's *raison d'être*. He then issued a statement about the club's disciplinary record that season (the players had amassed 12 red cards). 'I am extremely unhappy with that record,' he said. 'It has been costly to the club, and I do not think you can blame referees for that. It has to be laid at our own door. I would have to say that the manager is responsible in a way.' Chilling reading for Burns. On 2 May 1997 he was effectively sacked as a couple of thousand people demonstrated outside Celtic Park, against McCann this time. Burns, when assessing his time as Celtic manager, came out with this stinging rebuke of his boss: 'In Fergus's world, there have to be two columns in the ledger, which are profit and loss. In mine, the columns read hopes and dreams.'

These hopes and dreams were shared by the multitude of Celtic supporters in season 1997/98 when stirrings of a reawakening were kindled by the side under a new manager, Wim Jansen, a Dutchman who had played for his country in the final against Argentina in 1978. They won the Coca-Cola (League) Cup final on 30 November 1997, beating Dundee United 3–0, and then beat Rangers 2–0 in the New Year derby at Celtic Park. Both clubs then moved into the closest head-to-head clash they had had in years. Both kept to within a point or two of each other until the last day of the season when Celtic achieved a 2–0 win over St Johnstone at Parkhead to win the league for the first time in a decade. As far as the club and its supporters were concerned, the greater achievement was preventing Rangers from reaching that mystic ten-in-a-row figure. Under any other circumstances in football you might have concluded that after such a season Jansen, now of folk hero status, could dictate his own terms for longevity at Celtic Park. In fact that St Johnstone game was his last as the Celtic manager. To be blunt, he did not like his job under McCann and the man he had appointed as general manager of the club, lawyer and football commentator Jock Brown. They clashed frequently, according to Jansen, who astonishingly said as he looked back from Holland, 'My relationship with Jock Brown was bad from beginning to end. In the past few months I couldn't even speak to him. In fact I wanted to resign just two or three weeks after I took the job but they wouldn't accept it.' This seemed mystifying to most people, for Celtic had discovered a winner. So there was nothing all that surprising about the popular outrage over letting this man go, with the implication in some statements that they would have sacked him eventually anyway as his views on the future did not chime with theirs.

On 1 August 1998, when the Scottish League flag was raised at Celtic Park, McCann was roundly booed by a considerable element of the crowd as he stood on the track intent on savouring the moment. It was intensely embarrassing for us onlookers, so even this tough little man must have been cut to the quick. I recall at the time being astonished by this, because his critics were sitting in the very stadium that was a tangible product of all the efforts he had put in to turn this club around. We could all easily recall when the place had been, as recently as the early 1990s, a dour reflection of a past age of tramcars compared to the supersonic lustre of Ibrox. Now it stood in the east end of the city as a landmark of defiance and stubbornness which McCann, with all his faults, had personified. Some 60,000 seats and a season-ticket public of over 50,000 did not seem to merit ridicule. Of course, many of these supporters had indulged in the biggest share-issue in British football in late 1994, when the club raised a capital base of over £20 million from the combined total raised from the oversubscribed initial share-issue and a supplementary one. But you cannot satisfy a public that feeds on the goodies they are supposed to see on the field. He was being seen as an impediment to any manager who wanted the purse-strings loosened, and his 'sackings' of people were viewed as insensitive and counter-productive. The media, generally speaking, were hostile too, having picked up the vibes from the terracings. Still, as David Low put it in a feature he wrote for the *Herald* in February 2004, 'It is convenient for many to forget that when McCann arrived, Celtic were essentially homeless with a turnover of £8.7 million compared with £15.9 million for Rangers. By the time he had left, the stadium had been bought and paid for, Celtic had won the SPL Championship and Celtic's turnover had grown to £33.8 million against Rangers' £36.5 million.'

It really is difficult not to see the McCann phenomenon as anything other than beneficial to the Celtic supporters. Where would they now be sitting had he not returned to his native land? Yet there are people who still resent the fact that he, as they put it, 'walked away with £40 million' when he eventually sold out and left. Low explained that in strictly commercial, free-market terms. 'He took a gamble. It paid off. He could have lost out, but the market at the time, when he released his shares, was buoyant. He got the value of what that dictated. It could have been worse. He played absolutely straight on that. He told us all, from the very beginning, what he intended to do with his plan, and it worked out.' Celtic, though, in 2005, are still without a training facility to match the ambitions of the club, still without a proper youth academy, and still finding it hard to raise the cash to buy more quality players, to the disgust of their support. On Saturday, 2 April 2005, I witnessed Celtic chairman Brian Quinn, regarded by the fans as the figurehead of an apparently parsimonious board, being roundly booed by a significant proportion of the nearly 60,000 crowd at half-time, with Celtic about to lose 2–0 to Hearts. It conjured up the memory of the hostility directed towards McCann out there in the open. In terms, therefore, of the huge profit he made out of the dealings, part of which might have usefully benefited the club he undoubtedly saved, the Dempsey remark about the cash register replacing the heart and soul of the club has a certain resonance. In June 2005 one of Celtic's most important players under Martin O'Neill, captain Jackie McNamara, was transferred to Wolves despite the fact that he fervently wished to remain at the club. In failing to be offered the right sort of contract by Celtic his bitterness was encapsulated in his simple valedictory statement: 'The businessmen got rid of me.' This would tend to strengthen the Dempsey view of the current club. However, it has to be borne in mind that Jock Stein in the 1970s, in an entirely different Celtic ethos, broke up the Lisbon Lions more quickly than he should have and transferred Willie Wallace, John Hughes, Tommy Gemmell and Davy Hay quite ruthlessly, all of whom wished to stay. As the French say, the more you change the less change there actually is. So people are still divided on that core issue of the character of the club. The fact is that a massive stadium is there for people to be proud of, which McCann achieved against all the odds. The fact is that in the process of the ensuing and recurring battles between Rangers and Celtic, the playing side of that rivalry became even more prominent than it had been before McCann ventured on the scene. The fact is that Scottish football would become even more imbalanced between the Old Firm and the rest. The fact is that in the buying of foreign talent to strive for success a blight would descend on Scotland's international team. So you could be tempted to say that neither Dempsey's nor Low's reflections encapsulate that turbulent time of passionate conflict, and that for a better one we could reach out to the poetic summary of the Battle of Sheriffmuir of 1715:

There's some say that we wan,
Some say that they wan,
And some say that nane wan at a', man.

That last line, in particular, would chime with the feelings of two men who took teams to World Cup finals believing the Old Firm were now as helpful to the international team cause as another discovery of Reactivan pills in the travelling bags.

CHAPTER TWENTY
A SOUR VINTAGE

The night before Scotland played Brazil in Paris, on 9 June 1998, the centre of the city became paralysed. Paris likes to party, and they had the perfect excuse to do so then, in celebration of the coming of the World Cup to their country. They take to the streets readily there, as if traffic at a standstill and aching ribs from trying to make passage for yourself on the throbbing pavements is a civic duty as important as paying taxes. One particular thrombosis was making a side street almost impassable, near the Place de La Concorde, where they used to guillotine the aristocracy during the Revolution. Many of the crowd in that congested, milling street were wearing kilts. Some of those in tartan had taken to begging with a desperate brother-can-you-spare-a-dime look on their faces. They had no tickets for the game the next day. They clutched at your arm as you passed, with plaintive looks on their faces. It was as close as an elegant, upmarket arrondissement of Paris could muster to reminding you of the deprivations of the Depression.

The supporters had congregated because they had obviously heard through the Tartan Army grapevine that a special pre-World Cup party was being held in the Buddha Bar, just behind the famous Hotel Crillon, for some of the luminaries of Scottish public life. Sean Connery would be there, as well as Ewan McGregor and his sidekick Ally McCoist, about whom there was much chat concerning an incident in Paris's 'Auld Alliance' bar in which it was alleged he had been witness to Stan Collymore apparently 're-designing' his girlfriend Ulrika Jonsson's features. That last piece of tittle-tattle was the very stuff of pre-World Cup gossip, without which you felt you could not actually have kick-off at all. But the crowd outside had not come to gape but to barter with the great and the good. The party-goers included writers, actors, journalists, broadcasters, business tycoons and editors of Scottish newspapers, all of whom ran the gauntlet in the ticket frenzy. Connery was no exception.

In the bowels of this restaurant the party organisers made an announcement that the great man had arrived. There were at least 300 assembled at tables in one of the most fashionable of Parisian howfs. Then he appeared at the top of the stairs, but not alone. As he slowly made his way down towards us, he was accompanied by the leader of the Scottish National Party, Alex Salmond, who had sped away from us on first intimations of Connery's presence to join him and effect a grand entrance. Double -o-seven, and the event, had been hijacked. They made their way slowly towards us in tandem as if they were about to present their credentials at the Court of St James after Scottish independence, and the assembled and well-oiled company rose, as to a man, and cheered them to the rafters. Salmond had a beaming and proud look on his face, as if Connery had whispered to him that he could get him the role of Q in the next Bond film. Milking it for all he was worth, Salmond brought him to our table. To his credit Connery seemed slightly taken aback by all this fuss, and those of us who felt our stomachs churning at this quasi-political stunt at what purported to be a footballing event were assuaged by the man himself, who just wanted at that stage to talk football and echoed some of the worries about the current Scottish team that he had expressed in Spain in 1982. The contrast between the perplexed Connery on Scottish football and the assured polish of the screen Bond was stark. Sadly, later that evening, the political overtone rebounded, for after much drink had been taken Connery took over a microphone and delivered an incoherent rant about independence which ended in the previously unthinkable phenomenon of this iconic figure being roundly barracked. The crowd were not having it. They were there to stoke up for a football match, not to be reminded of the Declaration of Arbroath. It all left some of us with a slightly queasy feeling, and it reminded me of Argentina in 1978 and of how a result by the Scottish national team could be seen by politicians to have some currency at the ballot-box.

This party would not have been held anyway had Scotland not been drawn against Brazil. Paris and the Brazilians was a particularly intoxicating cocktail for the Scots, and to hell with the result. We veterans of Scotland–Brazil games were almost haughtily sanguine about it all. I had watched all eight previous contests, bar the game in Rio in 1972. Brazil fever never goes away, but the more you experience it the more controllable it becomes. There is the sustainable reverence, the admiration, the feeling that rubbing shoulders with the aristocracy for an afternoon will do you good even it means they will set the dogs on you by the end of the day. But rarely did the Brazilian demi-god superiority surface in all the years of the contests in which Scotland was involved with them. Some of it, of course, notably in Seville, but not as much as we so often anticipated. There was the 1–1 friendly draw at Hampden in 1966, when Jim Baxter was peerlessly brilliant; the 1–0 defeat at Hampden in 1973, when a Derek Johnstone own-goal decided the match; the goalless draw in Frankfurt in 1974; Rio in 1977, when Scotland were certainly outplayed, though the 2–0 victory came only in the last 15 minutes; the toe-poke provocation of Narey's in Seville in 1982 which did prompt touches of Brazilian brilliance; the 1987 Rous Cup defeat in a bland, meaningless game at Hampden when Rai and Valdo scored a goal each; and Turin in 1990, when in a dreadful game played in the dreadful Stadio Delle Alpi, Muller scored the only goal of the game to put Scotland out of the World Cup. To me, these Brazilian sides were simply ersatz reminders, with the possible exception of Seville, of how magical they really used to be, and of how they looked as if they might be slipping towards myth. For they still had this aura about them which mesmerised too many people into seeing qualities that simply were not there.

On the other hand, nobody, so far as I could tell, actually enthused about the Scottish side. When they walked on to the pitch at the Stade de France, jauntily wearing their kilts, to inspect it before the Brazil match the following day, you felt that dungarees would have been more appropriate to reflect the work ethic, the stubbornness and good organisation that had got them to the finals. Craig Brown's sober approach to management did not strike a chord with many, and sometimes aroused hostility. But on this occasion the people who had come to Paris were deeply supportive, as the World Cup finals tend to soften criticism, for just a little while. However, for years now it had increasingly felt like a duty to attend Scotland's games, not an exhilarating pleasure. That more dyspeptic mood amongst the Scottish crowds had emerged in 1986. And I remember, very specifically, the day when I and the others who were there started to wonder what sort of future we were letting ourselves in for.

It was 22 June 1986 in the Azteca Stadium in Mexico City, the day of the famous 'Hand of God' game. At half-time in that match between England and Argentina we repaired to the back of the stand for a refreshment. There were about six Scottish journalists in the group. Apart from marvelling at the performance of the pint-sized (now gallon-sized) Maradona's performance, we were discussing the topic of the moment amongst the media – namely, who would be the next Scotland manager? Alex Ferguson had departed with the Scottish team by that stage and was getting out of his temporary post like a bat out of hell, given that he had learnt the job carried too much unwanted baggage over which no national manager would have control. Sundry names were being bandied about, but nobody had a real front runner in mind. Jim McLean? Unlikely. Billy McNeill? A definite possibility.

As we discussed this we were joined at some juncture by an unassuming, genial and certainly popular figure who appeared out of the crowd from virtually nowhere. He was Andy Roxburgh, then head of coaching at the SFA who had been left behind to do technical studies for FIFA. At some point in the conversation somebody light-heartedly asked if he would be interested in the post. It was as if somebody had made the preposterous proposal to make the head prefect the headmaster. He politely evaded the question, amid a frisson of nervous chirping amongst us, for we did not want any more embarrassment for the fellow. I cannot remember his exact words, but we had the feeling there was no outright rejection of the notion put to him, and that conversation, brief though it was, stayed with us, intriguingly, for the rest of the day. Nor did it completely leave our minds thereafter, even though we all became embroiled in the 'Hand of God' post-match hubbub, histrionically commiserating with any Englishman we could find. On our flight back home we discussed this nagging thought and eventually dismissed it. Weeks later Roxburgh was appointed Scotland's team manager. It shook us. It stunned virtually every club manager in the game. It bemused the public. It even surprised his closest professional friend, Craig Brown. In one fell swoop the SFA had altered the course of national team management and presented a decent, intelligent and totally dedicated man with a task quite beyond him.

Roxburgh had always been an approachable and extremely articulate coach who handled youngsters well, coming as he had from the teaching profession. He had, of course, played professional football, both with Partick Thistle and Falkirk, where he played alongside Alex Ferguson. It could hardly be hidden, though, that as part of the advance party for preparations in Santa Fe for the Mexico finals he had departed the scene before the Scottish team arrived, because Ferguson simply did not want him around the place, not having held him in the greatest esteem, to say the least. So the immediate aftermath of his appointment was to visualise perhaps the toughest task any national manager could ever have. Brutally put, he started off by being a less credible figure compared to the models we had had before him. And I knew, right from the outset, that even were he to achieve unprecedented success there were many on the terracings, and behind mikes and laptops, who would never accept him as the genuine article. Perhaps more significantly, outside the unwarranted prejudice against him personally, the Scottish domestic game would not provide him with the answers all of us sought, for the betterment of the national team. The Old Firm, led by Rangers, were changing. No Scottish manager prior to 1986 had had to cope with such a devastating dilution of his potential resources. Major players were on their way out, or were past their best (namely Souness and Dalglish). That quality was never replaced.

But throughout his reign, Roxburgh was strongly supported by SFA secretary Ernie Walker, who, it could be said, was the man who had effectively appointed him. By the mid-1980s Walker was as influential a secretary as any there had ever been. He had become tired of the orthodox route of appointing former international players or club figures of renown to the post. He also thought there were no candidates who could hold a candle to Jock Stein, whom he had come to adore. He deliberately persuaded his international committee to go down another route altogether, and as a consequence we were into new territory. But, unlike the pioneers of old, the SFA were going to find it hard to draw the wagon trains into a circle to fend off marauding critics.

From Roxburgh's first outing on 10 September 1986, against Bulgaria, which ended goalless, until the Rous Cup game against Brazil at Hampden on 26 May 1987, which Brazil won 2–0, Scotland recorded only one win out of seven games. The fact that that win was a 3–0 beating of Luxembourg at Hampden did not lend itself to lyrical endorsement of him in the media. It is not so surprising that the task he had taken on soon began to affect him. On the eve of the Rous Cup match with England on 23 May 1987, I travelled along with my BBC commentating colleague Barry Davies to see the Scots in training at Girvan on the Ayrshire coast. Roxburgh was first off the team coach, and for coaching purposes began to distribute the indispensable traffic cones around the pitch, like a Klondyker marking out his claim. When he saw Davies and me, he pulled me aside and said, 'You've let me and the boys down. That man [he nodded in the direction of Davies] will go back and report all this to Bobby Robson. It'll do us no good.' We thought he was joking. He wasn't. He did not order us out, but as we would use any excuse to avoid the tedium of watching a training session we simply upped and went, thinking how odd it would be if the man who was supposed to set a new standard had, in record time, become your orthodox paranoiac managerial moaner.

On balance I put it down to no more than testiness, but it certainly did not encourage me to believe he was of the right stuff. It is clear he had much to offer the Scottish game, and anybody who came into contact with him throughout the entire structure of Scottish football, particularly at grass-roots level, could not speak highly enough of him. But he was an easier touch than some who had preceded him, like Stein and Ferguson, who could turn men into slavering wrecks if they so much as hinted at dissent. Roxburgh was essentially a civilised communicator who, in general, would go out of his way to avoid confrontation with anybody. It did not work to his advantage as it made him seem vulnerable and soft. As a consequence, we in the media waded in liberally when it suited us. And we had plenty of opportunities to do so.

In Cyprus, for example, on 8 February 1989, in a World Cup qualifying game in the Tsirion Stadhion in Limassol, I experienced during commentary a feeling that was something akin to a panic attack. As the game on the gritty surface drew to a conclusion with the score still 2–2, a feeling of indignation at being held by a team of little quality, however much Scotland were trying, was giving way to one of almost terminal disillusion. I remember as a boy listening to the radio in 1949 to the news that Belfast Celtic had beaten Scotland in a game in New York. I could not have known at the time that the Scottish team had drunk Manhattan dry the night before the match and were treating the whole enterprise as a bit of a joke. It was simply an astonishing, deeply wounding piece of news. Then came the traumas of Argentina. We needed no more of that on a holiday island. I was struggling to try to make sense of how a team of 'wine-waiters', as Shankly would have described them, could possibly be torpedoing Scotland's chances of reaching the finals in Italy. And they had taken a 2–1 lead after 47 minutes, though Richard Gough had equalised seven minutes later. Now, looking down at our watches, we noticed that the time had crept up to almost 97 minutes. Then up stepped

Gough again to head the winner from a long throw-in by Roy Aitken. The explosion of relief on the Scottish bench was perhaps understandable, but to me and others almost risible. This was Limassol, not Rio. Triumph has to have its proper balance of response. Scotland had won because the pre-match warnings of time-wasting by the Cypriots, constantly aired by Roxburgh, had got through to the East German referee Herr Kirschen, who had acted accordingly. That added-time winning goal did not satisfy many of us. The contrast between the euphoria on the trip back home within the official party and the more sober assessment of the standard of play by the media present could not have been more distinct. It did not seem to matter at the time that France, in the same qualifying group, had dropped a point in Cyprus. The trend of mundane, ordinary fare being served up was the worrying factor.

It is certainly true that one month later, on 8 March at Hampden, Scotland beat France 2–0 with a goal in each half by Maurice Johnston, then with Nantes. But I always felt that only one team played the real football that night – France. They had players like Battiston, Blanc, Sauzee and Papin – thoroughbreds all. Those who were there will remember the appalling conditions of heavy rain and a sluggish pitch which defied fluidity of play; had the conditions been drier and thus afforded the French the kind of passing surface on which they excelled, I think the result would have been different, for they commanded much of the game, without the killer touch. That added-time goal in Cyprus and the topsy-turvy result against the French added to this odd contradiction of welcoming the possibility of reaching Italy for the finals in 1990 despite the deep dissatisfaction about the performances. The last qualifying game, against Norway at Hampden on 15 November in front of 63,987, evoked images of the infamous Dorando Pietri's finish to the Olympic marathon in London in 1908. Scotland staggered over the line, disorientated and looking as ready for a World Cup as a pub team from Duntocher. Needing only one point out of the last three qualifying games had seemed a simple enough task. But it went to the wire, for they had lost the two preceding games, to Yugoslavia and France. Ally McCoist scored a minute before half-time to provide a lead against Norway. Then, with only two minutes to go, Leighton in the Scottish goal fumbled a shot from Johnsen and the ball slipped under his body for the equaliser. Somebody up there seemed to be suggesting it might be better not to qualify at all. Still, who would have wanted to miss a trip to Italy?

Certainly not the media, myself included. We diluted our frustration with the dreary ordinariness of the Scots and played up the prospects of rubbing shoulders again with some of the greatest.

On the eve of the Brazil match in Paris in 1998, Craig Brown looked back on that World Cup in Italy eight years earlier, when he was Roxburgh's right-hand man, and regretted that he was not blessed with the sort of players his predecessor could field. Brown had no Johnston or McCoist up front. Johnston had in fact scored six goals in eight qualifying matches prior to Italia 90 – a veritable harvest compared to the meagre bounty of succeeding Scotland strikers. Roxburgh also had McLeish of Aberdeen, Malpas of Dundee United, MacLeod of Borussia Dortmund, Roy Aitken, then with Newcastle, and Stuart McCall of Everton – all experienced in European football at the highest level. Brown had decent professionals under him, but not that spread of quality and experience. He had lost the greatly influential Gary McAllister, which left him with a void in midfield he could not adequately fill. Colin Hendry, his captain and centre-back, exemplified what Brown's teams were all about: good organisation, hard work, assiduous application of the game plan, and sometimes, as a result, looking deadly dull and predictable. It divided the fans. Boring so often, lacking the gems of innovation and creativity which many of their opponents could muster, but nevertheless getting there eventually – that was the Brown team. As bitter criticism was occasionally heaped on his head, what we did not realise at the time, and perhaps still do not, is that this was the prototype of what Scottish teams of the future might, perforce, have to be.

But back in 1990, when Brown was still an assistant, Costa Rica on 11 June seemed to rhyme with catastrophe. A Third World kid against an ancient, toothless crone might have been another way of illustrating the tenor of the game, as Scotland seemed decrepitly incapable of mustering even a single goal. They went down 1–0 to a Cayasso goal just after half-time having, in my view, been afflicted initially with World Cup caginess. They had applied caution – the very antithesis of what it should have been against lads who looked as if they could, and should, have been blown away by one gust of Scottish endeavour. It was all so timid and measured. In that incredibly atmospheric stadium the barrage of noise coming from the Scottish supporters seemed increasingly and garishly out of tune with what they were watching. If you play like that and are beaten, you deserve what you get. I knew the vitriol that had built up since Roxburgh's appointment would blossom in various creative ways after that. Witness Robert Philip's comments later that month in *Scotland on Sunday* when he dismissed Roxburgh as 'a theorist whose main claim to fame is he once scored a hat-trick for Partick Thistle in the Scottish League. Andy Roxburgh should not be hounded back into the headmaster's study, but his undistinguished tenure must end with the final whistle against Brazil on Wednesday.'

Rapallo on the coast became another place of pining and drowning of sorrows. In summer, Italy is a hard country in which to retain depression for too long, but when we learnt that after the Costa Rica game Maurice Johnston had resorted to that great anti-depressant called champagne and had drunk copious quantities of the stuff in the company of some budding Sophia Lorens, in breach of curfew and in full view of a tabloid paper, the gloom hung around longer than we thought it would. Driving in on the evening of 16 June, apprehensively, to the stadium in Genoa where Scotland were to take on Sweden, I was not to know it would be my last live television commentary for the BBC, nor that the Scottish players had powers of redemption within themselves. I was surprised more by the latter than the former, for I had annoyed certain people with my outright criticism of the side in the previous game and I was prepared to be even more critical this time, even though I knew I would be arousing the ire of those who wished to peddle fantasies about the ability of the Scots. In fact I had nothing but praise for them that night as they roared into the game and were one up through Stuart McCall after only ten minutes. With nine minutes to go, Johnston, having shrugged off his penchant for Dom Perignon, scored another from the penalty spot. Stromberg did score one for Sweden a few minutes later, but the evening belonged to the maligned Scots.

This, of course, did not necessarily convince us that we could roll over the Brazilians in the next game four days later in Turin. Up there, in the ghastly Stadio Delle Alpi, which even the home Juventus supporters now shun, we were pleased to see the Alps in all their majesty from the back of the stadium. But that is all the evening had going for it. The only goal of the game came nine minutes from time. History has a habit of repeating itself, as we know, and I witnessed that as Leighton, whose incompetence had come between Fergie and me in the past, boobed yet again, fumbling an Alemão shot and allowing the stocky striker Muller to push in the rebound. I flew home wondering who would go first, me or Roxburgh. I beat him to it and left BBC Scotland one month later to pursue another career with BBC London. Roxburgh lasted until 8 September 1993, the date of his final game in charge.

He was effectively on his way out before that, though. On 28 April that year I travelled to Portugal to cover Scotland's game there for Radio Clyde. Perhaps radio commentary accentuates the awfulness of heavy defeats, largely because you have to paint scenes lavishly, emphasising what people cannot see for themselves. Describing those five Portuguese goals was like trashing your own dysfunctional family to a hostile public. The defeat was bad enough, but lying at the core of it was a dispute and a story that ought to have been a warning to Craig Brown of what he would have to face up to when he was offered the post several months later. The rumour spread quickly around the media that Scotland's tactics that night in the now tawdry-looking but still vast Estadio Da Luz in front of a smallish crowd of 28,000 had been influenced by a Lisbon taxi driver who had informed his passenger, the Scottish assistant coach Craig Brown, that Figo would be playing instead of Barros. A taxi-driver as a coaching informant? What next? Window cleaners? Plumbers in the know? This story was manna from heaven for the media, determined now to heap any kind of ridicule on the entire Scottish coaching staff. The truth of the matter is that Brown did indeed have this information passed on to him in a taxi, but by his fellow passenger that day, the man who is now Sir Bobby Robson, who at that time was coach of Sporting Lisbon. It is of no great relevance to the final outcome, to be honest – although Barros did play, not Figo – for Scotland were overwhelmed. The home side could have played any system that night and still won. It had become noticeable that Scottish morale was so low that the ancient Eusebio could have been fielded by the Portuguese.

The more crucial point was that if such a loose story as that was being used to discredit both he and Roxburgh, Brown must have known that life would be hell for him when he took over, as he did after Scotland drew 1–1 with Switzerland at Pittodrie and therefore failed to qualify for the World Cup finals in the USA. Not only would Brown be facing a public and a media who felt appointments as such were coming from a clique, he still had to contend with a figure who most certainly had caused dissension in the Scottish camp – Richard Gough, the captain of Rangers at the time, who although now on amicable terms with the pair of them had little respect then for either Roxburgh or Brown, and in the former's case was openly hostile about the manager's tactics. He never played again for Scotland after that night in Lisbon, but the legacy of his dispute with Roxburgh went to the root of the criticism of the SFA's policy – that both men were simply unsuited to the task. The press had taken sides and felt that Gough was a more credible figure than the coaches. So the climate had been set for a war of attrition between the doubters, among whose number were major figures in the media, and the determination of this man to prove them wrong. I thought at the time, whatever admiration I had for his pluck, that he had little chance of success.

Under Brown, Scotland performed creditably in the European Championship finals in England in 1996. The game against the hosts at Wembley on 15 June was miserably memorable for the Scots because of the missed penalty by Gary McAllister – after which, unfairly, he would never recover his relationship with the Tartan Army – and Paul Gascoigne's brilliance shortly after that which produced the second England goal in their 2–0 victory. But it was only a goal scored by Holland at Wembley late on in their game against England, at a time when they were losing 4–0, which put the Scots out of the second stage on goal difference. So although the champagne was flowing that happy night in Paris in 1998 before the Brazil game, optimism was garishly unconvincing.

The French campaign turned out simply to be a sort of mirror image of the Italian one: one proud but unsuccessful game, another excellent effort after that, and then, of course, the almost inevitable disaster. In the Stade de France on 10 June, a John Collins penalty after 38 minutes equalised the goal scored by Sampaio for Brazil after only four minutes which had sent shivers down the spine. The appropriate French phrase *après moi le deluge* came into my mind in the Eurosport commentary position, although I refrained from tempting providence. But that was not to be. The Brazilians were flashy but unconvincing; Scotland were terriers. That could not prevent a 2–1 defeat, a tragic own-goal by Tom Boyd as he attempted a clearance late in the game making the difference. So there was reason to take a kind of controlled celebratory mood to the streets of Bordeaux, which, of course, offer ample opportunities for relaxation. Six days later, to a background of revelry as Norwegian and Scottish supporters mixed harmoniously, the two countries drew 1–1 there, Scotland's goal scored by Craig Burley. The Tartan Army's resourcefulness proved it knew no bounds that day, for one of them tried to pickpocket my co-commentator, the former England captain Bryan Robson, but after failing to do so turned round and asked him for an autograph. That audacity was not matched by the Scots team in the final game in St Etienne on 23 June. They lost out 3–0 to fresh, inventive and speedy football played by the Moroccans, and one of Scotland's more reliable players, Burley, was sent off.

It was as bad as it gets. And it confused again. The misery of that night walking back to the hotel was simply compounded by the recollections of two other matches in which Scotland had performed tolerably well. But I knew Brown's position had hardly been strengthened, although he did have the capacity to pick himself up well. The next time I saw him after that was in the same stadium in St Etienne on the night Beckham was sent off against Argentina, when I was commentating for Eurosport while he was working for BBC Radio Five Live. It was as well for him personally that he kept his articulate public image on the boil through radio to prove he was not going to be swamped by events. He certainly had become accustomed to hostility. He once told me a journalist had bumped into him on the way back from a defeat and told him he was going to savage him in a column. 'Nothing personal, you know,' he was told. And when he remonstrated about that insensitivity, he was informed, 'That's showbiz!' In fact, Brown and Roxburgh belonged to another tradition, far removed from treading the boards.

CHAPTER TWENTY-ONE
'THEY USED TO GROW ON TREES'

'Those who can, do; those who can't, teach.' That aphorism was not coined by a tabloid, but by George Bernard Shaw, in an age when footballers wore handlebar moustaches and their shorts came down well below their knees. But you might have thought it was a contemporary barb had it been brought to your attention for the first time during the respective periods as Scotland manager of Roxburgh and Brown. They were not only perceived to be clones, they were ex-educationalists: one a former headteacher, the other a lecturer and author of books on education. Worse, they were seen to be part of a kind of cabal of coaching, sucking the vitality out of the game at its very roots, which unfairly attained the label the 'Largs Mafia', referring to the place on the Ayrshire coast where many coaching courses were held, at the Inverclyde National Sports Centre. Roxburgh and Brown attended and ran courses there. Brown, who becomes particularly incensed about that tag, is not slow to list the former alumni of these courses, including Alex Ferguson, Jim McLean, Walter Smith and other foreign notables, just to shed a different sort of light on the judgements made of the work carried on there.

He believes the poisonous implication behind that phrase stemmed from Steve Archibald. The former Aberdeen, Spurs and Scotland international had wanted to be fast-tracked for a coaching award to get the job as manager of Espanyol in Barcelona. He completed only half of the course, attaining a grade that was lower than required for the Spanish job, and Brown and the others refused to expedite matters, as that would have been grossly unfair to those who had completed the requisite examinations. The Spanish management took one look at the lesser qualification Archibald was showing them and rejected him. So he lashed out, Brown claims, at what he termed the 'Largs Mafia'. The phrase was eagerly taken up by others, and it sticks to this day. It suggests the primacy of theory over the harsh practicalities of motivation and inspirational leadership, such as were demonstrated by Stein – a man who most certainly paid scant attention to coaching awards. However, those still pegged down in that 1960s era ignore the fact that nowhere in world football is there an internal domestic structure without a regulated coaching system. The fact that a Spanish club demanded a coaching credential of global value before considering a man for a job is proof enough of the significance of Largs and of the trend towards a coaching culture throughout the entire world game. It is here to stay, and rightly so.

Could others have done better than those two men, in similar circumstances? In many quarters you will get a resounding 'Yes!' to that. Of course the difficulty is in proving such a proposition. The criticism Roxburgh and Brown had to endure was coloured by a contempt at times which suggested neither of them could hack it because they had little of the stature or the level of achievement of those who had preceded them. They were of the wrong stock. But it is as well to remember that some distinguished figures in that post were hounded as well. I recall the first time I was shocked at the level of animosity that could be directed towards a national manager. It was at Wembley on 22 May 1971, immediately after England had beaten Scotland 3–1. I was sitting in a large limousine which had been provided by a sponsor from the car industry. Scottish supporters streaming out of the ground recognised my face behind the window, and, making the rather odd assumption that the other six people beside me were from the SFA, they surrounded this completely new vehicle and started to rock it to and fro. As the cry 'It's the SFA!' spread around the area, others flocked towards the car and tried to join in. The poor chauffeur, hemmed in by other cars, could not move away. The men beside me were terrified. The car seemed to be leaving its wheels. The noise was so great that I could not convey the fact to the pack outside that I would not have been seen dead in the company of the then SFA International Committee. It was only when the police eventually arrived that they fled. And why all this? They were after the blood of the Scotland manager at the time, Bobby Brown, the former Rangers goalkeeper, as honourable a gentleman as ever had to think of hiding himself in the team hamper when coming out of a ground. But he was failing, and thus they were after him.

It is a reminder that there never has been a Scotland manager who did not have the public turn on him at one stage or another, and with varying degrees of vitriol. Some, because of previous stature, like Stein, could call on a credible club track-record and power of personality to provide insulation of a sort. This is something neither Roxburgh nor Brown could resort to. Is it disreputable to call on statistics, even though Mark Twain's warning of lies, damn lies and statistics should prepare us not to swallow everything produced? Of course not. The results under Brown, Roxburgh and Stein are worth examining:

Stein: Played 68 Won 30 Drew 13 Lost 25
Roxburgh: Played 63 Won 23 Drew 19 Lost 21
Brown: Played 69 Won 31 Drew 18 Lost 20

Naturally they do not tell the whole story, but they are hardly a decisive rejection of the style of management the SFA decided to pursue with these two men. If the governance of any football team was determined exclusively by playing experience at a high level then Jose Mourinho would never have emerged from obscurity. Berti Vogts won nearly 100 hundred caps with West Germany, but his appointment in March 2002 to the SFA post was disastrous. He was simply out of tune with the Scottish environment and character, a 'celebrity' appointment that astonished my German broadcasting friends at Eurosport who never rated him as a manager and felt that any success he had had with his national side sprang from the work done by others before him. So, Brown and Roxburgh would be perfectly entitled to wield the above statistics at some of the men who made their lives hell when they were in office. Those statistics do not necessarily cover them in glory, but they at least indicate that Ernie Walker, the SFA secretary, was entitled to lead us away from conventional thinking. They had stuck to orthodox ways in the past and it was time to change, he thought. If nothing else, he forced us to rethink the values of football management.

Neither is it an ingenuous defence of these two men to note the increasing friction caused by the conflicting demands of club and international football, which would have taxed even the sublime managerial genius of a Ferguson or a Stein. For when Roxburgh accepted the role, just as Souness was taking over at Ibrox, Scottish football was about to be transformed by as great a clash of interests as the game had ever seen, and it persists into the new millennium. With the outpouring of money at Ibrox and the inflow of foreign talent to the club, so began a process taken up by others, and just as spectacularly by Celtic in later years, that would be as useful to the production and development of young Scottish talent as Herod's kindergarten policy was to the first-born of Israel. This did not instantly impinge on anybody's consciousness, but there was another factor that certainly did. With the emphasis placed on the Rangers revival and the recurring efforts of Celtic to keep pace with them, which they failed to do until the McCann period, the focus became more intense on club rather than international football. The great urban masses of Glasgow and the West of Scotland, who used to support Scotland, were now engrossed in big-spending clubs, instant success and foreign names to conjure with, and as a consequence were losing interest in the national side. There were signs to indicate that this was a global phenomenon too, hence the subsequent efforts of FIFA to regulate commitments to international football more rigidly. But in a country of just over five million people the importation of so much talent was of little help to men who needed Scots playing regularly for the best clubs.

Foreigners had always been welcome here, though. Jerry Kerr with Dundee United in the early 1960s and Hal Stewart at Morton, at about the same time, had raided Scandinavia, as if in revenge for what the Vikings had done to us, and had come back with some useful players. But from the late 1980s it became a flood. Before Souness came to Ibrox in 1986 there was a mere sprinkling of foreigners around the clubs; six years later there were 180 non-Scots with clubs in all divisions; by 1996 there were 238 throughout the entire league system. In season 2004/05, in the SPL alone, there were no fewer than 144 registered foreign players. But more significantly, in actual playing terms, the number of foreigners who played in the first two games of that season was 60, or a third of the selections. In a league of 12 teams this represents a huge influence. Of course, the Old Firm represented the largest share of that, but certainly it was far from limited to them. It was barely credible to talk about the 'Scottish' game any longer. Potential native talent was being elbowed out, for whatever valid club reasons. Would there be any way back from this?

With the ending of the Souness–Dalglish international era, talent of the calibre of those two men evaporated. The Jimmy Mason I mentioned in my first chapter, Billy Steel, 'Jinky' Johnstone, Jim Baxter, Charlie Cooke, Willie Hamilton at Hibs, Bobby Murdoch of Celtic, Denis Law, Alan

Gilzean, Ian St John, just to mention a handful – and no disrespect to the others who were close to that calibre over previous generations – now represented an almost extinct species. As Willie Waddell once growled at me about the huge supply of naturally gifted players in the past, 'They used to grow on trees.' Shake a branch and off would fall a talent. Dutch Elm disease had obviously now set in. The most popular target for those looking for a quick explanation is the Scottish schoolteachers' strikes of the 1980s, and particularly the targeting of schools football in 1985. The serious dearth of talent is generally attributed to that. Before then we seemed to take for granted that shaking that branch would last for ever.

After all, in one of the most famous schoolboy games of all time, played at Wembley on 7 June 1980, we witnessed a Scottish performance that seemed to be no more than a confirmation of the innate ability of succeeding generations to produce equal amounts of skill and endeavour. Captained by the admirable young Paul McStay, who was later to be one of the great Celtic players, they were full of class and promise for the future. John Robertson, who was capped 16 times at senior level, became Hearts' record goalscorer, and who in 2004 was appointed manager of the club only to be shamefully ousted seven months later with the club now in Lithuanian ownership, played on the right wing that day. He can hardly forget it. 'I remember it well because it is the only time I ever played there,' he said. 'It was a baking hot day which would have melted you, and I know you might not believe this, but before the game the president of the English Schools FA came into our dressing room and said to us that if we were going to beat his side then he hoped it would be by a big score like 5–4 in an entertaining game. And that, as you know, is exactly how we beat the English. We were 2–1 down at half-time but we scored three goals in the first ten minutes of the second half, and that was us on our way.' Of the team that day, the majority of the players went on to play senior football at a respectable level. But only three made it through to the senior international side: Robertson, McStay and Ally Dick, although the latter's career eventually stalled badly. This was a team that not only achieved a memorable victory that day but executed a clean sweep the same season, beating all opposition. So, if you like, there was 'wastage' even in a period that offered so much promise, suggesting that this would always be the case.

Then came the teachers' strikes of the mid-1980s, especially that of 1985. These have been blamed for many of the ills, but it is something of a myth. It is certainly true that the teachers' union, the Educational Institute of Scotland, hit schools football in their salary dispute with the government. They knew Saturday mornings were areas of vulnerability for those teachers who gave of their time devotedly, without payment, every school week. The EIS did not care about any other sport; it was football they were after, because of the 5,000 teachers then involved in schools football 4,000 plus were members of the union and were expected to withdraw their labour. Most of them did, for various periods. By the 1986/87 period and the ending of the disputes, schools football activity had almost halved. In 1982, 357 secondary schools were involved in the Scottish Schools FA; by 1990 the total was down to 238. But it recovered to 325 in 2005, though that figure is skewed for the simple reason that because of amalgamations of schools and the disappearance of others, there are fewer in existence and pupil rolls are falling. There are simply fewer kids around to be included in football. In 1990/91 there were 556 school teams involved in all competitions at all grades; by 2005 the number was 829 – an increase of almost 50 per cent. So there were more schools and teams involved, only with fewer pupils to participate because of falling school rolls as a result of the declining birth-rate.

Thus, evidence of recovery is unmistakeable. There is no sign whatsoever of a savage decline as a long-term result of the strike. On the contrary, while there might have been a very temporary lapse, the organisation of schoolchildren suffered only minimally and has bounced back considerably. It is true that some teachers, particularly physical education specialists, never returned to supervise matches, but as David Little, the SFA's Scottish Youth Development Officer, points out, as school participation fell, youth club football immediately filled the vacuum. 'Any boy who could play the game to a decent level got a game of organised football,' he said. 'Hardly anybody of note missed out.' There are now, in 2005, 40,000 boys and girls in youth club football under the auspices of the SFA, controlled and organised in a way that did not exist in the early 1980s.

These figures simply do not account for the disappearance of the kind of dream players of the past. In addressing this problem a crucial factor is the SFA's attitude to youth football up to the age of 14. That age range is demarcated by the concept called, perhaps unfortunately, 'non-competitive football'. On initial reading, that might make us much sense to the general public as talking about non-sexual sex. It requires further scrutiny because it is central to the dogma that emanates from the coaching philosophy of the governing body, upon which depends the shape of the game to come. Football without prizes? Without trophies? Without recording results? Without identifying winners or losers? It all suggests it comes from the discovery of a long-lost chapter of *Alice in Wonderland*.

But a champion of all this is a man who learnt early in his coaching life under Jim McLean that preparation for a footballing life can be a deadly serious business and he himself would play no part in flippancy in the game. Walter Smith, the former boss of Rangers and Everton, was appointed Scotland manager on 2 December 2004. Bring up with him the subject of non-competitive football and you tap into a strong belief born of a reverence for a lifestyle long since gone and a conviction that all is far from lost. 'Of course you've got to be competitive,' he said, 'but it depends where and when. In the past we would go out and play in the street, or round the backyards, or on waste ground anywhere. You could lose by a score 19–18. You would go back home, have your tea, then go back out again until it was too dark to see, and this time you might win. So what was happening? There was firstly a hell of a lot of football played. It was all we had for play. There was competition, even though you didn't get a trophy for it. You just wanted to beat your pals. And you did that by playing, playing, playing. You developed skills in how to beat people, when to pass and not to pass. Nobody was screaming instructions at you; you just did it through the sheer number of times you played. We learnt all the basic stuff in that environment without anybody instructing us. That's how we got Jimmy Johnstone or "Slim Jim" Baxter or an Ian McMillan. These players were skilled enough to compete anywhere eventually because they never stopped playing football.

'It's that ingrained quality you've got to have before you start thinking of putting on a specific football jersey and thinking of winning a cup. Why should we put kids in those specifically competitive situations if they haven't yet developed the skills to compete properly? And it's no good thinking you can start the real competitive stuff at the age of 14 if they are still not good enough. The die is cast by then. All the right stuff has to be developed years before that. Now, when we had a huge bulk of young boys playing football all the time like that it was inevitable that you would get a percentage of really great players. That bulk has diminished, so it's no surprise they don't emerge the way they used to. So the problem is how to get more kids playing more often. That's what the so-called "non-competitive" football is all about. We can't put them back on the streets any longer because it is a different age. Kids are accustomed to better standards everywhere. To get back to where we were we have to create the circumstances of the past in a modern manner. We've ignored that for too long. We need large, safe play areas, purely for kids, all over the country where they can play to their hearts' content, morning, noon and night, like they have provided in the likes of Norway – not just for football but for all sports. Too many people are missing the point. You can talk about all kinds of factors, like the teachers' strike. But they are all irrelevant to the real crux of the matter, and that is not enough kids play football between the ages of five and 12. Believe you me, that's what it's all about! That's what we've got to work on!'

The intensity with which a man like Walter Smith extols the virtue of 'non-competitive' football can hardly be ignored. Jimmy Johnstone, the great winger of the Lisbon Lions, once recalled for me that kind of 24-hour obsession with a football which was so typical of boys before the Second World War and in the decades up to the 1970s. 'I used to play in the parks and in the streets until it was too dark, and then I would play up and down our hall, at all hours, dribbling and kicking a ball and making a hell of a noise doing it. But the old woman living below us never once complained about me. And she was a Protestant too!' Jim Moffat, part-time manager of the Scottish lower-division club East Fife, which has produced some great players, is also head physical education teacher at the local Bell Baxter School. He straddles both dimensions of football and is in a favoured position to make assessments. 'There is value in seven-a-side football,' he said, 'but the emphasis has gone too far, although I admit that when you see boys resorting to eleven-a-side football you begin to be aware of them losing their fine touch on the ball. But playing a full-side game has to come some time, and it would be wrong to deny it altogether for primary kids.' Michael O'Neill, the Director of Education for North Lanarkshire, a football enthusiast and a member of various SFA initiatives, is a strong advocate of the approach, although he does have reservations about the tag 'non-competitive'. 'We wanted children to take part and to enjoy football,' he said. 'We run festivals of seven-a-side football for kids from the Primary One stage right up the school age range. Games last seven minutes. We rotate the teams to play one another. You should see the competitive way they play even though we are not awarding any trophies to go with the results. They go at it hammer and tongs. Everybody gets a certificate. And everybody gets really involved where previously in eleven-a-side football you would see boys standing doing nothing for part of the time. This is the way to develop skills.'

Of course there is value in the shorter version of the game, and the SFA might have clarity of purpose about the policy, but others steadfastly do not see it that way and view the wholesale rejection of prizes and trophies as ridiculously extreme. They are worried that the official line in the future will prompt people to turn away from assisting in youth football in resentment at the classic 'You'll play wi' ma ba' or no' at all.' This central nub of non-competitiveness seems to run counter to the Report of the Review Group on Physical Education set up by the Scottish Executive in 2004 which states in one of its paragraphs, 'Competition is part and parcel of sport and young people need to learn how to prepare for an event, to take part and to win or lose well.' And it certainly does not chime with an HMI Inspector of Schools report on improving physical education in schools, which also states, 'When handled well, competition motivated pupils to try harder and seek new strategies for solutions, thereby raising the levels of achievement.'

It did surprise me to come across people deeply involved in schools and youth football, in 2005, unwilling to be identified as opponents of this 'non-competitive' system. An SFA community coach in Fife told an organiser of a local tournament on one occasion that he had better not attend it because a trophy was to be presented at its conclusion. Such dogma, though, always produces its heretics, and Jim Moffat, teacher and professional coach, you could say, might be one. 'Nowadays we don't seem to want children to experience failure,' he said. 'We protect them from it. But if you do that you can eliminate the drive to succeed. Certainly you can watch kids playing with great enthusiasm in a series of games even though there is no trophy at the end of it. It can really be competitive. But the kids award their own prizes by knowing who are the best players and which the best teams. That is in their heads. To hold back a prize for the winners is consequently artificial.' Michael O'Neill, from the point of view of an educational administrator, while an extremely influential advocate of 'non-competitive' football, pours scorn on the extreme views. 'We have to find the right balance,' he said. 'I am not utterly opposed to trophies, but I do know that too much emphasis was placed on winning for its own sake in the past, with parents caught up in all of this, bawling from the touchlines to their kids. All that was doing us no good.' Few would disagree with that.

But relationships in some areas are not as smooth as they ought to be. One such is that between schools and professional clubs. The bigger clubs forbid their young signings to take part in schools football, and they miss out on the great Saturday-morning tradition, much to the chagrin of their mates. (St Ambrose School in Coatbridge, for example, were in three Senior Shield finals in 1999, 2002 and 2003, and lost them all. They would have been better equipped for these games had Celtic not barred three of their signings from playing for them. Inverkeithing won the senior schools trophy in 2005, and it was no coincidence that a boy was playing for them that day who had not been permitted to do so during the previous rounds because he was on Hibs' books. He was subsequently released by that club to Falkirk, who permitted him to play in the final.) This policy of the clubs in the SPL is certainly denying kids the important socially bonding experience of playing, particularly through puberty, with their mates. We have to suspect that if you are withdrawing an important element of the 'growing-up experience' from certain lads then you are doing nobody any good. For being isolated in that way from their peers puts a special pressure on them. They have to 'make it' or else. And too many simply do not.

The loss to the game of potential talent slipping through the net has always been a defect, but it is now an epidemic. In the late 1990s great credence was given to football academies to stem this. While commendable in concept, they are conversely arousing too many expectations and producing too many casualties. Evidence of that trend comes from south of the border where the FA, in a census they carried out, discovered that the football academies of the Premiership would be lucky if they produced even a couple of boys capable of making first-team football, and that virtually all of the rejects gave up the game altogether. Many turned to rugby instead. Walter Smith has seen the figures. 'Do you know that 80 per cent of those who went into those academies never kicked a ball again in earnest after they left? And I will tell you why: they were not good enough in the first place. That is why there is a high casualty rate. People think that you can get a fair percentage of success just by putting kids in there and pushing them through the system. But I go back to what I said about early development. If they don't possess the skills before they are "taught" then they are not going to make it. Not enough boys going into these academies have played enough football in the natural way that I have been describing. So, although I approve of academies, we cannot expect them to be solving all our problems. Before we have structured football we must have loads of unrestricted, freewheeling football where boys can play more often and learn through hard personal experience. The necessary coaching for what is a team game only comes after that.'

Although no comparative study has been made in Scotland, the anecdotal evidence suggests that many rejects from our academy system disappear completely from football. Build up a young man's anticipation of a glowing career in the sport he loves, then tell him he is not wanted, and you have a potential recruit for the French Foreign Legion. For example, in mid-April 2005 Hearts released seven boys under the age of 11 from their coaching scheme, probably because it was considered they would not make the grade expected of them. They were what one official SFA website once referred to, rather insensitively it has to be said, as 'jersey-fillers' – that is, boys who make up numbers to ensure that the more talented get proper games. But the distinct possibility is that those who have been promised a career but who are then told they are not going to make it are as likely to give up football as those who have shown less promise from the outset. We are left to wonder how much wastage there will be in the Old Firm academies of the future, and just how meaningful and economically viable are the vast sums of money that have been poured into the likes of the palatial Rangers training ground and academy, in an age when the instant fix and the buying of ready-made talent will persist as far as the eye can see for these two clubs in particular, despite financial constraints. But the financial costs involved for all clubs, for a modest return in the pursuit of quality players, and the human price paid in the waning interest in football of the 'failed' kids, might be too high. Certainly the non-competitive ethos does not seem to belong to the football world I inhabit, nor to the habits and instincts of kids, whom I used to teach in that age group. The man who taught pigeons how to play the piano by offering them prizes or rewards for their efforts showed us the importance of incentives in gaining skills. To completely outlaw the trophy as an object of desire seems an unnecessary emasculation of the instinct kids have to succeed in any walk of life, not least on a football field. Ironically, Germany and Holland, who were the prototypes for our conversion to seven-a-side 'non-competitive' football in the first place, are now born-again believers in eleven-a-side competitive football at the younger levels. They seem to have left Scotland behind, as have other nations, in their emphasis on physical education in schools.

I once asked Jock Stein, during the World Cup in West Germany in 1974, what was the basis of any football success. He answered in one word – fitness. From that comes the outcropping of natural skill, which as Michael O'Neill accepts has to be given the earliest encouragement in primary schools, and as a whole the educational system has to provide the alternatives to compensate for the disappearance of the habits of a more robust age. So as Scotland in 2005 assesses its future development of the national game I am aware of a certain tension in and amongst the tender shoots as there is no unanimity over the way to develop Scotland's youngsters. What is certain is that the nation needs more involvement in sporting activity. In an age of concern about the supervision of children stemming from the tragedy of Dunblane in March 1996 and instances of child abuse, it is no simple matter for any adult volunteer to become involved in any sport, not least football. While this is understandable, the bureaucratic necessity of checking backgrounds, even for the simple exercise of driving other children to a schools football match, can be a turn-off for parents.

Yet it is volunteers football needs at these younger stages. It can't all be left to schools. The Scottish Executive is earmarking £30 million annually for the development of youth football, but as their first allocation of £9.9 million in 2005 is being directed towards the professional clubs to help them with their football academies and Youth Initiative Schemes, and none to amateur grass-roots football which is reliant on volunteer effort, this money could be seen as merely a hidden subsidy for clubs struggling financially. It is a strange order of priorities not to finance encouragement at the most basic levels of football, where voluntary effort and the development of coaches is desperately needed. And although it would be foolish to dismiss the conventional SFA view on 'non-competitive football' outright, as it is well intentioned, if that body becomes too dogmatic about trophy-less football it could further deter adults from becoming involved in the organisation of the game. It is certainly difficult for many to ally the 'non-competitive' ethos with the memory of a Billy Bremner, for whom a concrete wall was but a minor impediment, or a Dave Mackay, who once lifted Bremner up with one hand and almost throttled him, and who shied away from no man. And will a skilful Baxter emerge from the seven-a-side ethos? Only if this does not dilute that gallus impulse to be seen publicly, trophy in hand, as simply the best.

There are two dates that ought to scare anybody harbouring fanciful notions of a return to the good old days of Scottish international football, when the streetwise kid rose to wear the international jersey. ('What do you mean by "good old days"?' Ernie Walker would say to me from time to time. 'Our national team never won anything.') They are 4 March 2000 and 8 September 2001. Those who took part in that party in Paris, Sean and all, spending great sums of money to demonstrate their commitment to Scottish international football, should regard these dates as sinister. They are when both Rangers and Celtic started matches with eleven non-Scots for the first time in their histories, and thus sent us the message that they were no longer benefactors of the Scottish international game. In their domestic rivalry, with their squads loaded with overseas players, they sent us spinning into the new millennium on the wings of the same age-old acrimony.

CHAPTER TWENTY-TWO

BLOODY SUNDAYS

A Sabbath in Edinburgh in the third millenium is certainly different from what it was when I was a boy visiting the capital and felt then that if you so much as blew your nose on the holy day it would be an act of sacrilege in the city of John Knox. Now on Sunday, 22 May 2005, at lunch-time in a traffic jam on the outskirts, as shoppers made for the huge shopping complexes at South Gyle, where Rangers' chairman David Murray's empire is sited, this was the modern Edinburgh, blighted by traffic and concerned more about the sales in the Mall than the Sermon on the Mount. The day, you felt, promised nothing to compare with the breath-stopping intensity of that other Sunday, 25 May 2003, when two Old Firm tribal tectonic plates rubbed together and the earth shook. It seemed, by comparison, rather ordinary. The distant thought occurred that given the snail's pace of the traffic we might not reach Easter Road, Hibernian's ground, in time for kick-off at two o'clock. It was the only tension you felt on a day that seemed to have a pre-ordained pattern to it. There was a commentary to do; the last of the season in the Premier League.

Hibernian, youthful, effervescent, who had delivered a master class in passing to the more mature Celtic earlier in the season, which had even the hardened Parkhead standites murmuring in appreciation, were to play Rangers. Yet the day seemed to promise nothing other than a predictable outcome as Celtic edged towards another title and their last game, against Motherwell at Fir Park, a day that looked from any angle to have a set agenda of triumph. On arrival at the Hibernian ground, with half-an-hour to spare, I noticed a group of Rangers supporters holding a banner stating 'Keep Believing'. It had nothing to do with a distaste for Edinburgh's headlong rush into materialism and need for spiritual re-awakening, but a simply stated plea to the Rangers players that they could, after all, win the league championship, although trailing Celtic by two points going into the last 90 minutes. It conveyed the stubbornness you would normally associate with lost causes. That particular banner disappeared half-an-hour into the game as the Hibernian supporters, crooning the Proclaimers's 'Sunshine Over Leith' anthem were announcing to the Rangers phalanx that Celtic had indeed, as expected, taken the lead at Fir Park. But it was to be unfurled again much later that afternoon.

The game with about 15 minutes to go has become a crushing bore. It is reminiscent of that black hole of a match we had to endure watching West Germany and Austria in 1982 eke out a pre-determined draw in the World Cup in Spain. The fact that Rangers Nacho Novo scores in the second-half for Rangers to give them a 1-0 lead does not alter the fatalistic shadow that hangs over the match. For Rangers, at that stage, are still second-best in the land and Hibs are virtually qualified for Europe for the first time in three years. Nothing, seemingly, can alter that fact as the game enters a phase which is reminiscent of the terminal stage of a summer picnic with a beach ball being pinged around by men who have just finished a monumental tuck-in, as meaningless short passes alternate with tepid tackles which would not bruise a delicate meringue. They have accepted their fate. It is all over. The game is hanging there like Monty Python's deceased parrot. And then ... the noise. There are about five minutes left of the game. It is an alert. But what does it mean?

The massed ranks of Rangers supporters hemmed in at one end of the ground are erupting in such a display of emotion it can only mean one thing, that something significant has happened in the Motherwell-Celtic match which they know about and I certainly do not. I have no communication with anybody as I am voicing the commentary for Scottish Television only for recorded highlights the following day. We are not transmitting live. Nobody is feeding me information. But there they are dancing and singing at the Rangers end. I have to be careful not to read too much into this. For although transistor radio communication is now the norm at football matches, and many ears would have been held to the 'trannies', with Rangers requiring a win and Celtic having to drop two points for the title to go to Ibrox. But false alarms have also been spread by terracings in the past. I have to be cautious. I look across to the Rangers bench. There is certainly a frisson of extra movement around that area but not enough to convince me that something extraordinary has occurred. The Rangers manager Alex McLeish betrays only a sudden alertness where previously he has looked inured to anti-climax. But nothing more than that. What is going on? When I hear the second loud eruption from the Rangers end

I am compelled to do something about it. For the first time in my career in broadcasting during a game, I take off my headphones, lay down the mike and walk along the television platform to where Trevor Steven, the former Rangers and England player is standing. He has been in communication with the broadcasting station he is serving that day and he simply says, 'Motherwell have scored. It's one each at Fir Park.' What he himself does not know is that Motherwell have scored a second goal. That is what the second roar signifies. The Rangers squad assume that the eruption is about the game ending at Fir Park and it is not until an hour after the game that Barry Ferguson realises Celtic have lost, not drawn, although it makes no difference as Rangers, he wrongly assumes, have won the title on goal difference.

I return to my station, partly stunned. Another championship won by visitors at Easter Road? After all, I have experienced it five times before – 1973, 1975, 1977, 1980, 1994 and now this. It is difficult to take in. In the Rangers technical area the technical squad and substitutes seem now to be making a fair go at dancing a chaotic version of the 'Dashing White Sergeant'. Ten minutes previously they have looked as if bored out of their skulls and sucked dry of all enthusiasm. Now, as if brought back to life by a defibrillator they are in ecstatic spasm. They have just learned they have won the league title. In the middle of this mayhem stands a man whose face seems to be contorting into a myriad of expressions that challenge simple description. It shifts between incredulity, relief, joy, and enviable restraint. Alex McLeish has triumphed in front of many of his own supporters and amongst the media, who if Celtic had not blown two goals in the last two minutes at Fir Park might have wanted his carcass thrown to the wolves. Redemption and crucifixion has never been so finely balanced in this, the mother of all finishes.

The Rangers players had not rehearsed an encore. They had even travelled to Edinburgh garbed only in their track-suits such was the feeling that this would not be the day for celebration, but back they came on to the pitch to a jubilant support who had turned up out of habitual loyalty and who now had to play their part as conquerors; the sort of thing they believed they were born to be. One tiny figure stood out for me as the Ibrox squad rollicked in sheer uninhibited incomprehension at what had just struck them; the goalscorer Nacho Novo. He was acting as if he had been born in Govan and had stuck his tongue out at a Celtic jersey all his life. He is, of course, a Spaniard who in the previous weeks had been finding it as difficult to find the net as he does finding the right word in his fractured English sentences. He represented the new dimension of Old Firm rivalry.

The foreigners did not dilute the nature of the continuing struggle between the Old Firm. They replenished it. The idea of a kind of 'continental cool' possessing both clubs through the introduction of lads who knew nothing of the 'Fields of Athenry' or 'Derry's Walls', which some of us felt might transpire, gradually disappeared as players from strange sounding places began to look less like mercenaries and more like tribal loyalists. The absorption into the extremism of the old Catholic-Protestant days, of support and inspiration for the players, was accomplished by these strangers with ease. They seemed to be both immune to the social inferences of that and inspired by them. Practically overnight they would pick up an understanding of the implications of defeat and victory in that fixture.

Rangers, of course, were more affected. They were now prepared to take a deep breath and put the past well and truly behind them and demonstrate that Mo Johnston was not just a temporary aberration. To their credit, this they did in style. Walter Smith, as Rangers manager, went to deepest Tuscany and brought back Lorenzo Amoruso, who for all his eccentricities played for Rangers with the gusto of a re-born John Greig. Whether he understood the Protestant anthems serenading his efforts I cannot attest to, but the Italian Roman-Catholic captain of the club confounded those who felt that they would never see the likes. Indeed my ears were assailed at Tynecastle one day as I watched him captain Rangers to another victory. It was a chant coming from the Hearts supporters, towards their opponents at the other end of the ground to the tune of 'Guantanamera': 'Oh, you have more Tims than Celtic' referring to what we might describe diplomatically as their more cosmopolitan outlook. By that time, into Dick Advocaat's second season as Rangers manager, the signing of 'those of the other kind' was so passé that we were no longer into a head count.

The Dutchman would have accepted nothing else, of course much he did share with Martin O'Neill when the Irishman on the scene. Neither of those men, who chose the histo foreigners on those two aforementioned dates becoming nannies to the Scottish national s agenda: their supporters demanded inst in the main was not good enough f in European football were altered a few years ago, to great satisfaction at Ibrox and Parkhead, out came the cheque books and millions of pounds left this country as the foreigners poured in. Between the years 1999 and 2002 the Old Firm spent an estimated £103.2 million on buying 53 players (Rangers 27 and Celtic 26) but only £9.3 million (less than 10 per cent) was pumped back into the domestic game through purchases from Scottish clubs – although not necessarily Scots-born talent. They spent only £5.2 million on players of Scottish nationality.

This trading policy of the country's two biggest clubs was, overwhelmingly, the major contribution to a severe balance of payments deficit in the market for talent that ran counter to Scotland's role as a net exporter of footballers, according to a *Soccer Investor* report of 2002. As a consequence, a source of income which historically transfused the domestic game, namely the readiness (indeed necessity) of other native clubs to sell players to the Old Firm, had been drastically reduced, the knock-on effect being such that it would bring venerable clubs such as Dundee, Motherwell and Dunfermline perilously close to bankruptcy. Meanwhile, in the course of embarking on this spending spree, whilst shipping out 43 players between them for a combined total of £41.03 million, Rangers and Celtic were conjointly running up a trading deficit of £62 million. Nobody seemed to mind. The bitter rivalry between the two produced an indifference to the balance sheets of the clubs. Most supporters – witness the public pressure for more spending which caused friction between Martin O'Neill and his chairman Brian Quinn in April 2005 – could not have cared less about debt or where the money came from as long as the clubs could produce quality players. There was not even the merest hint of financial problems lying ahead. And the two managers self-indulged, but in different ways.

Advocaat became Rangers manager on 1 June 1998. In the tradition of historical sobriquets like Attila the Hun, Vlad the Impaler, and Ivan the Terrible, Advocaat could well be known as Dick the Profligate. He used a cheque book like it was his Excalibur, drawn not from a stone but from his chairman's ready paw. He took over from Walter Smith after Rangers had committed the long-term tactical blunder of announcing on 27 October 1997, ̣ months ahead of the close of the season, that he would be leaving the ̣ Celtic, though, to the last game to beat St Johnstone at Celtic Park ̣ ̣urday 9 May 1998 and deny Rangers their ambition to ̣ ̣s heralded the entrance of the Dutchman.

The impression Advocaat gave, as he established his own rigorous belief in discipline, was that he had come upon a group of libertines who required a puritanical purge. Conditions were established which reminded one of boot camp. The drink-together-and-play-together ethos of chumminess of the Smith era was expunged by this man with a more Cromwellian outlook. Arthur Numan, the left-sided ex-Rangers defender who captained PSV Eindhoven under Advocaat, admits that to avoid the Little General's booming voice in Holland, for at least part of the time, that when he would win the toss he would make sure he would be playing on the opposite side of the pitch from the bench so as to give his ears a rest. All that pitchside aggression proved initially successful in Scotland. Nobody can detract from the manner in which he transformed Rangers into an organised functional unit that won five out of the six prizes in Scottish football in his first two seasons.

At least part of the Rangers success, from 1998 to 2000, can be put down to the sheer ineptitude of the way Celtic were going about their business, from top to bottom. The Alan MacDonald, Kenny Dalglish, John Barnes triumvirate proved disastrous in that time. The coming of Martin O'Neill changed everything. It immediately altered the perception of an invulnerable Advocaat, and, after a year of O'Neill, gave some of us pause for thought that the Rangers manager, in winning five trophies in his first two years (the treble, and then the double of League and Scottish Cup), had been given a relatively easy ride. However, it is the Dutchman's legacy for the club that is a more compelling study.

On 23 November 2000, when Tore Andre Flo, formerly of Chelsea, walked into the Ibrox press room that morning, he looked more like an American college kid just recruited for the basketball side, than a £12 million striker. Tall, spindly, boyish, smiling shyly, instead of the growling predator we might have expected for that amount of money, there was even then an aura of disbelief in the room that so much money had been spent on a man who had not covered himself in glory in the south. It was put more trenchantly at the time by a former Rangers striker, Mark Hateley, who had openly questioned the transaction and called it 'an awful big gamble'. When, during the conference, Flo answered some questions and said, 'I like to think of myself as a skilful player,' Advocaat muttered quickly in support, 'Tell that to Hateley', with a testiness which could be taken as an admission that he was, after all, taking a massive gamble. The fact that the striker scored in his debut game against Celtic three days later at Ibrox, might have suggested sound acumen on Advocaat's part. But Hateley was right and the Dutchman wrong. In the context of such sums of money it was a catastrophic mistake. Flo cost Rangers double the money it did for O'Neill to bring Chris Sutton to Celtic from the same club. In 2005, Sutton was still there scoring goals, while Flo was a displaced person somewhere in Europe and ultimately would head back to his native Norway.

Then there was the other avenue that Advocaat set his mind on, financially at least – something that even yet burdens Rangers. It was about bricks and mortar. A civil engineering project was initiated at Ibrox stadium to increase the seating capacity and to establish a hotel at the Copland Road end. Test pile-driving was going on one day. As the hubbub of work continued apace, John Greig, in his capacity as PR officer for the club, strode across the pitch towards the workers. He told them they had to stop all that they were doing, immediately. At first, the civil engineer, in charge of the project, thought the request was related to the noise they were producing. But when he pursued this with Greig, he was told that the whole plan was being ditched. And then the astonished man was informed by Greig, with an added warning to say nothing to the press, that he had just come from a board meeting at which Advocaat had threatened to leave the club immediately if they did not put an end to this work. He wanted the money spent on a new training facility, or else. That was to prove a fateful day for Rangers. For although nobody can deny that Murray Park, which they then proceeded to construct virtually to his specifications, is a superb, luxurious training complex, which ranks with the best in Europe, it was built to the gurgling sound of Rangers remorseless descent into huge and crippling debt, which was estimated in 2004 at £80 million. Even now that simply does not make any financial sense. The tangible rewards for any such training complexes and academies, as I have already argued, are distinctly unpredictable. What is not, is the effect that it was going to have on another generation of Rangers managers weighed down, as they certainly would be, by so much debt. With increased ground accommodation, and a hotel, Rangers would at least have seen tangible income at a time when the well was running dry.

It also indicated the stranglehold Advocaat apparently had on his chairman. There was a positive side to this, in the sense that David

Murray always strongly backed his managers and offered little resistance to their demands and dug deeply into resources to do so. That seems an ideal relationship, sought after by any manager. Rangers had the advantage of seemingly being able to act more speedily than Celtic because of the pre-eminence of the man who really controls the purse strings, as opposed to a chief executive at Parkhead who has to work within the plc system. When Murray came back heavily into the club in 2004, after having moved aside for a period, and injected the club with more cash to limit their deficit, the effect was immediate. In the close season of 2005 Rangers went smartly about their business of making new signings, aided by the flamboyant use of Murray's private jet to bring in new men from abroad. It made Celtic, for all their huge support and massive commercial clout, seem as if they did not belong in the fast lane which they always claimed to aspire to. The Rangers supporters, blissfully unaware of the long-term consequences of such an extravagant outpouring of funds, turned up to wallow in the club's superiority. They had woken up with a start though when Martin O'Neill arrived at Celtic Park in June 2000.

His appointment was not entirely straightforward. At one stage Guus Hiddink, then with Betis in Spain, was strongly in the frame and it was said at the time that only the late intervention of Dermot Desmond recommending O'Neill, who had changed his mind after firstly rebuffing the Celtic job, altered the course of events. And if ever there was a template established which set the mould for the relationship between the two clubs over the next five years it was at Parkhead on 27 August 2000, when Celtic won 6-2 in O'Neill's Old Firm debut.

However, that does not tell the whole story, even though that statistic seems conclusive enough. For the overall impression was of two philosophies of football confronting each other. Advocaat instilled the basic Dutch notion of passing your way out of trouble into advantageous situations. O'Neill's seemed simpler, stronger and more effective. The ball went from back to front as expeditiously as possible, to men who relished such quick direct service. Rangers had become in contrast, neat, precise, but astonishingly brittle at times. O'Neill would build in a more powerful infrastructure to his side with the initial acquisition of players like Sutton, Thompson, Lennon and later a towering defender in Bobo Balde. The Opta analysis towards the end of season 2002/03, for example, indicated that Rangers had made 10,725 passes in the opposition half, while Celtic had made 9,670. Celtic's crosses into the box were recorded at 923, Rangers 759. In a less statistical sense, those of us who had been watching the Old Firm through the years were witnessing a dramatic role reversal. Celtic were playing like Rangers teams of old. They now had big strong players who looked dependable, aggressive, lustful for success and supremely confident. Much of that derived from that single 6-2 victory.

And he had Henrik Larsson. Think of how the Gatling Gun revolutionised battlefield operations with its repetitive mechanism and you sense the scale of how Larsson diverted the quixotic but never entirely predictable Celtic style into almost remorseless success. When I had watched him making his debut for Celtic against Hibernian at Easter Road on 3 August 1997, he bombed. With almost his first touch, after coming on as a substitute, he made a wayward pass to Chic Charnley of Hibs who scored a superb goal. A well-known Celtic supporter described Larsson to me afterwards, in so many words, as a waste of time. His total of 242 goals in 315 appearances in his Celtic career would be a reminder to everyone who dismissed him that day as a waste of money, of the wisdom of suspended judgement.

So for all that we might have bemoaned the demise of the Scottish player during the decade, the foreigners had enriched the game in ways that could only inspire, not deter, the young to put on football boots. Both Brian Laudrup and Paul Gascogine had elevated domestic football to different heights with Rangers. The Dane brought professional finesse with long, sinewy runs, which made some Rangers sides seem better than they actually were. Gascoigne, who was never able to shuffle off the controversies surrounding his personal idiosyncrasies, was nevertheless a combination of cabaret act and ruthless destroyer with fits of brilliance that were unique to the Scottish game. His hat-trick against Aberdeen in a title decider at Ibrox on Sunday, 28 April 1996 was one of the most accomplished I have ever witnessed. His 40-yard run for his second is arguably one of the best solo goals ever scored in the Scottish game. Scottish football's foreign accent was pronounced but perfectly translatable for a rapidly adoring public.

But in one sense it was beginning to go sour at Ibrox, where the Dutch colony was being blamed for dressing-room discord. As talk increased of Dick Advocaat 'losing' the dressing room, he recognised his own growing impotence and secured a move to have himself elevated to

Director of Football at Ibrox, which again would not have come cheaply for Murray. He obviously still enjoyed the enormous trust of the chairman, even though it was clear he could make monumental mistakes. It was he who chose Alex McLeish, then Hibernian manager, as Advocaat's successor in December 2001.

This surprised many people, not least the vast Rangers support. The general media perception was that the club needed someone of proven managerial ability, at as high a level as was available at the time. But while we know that George Graham would have jumped at the job, Rangers were limited in the amount of money they could afford on any personality. McLeish therefore came to Ibrox on the back of pragmatism as much as anything else. Thus began a new duel that was to end with O'Neill and McLeish winning seven trophies each before the Celtic manager left. But while Old Firm contests are portrayed in that personal way these statistics hardly lend insight into the true nature of the struggle between these two men. To start with Celtic in that time fared better in Europe, but not without anguish. When they fell to a despicable refereeing decision by German referee Hellmut Krug in the Stadio Delle Alpi in the Champions League in September 2001 – when he awarded a penalty and the Glasgow side lost 3-2 in a game they could clearly have won – we witnessed for the first time what the success of this club meant to O'Neill. It brought out the distinct difference between the respective managers. He entered the press room afterwards, pale, distraught, and with a voice which hinted at a tremble. We had seen his volcanic reaction to events on the field, from afar, during games, but now we were close to the inner man, tormented by what he thought were the injustices in life.

We saw this again in the San Siro, after the Champions League game against Milan, on 29 September 2004, when , after Celtic had mounted a fightback to equalise 1-1 and clearly had the home side on the run, they conceded two goals in the last ten minutes to lose 3-1. In front of the assembled throng of pressmen after the game, we saw a man utterly crushed by events. There was no fulmination as we might have witnessed from a Fergie or a Stein. Phone the Samaritans, you had to think. What we were not to know at the time was the draining effect his wife's protracted illness was having on him. But, in a trade in which the most distinguished managers are the worst of all losers, he suffers in defeat like no other manager I have ever known. Although when he paraded with Neil Lennon in front of his own support, after losing 2-0 at

Ibrox on 20 November 2004, his fist clenched in the air, you felt that he was also fuelled by the spirit of defiance on behalf of a community and his vilified player, as if he was demonstrating he had let them down, but that he wouldn't allow it to happen again. It might have caused mayhem were it not for the fact that it induced such a sense of bewilderment in the stadium amongst his opponents, that it passed without major incident although the scene was eagerly, and not surprisingly, plundered by the media.

McLeish, on the other hand, remained upright and measured in his response that day. Since arriving at Ibrox he had faced, from time to time, howling criticism; on the island of Madeira, after a defeat at the hands of the undistinguished Portugese side Maritimo on 16 September 2004, the Rangers supporters there besieged the bus, howling for his resignation. John Robertson, then the Inverness Caledonian manager, made an interesting comment to me after the game his club played at Ibrox on Sunday 19 September (Rangers won narrowly 1-0 but had been outplayed by the newly-promoted visitors for most of the match). 'I sensed that a lot of the Rangers supporters wanted us to win that day, just to bring the whole issue to a head.' He had not actually needed to tell me that as I could sense the sullenly critical atmosphere myself. At the back of our commentary position, which houses some of the high-flyers of the Rangers support in the front of the central stand, you did not need to look far to find men who would offer contemptuous comment on the manager's abilities. That sort of hostility bubbled up, then died down again, according to results, but you feel it is still there and is certainly not a spent well, despite their last league win. McLeish, therefore, does command respect for maintaining a sober, and at least on the surface, unemotional demeanour in the face of such swings of fortune.

Throughout the O'Neill period, though, you always felt that Rangers were playing catch-up, hanging on at times with grim determination to wring something out of the contest and which, of course, they did most dramatically at Easter Road in 2005. But season 2002/03 separated the two men dramatically in a more drawn-out torturous way. For although the records show that O'Neill won nothing and McLeish lifted the treble, it never felt like the beginning of a golden era for Ibrox in an age when money counts as never before and their cupboard was now bare. It is indisputable that what largely aided Rangers to win that treble was Celtic's inability to cope with their own success in Europe. It was not the only factor but when a club reaches a European final, has played more games overall but is only pipped by a single goal in the title race then they are entitled to seek solace in claiming to have sacrificed achievement for enhanced prestige.

The Parkhead club was heavily involved in Europe in 2002/03. It is for this period that O'Neill principally will be remembered. Eliminated from the Champions League, they were making sometimes spectacular progress in the UEFA Cup. They had eliminated Suduva of Lithuania, Blackburn Rovers, Celta Vigo, Stuttgart, Liverpool and Boavista and were now heading for the final. Superstition was running deep, as students of coincidences noticed that each team they had conquered had a V in their name somewhere (if you allow for the Voetbal in Stuttgart's full name) and so did Seville, the venue for the final. The portents looked good, in that sense, even though they were to play the highly talented Porto who could claim a real artist in their midst, the midfielder called Deco.

This was not so much a cup final as a demographic phenomenon, a massive tribal movement barely known in Europe since the Middle Ages. A whole community seemed to uproot itself and take to the Iberian peninsula, as if they wished to take up permanent residence there. Nobody has come up with a finite number as to how many Celtic supporters actually travelled to the Estadio Olimpico on 21 May 2003 – that would be impossible to determine. The figures simply soared every time you read a newspaper. The favoured estimate became 80,000. It is safe to say that only the weak and infirm were left behind as countless thousands made the journey. Immediately, comparisons were being made with Lisbon of 1967. But this was essentially different. It was a much bigger exodus. It is a safe guess to make that, back then, only a handful would ever have been abroad before. Or could have afforded to. In 2003 the vast majority were already experienced in travel to the sun through the blessings of the inexpensive package holiday. They knew the ropes. This was a relatively more affluent crowd. The size of it was a reflection of the social changes undergone in Scottish society. People in general were much better off than they had been three decades earlier.

The narrow streets of the ancient city were jammed with supporters, the whole holiday spirit maintained in a spectacular display of good nature – evidence of the awareness of the value of model behaviour. An internal but natural feeling of self-policing seemed to run through the throng. That was just as well, for it helped cushion the disappointment of being beaten 3-2, by a Porto side which could play some excellent football but betrayed histrionics which went beyond even the style of those crowd extras in John Ford movies, ten of whom could fall from a horse after only one rifle shot by John Wayne. Their desperate diving tarnished their overall performance, which in a footballing sense was simply better than Celtic's, it has to be said. But it was the scenes in the city that people remember mostly. Rod Stewart, for example, suddenly popping out of a limousine and standing by a fountain to give an impromptu concert to the Celtic thousands. Pat Woods, who has followed Celtic for 50 years, described it this way: 'The citizens of Seville were bewildered – it was as if they had woken up to find themselves strangers in their own city.' Celtic, wounded naturally by the defeat, took great consolation, nevertheless, from the praise heaped upon their community for their general conduct. Celtic had no time to take breath though.

The last days of the 2002/03 championship battle were shot through by nerves and suspicions. There is little doubt that the passage of time, not least in the period covered in this book, had done little to allay suspicions lying at the core of Celtic Football Club that an institutional bias favours Rangers. O'Neill is an intelligent man, but he seemed to have reached the conclusion of his predecessors that the odds are stacked against the club in any crunch situation with his great rivals and that those in authority paid them no favours. When the manager learned of the SPL's decision to play a crucial, Old Firm league match only 63 hours after Celtic's semi-final UEFA tie with Boavista in Portugal, O'Neill was quoted in the *Celtic View* of 16 April 2003 as saying: 'This wouldn't have happened if Rangers had been involved in a semi-final. There's absolutely no way it would and, in that situation, I wouldn't have wanted to play them on that date in any case.'

It was not only a surfacing of the subterranean strand of mistrust that ran through their management, about the way Scottish football was administered, but also extremely shrewd. He knew he would get a response from both his players and his supporters that would be like a gesture of defiance against a perceived injustice. He did. Celtic won 2-1. Rangers, on the other hand, have always traditionally believed that opponents, who were Celtic inclined, would never pull out the stops against their favoured club if it meant it would aid Ibrox or anybody else.

Witness what Sandy Jardine previously said about the dramatic conclusion when he was with Hearts in Dundee and Celtic were playing St Mirren at Love Street in May 1986. Rangers followers fervently believed that when Celtic thrashed Dundee, managed by former Celtic player Jim Duffy (the match ending 6-2 on 14 May 2003 with Rangers having two matches to play and Celtic only one), no real opposition had been offered. Fantasy, tinged with hatred, can conjure up incredible scenarios.

On Sunday, 25 May 2003 Rangers played at home to Dunfermline, while Celtic were away to Kilmarnock. They were equal on 94 points and with the same goal difference. As the fortunes swung one way and the other throughout the afternoon, Rangers took the title by one solitary goal, +73 to +72, winning 6-1; Celtic, with Thompson missing a penalty, defeated the home side 4-0. But as Ian Paul wrote in *The Herald* the day after the league decider: 'We may never see the likes of this finale again, and maybe for the health of the nation that is no bad thing.' But, of course, we did see another finale that was to test the human capacity either to resist shock or how to survive 'benders' lasting days on end. Both these close-run Sundays in 2003 and 2005 brought out the worst in some people. You felt a poisonous McCarthyite atmosphere had been generated in which you might be hauled up in front of some committee to avow or disavow your loyalties, as everyone suspected everyone else of having a hidden loyalty. Even among media colleagues there is an undercurrent of suspicion that you are withholding 'the love that dare not speak its name.'

Both O'Neill and McLeish handled this as delicately as they could but were also helped by the changing nature of dealing with the public and media. You could argue that Tommy Burns and Walter Smith were the last in the tradition of Old Firm managers to be openly accessible to the media and therefore indirectly to the public. Stein initiated press-conferences in Scotland when he arrived at Celtic Park to the discomfort of Rangers manager Scot Symon, who regarded the Fourth Estate with some disdain. When asked once if a match might be postponed because of fog, he offered the reply 'No comment.'

Stein's meetings with the press were more like group-therapy sessions compared to the neatly PR-groomed conferences which now take place and whose soundbites lead so often to guessing games, not to clarification. It is not that Stein and Waddell could not manipulate or 'spin' but they were more often forthright and accessible, especially if you had impromptu banter with them on foreign trips. This modern distancing from the public, in which managers are distinctly corralled by ever present press officers, and which rarely leads to a lengthy, meaningful face-to-face conversation, seems to suit them. For it protects them largely, although not invariably, from indiscretion and tends to mute the way that questions are shaped for them. It recalls the techniques the novelist Thomas Pynchon ascribes to paranoiacs: 'If they can get you asking the wrong questions, they don't have to worry about the answers.'

Does that really matter? Transparency should matter to people who fork out fortunes to follow a club. But too often it does not exist, as witness the guessing game the Celtic supporters went through, post-Seville. In the last couple of years of O'Neill's management, not only was the air rife with rumours that his rolling contract simply meant he was playing the waiting game until the post at Old Trafford became available, but that he was disturbed that it was highly unlikely significant funds were going to be made available to him in the future. He hinted at that several times. All this led to heated conjecture. It was not until a mistaken call by the Celtic chairman Brian Quinn from his mobile phone to an unsuspecting girl in the English Midlands – he thought he was actually speaking to the club's PR office (the text of which was quickly dispatched to the *Sun* newspaper) speaking almost sarcastically about his manager – revealed the depth of mistrust which actually existed between himself and O'Neill. A curtain was rolled back to suggest that Celtic had a deeply unhappy manager sending out a tired-looking team to win a title in the last few months of season 2004/05.

The weakening financial status of Celtic was never fully explained to their large support and should have been. Too many were deluding themselves that adequate funds would be made available to regenerate the side. Lost amidst the false optimism was the lone voice of chief executive Peter Lawwell, who in an interview with some of us, but wishing curiously to be anonymous on that occasion, alerted us to the fact, in December 2004, that Celtic had actually reached the very limit of their borrowing facility. There was no money left. This information never reached the supporters but should have; candour would have paid off better. It suggests that perhaps they were rather shamefaced to admit that position widely to a vast support who crammed the stadium, week in week out, bought lavishly any Celtic outfit or trinket on the market, could summon up 3,000 supporters alone in Las Vegas for a North American convention that year and yet the club had to plead poverty. Admittedly that would have been a hard position to explain. This was especially so in contrast to Murray's venture at Ibrox to dilute their problems with a share-acquisition amounting to £50 million and making their financial situation more tenable.

The records, of course, show that two goals lost late on that Sunday afternoon in May 2005 at Motherwell cost Celtic the League. There is more to it than that if you firstly consider the background. It is a game all of us expected Celtic to win and should have. But listen to O'Neill speaking just a couple of days before that match at Fir Park when asked about his immediate future and as reported in the *Daily Record* on 21 May: 'These five years have been pretty decent and there's as good a chance of me being here than not. But if you are asking if I will be leaving to go to another football club then the answer would be no.'

The media were mystified. His press-conferences could frequently lead us down so many philosophical avenues that some pressmen might have needed a cryptographer to decode their shorthand notes for them. But they were also stimulating for that reason. But this time it sounded more like a man desperately keen to add something more than he could admit publicly, and in the process was needlessly introducing a note of confusion on the eve of an important game. The uncertainty in his words was in direct contrast to the studied, careful and intelligently positive way he had gone into crunch matches in the past. No matter that the players rightly had the greatest respect for him, words like that could hardly have been a tonic. As we had seen in earlier games, a staleness had stolen its way into his side and from those who were involved in the match that day at Fir Park we discover that this was a grumpy Celtic team.

There was a lot a back-chat going on between some of the players which was hardly harmonious. Indeed two players looked as if they were about to come to blows at one stage. They should have been buoyant, but were not, as others sniped at each other. This does not explain why it could lead to an Australian player scoring two goals against them in the last couple of minutes to lose them the title, which had its freakish element to it, but it might indicate that despite what we predicted, Celtic were perhaps more of a spent force than we actually recognised. A team with a deeply unsettled manager, an increasingly disillusioned captain without a decent contract offer and jaded players was not the ideal mix for such a challenge. A game that required a positive edge to it was surrounded by too much Celtic indecision. It puts the loss of a title into a more logical context.

O'Neill waved farewell to Scottish football with the Scottish Cup of 2005 as his last trophy and companion. McLeish, with at first undisguised incredulity, had taken another title and could have turned nasty with his detractors. Somehow, though, he seemed to be adopting that John F. Kennedy dictum: 'Forgive your enemies. But don't forget their names.' Sundays will never be the same again for those two men. But whilst there was a dramatic change in personnel from O'Neill to Gordon Strachan as manager at Parkhead in 2005, Celtic and Rangers had this much in common. They could no longer recruit the highest level of player. Craig Bellamy in his loan period with the club was an outstanding success, entranced the Celtic support, but was too expensive to keep. Their historical strengths had been undermined by the passage of time and by the closed, limited environment within which they had to try to prosper. They no longer had the financial clout that outward appearances of large grounds, packed weekly with supporters, seemed to indicate. All this had prompted a major strand of thinking, particularly at Celtic Park, as the Old Firm were beginning to warm to Dr Johnson's remark: 'The noblest prospect which a Scotchman ever sees, is the high road that leads him to England!'

CHAPTER TWENTY-THREE

SURVIVAL

On 23 April 2001, in the Eurasia restaurant in Glasgow, Scottish Television held a dinner for some of the leading personalities of the Scottish Premier League and representatives of the leading political parties. It was a convivial occasion chaired by the head of the media group SMG, Andrew Flanagan. But it was also an opportunity to talk about the problems facing football in the country, and its relationship with the media. The Old Firm were not represented, but, like Banquo's ghost in Macbeth's banqueting hall, they were there in spirit, for you can never escape their clutches, and the men there knew it. One of the points mulled over was the possibility of the Old Firm leaving Scottish football altogether and joining the Premiership in England. It was never dismissed as outlandish; in fact, it was talked about over the coffees and liqueurs as a distinct possibility. The move south was made to appear feasible, if not downright inevitable, just as the Old Firm would have liked it to sound. From time to time the issue had been surfacing in the press, and the impression was invariably made that it would only be a matter of time before it happened. The idea was gathering momentum. And so, life without the Old Firm was being contemplated, as either a Domesday scenario for the rest of the SPL or the beginning of a new age for clubs that had suffered under their tutelage too long.

We discussed the interesting phenomenon of Hibernian, as an example of life without the Old Firm. They had been relegated from the Premier League in the 1997/98 season and had proceeded, the following season, to play a number of games that attracted gates significantly higher, in percentage terms, than the average from the previous season in the higher division (apart from their Old Firm matches). In the lower division Hibernian beat Falkirk on 12 December 1998 in front of a crowd of 12,572, which was 10.7 per cent up on the previous season's average. On 26 December 14,106 watched them beat Ayr United 3–0 (24.2 per cent up), and on 2 January 1999 the game against Raith Rovers, which Hibernian won 5–1, attracted the season's record crowd of 14,703 (29.4 per cent up). These specific figures were not bandied about at that particular meeting, but those present knew in general terms that Hibernian had seemed to prosper even though the Old Firm were out of the equation. The Edinburgh supporters had the possibility of seeing a league trophy won, whereas in the higher division that was out of the question. The fact that people were getting a more tangible reward out of buying their season tickets had obviously become a potent force in selling the game to them, even at a lower level. Therefore the concept of a more competitive league without the Old Firm was a tantalising one, and it was taking hold with those who thought it through sensibly. Nothing stimulates interest with the public more than the uncertainty of results.

In August 2003, at half-time during a match against Dundee United that Celtic were winning 3–0, a Celtic season-ticket holder came to me at the commentary position and described the unusual dilemma he and others around him faced. 'I spend £400 for my ticket,' he said. 'I could have gone home after 20 minutes. The game was over then. There is no competition. I sit here looking at my watch just waiting for the end. That can't be healthy. I enjoy the European nights much better. Why? Because I am never sure if we are going to win or not. Sure I want us to win. But how long can we pay up to watch a game that's finished before half-time?' At that stage Celtic's almost automatic superiority was whetting the appetite for a departure from Scottish football altogether. Some fears surfaced, though, that without the Old Firm Scottish football would degenerate into something like the league in Northern Ireland, where the honours might swing around more evenly, as they also do in the Republic of Ireland, but in a league of much poorer quality. But you only need savour the Edinburgh derby, or sample the hostility of the Dundee derby, or even the competitiveness of Kilmarnock against Ayr, to note that Scottish football has a robustness the other Celtic nations cannot match. That tradition ensures that the comparison with Ireland does not stand close scrutiny. To add to that I had found among ordinary supporters hardly any evidence of anyone wishing to mount a campaign to prevent the Old Firm taking their leave. People were alert to this possibility without fearing the consequences, and were prepared to be positive and optimistic. It is a view I share.

But what we did not argue through around that table was whether this notion of their leaving had any real substance. In later months we had hints dropped, mostly from Dermot Desmond, the major shareholder in Celtic, that the club would inevitably leave Scotland for England. There was not a shred of evidence to substantiate that claim. At the time of writing there is still nothing to lend credence to it. Indeed, those still pursuing the idea could be accused of peddling fantasies. These are built principally around what they consider to be the potential driving force, Sky Television. Prior to Sky there was BSkyB, which had grabbed Scottish football even before Sky bought the rights for the Premiership in England. Indeed, Scottish football could be said to have been the cornerstone of Sky's development in sport. But there was a fall-out, eventually, between the new Sky and the SFA, so the satellite company backed off Scottish football until they came back in December 1994. In January 1995, a three-and-a-half year contract was signed at around £10 million a season. In 1998 a new deal was struck, earning £40 million over four years. Scottish football had never had it so good.

But in December 2001, during the last season of the contract, Colin Davidson, head of Sky's Scottish football output, took a phone call from a journalist who said that he was about to run a story indicating that the deal was now in jeopardy. From that point on Sky were made aware of the SPL's plans to develop their own television channel. Roger Mitchell, chief executive of the SPL, and Vic Wakeling, Head of Sport at Sky, then went into negotiations, and effectively Mitchell walked away from a deal. The SPL would in fact have launched their own channel had not the Old Firm, near the midnight hour, seen the enormous practical difficulties of this and the almost naïve approach that was being made on ill-thought-out assumptions, and voted against the proposal. The SPL, in desperation, resorted to a ludicrously cheap deal with BBC Scotland, who in covering the games professionally were paradoxically encouraging people to sit at home and watch football. Empty seats in stadiums stared viewers in the face. Scottish football was in big trouble again. Although a deal was eventually struck with the Irish-based satellite company Setanta, which provides subscription coverage of games, there is little doubt many of the clubs pine for the days of Sky and regret the day Mitchell ever mentioned an SPL television station. It is this trust in the financial clout of Sky which still promotes the myth that they will provide the leverage to lift the Old Firm into English football.

There has never been a word of support for this notion from Sky, even though their name is constantly linked with an Old Firm exit strategy. Their silence on the matter suggests not complicity, as is strenuously promoted by the fantasists, but acceptance of the fact that they will be in no position in the foreseeable future to influence the structures of football anywhere, not least in England, with the entrenched views of clubs there: if they are the dominant ones, like Manchester United, Arsenal, Chelsea and Liverpool, they do not want the Old Firm; if they are outside that group, they would not welcome any more giants in their arena. With UEFA also trying to consolidate the national domestic bases of football with their long-term commitment to limiting the number of foreigners any club can use in European tournaments in the future, the climate certainly does not exist within that exalted body for support of the kind of cross-border development which a move to England by the Glasgow clubs would entail. It is important never to say never in football, but the closer you examine the possibility of this, the more remote it seems.

The dilemma and paradox is that the signs are there that the armchair is becoming, more insidiously, the preferred option for too many. On 3 May 2005 the Liverpool–Chelsea Champions League semi-final match was watched by 862,000 viewers in Scotland and peaked at one stage at just over one million. This represented 42 per cent of the viewing public, and, interestingly, was a bigger percentage than in England, where 34 per cent was achieved. If you discount a proportion of women, you might say that almost half the adult male population in Scotland watched a match with not one Scot in either team – something unthinkable in the days of Bill Shankly and Tommy Docherty. It shows the astonishing appetite for football in this country. But that might increasingly be satisfied only by watching pictures of high-quality football from other countries, which might seriously undermine loyalties to Scottish clubs. A more insidious trend is that Setanta's essentially pay-per-view service, however admirably it is produced, has many fewer clients than either Sky or the other terrestrial companies. This has two effects. A pub-culture of watching football has taken a strong hold on the viewing public as many shun watching these games in their own homes and opt for the local. And fewer kids are watching Scottish football on the box. The less you exhibit the native product to them the less likely they are to want to emulate its practitioners and to develop an appetite for the domestic game.

A consensual approach to television contracts is the only way forward, despite the major possibilities in the internet age for clubs to develop their own channels. Lawrie McMenemy once reminded me of the time Martin Edwards walked out of a Premiership television meeting, frustrated by lack of progress on a new deal with the respective channels, and loudly proclaimed that Manchester United would go its own way and cover its own games. Before he reached the door, Ken Bates, then chairman of Chelsea, simply asked, 'Yes, but who are you going to play against?' In short, nobody can declare unilateral breakaway in league football; you have to carry others with you. So no matter the potential inducements for the Old Firm to break out on their own in the future, they still have to remain part of an agreed structure. What is certain is that Sky will not return to Scottish football in a major way, and that the pros and cons of the Old Firm leaving for the south is a wholly distracting matter that seems to be a sop to their supporters, led particularly by Celtic sources, to allay the customers' frustrations (like the season-ticket holder mentioned above) at playing in an entirely predictable league. So the future of Scottish football is inexorably bound up with the problems of how the rest can co-exist with those two clubs and make it more competitive.

One guest at that dinner that night was a man prepared to speak out frankly and creditably about his own mistakes in the late 1990s, and in doing so he reflected much of what had gone wrong with Scottish football over the past decade. He was John Boyle of Motherwell, sufficiently well off in the world to have that restaurant stock a preferred wine especially for him. He bought the club in the summer of 1998 from the previous owner John Chapman and threw money at it. Motherwell had long been run on traditional and prudent lines. They sold the likes of Tom Boyd to Chelsea in May 1991, three days after he captained Motherwell to a Scottish Cup victory, to finance the building of a new stand. They transferred Phil O'Donnell to Celtic in September 1994 and built another one. It was the prototype Scottish club way – sell and develop. Boyle wanted to use his money to elevate the provincial club to a higher status and take on the Old Firm.

We had heard it all before. Perhaps nobody had warned him. But any man who has made £40 million in selling out his greatly successful travel business by working hard and taking risks, and who is looking around for an outlet for his cash, is entitled to spend it on whatever he fancies. He chose the Lanarkshire club. He was not averse to a down-to-earth self-scrutiny, as we were about to learn over that dinner, for apparently he would tell his staff at Motherwell that in his younger days his mother would warn him that life could teach you the following lesson: one day you can be a peacock, the next you can be a feather-duster. We were not staring at a feather-duster exactly, but certainly at a very contrite gentleman. He represented one of the unhealthiest trends in Scottish football – throwing money around. Both Rangers and Celtic, we learnt, paid out 66 per cent of their turnover on wages during the first two seasons of the new millennium; a healthy median should have been around 50 per cent. But in trying to compete with the Old Firm, and buy their way to a different status, the average wage bill for the rest of the SPL clubs was, incredibly, 90 per cent of their turnover. For Dundee, Dunfermline and Motherwell it was actually over 100 per cent. This is like sighting an iceberg and allowing the band on the foredeck to play on without shouting a warning. Astonishingly, because of their massive combined turnover, the Old Firm's wages-to-turnover ratio was 27 per cent lower than the rest, not higher. This crazy situation could not carry on indefinitely. Boyle owned up that night with admirable candour. 'We failed,' he said bluntly. 'We tried everything we knew, but we failed. We couldn't bring the people in. I have to be honest and admit that. We gave them all kinds of inducements, but it just did not work.' Then he went on to add another interesting dimension to his gospel of despair: 'And I'll tell you the main problem at Motherwell: we couldn't stop buses leaving the town, going into Glasgow to support Rangers and Celtic. And the reason for that is sectarianism. The sooner all kids go to the same schools, without any division, the better for all of us.'

He had lobbed his own tiny bomb into the discussions. In a few words he had encapsulated much of what affected Scottish football: the disparity in income between the Old Firm and the rest; the overweening ambition of those who felt they could buy themselves an elitist ticket; and the sectarian tribal loyalties established in the cradle and nurtured ever after. When Motherwell went into administration a year later, in April 2002, the inevitable feeling was 'Who next?' You could hardly believe that they alone were to be victims of the draught blowing through the game. Boyle had paid extravagant wages out of his own pocket, but could cushion the shock of this outcome – in order to come out of administration he had to write off £8 million of his own money – much better than the players and other employees, whose contracts thereafter were worthless to them. Dundee and Livingston were the next to move into administration, as the SPL tried to impose some probity by deciding to deduct ten points from those clubs that could not move back out of that situation by specific dates.

But in the final analysis, the mentality of Scottish football was fundamentally changed in the year 1974 when it was decided to reconstruct the leagues, from which legacy the game still suffers an almost incurable ailment. It was then, as we have mentioned elsewhere, that the elitist top-ten division was established. From its inception the following season, 1975/76, the fear of losing, the dread of relegation (which eight of the clubs had to face up to realistically every year as the Old Firm would never be placed in that situation), and the emphasis on defending became the prime motivations in football tactics. The only thing that visiting teams to Ibrox and Parkhead failed to bring with them to their stadiums after that date was a joiner to board up their goal. Things would never be the same again. You could say the age of the purist was over from 1975 onwards. Before that year there seemed room for clubs to breathe and to develop talent in a much bigger league; after that year, risk-taking was out. Buying your way out of trouble became modish; gambling on youth could be regarded as foolhardy. Foreign duds proliferated as a result. Players became fed up of seeing the same faces against them so often, as they could match each other six times a season. They knew each other so well that the element of surprise was virtually obliterated from game plans. Survival at all costs produced a level of football that might certainly have been dramatically engaging at times, but where had the quality gone?

The argument against an increase in the top division to 16 clubs is well documented. The principal objection is that it would produce many more meaningless games. It is a fair point. But the price for not going that way is simply to worsen our lament for the disappearance of the kind of quality football a division with a bigger safety net would, I believe, inevitably produce. For whatever compelling commercial challenges the clubs thought they had to combat and adjust to in the mid-1970s, the changing social conditions through the decades have failed to insulate Scottish football from the very perils they believed confronted them then. The clubs that formed the first Premier Division were Rangers, who had just won the last old-style championship, Celtic, Hibernian, Dundee United, Aberdeen, Dundee, Ayr United, Hearts, St Johnstone and Motherwell. All of these clubs are now suffering financial hardship to one degree or another, and several of them are now perilously close to catastrophe as they struggle with historic debt they might never be able to clear and which could still lead to their demise. In 2005 it was calculated that the total debt of all the SPL clubs was over £100 million, with approximately £40 million of that carried by the Old Firm. In those terms the mid-1970s turnaround can be seen as a commercial flop. The sacrifice for that reconstruction has been too great. For too much has gone by the wayside: attacking football, the priority given to the ball player, the stylist, the show-off, the self-indulgent, the eccentric, all of which could be seen on ash-pitches in amateur football right through to the grassy plains at the top level. Not so now. That halcyon age of the purist only stands a chance of revival in a league embracing more clubs in the top division. But the suggestion of going back to 16 clubs is seen by too many, sadly, as like advocating the reintroduction of the hansom cab. Yet the Scottish footballing flower is hardly in full bloom as it is.

The QE2, almost four decades on from that evening in April 1967 when Third Lanark's final line-up saw the liner's hulk in the stocks as they travelled to Dumbarton, is still sailing the seven seas. Scottish football remains afloat too, albeit with the feeling that at any moment it will be all hands to the pumps. We do not build majestic liners on the Clyde any longer, just as we have no claim to apply that generic term of quality 'Clyde-built' to our national game. As uncertainty about the finances of football continually percolates through our thinking in the year 2005, and the Old Firm might now be coming to terms with the fact that they will be part of Scotland's culture for as far as the eye can see, our history compels us to assume that Scottish football will survive Death Row. It is both a risky assumption and the only available one to cling on to. In spite of the financial recklessness which afflicted the game, the banks themselves are clearly aware of the social implications of closure. Perhaps more cynically, you might say that keeping a club afloat is a better option in the long run, as foreclosing definitely loses money for all involved. Propping up a football club is more than just tending a cemetery, though. For all its faults, football still links past with present in a practical, living way that is preferable to having our social history presented to us merely in museum form.

A visit to the south side of Glasgow reminds you of that. For Third Lanark's former stadium, Cathkin Park, is now a sedate public park, with a football pitch in the middle which is played on only by obscure amateurs, and with a perimeter around which mothers push prams. It partly retains its bowl shape, and although fringed by trees and bushes, rusting stanchions are dotted around, reminding you of those thousands of supporters over the years who used to lean or have their ribs crushed against them as the stadium groaned with heaving crowds when the Old Firm were there. They look like anchors to the past. Damien Hirst might have concocted this as an entry for the Turner Prize for modern art, symbolising the life and after-life experience of football. It is not so much a depressing sight, more a caveat, to remind us that a failing Scottish football culture is as wounding a blow to our self-esteem as the disappearance of our traditional manufacturing industries.

As the late Hugh Brown, the former principal of the Scottish School of Physical Education at Jordanhill, and father of ex-Scotland manager Craig Brown, used to say to me, 'You could always tell how well a mining community was doing by seeing how spruce the junior football ground looked in the villages.' Employment, pride in community, fitba' – they were interlocked. We cared even for those handfuls of people who turned up to watch professional football in the lower divisions. Some would argue that there are now too many clubs chasing too few people. Of course there are. But tell that to the stalwarts who still want to turn up at grounds around the country weekly, though they barely outnumber the players on the field. Navigating through these years has taught me not to dismiss lightly anyone's love of the game as an anachronism or an irrelevance. The weak as well as the strong belong to our tradition. For Scotland was a bulk exporter, not just of footballers, but of a native indomitable spirit which they carried with them and imbued in others. 'Have boots will travel' might have been the motto of those men who played at all levels of the English game in particular. The hardy Scots pro was part of the bedrock of football in the south, from the lower divisions upwards. At the highest level he is personified by Sir Alex Ferguson, who might yet turn out to be the last of the great Scottish footballing gifts to the world. But it would not be in our nature to slam the door on the future and all its limitless possibilities.

'Scots? Wee boys looking for fairy tales,' said Gordon Williams's drunk punter on that Glasgow bus. He has something. He would find acknowledgement of that in the imagination of football addict and Hibernian supporter Irvine Welsh, with whom I now have a special affinity. It happened like this.

It is the mid-1990s. Andrew Macdonald, the Scottish film producer, asks me if he can use part of my commentary on the Scotland–Holland match in Mendoza in 1978 as a background track to a sequence in a film he is making – and can I record a version of the Archie Gemmill goal with even more zest and punch than I had delivered in Argentina (even though I thought my voice had soared exultantly over the Andes that day at one particular point)? The director of the film, Danny Boyle, sits beside me in the recording booth in London and coaches me in the tone of voice he expressly demands for this scene. I do as I am directed and think no more of the context until a year later I see that film, Trainspotting, from the Irvine Welsh novel of the same name, in a cinema on the Champs Elysées one afternoon with some French friends.

We spill back on to the pavement afterwards, duly stunned. The film is already a hit, and standing there blinking in the Parisian sun I suddenly realise that millions around the world will learn, from a single scene in the film, more about the Scottish football mentality than a two-hour documentary illustrating the peaks and troughs of the game. In the film, boy meets girl, girl is not initially chuffed, boy uses the patter, girl relents, and the boy's memory bank, amongst other things, is stimulated at just the right moment. The naked Ewan McGregor, playing Renton, is seen lying back in his bed, with his 'pick-up' of the night Diane straddling him with obvious delight. Intercut with that we see pictures from a television video of a tiny figure in a Scottish jersey picking his way amongst orange-clad figures, in synchronisation with the actions on the bed. And just as my voice describing this action is screeching loudly enough to reach the ozone layer, as the ball crosses the line, Renton and Diane attain their howling climax – all three of us sounding as if unified in orgasm.

Heavily staged? Yes. Cunningly scripted? Of course. True to life? Absolutely. The blend of reality and fantasy in an Edinburgh sit-com relates to an inexhaustible passion. Renton relaxes in post-coital satisfaction and breathes the defining words, 'I've never felt like that since Archie Gemmill scored against Holland in 1978.' No greater compliment can ever have been paid to any lady, anywhere, at any time. If images of Scottish football in full blossom can be portrayed to the world as being able to penetrate even the intimacies of the bedroom, then we need never fear for the game's longevity.

INDEX